Adobe Illustrator
SCRIPTING
with Visual Basic and AppleScript

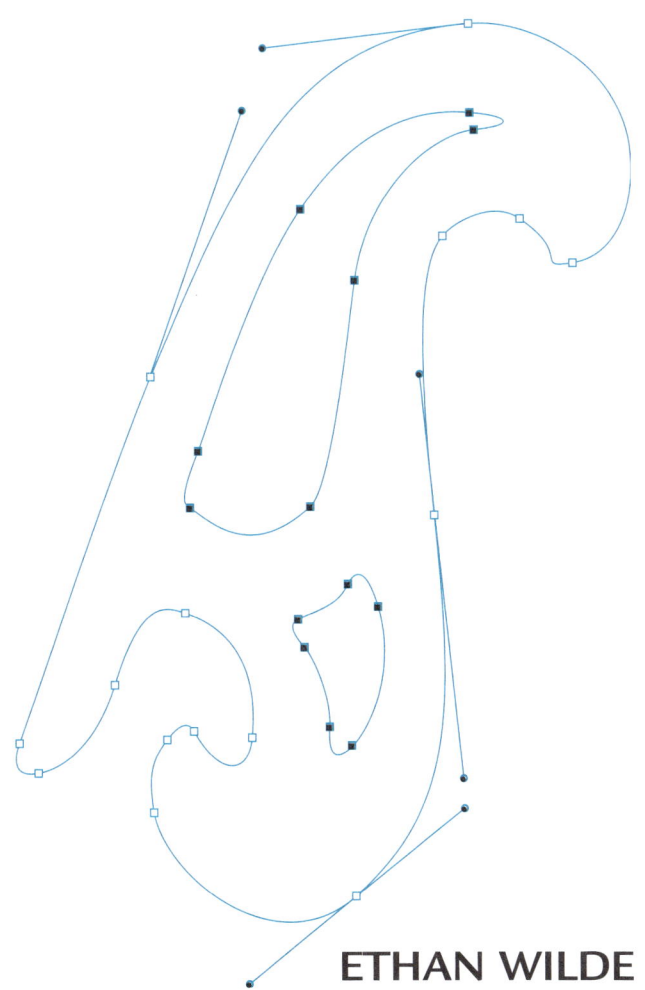

ETHAN WILDE

Adobe Illustrator Scripting
Ethan Wilde
Copyright ©2003 by Ethan Wilde

This Adobe Press book is published by Peachpit Press.
For information on Adobe Press books, contact:

Peachpit Press
1249 Eighth Street
Berkeley, California 94710
510-524-2178 (tel), 510-524-2221 (fax)
http://www.peachpit.com

To report errors, please send a note to errata@peachpit.com
Peachpit Press is a division of Pearson Education
For the latest on Adobe Press books, go to
http://www.adobe.com/adobepress

Editor: Kelly Ryer
Production Coordinator: David Van Ness
Interior Design: Mimi Heft
Cover Design: Mimi Heft, Michael Mallery
Copyeditors: Brenda Benner, Kathy Simpson
Compositors: Maureen Forys, Kate Kaminski
Illustrations: John Farnsworth
Index: Emily Glossbrenner

Notice of Rights

All rights reserved. No part of this book may be reproduced or transmitted in any form by any means, electronic, mechanical, photocopying, recording, or otherwise, without the prior written permission of the publisher. For information on getting permission for reprints and excerpts, contact permissions@peachpit.com.

Notice of Liability

The information in this book is distributed on an "As Is" basis, without warranty. While every precaution has been taken in the preparation of the book, neither the author nor Peachpit Press shall have any liability to any person or entity with respect to any loss or damage caused or alleged to have been caused directly or indirectly by the instructions contained in this book or by the computer software and hardware products described in it.

Trademarks

Throughout this book trademarked names are used. Rather than put a trademark symbol in every occurrence of a trademarked name, we state we are using the names only in an editorial fashion and to the benefit of the trademark owner with no intention of infringement of the trademark. All trademarks or service marks are the property of their respective owners.

ISBN 0-321-11251-2

9 8 7 6 5 4 3 2 1

Printed and bound in the United States of America

Acknowledgments

Creating a book about scripting takes a great deal of help, I can tell you from personal experience. My list of greatest supporters and those to whom I owe the most gratitude starts with my editor, Kelly Ryer, who unfalteringly led me through to the end of this text. She tracked me down when I fled, reassured me when I missed my deadlines and watched out for my well-being throughout the process. Thank you Kelly—I can easily say that I couldn't have done this without you. Next on the list is ever-reliable and supportive Marjorie Baer, Executive Acquisitions Editor at Peachpit Press, the parent of Adobe Press. Marjorie is an ever-encouraging and calming soul who consistently imparts wisdom in every encounter I have with her. Everyone else at Peachpit Press has always been an ally and great support—a real family of people dedicated to great computer books.

I can trace the start of my scripting relationship with Adobe back to 1998, when I had the good fortune to meet Susan Dumont, Lead Engineer for Adobe Systems' Core Technologies Scripting Group. Susan sensed my enthusiasm and interest in her team's efforts to implement scripting in Adobe's product line. She gave me many chances to work with the team who implemented scripting in both version 9 and 10 of Illustrator. It is with great sadness that I learned of Susan's passing earlier this year. She was an extraordinary person and the scripting community has lost one of its pioneering engineers. Her compatriots at Adobe, including the brilliant engineer Jesper Storme and the savvy Illustrator product managers Leon Brown and Mordy Golding, continue to deliver what are arguably the best scripting implementations ever seen in commercial applications (in three languages no less: AppleScript, Visual Basic, and JavaScript)!

The scripting language of my heart, AppleScript, continues to expand and thrive thanks to the ever-growing development team at Apple. Special shout out to Jason Yeo, Chris Nebel, Chris Espinosa, Sal Sogohian and the rest of the AppleScript team. I can't wait to get my hands on AppleScript X, a fully-object-oriented and re-engineered version of the AppleScript language—coming soon to a Mac near you. AppleScript has always kept me inspired by its ability to deliver powerful results with relatively simple scripts.

Finally, a few last words of thanks to those other individuals so important to this book. John Farnsworth is an illustrator of rare talent and his illustrations and information graphics add a great deal to this book—thank you John. My staff at Mediatrope—Megan, Eric, and Lisa—has supported my writing process by "taking the heat off" and carrying extra burdens for me. My family, Ted and Maya, for pulling together through the hard times we dealt with as my mother passed away last fall. To my long-time partner and new wife, Tania, thanks for bearing with me through another difficult book birthing process.

Table of Contents

1: Introduction 1
What You Need to Use This Book 2
Using This Book With Mac OS 4
Using This Book With Windows 6

2: Choosing to Script 9
Deciding If You Need a Script 11
    Do You Need to Make an Action? 12
    Will a Variable Palette and Datasets Solution Work Best? 13
    Do You Need to Write a Script? 13
Creating Documents for Use as Templates 13
    Creating Documents for Use With AlterCast 14
Using Actions With Illustrator 16
Using the Variables Palette and XML-Based Data Sets 17
Creating Scripts for Illustrator 19

3: Scripting Basics 23
Using AppleScript and Script Editor on the Mac 24
    Scriptable Applications and Their Dictionaries 27
    Using Scripting Additions 28
Using Visual Basic and the VB6 Integrated Development
Environment (IDE) in Windows 29
    Scriptable Type Libraries and the Object Browser 32
    Including Type Libraries in Your Visual Basic Script 36
Scripting and the Object Model 38
    Object Classes 39
    Object Inheritance 40
    Collections of Objects or Elements 40
    Referring to Objects 40
Writing Comments in Your Scripts 41
    Dealing With Long Lines in Your Scripts 43
Numbers, Text, and More: Using Values 43
    Working With String Values 44
    Working With Numeric Values 45
    Working With Boolean Values 46

- Date Values. 46
- Lists or Arrays 47
- Object Reference Values. 48
- More Value Types. 50
- Variables: Places to Save Values 51
- Expressions and Operators. 52
- Commands or Methods 54
- Conditional Statements and Comparisons 55
- Using Else Statements 56
- Combining Comparisons 57
- Control Structures 58
- Interacting With Users 59
- Functions and Subroutines. 61
- Calling Functions and Subroutines. 63
- Testing and Troubleshooting Your Scripts 63
- How to Handle Errors in Your Scripts 65
- Ways to Save Your Scripts. 67
- Saving Your Script As an Application 67
- Scripting Illustrator's Object Model. 68
- Looking at Illustrator's Objects and Commands 71
- Writing a Script for Illustrator 72
- Adding Features to Your First Script. 73
- Using Measurement Units and Coordinates in Scripts 76
- Coordinates 77
- The Zero Point. 78
- Position, Width, Height and Bounds 80
- Using References to Illustrator Objects 81
- Working With Objects in Documents and Layers 84
- Working With Selected Objects 86
- Working With Paths and Points 90
- Working With Color 92
- Working With Fonts 95
- Working With Text Art Objects 98
- Using the Power of Transformation Matrices 99
- Launching and Quitting Illustrator 103
- Limitations of Scripting Illustrator. 104

4: Script Recipes for Illustrator ... 105

A Modular Approach to Scripting: Using a Cupboard Full of Scriptlets ... 106
Script 4.1: Batch Processor of Files in Nested Folders ... 106
    AppleScript ... 110
    Visual Basic ... 111
Script 4.2: Batch Processor of Open Documents in Illustrator ... 113
    AppleScript ... 113
    Visual Basic ... 114
Script 4.3: Batch Processor of All Objects in the Current Document ... 117
    AppleScript ... 117
    Visual Basic ... 120
Script 4.4: Batch Processor of All Objects in the Current Selection ... 123
    AppleScript ... 123
    Visual Basic ... 126
Script 4.5: Creator of New Document with Default Settings ... 130
    AppleScript ... 130
    Visual Basic ... 132
Script 4.6: Exporter of Current Document ... 134
    AppleScript ... 135
    Visual Basic ... 144
Script 4.7: Remove Unused Swatches, Symbols, and Styles to Reduce File Size ... 152
    AppleScript ... 154
    Visual Basic ... 157
Script 4.8: Make Duplicates of A Selection with Step-and-Repeat ... 162
    AppleScript ... 164
    Visual Basic ... 165
Script 4.9: Collect Files for Prepress Output and Generate Font Report ... 167
    AppleScript ... 169
    Visual Basic ... 171
Script 4.10: Autocomplete a Title Block with File and User Information ... 174
    AppleScript ... 180
    Visual Basic ... 182
Script 4.11: Create and Export Animations Based on Math and Physics ... 184
    AppleScript ... 186
    Visual Basic ... 188

Script 4.12: Convert Multipage PDFs to Multiple Illustrator Files 191
    AppleScript 193
    Visual Basic 194
Script 4.13: Resize and Embed All Raster Art for a Specific Resolution. . . . 195
    AppleScript 197
    Visual Basic 201
Script 4.14: Create and Work with Parametric Shapes in Documents. 205
    AppleScript 209
    Visual Basic 212
Script 4.15: Use Tags to Attach Searchable Data to Objects. 215
    AppleScript 219
    Visual Basic 223
Script 4.16: Use a Web Service to Translate Text in a Document 227
    AppleScript 232
    Visual Basic 234
Script 4.17: Slice by Guides and Export for Web Use 236
    AppleScript 238
    Visual Basic 244
Script 4.18: Create a Two-up Booklet Imposition 252
    AppleScript 255
    Visual Basic 259
Script 4.19: Merge Database Text with Template
to Create Custom Documents 269
    AppleScript 279
    Visual Basic 282
Script 4.20: Import Database Data into a Document as Datasets 284
    AppleScript 287
    Visual Basic 289

5: AppleScript Reference 293

AppleScript Language Reference 295
    Illustrator's Object Model 295
    Primary Objects. 296
    Page Item Superclass of Objects 311
    Text Superclass of Objects. 331
    Swatch Palette Color Objects. 341
    Basic Color Definitions 349
    Objects Related to Save, Export, and Open Options 354
    Other Objects Contained in Document 374

Other Objects Contained in Application 383
　　　The Matrix Object Class 383
　　　Special Page Item Creation-Only Objects 386

6: Visual Basic Reference 389

Visual Basic Language Reference 391
　　　Illustrator's object model. 391
　　　Primary objects 392
　　　PageItem superclass of objects 408
　　　Text superclass of objects. 436
　　　Swatch-palette color objects 446
　　　Basic color definitions 452
　　　Objects related to save, export, and open options 457
　　　Other objects contained in document 475
　　　Other objects contained in application. 484
　　　The matrix object 485
　　　Important Value Enumerations. 485

7: Learning More 489

Books. 489

Magazines 490

Web Sites 490

Index 493

1: Introduction

If you use Adobe Illustrator, you probably need this book. Let me tell you why.

The creative process is fundamental for visual design and illustration, but certain aspects of the actual work of illustration and page layout are anything but creative. When you think about the work you do, chances are good that you spend most of your time doing similar tasks over and over again. In fact, you'll probably notice that the time you spend placing and replacing images, correcting errors in text, and preparing files for printing often reduce the time you have available for doing creative work. Wouldn't it be great if you had an assistant—one that wouldn't mind doing most of the boring, repetitive tasks for you? Illustrator's built-in scripting and automation support give you that kind of help. Think about your work—is there a repetitive task that's driving you crazy? If so, you've identified a candidate for a script. With a small investment of time, you can write a script for Illustrator that will automate many of your least-favorite time-consuming tasks.

You can start with short, simple scripts that save you a few seconds every day and move on to full-fledged script-based solutions that work all night while you're sleeping. And Adobe Illustrator 10 includes new automation technologies, such as the Variables palette (shown in **Figure 1.3**), that are guaranteed to save you time.

To start scripting, you'll always ask yourself two key questions. In what conditions do you need to do the task? What are the steps involved? Once you understand the process you go through to perform the task, you'll be better prepared to write your script. This book will teach you how.

What You Need to Use This Book

All of the scripts in this book require Adobe Illustrator 10 for Mac OS (**Figure 1.1**) or Windows (**Figure 1.2**). Scripts in this book are written using AppleScript for Mac OS and Visual Basic for Windows. Be sure to use the language appropriate for your operating system. Adobe Illustrator 10 also supports scripting with JavaScript. Some basic JavaScript code examples are also included in this book.

Figure 1.1 Adobe has done a good job of integrating Illustrator 10's appearance with that of Mac OS X's new Aqua interface.

Complete sample code for both AppleScript (**Figure 1.4**) and Visual Basic (**Figure 1.5**) is included for all scripts. You will need to have a script-editing application for your system to create and edit scripts.

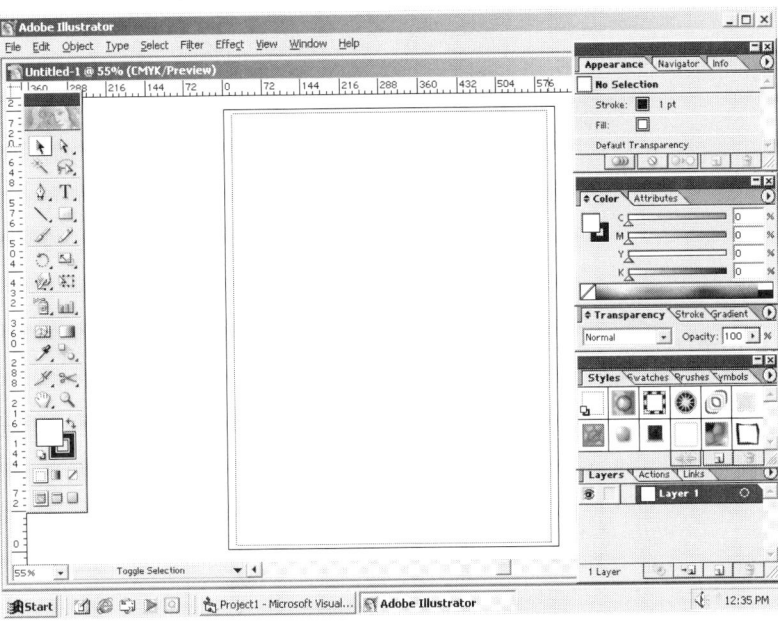

Figure 1.2 *Users of Adobe Illustrator 10 on either Mac or Windows will find little difference other than the "skin"—here's Illustrator 10 running in Windows 2000 Professional.*

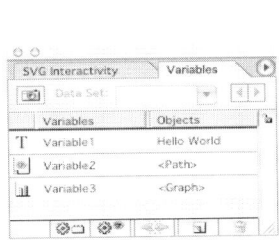

Figure 1.3 *By using variables in your documents, you can take snapshots of the states of objects in your document, changing their values and visibility, for example.*

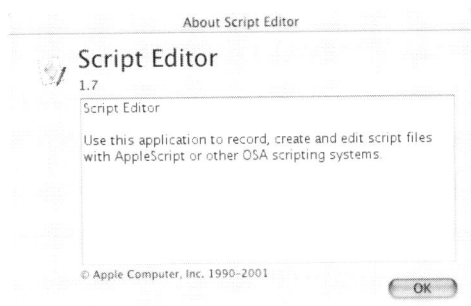

Figure 1.4 *The About window for Script Editor 1.7 from Apple—the primary script development tool used in this book for AppleScript on Mac OS.*

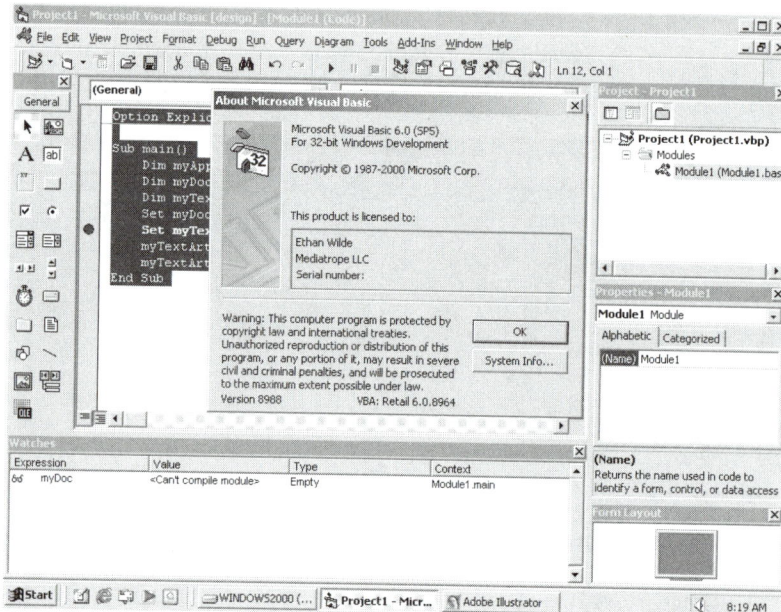

Figure 1.5 The About Visual Basic window from Visual Basic 6.0—this will be the development environment used in this book for writing Visual Basic on Windows.

Using This Book With Mac OS

To write scripts on the Mac, you must have Mac OS 8.6 or later. You will also need AppleScript and a script editor installed. AppleScript and the Script Editor application from Apple come installed on all supported versions of Mac OS. **Figure 1.6** shows the standard Mac OS X icon for Script Editor. In the unlikely event that these items are not installed on your system, install them from your original system software CD-ROM.

Figure 1.6

The standard Mac OS X icon for Script Editor 1.7.

Once you get the scripting bug, you may find you want debugging and productivity features not found in Script Editor. For Mac OS X 10.1.2 and above, Apple also provides AppleScript Studio, a complete development environment for creating Mac OS X applications. It's part of the Developer Tools installation available to Apple Developer Connection members. Basic online membership is free with registration. **Figure 1.7** shows the Project Builder environment with an open AppleScript Studio project. Project Builder is one half of a pair of applications that Mac OS X developers use to create Cocoa and Carbon applications—it lets you write code like the Script Editor. Interface Builder is the other half of Apple's development suite that AppleScript Studio projects are created in—it gives you a full user interface for your scripts.

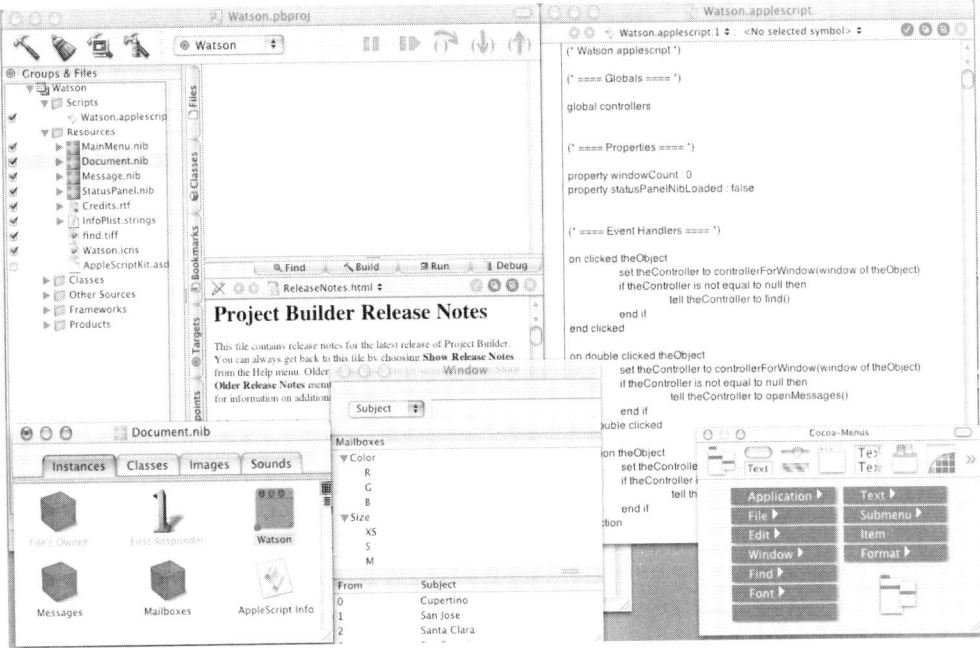

Figure 1.7 An open AppleScript Studio project in Project Builder and Interface Builder. AppleScript Studio, free from Apple, allows users to create Mac OS X applications using AppleScript.

Third-party script editors, such as Script Debugger from Late Night Software (www.latenightsw.com) provide additional features that will help you develop scripts more quickly. **Figure 1.8** shows the windows of Script Debugger with its debugging options enabled.

This book uses Script Editor 1.7 from Apple for all examples. Users of AppleScript Studio can use all of the scripts as-is, but may want to add user interface controls for capturing user input.

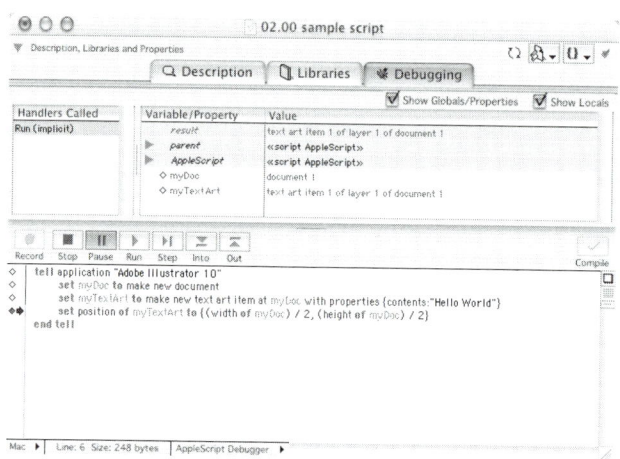

Figure 1.8 *The windows of Late Night Software's Script Debugger 3.0 with a script opened in debugging mode.*

Using This Book With Windows

To use Illustrator scripting in Windows, you must have Windows 98, Windows NT 4.0, Windows 2000, Millennium Edition, or Windows XP. You will also need the Microsoft Visual Basic development environment or one of the applications that contain a Visual Basic editor. Many applications that support the Visual Basic for Applications (VBA) language contain a built-in editor. Applications that contain a built-in editor include Microsoft Word, Microsoft Excel, and Visio. You can use any Visual Basic editor to create your scripts. However, serious scripting requires the Visual Basic development environment (**Figure 1.9**).

For consistency and ease of use, this book will use the Visual Basic Integrated Development Environment (IDE), which is available from Microsoft. The Microsoft Visual Basic IDE development environment comes in a variety of packages, all of which provide everything you need to script Illustrator.

In this book, we use the Microsoft Visual Basic development environment's editor. This editor must be purchased—it is available in a number of versions, including an educational, standard, and enterprise package. The prices vary from about $100 up to many thousands of dollars for an enterprise package.

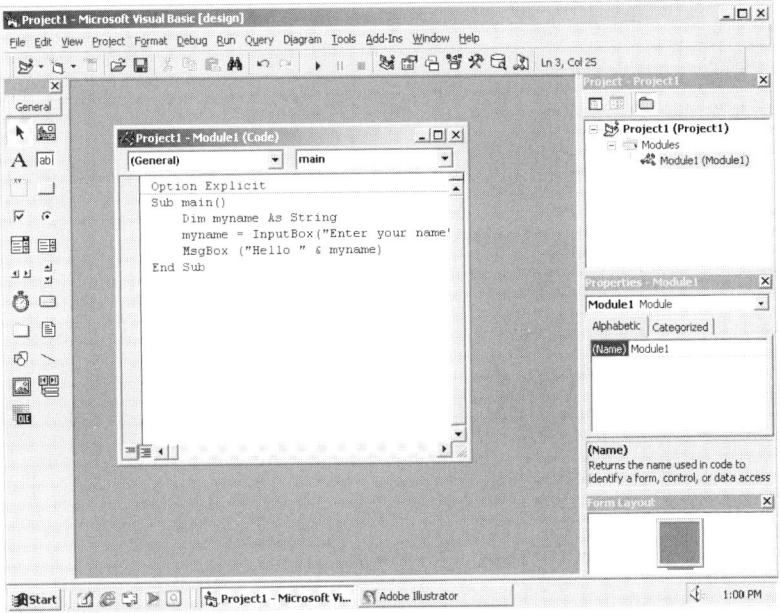

Figure 1.9 *An open project in the Visual Basic development environment.*

2: Choosing to Script

In this book, the word "automation" is used to describe all of the techniques you can use to make Adobe Illustrator do things on its own. Yes, that's right, automation makes Illustrator a slave to your desires. There are several basic automation techniques that allow Illustrator to operate automatically. These techniques include using scripts you write and actions you record inside of Illustrator. You can also use the Variables palette to import data from external files into Illustrator as datasets. Using automation, you can work with your existing documents, create new ones from scratch, or use documents you create for use as templates.

As you may already know, not all applications can be automated. Historically the few illustration and graphics applications that have incorporated automation technologies such as scripting have provided only limited access to the application's full feature set. Adobe has set a new standard with Adobe Illustrator 10—it is easily the most scriptable illustration application available today. In addition to providing great scripting support "under the hood," Adobe has incorporated advanced access to automation tools in the user interface itself. Many of these approaches are accessible through the standard user interface of Illustrator. The Variables palette, for instance, shown in **Figure 2.1**, provides direct access to XML data. The Actions palette, shown in **Figure 2.2**, is the grandfather of automation tools in Illustrator. Adobe has enhanced this older tool by allowing you to call actions you create in Illustrator from the scripts you write. Illustrator even provides quick access in the user interface to scripts you've written from the built-in Scripts menu, as shown in **Figure 2.3**.

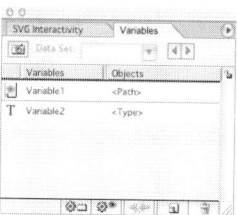

Figure 2.1 The Variables palette in Illustrator 10 lets you attach variables to the objects in a document, making them dynamically updatable by importing external data or simply by making snapshots of your changes with the capture button, shown as a little camera.

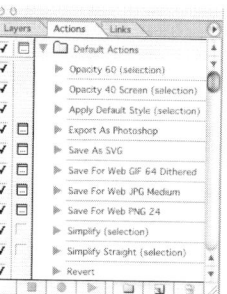

Figure 2.2 Actions in Illustrator can do many repetitive tasks for you without any need for writing scripts in AppleScript, Visual Basic, or JavaScript. What actions cannot do is make decisions using logic—that's something only scripts can do.

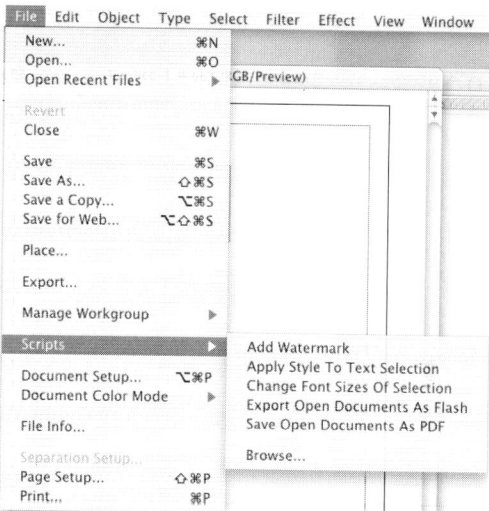

Figure 2.3 Scripting is so well-integrated into Illustrator 10 that it even sports a Scripts menu choice, File > Scripts, where you can run scripts directly from Illustrator—a great way to work with scripts that operate on all currently selected objects in a document.

Deciding If You Need a Script

Since there are so many ways to automate Illustrator besides scripting, it is a good idea to think ahead before embarking on any of your own scripting efforts. This flowchart might help:

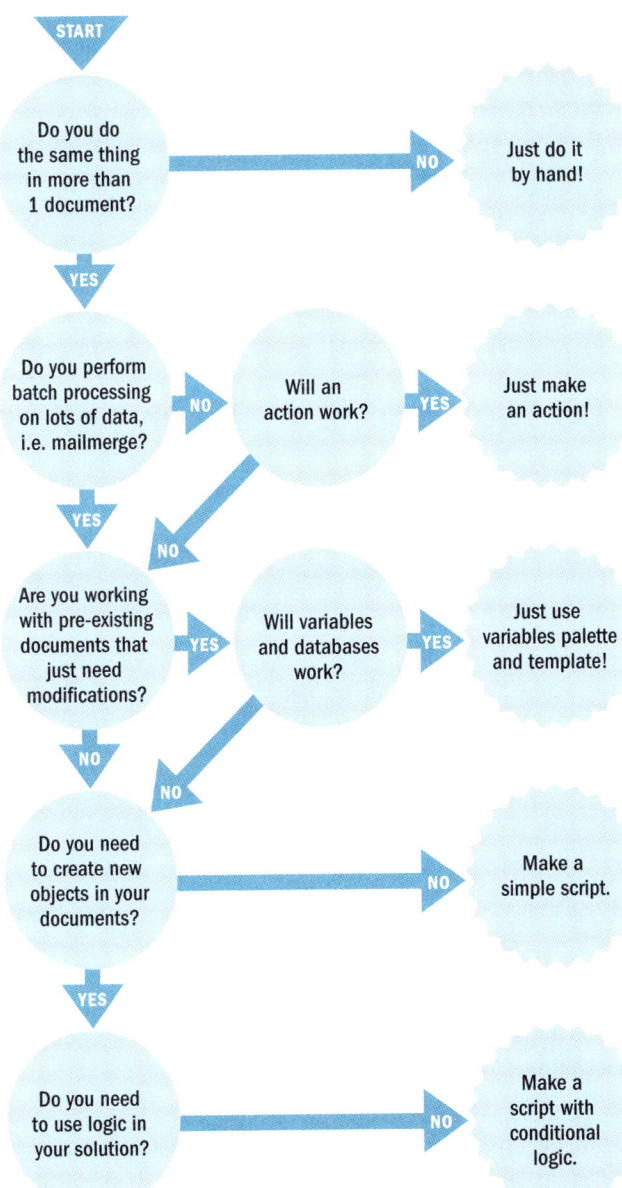

Ask yourself these questions before starting to create a script to automate Illustrator:

1. Do you need to change the same thing repeatedly in one or more documents?
2. Are you batch-processing a large amount of data in a "mail-merge" situation?
3. Are you working with pre-existing documents that each need to have some text, images, or graphs modified?
4. Do you need to create new objects in pre-existing documents?
5. Do you need to provide any logic in your solution? In other words, are there any decisions that need to be made during the process?
6. Do you need to do different things to each document depending on the individual details of the document?

Do You Need to Make an Action?

If you answered "yes" to only question 1, an action is likely to provide all the automation you need.

Do You Need Logic?

Boy, do you ever! Seriously, logic is the secret weapon of scripting. And what is this "logic" we speak of? It is not some obscure Vulcan body of knowledge reserved for Trekkies. Logic is the act of deciding something. You employ logic every time you make a decision for yourself. You evaluate certain criteria along the way, deciding at each juncture how to proceed based on the current evaluation. For example, the decision "Where should I go for ice cream?" leads you through the following questions:

a. What kind of ice cream do I want? Vanilla, chocolate, or pistachio?
b. What store has that kind of ice cream? Save-it, Eat-more, or Buy-less?
c. Are they open now? Yes or no?

Each question has a series of possible answers. Each time we choose an answer to a question, we determine a "result" and we move forward in the decision-making process based on the current result. This is logic in action.

The most basic questions have a "yes" or "no" answer. These questions are the foundation of logic. Scripting languages provide special ways to evaluate questions, such as the ubiquitous "If... then" statement. For example, If x=1 then quit.

Will a Variable Palette and Datasets Solution Work Best?

If you answered "yes" to questions 2 or 3, you can assign variables to the objects that change in your documents and use the Variables palette with datasets to batch-process or change your Illustrator documents.

Do You Need to Write a Script?

If you answered "yes" to questions 4, 5, or 6 in addition to any other, you need to create a script to automate the task.

Creating Documents for Use as Templates

While scripts can create documents completely from scratch, you can use any pre-existing document you have in conjunction with a script. When you set up a document to use with your scripts, it is good practice to observe some basic rules that will make things easier scripting-wise:

- Only documents that contain objects associated with variables can be used with the Variables palette.

- Naming any objects you plan to access from a script will help you reference and keep track of these objects in the code of your script. You can assign names to each of your document's objects by clicking on their entry in the expandable tree shown in the Layers palette (**Figure 2.4**).

- Placeholder text can be used very effectively in documents that you want to use with scripts. Think of placeholders as special words you put into your Illustrator document so your script can find them when it is running. You might want to include placeholder text in templates that you are going to use in batch-processing scripts that fill in specific text. I'll discuss the details of using placeholder text in templates later on in Script 4.19 in Chapter 4.

- Use your colors consistently. Adobe Illustrator allows only a single color model in any one document, either RGB or CMYK. However, your scripts can attempt to create colors in documents using either color model. The result of this is not ideal: Illustrator will choose an approximate color in the document's color space whenever you assign one from the other space. For example, if you try to assign an RGB color value to an object in a document with a CMYK color space, Illustrator will appear to let you do this, but the resulting color will be a CMYK approximation of the RGB color. **Figure 2.5** shows the standard new document window with color space options.

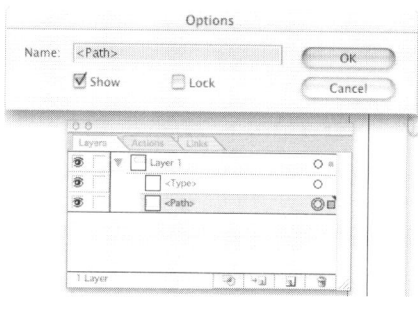

Figure 2.4 *Naming objects in your documents is a great way to make scripting them easier—and applying a name is as easy as double-clicking on the object's entry in the Layers palette to call up the Options dialog.*

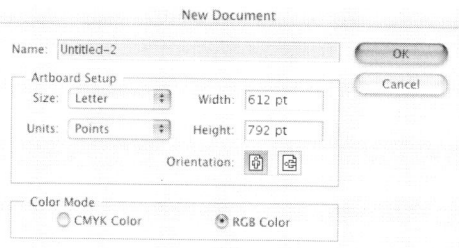

Figure 2.5 *Every new document in Illustrator 10 needs to have its dimensions and color space defined.*

Creating Documents for Use With AlterCast

Adobe's new AlterCast image server lets you easily update and maintain your Illustrator-designed visuals on frequently updated Web sites by automating the creation and repurposing of images. AlterCast works with many content management systems. It eliminates the tedious tasks of refining and reformatting images for specific purposes.

AlterCast enables you to reuse existing images by automatically generating variations based on different color modes, sizes, resolutions, and file types. Scripts can be developed to automate routine tasks, making it quick and easy to apply changes to a large number of files.

AlterCast supports the following:

- Import of GIF, animated GIF, JPEG, TIFF, PSD, and Adobe Illustrator (SVG) formats.

- Export of GIF, animated GIF, JPEG, PNG, PSD, SVG, WBMP, and I-mode wireless formats.

- The same range of image optimization settings available in Adobe Photoshop, Adobe ImageReady, and Illustrator.

- Image resizing and cropping.

- Color-mode conversion for print and Web.

How does this work, and how can you prepare your Illustrator files for use with AlterCast? **Figure 2.6** shows the overall architecture of the AlterCast system. The bottom layer of the cake, the Core Layer, includes two boxes: PSD libraries and SVG libraries. Illustrator is able to prepare SVG files for use in AlterCast's SVG library. Note that developing a complete AlterCast-based solution is beyond the scope of this book.

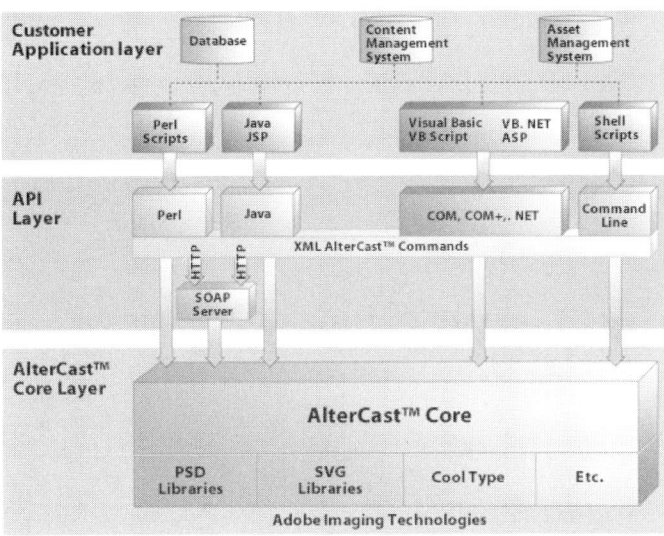

Figure 2.6 Adobe's chart explaining how the AlterCast image server fits into a working process. Smart scripters can make Illustrator 10 behave like an image server if they have the time to invest—but remember that Illustrator isn't designed to handle multiple requests the way that AlterCast's server engine is.

To Prepare a File for Use With AlterCast

1. Associate a variable with each object in your document that will be dynamically updated by AlterCast. For example, if you have some text that you want to be dynamically changed by AlterCast, associate a text variable to it. You can associate variables with text, graphs, placed images, and any object's visibility. These variables can be used by AlterCast to assign dynamic data from a database or other source.

2. You can also associate interactivity with the objects in your file by using the SVG Interactivity palette to assign JavaScript actions that will be triggered by any one of a series of JavaScript-based user events, such as on `mouseover` or on `click`. **Figure 2.7** shows the SVG Interactivity palette with an action assigned to one of the active document's objects.

3. Export your file as an SVG image. This will preserve all SVG interactivity as well as any variables you have assigned to objects in your document.

4. Once you have a valid SVG file, you can submit it to your AlterCast server's workflow.

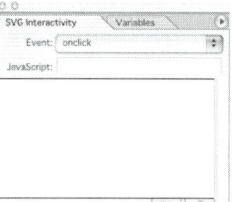

Figure 2.7 *SVG Interactivity is designed to let Illustrator document creators assign JavaScript-based actions to objects that then incorporate these actions as SVG files rendered in a Web browser.*

Using Actions With Illustrator

Illustrator actions are different from scripts. An Illustrator action is a series of tasks you have recorded while using the application—menu choices, tool choices, object selection, and other commands. When you "play" an action, Illustrator performs all of the recorded commands. You record, play, edit, and delete actions using Illustrator's built-in Actions palette. **Figure 2.8** shows the Actions palette with an action running.

Be careful not to confuse actions and scripting. Actions and scripts are both ways of automating repetitive tasks, but they work very differently:

- Actions use a program's user interface to do their work. As an action runs, menu choices are executed, objects are selected, and recorded paths are created. Scripts do not use a program's user interface to perform tasks. Scripts can execute faster than actions.

- Actions have very limited facilities for getting and responding to information. You cannot add conditional logic to an action. Therefore, actions cannot make decisions based on the current situation. Scripts are capable of getting information and making decisions and calculations based on the information they receive from Illustrator.

- A script can execute an action, but actions cannot execute scripts.

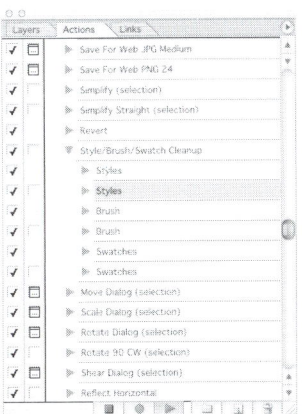

Figure 2.8 The Actions palette supports actions with a great deal of sophistication, including the ability to display dialogs to users and work with selected objects.

Using the Variables Palette and XML-Based Datasets

The Variables palette, shown in **Figure 2.9** and **Figure 2.10**, is new to Illustrator 10. It's a great new tool that works well on its own as well as integrates well into many scripting approaches.

So what is the Variables palette? It is a linking tool that lets you connect Illustrator objects' properties to external data. The data can be created in Illustrator and exported as XML or imported as XML from another data source. This means you can make a single template file, say for a business card, and link each of the text fields' content to fields in an XML-based data file. As you'll see later on in Script 4.20 in Chapter 4, using the FileMaker or Microsoft Access database software as a source for creating datasets in Illustrator is rather straightforward. Each record from FileMaker or Access

17

becomes a dataset in Illustrator's Variables palette. By using the XML-based dataset importing and exporting capabilities of the Variables palette, you can bring data in from any source, if properly formatted, just by importing an XML file.

Once you have a series of datasets in your Variables palette, you can easily switch between them by clicking the previous and next arrows in the palette. You can also jump directly to a particular dataset by using the pull-down menu provided in the palette. With a bunch of datasets imported, it's easy to switch between them and export each dataset as a unique file for printing or other uses. In Chapter 4, we'll create a simple script to perform the batch exporting of all of our current datasets.

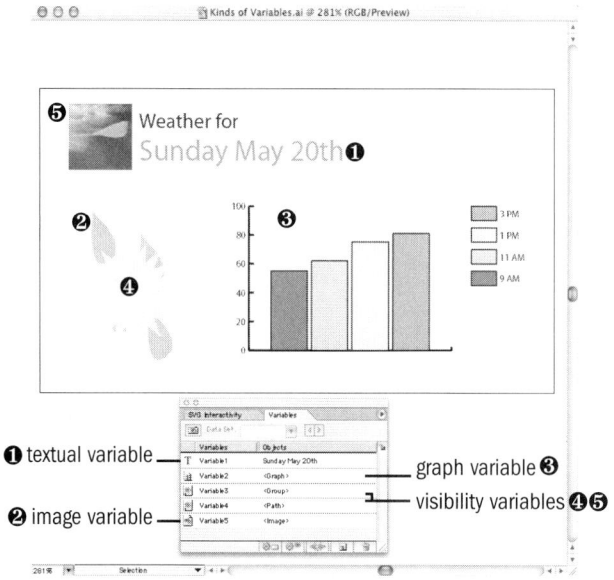

Figure 2.9 In Illustrator 10, there are four possible kinds of variables, each with specific capabilities. (1) A textual variable can be bound only to text art items—each dataset snapshot of this kind of variable stores the string of text contained in the text art bound to it. (2) Image variables can be bound to placed and raster art items—each dataset for an image variable stores the path to the linked art file. (3) A graph variable can be bound onto graph items—each dataset for a graph variable stores all of the values and settings associated with bound graph items. (4) and (5) Visibility variables can be bound to any page item—the dataset snapshot for a visibility variable stores the true or false state of the associated page item's visibility.

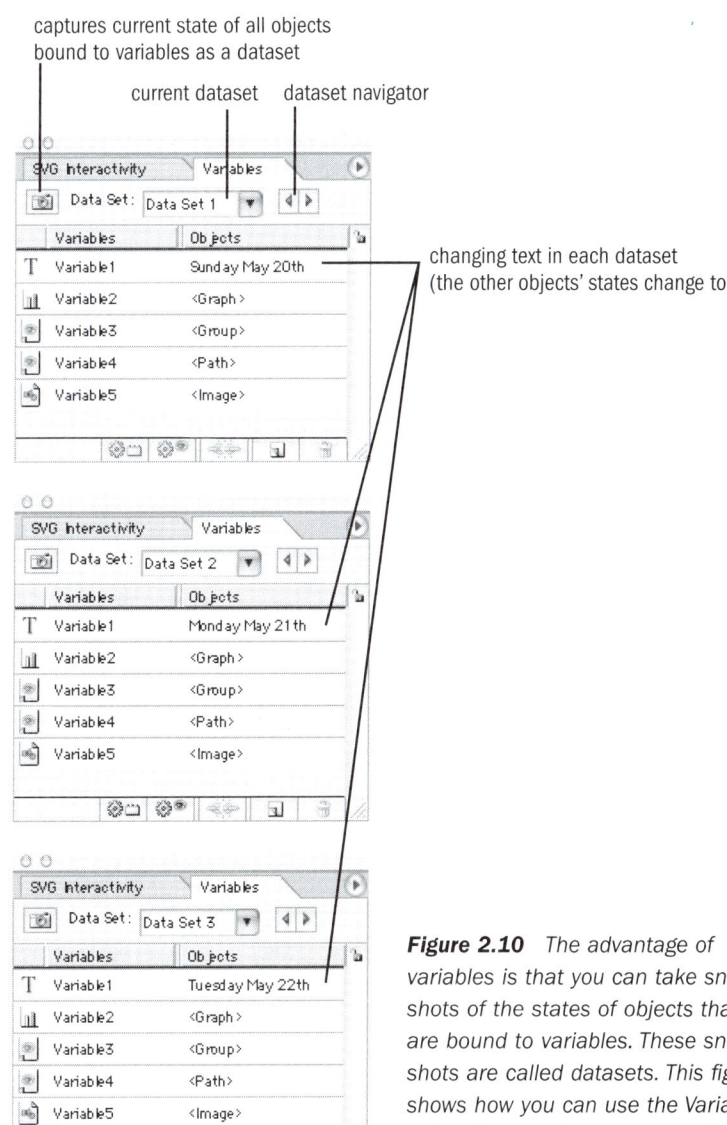

Figure 2.10 *The advantage of variables is that you can take snapshots of the states of objects that are bound to variables. These snapshots are called datasets. This figure shows how you can use the Variables palette's controls to create and navigate through datasets.*

Creating Scripts for Illustrator

Not everyone is a programmer, but most experienced computer users can write a script if they try. A script is a series of commands that tells Illustrator to perform a series of actions. These actions can be simple, like changing a single object in your current document, or complex, like modifying all of the objects in all of your Illustrator documents. Many of the tasks you can perform with Illustrator's tools, menus, palettes, and dialog boxes can be performed by a script (a notable exception is third-party plug-ins, which cannot be scripted at this time).

While scripting is a way to automate repetitive tasks, it can also be a creative tool. You can use scripts for creative tasks that would be too difficult or time-consuming to do manually. For example, you could write a script to systematically create a series of objects, modifying the new objects' position, stroke, and fill properties along the way. You could also write a script that accesses Illustrator's built-in transformation matrix functions to stretch, scale, and distort a series of objects. Without scripting, you'll likely miss out on the creative potential of such labor-intensive techniques.

Illustrator 10's scripting support offers the widest array of options for automating tasks. By writing scripts in any one of three common languages, you can control Illustrator's functions down to the finest level of detail. The scripting languages supported by Illustrator 10 are JavaScript (for both Windows and Mac OS), AppleScript for Mac OS, and Visual Basic for Windows. **Figure 2.11** and **Figure 2.12** show the text of simple scripts written in AppleScript and Visual Basic, respectively. All of the automation techniques covered in this book will rely on the scripting support built into Adobe Illustrator.

Why Didn't I Use JavaScript to Script Illustrator 10 in This Book?

OK, that's a fair question. JavaScript, with its roots in the Web, is probably the most widely known scripting language in the world as I write this book in 2002.

However, JavaScript is not a widely adopted application automation scripting language for all of my audiences. It is entirely possible to script not just Illustrator 10 in JavaScript, but also Mac OS X and Windows. But very few people do this—as a result, the development tools for working in JavaScript aren't well-tested or extensively used. It is simply harder to write and debug scripts in JavaScript for Illustrator than it is using the native scripting languages of the two platforms concerned.

There is a JavaScript OSA (Open Scripting Architecture) component available for AppleScript and Microsoft supports JScript, but script developers still predominantly work in their own platform's native scripting language: AppleScript for Mac OS, and Visual Basic for Windows. The good reasons for this fact include extensive documentation, reference books and online support communities for working with both AppleScript and Visual Basic. Relatively speaking, there is a dearth of information and support for using JavaScript OSA instead of AppleScript or JScript instead of Visual Basic for COM scripting in Windows.

The next chapter includes an introduction to the basics of scripting in Mac OS with AppleScript and in Windows with Visual Basic. If you are new to scripting, be sure to read this chapter. Concepts and approaches specific to the application are covered here, such as measurement units, matrices, and color models. Beginners who have never written a script before are encouraged to consult Chapter 7 for books on AppleScript and Visual Basic. If you're an experienced AppleScript or Visual Basic scripter, you may want to skip to Chapter 4 to get to the scripts!

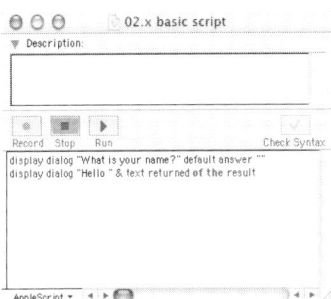

Figure 2.11 Writing AppleScript scripts means using a script editing application like Script Editor to create English-like statements that communicate with and control the Mac OS or applications like Illustrator.

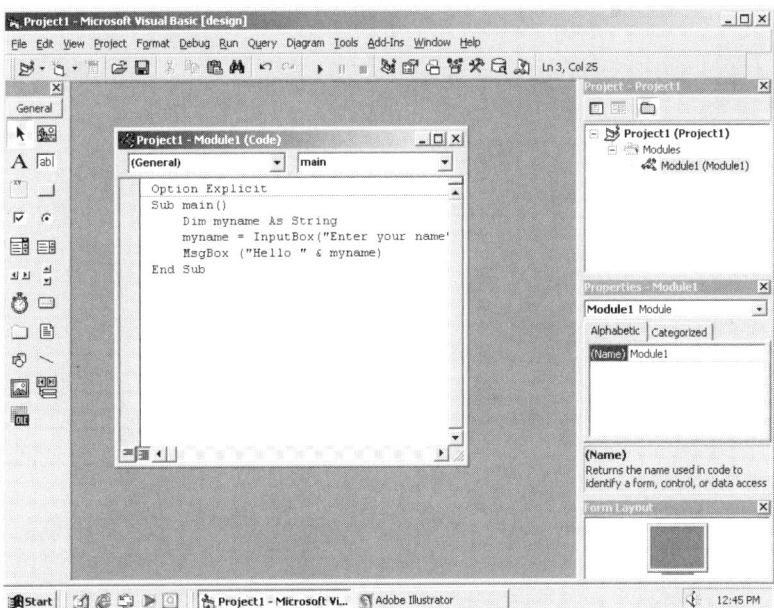

Figure 2.12 Writing Visual Basic scripts, just like AppleScript, requires the use of a script editing application, like Visual Basic 6.0's integrated development environment (IDE).

3: Scripting Basics

AppleScript and Visual Basic are scripting languages that make it possible for you to control many different applications on your computer. To gain control, you need to write scripts. To write scripts, you need:

- To be able to find out what commands each application supports and learn the syntax for those commands.

- A way to test them.

- A way to save your scripts when you're done creating them.

We'll use a script-editing application for all of the scripts in this book. To write AppleScript on the Mac, we'll use Apple's free Script Editor. To write Visual Basic scripting on Windows, we'll use Microsoft's Visual Basic 6.0 IDE.

So, to kick things off in this chapter, let's take a quick look at the Script Editor and Visual Basic IDE script-editing applications. In both applications, you'll be able to look at Illustrator's complete scripting vocabulary, or dictionary. You will also be able to inspect and use additional libraries of commands in your script-editing application. In the Mac OS, libraries of additional commands for AppleScript are called Scripting Additions (OSAX). In Windows, additional libraries of commands are called type libraries, and they're contained within dynamic linked library (.dll) files.

Using AppleScript and Script Editor on the Mac

When you write AppleScripts, you need an application that enables you to edit, compile, and save your scripts. For consistency and accessibility, all the scripts in this book were written with Script Editor. Every version of the Mac OS from System 7.1 through Mac OS X (including Mac OS 9.1) comes with AppleScript and Script Editor. **Figure 3.1** and **Figure 3.2** show you what Script Editor's application icon looks like in Mac OS X and 9.1, respectively, and **Figures 3.3**, **3.4**, **3.5**, and **3.6** show the four windows of Script Editor:

- **Script window:** The Script window (**Figure 3.3**) is where you create your script by typing script statements or recording your actions in a recordable application. AppleScript compiles your script and tests for syntax errors whenever you click the Check Syntax button in the Script window. When you click the Run button your script is executed from Script Editor. The Script window also has a description field that you can use to describe your script. If you roll over your script's icon in the Finder with Balloon Help on, the script's description is displayed.

Figure 3.1 The Script Editor application icon in Mac OS X.

Figure 3.2 The Script Editor application icon in Mac OS 9.1.

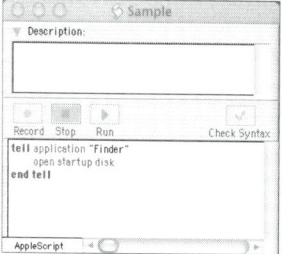

Figure 3.3 The Script Editor's Script window with a simple script showing.

- **Event Log window**: Open the Event Log window (**Figure 3.4**) from the Controls menu. It displays all events and results generated by a running script, which makes it extremely useful for debugging your scripts.

- **Result window:** Open the Result window (**Figure 3.5**) from the Controls menu. It displays the results of the last event.

- **Dictionary:** You can open the dictionary of every application or scripting addition in Script Editor. (I'll cover additions in detail in the "Using Scripting Additions" section coming up soon.) Dictionaries can provide help with proper syntax and teach you an application's script statements, events, and objects (**Figure 3.6**).

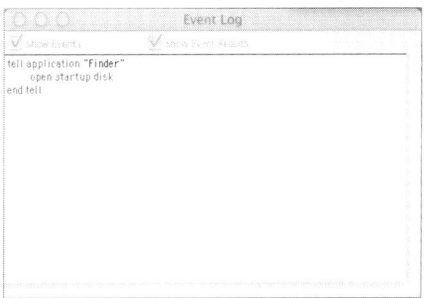

Figure 3.4 The Event Log window in Script Editor shows the events sent to other applications and their responses.

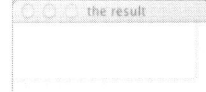

Figure 3.5 The Result window shows the returned result from the last script ran.

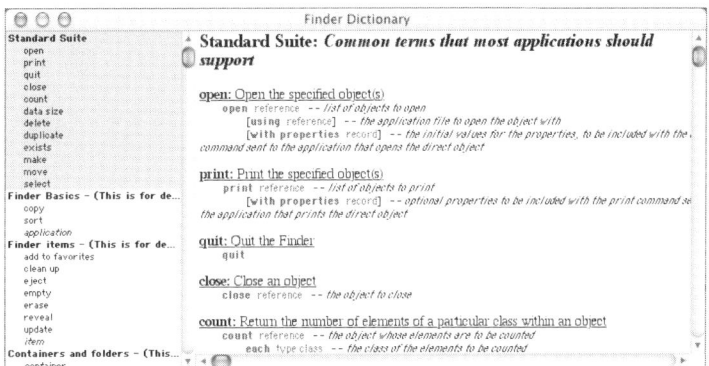

Figure 3.6 The Dictionary window of Script Editor displays the terminology defined for an application or scripting addition's AppleScript implementation—here we see the Finder's dictionary.

Finding the Script Editor

Use Sherlock (**Figure 3.7**) to locate the Script Editor application on your Mac. In Mac OS X, the Script Editor can be found in the AppleScript folder inside of the Applications folder, as shown in **Figure 3.8**. In Mac OS 9.1, the Script Editor can usually be found inside of the Apple Extras folder. **Figure 3.9** shows this folder in the Finder. Once you've located the Script Editor, drag it onto your Dock in Mac OS X or make an alias of it on your Desktop in Mac OS 9.1 for easy access.

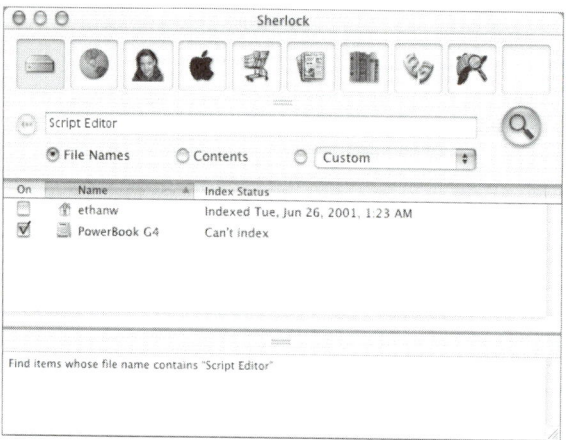

Figure 3.7 *The Sherlock searching application can help you locate the Script Editor application on your Mac.*

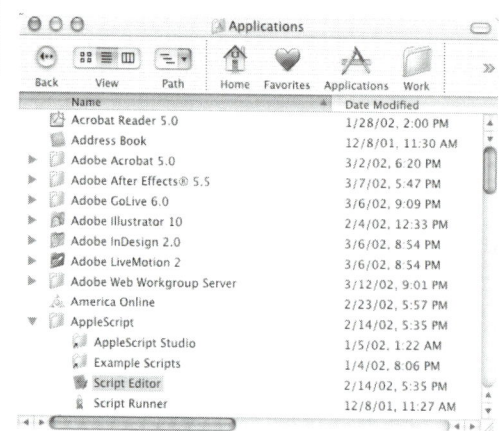

Figure 3.8 *In Mac OS X, the Script Editor can be found in the AppleScript folder inside of the Applications folder.*

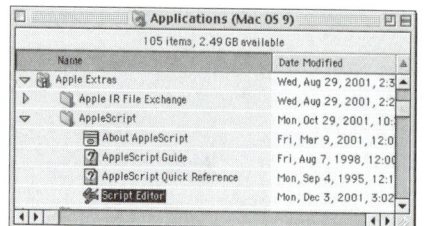

Figure 3.9 *The Script Editor application is found in the Apple Extras folder in Mac OS 9.1, as shown by the Finder.*

Scriptable Applications and Their Dictionaries

Any Macintosh application that supports AppleScript must have a dictionary. The dictionary defines the commands that the application will understand in AppleScript, from the most basic commands (such as Open) to commands that are unique to that application. Dictionaries also define all objects that you can reference with commands. Objects include things such as database records and fields, words and paragraphs in text documents, objects in drawing programs, and URLs in Web browsers. The dictionary defines what each object's properties are. Properties include filenames, window positions, and window sizes.

You can learn all the supported AppleScript commands and objects for an application or scripting addition simply by opening the dictionary in Script Editor. **Figure 3.10** shows how to open a dictionary from Script Editor's File menu. **Figure 3.11** shows a sample entry from Illustrator's dictionary.

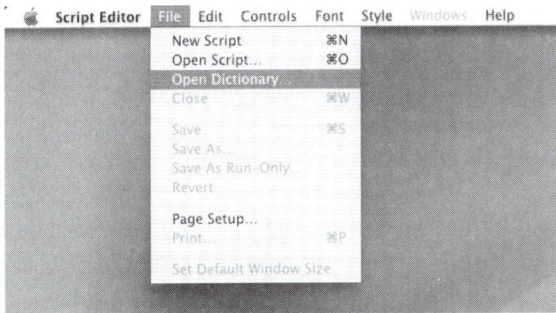

Figure 3.10 Opening an application or scripting addition dictionary is as easy as choosing File > Open Dictionary…

Dictionaries are the only guaranteed way to discover a scriptable application's commands and syntax. With some practice, you will become adept at reading dictionaries in Script Editor.

Use Drag and Drop to View a Dictionary

If you drag and drop the icon for a scriptable application or scripting addition onto the Script Editor icon in the Finder, Script Editor opens the dictionary for that file.

Scripting Additions and Mac OS X

Scripting additions must be rewritten to work with the Mac OS X version of AppleScript. While it is possible to use Classic scripting additions with Mac OS X via the Classic environment, this is outside the scope of this book.

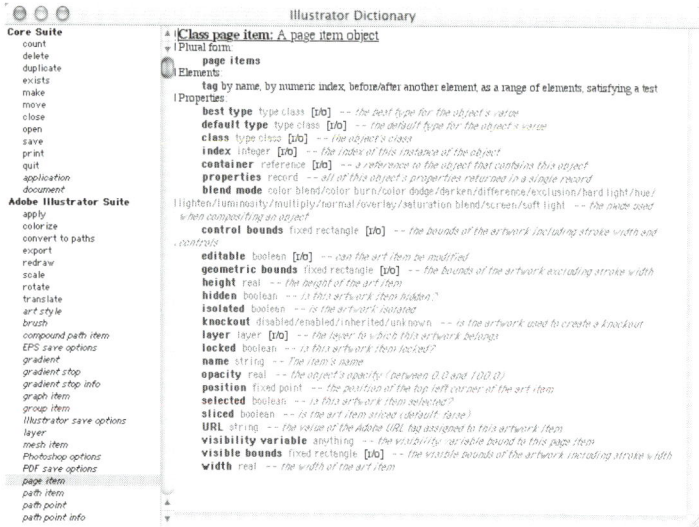

Figure 3.11 Adobe Illustrator's AppleScript dictionary is extensive, as shown by the Script Editor's Dictionary window.

Using Scripting Additions

Some AppleScripts rely on special files that add commands to AppleScript. These special files are known as scripting additions; acronym-toting geeks call them OSAX. OSAX stands for Open Scripting Architecture eXtension, which is the official way of saying that AppleScript lets you add your own command libraries. **Figure 3.12** shows the standard icon for scripting additions in Mac OS X. **Figure 3.13** shows the icon used for scripting additions in Mac OS 9.

Each scripting addition has its own dictionary of commands. These commands are added to AppleScript's set of commands when you put the addition in the proper folder for your system. Mac OS 9 uses a single Scripting Additions folder in your System Folder to hold active Scripting Additions. **Figure 3.14** shows the Scripting Additions folder icon for Mac OS 9. Mac OS X has more than one folder for active additions.

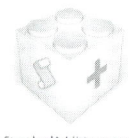

Figure 3.12 The standard system icon for a scripting addition in Mac OS X.

Figure 3.13 The icon used for a scripting addition in Mac OS 9.1.

Figure 3.14 The Scripting Additions folder icon in Mac OS 9.

Some scripting additions add powerful functions to AppleScript's basic command set, including text matching and replacement, control of system components such as control panels, and keyboard and mouse control.

Many of the scripts in this book use scripting additions. Wherever you need a scripting addition, I'll tell you where to get the addition on the Internet. Some scripting additions are available as freeware but many more are shareware. Be sure to support the Mac development community by purchasing any shareware scripting additions you end up using.

Where Scripting Additions Belong

In Mac OS X, there are multiple ScriptingAdditions folders. You can install additions accessible to all users inside /Library/ScriptingAdditions/. Users can also have their own additions inside ~/Library/ScriptingAdditions/.

In Mac OS versions 8.0 through 9.1, the Scripting Additions folder is located directly inside of the System Folder.

In versions of the Mac OS prior to 8.0, the Scripting Additions folder is inside of the System Folder's Extensions folder.

Using Visual Basic and the VB6 Integrated Development Environment (IDE) in Windows

There are many different applications that allow you to write Visual Basic scripts. You can write scripts using a Visual Editor in any application that has one. These include Microsoft Excel, Word, and Visio. Or you can use the Visual Basic 6.0 Integrated Development Environment (IDE) from Microsoft. This software package is available in a number of editions, any one of which will enable you to script Illustrator. In this book, we'll use the Microsoft Visual Studio 6.0 edition of the IDE. **Figure 3.15** shows you what the Visual Basic 6.0 editing application icon looks like in Windows. **Figure 3.16** shows the basic windows of the VB6 editing environment:

Figure 3.15 *The Visual Basic 6.0 editing application icon.*

- **Code window:** The Code window (**Figure 3.17**) is where you create your script by typing script statements. Visual Basic tests for syntax errors while you type in the Script window. You can open the Code window from the editor's View menu.

- **Toolbar**: The Toolbar, shown in **Figure 3.18**, provides access to many functions of the editor. When you're ready to test your script, just click the Start button in the toolbar to execute your script from the IDE.

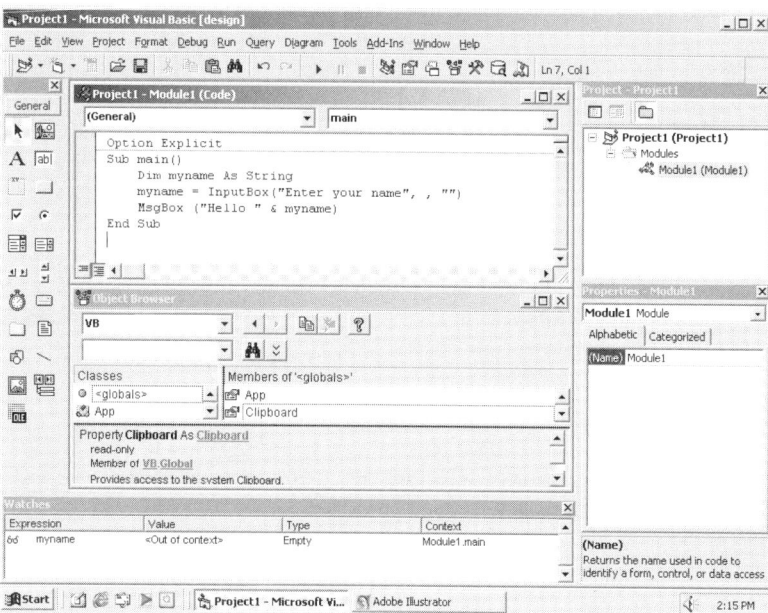

Figure 3.16 The basic windows of the Visual Basic 6.0 integrated development environment (IDE).

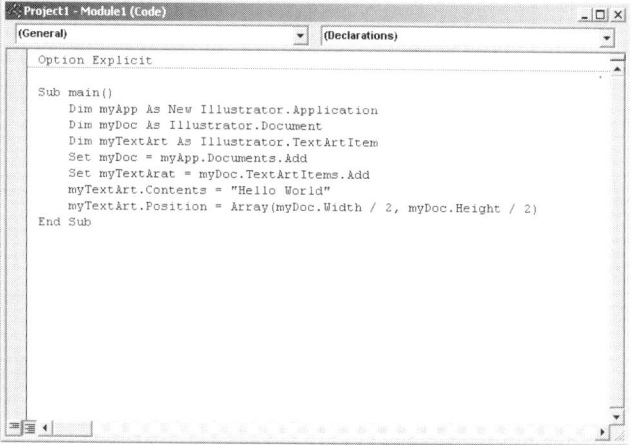

Figure 3.17 The Code window of the Visual Basic IDE is where you create your scripts.

- **Watches window:** The Watches window (**Figure 3.19**), which can also be opened from the View menu, displays the values of all variables being watched. To easily add a variable from your script to the Watches window, just select the variable in your Code window and choose Add Watch from the Debug menu. You can open the Watches window from the editor's View menu.

- **Object Browser window:** You can open and view the type library of every application or scripting addition in Visual Basic IDE. Type libraries can provide help with proper syntax and teach you an application's script statements, events, and objects (**Figure 3.20**). You can open the Object Browser window from the editor's View menu.

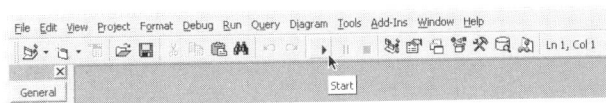

Figure 3.18 The Toolbar provides access to many functions of the VB editor.

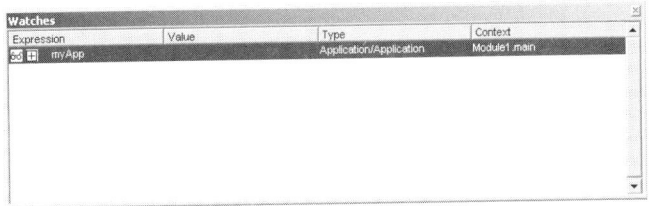

Figure 3.19 The Watches window displays the value of any variable being watched during script execution or debugging.

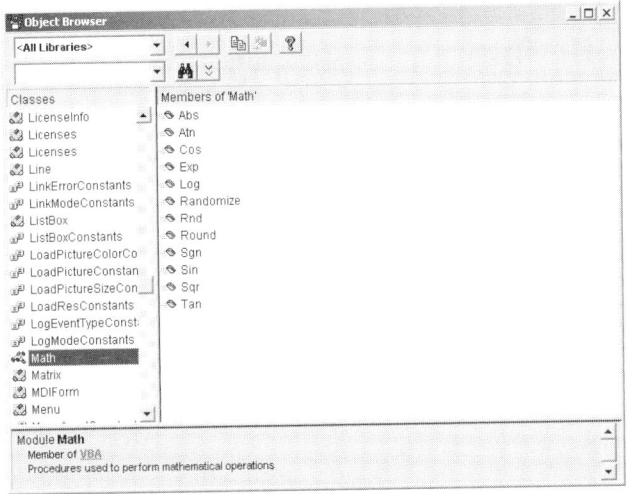

Figure 3.20 The Object Browser window lets you open and view every type library available on your system.

Finding the Visual Basic 6.0 Editor

Use Search for Files or Folders from your Start menu to locate the editing application on your PC (see **Figure 3.21**). Search for a file named "VB6.exe" if you are using version 6.0 of the Visual Basic editor. The editing application is installed in different locations depending on what edition you purchase. In Windows 2000, Visual Studio 6.0 installs the editor to the default location of C:\Program Files\Microsoft Visual Studio\VB98\VB6.exe.

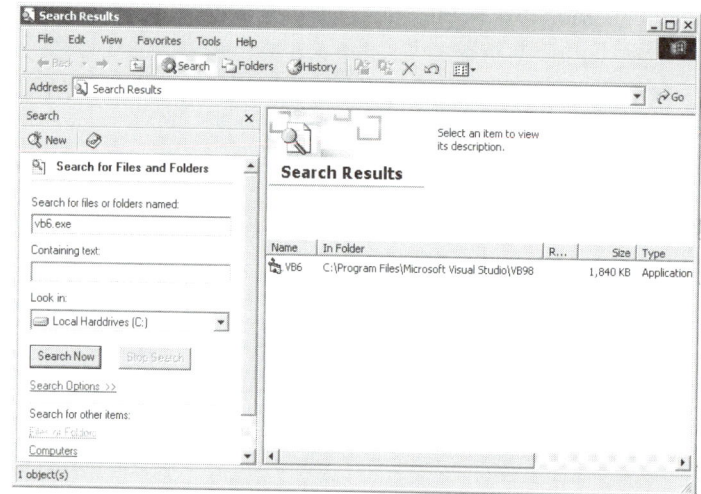

Figure 3.21 *Use Search for Files or Folders from your Start menu to locate the VB6 editing application on your PC.*

Scriptable Type Libraries and the Object Browser

Any Windows application that supports Visual Basic must have a type library that defines all of the application's objects you can script. The type library defines the commands that the application will understand in Visual Basic, from the simplest commands (such as Open) to commands that are unique to that application's objects. Type libraries also define all objects that you can reference with commands. Objects include things such as database records and fields, words and paragraphs in text documents, objects in drawing programs, and URLs in Web browsers. The type library defines what each object's properties are. Properties include things such as filenames, window positions, and window sizes.

Using the Object Browser, you can view all of the supported Visual Basic commands and objects for an application simply by opening the application's type library in the VB6 editor. **Figure 3.22** shows a view of Illustrator's type library from the Object Browser, found under the View menu.

Viewing the class library for an application is the only surefire way to discover a scriptable application's commands and syntax. With a little experience, you will become an expert at reading the Object Browser.

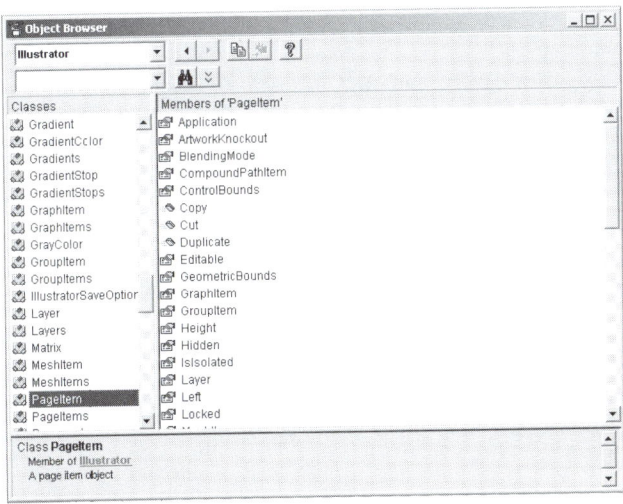

Figure 3.22 Adobe Illustrator's type library shown by the Object Browser window.

Printing a Type Library Definition

Visual Studio 6.0 includes the OLE/COM Viewer program that will provide text output of a type library's definition, similar to the view shown by the Object Browser. The Object Browser is not printable from the editing application, so the OLE/COM Viewer is the only easy way to get a printed copy of a type library. To use the utility, follow these steps:

1. Choose Run from the Start menu, as shown in **Figure 3.23**.
2. Click the Browse button in the dialog box that appears (**Figure 3.24**).
3. Navigate to the path C:\Program Files\Microsoft Visual Studio\Common\Tools\ to the OLEVIEW application, as shown in **Figure 3.25**.

Continues on next page

Printing a Type Library Definition (continued)

4. Double-click the OLEVIEW.exe icon to select the program. Click the OK button to run the program. If you don't have Visual Studio 6.0 installed, you will probably not have this file installed. It can be downloaded free from Microsoft's site at www.microsoft.com/com/resources/oleview.asp.

5. The OLE/COM Object Viewer is really for developers, so don't be alarmed by the very technical nature of the program. You just want to use it to view the guts of Adobe Illustrator's type library, so expand the folder in the left pane named "Type Libraries" so you can look for Illustrator's (**Figure 3.26**) type library.

6. Once you locate the Adobe Illustrator 10 Type Library, double-click its entry to open the ITypeLib Viewer, as shown in **Figure 3.27**. Once here, you can view the definition of each object in Illustrator's script library. You will see a lot more than the Object Browser ever showed you, but it is also harder to read. You can copy and paste as much as you want or all of the definition from the ITypeLib Viewer into any text-editing application to format and print it.

Figure 3.23 Selecting Run... from the Start menu.

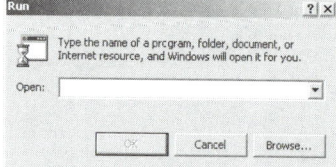

Figure 3.24 Clicking the Browse... button in the Run dialog box.

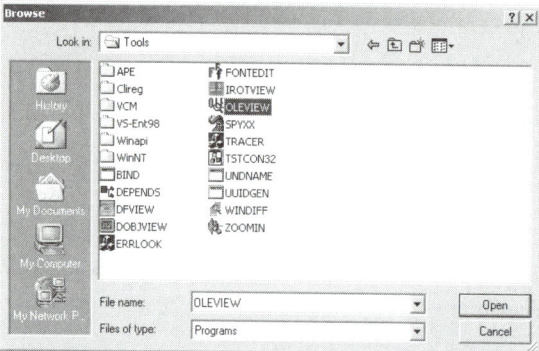

Figure 3.25 Navigating to the path C:\Program Files\Microsoft Visual Studio\Common\Tools\OLEVIEW.EXE.

Printing a Type Library Definition (continued)

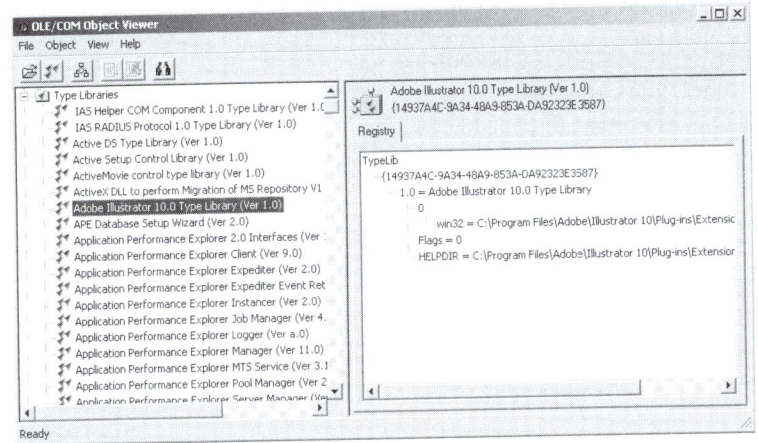

Figure 3.26 Expand the folder in the left pane named "Type Libraries" to locate Illustrator's type library, and double-click the Adobe Illustrator 10 Type Library to open the ITypeLib Viewer.

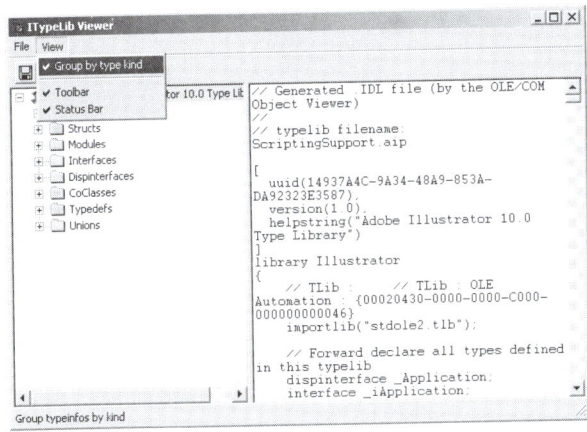

Figure 3.27 The ITypeLib Viewer shows the details about Illustrator's type library.

Including Type Libraries in Your Visual Basic Script

Some of the scripts in this book use special commands and objects found in other type library files that add commands to Visual Basic. These type libraries are often contained in dynamic linked library (.dll) files installed with different software packages. Microsoft has developed a great number of additional type libraries for use with Visual Basic to let us access ODBC databases, specialized XML-managing routines, and many other features.

You need to add a reference to each type library that you want to use in your Visual Basic script, including Adobe Illustrator's. You do this by choosing References from the Project menu, as shown in **Figure 3.28**. The Visual Basic editor will display the References window, as shown in **Figure 3.29**. From this screen you can choose to include in your project any of the available type libraries on your computer by checking the box next to their names. If you don't include a reference to the type library you want to use, none of the commands or objects it contains will be available to you. Again, this includes Illustrator, so we'll always add a reference to it in all of our scripting efforts.

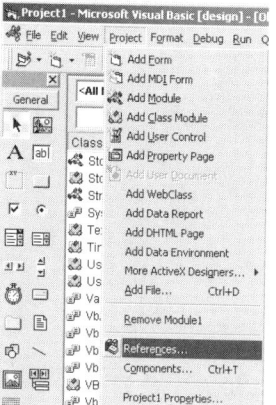

Figure 3.28 Choosing References from the Project menu.

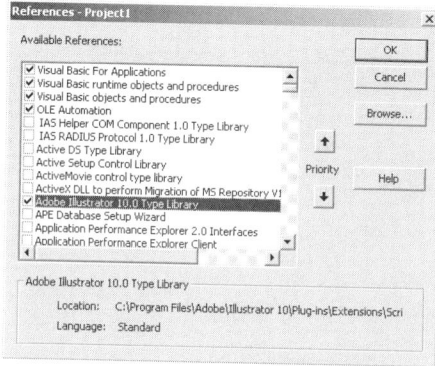

Figure 3.29 The VB editor's References window.

Each type library includes its own vocabulary of objects. These objects are added to your Visual Basic script's set of commands when you add the reference to the specific library in your Visual Basic editor.

Some type libraries add powerful functions to Visual Basic's functionality, including database access, file system access, and XML file parsing.

Many of the scripts in this book use various type libraries in addition to Illustrator's. Wherever you need to include a reference to a special type library, I'll tell you how to install this library if you don't already have it. Some type libraries are available on the Internet for free, but many more come as part of a commercial software package.

Where the Files Containing Type Libraries Can Be Found

In the different versions of Windows available, there are many places you will find external .dll files that often contain Visual Basic type libraries. As **Figure 3.30** shows, the References window will display the path (or as much of it as will show in its small dialog box) for any type library you want to locate. In this example, the Microsoft XML type library resides in the dynamic linked library file found at C:\WINNT\System32\msxml.dll.

As you browse around the References window in your Visual Basic editor, you'll see that the files containing the type libraries on your computer are installed in many different places. Leave all of the files where they were installed to prevent the likelihood of disabling their functionality.

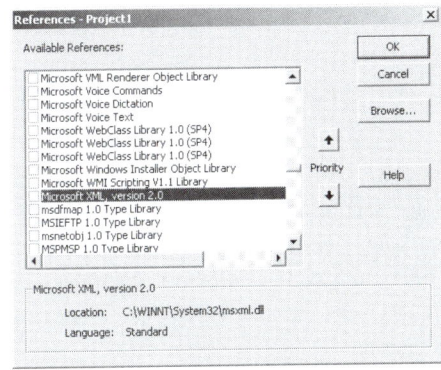

Figure 3.30 *The References window displays the path for any type library you highlight.*

Scripting and the Object Model

Now it's time to really get to the heart of what scripting is about: telling applications to do things for you. To make it as easy as possible for people to write scripts that control applications, most scripting languages treat applications and their documents as a group of individual objects rather than a single solid unit. Both AppleScript and Visual Basic use an object-oriented approach to let us control and create with our computer's software.

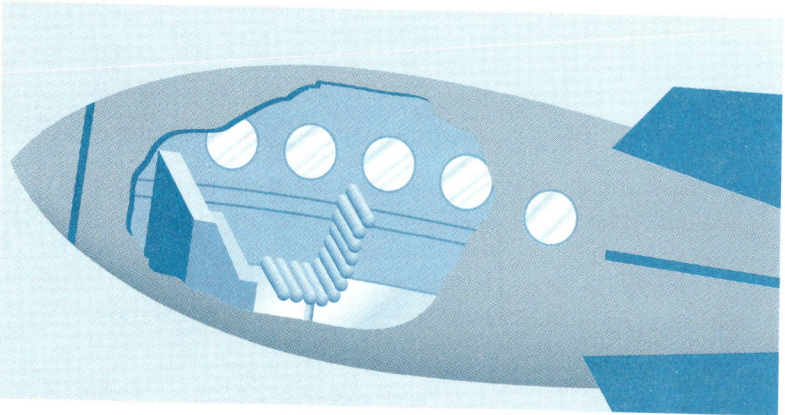

The terminology of object-oriented programming can be hard to understand at first. "Objects" belong to "classes" and have "properties" you manipulate using "commands" (AppleScript) or "methods" (Visual Basic). What do these words mean in this context?

You might think about this object approach as being like a collection of Lego blocks. Different pieces do different things, but you can use them all together in combination to do what you want to do. In object-oriented scripting languages, each important part of an application that is scriptable is given a name that we can use to refer to it. In Illustrator, for example, there is a document object that refers to an open Illustrator document. Each kind of object you see on your Illustrator tool palette most likely has a corresponding scripting language object name.

Imagine that using your Lego blocks you build a spaceship that responds to your commands (you can think of this creation as technologically advanced, or magical, or both if that helps!). The spaceship is an object, and its properties might include the number of windows, the color of the exterior, or the number of Lego blocks used in its construction.

When you write a script, you can talk to each object directly, or you can talk to them as part of the spaceship. You have to be very specific, though—you can't tell your Lego spaceship to open a window without telling it which window you want to open. So windows, just like all other objects, need some unique way of being identified so you can refer to them specifically. For example, we might want to say in a script: "Tell the spaceship to open the fifth window to the left of the docking port."

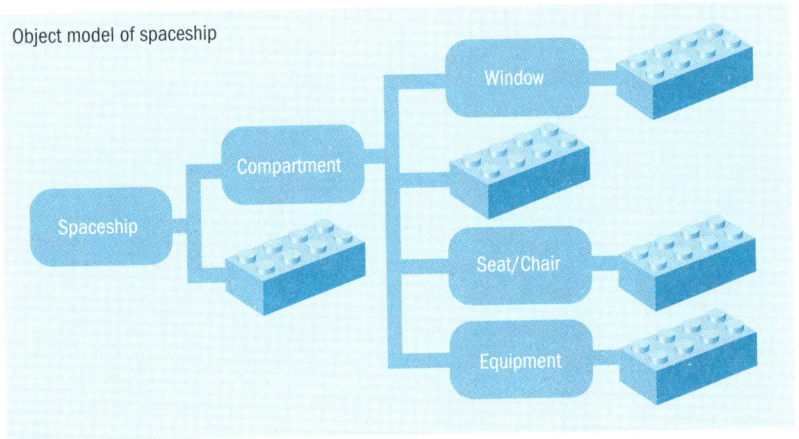

Object model of spaceship

Your Lego spaceship can also contain other objects, as shown by the diagram above. The objects within the spaceship are, of course, made up of a number of smaller objects (Legos). Since the spaceship is divided up into different compartments, we can also think of each compartment as another object in the spaceship. Then each window, seat, and piece of equipment is an also object inside of that compartment.

Objects also have properties that describe specific details about them, such as color and size. Imagine that the properties of objects in your Lego spaceship can be changed. You might say, "Chair, paint yourself blue." Because your chair can respond to the command "paint, " you'll soon have a chair of a different color.

Now let's apply this object model idea to scripting an application such as Illustrator. The Illustrator application is the spaceship, its documents are the compartments of the ship, and objects in your documents are like the windows, seats, and other things that fill up compartments in spaceships.

Object Classes

Just like in the real world, each object has inherent capabilities. Windows and doors, for example, can open or close—but the floor and ceiling cannot. This idea that objects have inherent capabilities lets us group things together in both our real and imaginary worlds. In scripting, similar kinds of objects are said to belong to the same class.

Objects with the same properties and behaviors are grouped into "classes." In the spaceship example, windows and chairs belong to their own classes, since they have unique properties, such as the number of panes for a window or the seat style for a chair. In Illustrator, every type of graphic object—paths, text, meshes, etc.—belongs to its own class, each with its own set of properties and commands. Properties such as visible bounds, width, and height, for example, are common to all page items.

Object Inheritance

Object classes may also "inherit," or share, the properties of a parent, or superclass. When a class inherits properties, we call that class a child, or subclass, of the class from which it inherits properties. So in our spaceship example, windows and airlocks are subclasses of a more general opening class, since they are both openings in the skin of the spaceship. In Illustrator, path items, for example, inherit geometric properties such as width and height from the page item class.

Classes will often have properties that aren't shared with their superclass. In our spaceship, both a window and airlock could inherit a property called "size" from the opening class, but the window class has number of panes property that the opening superclass doesn't. In Illustrator, path items, for example, have the property stroke color, which isn't inherited from the page item superclass to which path items belongs.

Collections of Objects or Elements

Object elements (AppleScript) or collections (Visual Basic) are objects contained within other objects. For example, rooms are elements (or collections) of our spaceship, contained within the spaceship object. In Illustrator, documents are elements of the application object, and page items are elements of a document object.

Referring to Objects

The objects in your documents are arranged in a hierarchy like the spaceship object—page items are in layers, which are inside a document, which is inside Illustrator. When you send a command to an Illustrator object, you need to make sure you send the message to the right object. To do this, you identify objects by their position in the hierarchy. You might, for example, write the following statement:

AppleScript
```
page item 1 of layer 1 of document 1
```

Visual Basic
```
Documents(1).Layers(1).PageItems(1)
```

When you identify an object in this fashion, you're creating an object reference. AppleScript and Visual Basic use different ways of creating object references, but the idea is the same—to give the script a way of finding the object with which you want to work.

Writing Comments in Your Scripts

Good scripting techniques always seem to take longer at first but save time later. You've probably heard this before. In fact, I find that good scripting techniques help not only when you come back to your script later, but also when you're in the process of creating it. Using clear variable names and writing well-commented, modular and reusable scripts helps keep your thinking clear and uncluttered.

Even more important than both of these techniques is the use of comments to annotate your scripts with additional information. **Figure 3.31** and **Figure 3.32** show what comments look like in Script Editor and the Visual Basic IDE, respectively. Comments are where you leave important notes for later visits to a script; they also help you clarify your thinking process while you're engaged in your scripting effort by letting you have some free space in which to outline your scripting approach.

Comments Pay Off Later

Be generous with yourself as you think through your scripting. Take the time to write out what you're doing while you're doing it. You will not regret this effort later, and it's a good way to keep yourself organized.

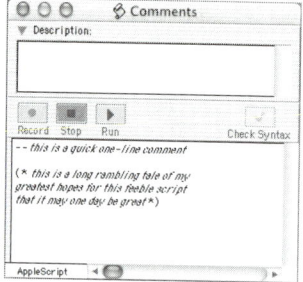

Figure 3.31 AppleScript comments in the Script window of Script Editor.

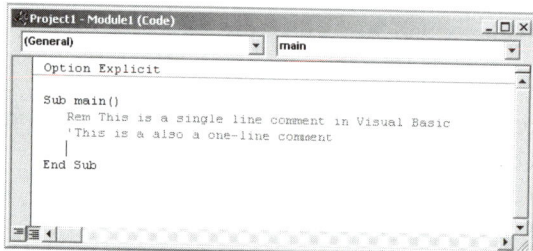

Figure 3.32 Visual Basic comments shown in a Code window inside of the Visual Basic editor.

AppleScript

AppleScript gives you two ways to enter comments in a script. The first syntax is for one-liners. You simply type two dashes to start a one-line comment:

```
--this is a quick one-line comment
```

AppleScript, always trying to be flexible, also gives the long-winded a chance to write many lines of comments quickly and easily. For a long comment, you start with an opening parenthesis and asterisk, and close with another asterisk and a closing parenthesis:

```
(* this is a long rambling tale of my greatest hopes for this
   feeble script that it may one day be great *)
```

Visual Basic

In Visual Basic, enter Rem (for remark) or "'" (a single straight quote) to the left of the comment.

```
Rem this is a comment
' and so is this
```

Dealing With Long Lines in Your Scripts

In this guide, standard lines of code are shown with blank lines above and below them. In some cases, individual script lines are too long to print on a single line, so they have been wrapped to subsequent lines.

In your scripts, however, you should follow the directions below for the language you are using.

AppleScript

AppleScript uses the special character (¬) to show that the line continues to the next line. This continuation character denotes a "soft return" in the script. You can enter this character in Script Editor by pressing Option-Return at the end of the line you wish to continue.

Visual Basic

Visual Basic uses a special character (_) to show that the line continues to the next line. This continuation character denotes a "soft return" in the script. You can enter this character in the editor by pressing Shift—(dash) at the end of the line you wish to continue.

Numbers, Text, and More: Using Values

A value in AppleScript or Visual Basic typically is a number, a string, a date, a list (or array), or a record (or dictionary collection in Visual Basic) that you use in a formula or store inside a variable. Values serve all kinds of purposes in your scripts. Values are manipulated by scripts and returned by applications as results of commands. You use values to exchange information—either between applications and your script or between lines of code within your script. When you send commands to applications, you usually send values with them.

In most languages, values have types, such as integer, string, or array. Types are also called classes in some languages; I'll use both terms interchangeably in this book. Visual Basic and AppleScript share many value types but treat each type somewhat differently. For example, AppleScript tries to set a value's type automatically unless it's explicitly defined. Sometimes you may need to do things such as coerce a string value to be a reference to a file. In those cases, you'll need to set the value types explicitly for your variables. This is consistent with Visual Basic, which prefers to have all variables declared, or defined, with a specific value type. The following sections discuss some of the most common value types and how you use them in a script.

Working With String Values

Strings are the one of the most ubiquitous value types you'll see in this book, because Illustrator documents often contain a great deal of text. A string is simply a series of characters strung together, such as "Hello there" or "Cool wig." AppleScript and Visual Basic let you work with string values in similar ways. You can access the individual characters of a string value, you can combine (or concatenate) string values together, and you can search for a matching string within a string easily. You can also coerce, or convert, numbers to string values for combining with other strings.

AppleScript

```
set x to "me"
set x to x & " and you"
display dialog (first character of x)
```

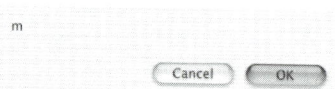

Figure 3.33 The sample code in Mac OS X generates a dialog with the letter "m" displayed.

In this case, after you set x to a string, you combine another string with the initial value. Then it's time to ask AppleScript to show the first character of that string by using the command `display dialog`. **Figure 3.33** shows the result of this code in Script Editor. In AppleScript, a string can also be referenced by its paragraphs and words as well as characters.

```
get the first word of x
```

Visual Basic

```
Dim x as String
x = "me"
x = x & " and you"
MsgBox (left(x,1))
```

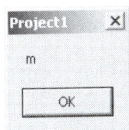

Figure 3.34 *The* `MsgBox (left(x,1))` *sample code generates a message box with the letter "m" displayed.*

In this case, after you define the variable x as a string, you set it to an initial value: "me". Next you combine another string with the initial value. Then it's time to display the first character of that string by using the command `MsgBox`. **Figure 3.34** shows the result of this code in Windows. In Visual Basic, three special functions, `left()`, `right()`, and `mid()`, let you access substrings within a string.

`MsgBox (mid(x,1,2))`

Working With Numeric Values

Numbers are the other major value type to contend with. And within the world of numbers, two basic flavors exist. There are those numbers that have no decimal point; they are the integers. Other than having no decimal point, they are free to be positive or negative numbers (depending on their own individual dispositions).

The other flavor of numbers—those with decimal points and little numbers after them—are the real numbers. Yes, that is what they are called, real numbers. Somewhat of an insult to our friends the integers, but there's nothing we can do about these names. A number is either an integer or a real number.

AppleScript

AppleScript tries to be as casual and carefree about value types as possible. Unless you insist on a type, AppleScript tries to pick one for you, based on the data stored in your variable. It therefore includes an unusual value type called just "number." Setting a value to this type in fact just leaves AppleScript to decide if the value is an integer or real.

```
set k to 1+3.5 as number
```

An integer is a positive or negative number without decimals.

```
set j to -2 as integer
```

A real value is a positive or negative number including decimals.

```
set q to 1.222 as real
```

Visual Basic

As noted earlier, Visual Basic is more strict about having you set value types. It also has more variations within the world of integers and reals. There is a short and long version of each numeric type so you can deal with "really big" numbers. Integers have a cousin called longs that can hold much bigger numbers, and real values are called either singles or doubles depending on how big a number they need to hold. We'd be fine using the smaller of each value type, but Illustrator tends to return values using the larger of each kind: long for integers and double for real numbers.

A long is a positive or negative number without decimals in the range –2,147,483,648 to 2,147,486,647.

```
Dim j as Long
j = 4000
```

A double value is a positive or negative number including decimals in the range –4.94065645841247E-324 to 4.94065645841247E-324.

```
Dim q as Double
q = 2.39393726712
```

Working With Boolean Values

A Boolean value can be only true or false. If...then statements always test a Boolean value, and Boolean variables are useful for storing the state of such tests. Think of them as being on/off or yes/no flags.

AppleScript

```
set x to false as boolean
```

Visual Basic

```
Dim x as Boolean
x = True
```

Date Values

Dates are their own value type; they specify a day of the week, month, year, and time. You can coerce a date into a string in both AppleScript and Visual Basic.

AppleScript

```
set i to the current date
```

Visual Basic

```
Dim i as Date
i = Now()
```

Lists or Arrays

The advantage of storing your values in lists (called arrays in Visual Basic) is that you can establish relationships between values easily and find values quickly. It also saves you a lot of typing time.

A list is an ordered (or linear) collection of values. You can create your own lists by specifying each element of the list when you define the list value.

Lists can be addressed as a whole or by individual values, also known as a list's items (or an array's elements).

AppleScript

To define a list is easy. In AppleScript, you can have numbers and strings intermixed as items in your list. These two lines of code show the value 1. **Figure 3.35** shows the result of the following code in Script Editor.

```
set k to {"apple","orange",1,2,3}
display dialog (item 3 of k)
```

You can add a new value to the end of a list by using the concatenation operator, &.

```
set k to {"apple","orange",1,2,3}
set k to k & "hey"
```

You can also modify individual items within a list. If you want to change the value if a single item, just reference it by number.

```
set item 2 of k to "banana"
```

AppleScript can tell you the length of a list easily.

```
set x = to count of items in k
```

Figure 3.35 The sample code in Mac OS X displays a dialog with the number "1" showing.

Visual Basic

To define an array in Visual Basic is straightforward. Normal arrays in Visual Basic allow only one value type in them, and you also must declare how many elements will be in the array. **Figure 3.36** shows the result of the following code in the Visual Basic editor.

```
Dim k(5) as Integer
k(0) = 1
k(1) = 2
k(2) = 5
MsgBox(k(1))
```

Figure 3.36 The sample code in Windows displays a message box with the number "2" showing.

Visual Basic has a special value type called a variant array to hold numbers and strings intermixed.

```
Dim k(5) as Variant
k(0) = "apple"
k(1) = "orange"
k(2) = 1
K(3) = 2
```

You can define and populate an array in one line in Visual Basic using the Array function.

```
k = Array (1,2,4,7)
```

Visual Basic uses the UBound function to tell you how long an array is.

```
x = UBound(k)
```

Object Reference Values

Objects are the things in applications or your system that respond to script commands. Application objects are objects stored in applications and their documents, such as text objects, database objects, and graphic objects. Objects can contain data in the form of values, properties, and elements that you can access or change from your scripts.

Each object belongs to an object class. Each object class is a category that defines an object's kind of properties, commands, and contained objects that you can access from your script. Object classes include applications, documents, windows, databases, fields, graphic elements, and characters.

An object's properties contain values, and elements are themselves objects that can be referenced separately from your script. **Figure 3.37** shows how Script Debugger on the Mac OS lets you see the Object Model view of Illustrator's dictionary entry for the text object class.

An object reference value holds a pointer to an object, like an Illustrator document or a file on your hard drive. Both AppleScript and Visual Basic use this value type to access the objects of specific applications. We will use object reference values extensively when we script Illustrator.

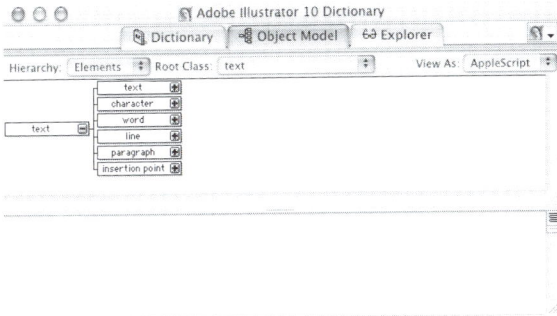

Figure 3.37 *On the Mac, Script Debugger lets you see the Object Model view of Illustrator's dictionary entry for any object class, in this case the text object class is shown.*

AppleScript

In this case, an alias reference will be stored in variable d, which points to the startup disk.

```
tell application "Finder" to set d to the startup disk as alias
```

And What About Constants?

Constants are values predefined by AppleScript and Visual Basic. You cannot change these terms, but you can use them in your code to make scripting easier. After all, using the constant tab in AppleScript or vbTab in Visual Basic is easier to remember than trying to generate an ASCII character 9, which is what a tab character is.

Visual Basic

In this case, a folder reference will be stored in variable d, which points to the startup disk. **Figure 3.38** shows the Watches window displaying the contents of the variable named d after running the following script in Visual Basic:

```
Dim fs As New FileSystemObject
Dim d As Folder
Set d = fs.GetFolder("C:\")
```

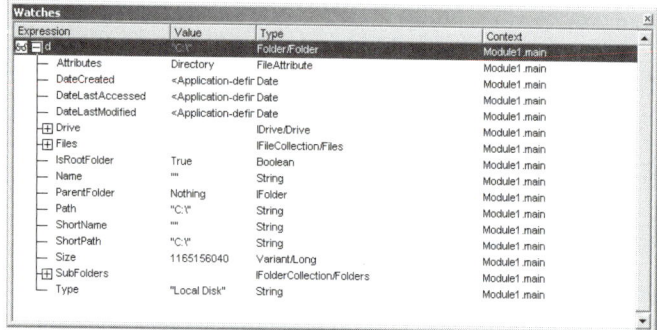

Figure 3.38 *The Watches window in the Visual Basic editor displays the contents of a variable after running a script in Visual Basic.*

More Value Types

AppleScript and Visual Basic each support other value types, including records (in AppleScript) and dictionary collections (in Visual Basic) that let you define lists of properties. See Chapters 5 and 6 for language-specific references that cover each language's value types in depth.

AppleScript Value Types

VALUE TYPE	DEFINITION	SAMPLE
Boolean	Logical true or false.	true
Integer	Whole numbers (no decimal points). Integers can be positive or negative.	14
Real	A number that may contain a decimal point.	13.9972
String	A series of text characters. Strings appear inside (straight) quotation marks.	"I am a string"

AppleScript Value Types (continued)

VALUE TYPE	DEFINITION	SAMPLE
List	An ordered list of values. The values of a list may be any type.	{10.0, 20.0, 30.0, 40.0}
Object reference	A specific reference to an object.	document 1
Record	An unordered list of properties. Each property is identified by its label.	{name: "you", index: 1}

Visual Basic Value Types

VALUE TYPE	DEFINITION	SAMPLE
Boolean	Logical true or false	true
Long	Whole numbers (no decimal points). Longs can be positive or negative.	14
Double	A number that may contain a decimal point.	13.9972
String	A series of text characters. Strings appear inside (straight) quotation marks.	"I am a string"
Array	A list of values. Arrays contain a single value type unless the type is defined as Variant.	Array(10.0, 20.0, 30.0, 40.0)
Object reference	A specific reference to an object.	Application.Documents(1)
User-defined	A collection of elements referenced by a key and stored as a key-value pair.	Var.name = "you" Var.index = 1

Variables: Places to Save Values

A variable is a kind of container that serves as a placeholder for any information you need to manipulate or share with other applications. Variable names in AppleScript and Visual Basic follow a few rules:

- They must start with a letter.
- They can contain only letters, numbers, and underscores (_).
- They cannot be words that are reserved for commands or objects.

Different scripters have different attitudes about naming variables. Some type short, cryptic variable names in the interest of expedience. I suggest using descriptive variable names, even if it means a little extra typing.

AppleScript

In this example, the command set tells AppleScript to set the variable x to the string value "me".

```
set x to "me"
```

Visual Basic

Visual Basic likes to have variables defined before being used with the Dim command. This is good practice and we will do so in all of our scripts.

```
Dim x as String
x = "me"
```

Expressions and Operators

AppleScript and Visual Basic both let you perform many operations on values and variables. The type of operator you choose depends on what you are trying to accomplish and the kind of value that your variable holds.

In both languages, you can combine strings by using the concatenation operator, &, as follows:

AppleScript

```
set x to "Hello " & "World"
display dialog x
```

Assigning Value Types to Variables in AppleScript

Variables come in many flavors, including strings, numbers, and Booleans. When you assign a value to a variable, you can tell AppleScript what kind of value it is. This is important, because commands often expect to receive values of particular types. We'll look at types in "Numbers, Text, and More: Using Values" later in this chapter.

Properties Are Like Persistent Variables

In both Visual Basic and AppleScript, your script can define its own properties. Properties behave differently in each language. Refer to Chapter 7 for books that cover each scripting language in more detail.

In AppleScript, you can also add items to a list by using &. **Figure 3.39** shows the result displayed in Script Editor when you concatenate an item onto a list.

```
set z to {"apple","pear"} & "banana"
```

Figure 3.39 The Result window of Mac OS's Script Editor displays the results of the last script run.

Visual Basic

```
Dim x As String
x = "Hello " & "World"
MsgBox(x)
```

Figure 3.40 shows the result of running the preceding script in Visual Basic.

Figure 3.40 The message box window in Windows is displayed by the MsgBox() function.

Operators perform calculations (addition, subtraction, multiplication, and division) on variables or values and return a result. For example:

```
mywidth/2
```

would return a value equal to half of the content of the variable `mywidth`. So if `mywidth` contained the number 20.5, the value returned would be 10.25.

You can also use operators to perform comparisons (equal to, not equal to, greater than, or less than). For example:

```
mywidth > myheight
```

would return the value true if `mywidth` is greater than `myheight`, or false, if it is not.

Some operators differ between AppleScript and Visual Basic:

AppleScript

For example, AppleScript uses the nonequality symbol to test "not equals" (≠, use Option- = from keyboard).

```
if x ≠ 2 then display dialog "Hello
```

Visual Basic

Visual Basic uses the greater and less than symbols juxtaposed: <>.

```
if x <> 2 then MsgBox ("Hello")
```

Also different is the divide-without-remainder operator. This is `div` in AppleScript and `\` in Visual Basic.

You can use many operators in both languages. The table below lists numerical operators. The "Combining Comparisons" section later in this chapter discusses logical, or Boolean, operators.

Numerical Operators in AppleScript and Visual Basic

OPERATOR	MEANING	SAMPLE
^	Raise to the power of	2^4=16
*	Multiply	1*3=3
+	Add	2+7=9
-	Subtract	5-2=3
/	Divide	8/2=4
mod	Divide, returning remainder	11 mod 2=1

Commands or Methods

If objects are "nouns" and properties are "adjectives" in our scripting systems, then commands (AppleScript) or methods (Visual Basic) are the "verbs"—they're the parts of the script that make things happen. The type of the object you're working with determines which methods you can use to manipulate it.

AppleScript

In AppleScript, use the `make` command to create new objects, the `set` command to assign object references to variables and to change object properties, and the `get` command to retrieve objects and their properties.

```
tell application "Illustrator"
    make new document
    set mydoc to document 1
    get width of mydoc
    set mywidth to the result
end tell
```

Visual Basic

In Visual Basic, use the Add method to create new objects, the Set statement to assign object references to Visual Basic variables or properties, the assignment operator (=) to retrieve and change object properties.

```
Dim myapp as New Illustrator.Application
Dim mydoc as Illustrator.Document
Set mydoc = myapp.Documents.Add()
mywidth = mydoc.width
```

Conditional Statements and Comparisons

One of the most powerful features that scripting offers you is the ability to introduce logic along with automation. At its most basic, logic means making decisions based on comparisons between values. These values can be stored in variables or used literally.

To put these comparisons to good use, you need a command to use with them. The hands-down conditional favorite in both AppleScript and Visual Basic is

if…then…else…

The following examples show some comparisons that use the if command. You can use basic comparisons with numbers, strings, and Booleans to good purpose.

AppleScript

The second example is the same, except that the command is written in words rather than symbols. AppleScript lets you do this for added clarity. You can generate the ≤ and ≥ characters by pressing Option-, (comma) or Option-. (period).

```
if 4 > 2 then display dialog "Yes"
if 1 < 8 then display dialog "Yes"
if 3 ≥ 1 then display dialog "Yes"
if 1 ≤ 3 then display dialog "Yes"
if 3 = 3 then beep
if 1 ≠ 2 then beep


if 1 is less than 8 then display dialog "Yes"
```

```
if 4 is greater than 2 then display dialog "Yes"
if 3 is greater than or equal to 1 then display dialog "Yes"
if 1 is less than or equal to 3 then beep
if 3 is equal to 3 then beep
if 1 is not equal to 2 then beep
```

Visual Basic
```
if 4 > 2 then MsgBox ("Yes")
if 1 < 8 then MsgBox ("Yes")
if 3 >= 1 then MsgBox ("Yes")
if 1 <= 3 then MsgBox ("Yes")
if 3 = 3 then MsgBox ("Yes")
if 1 <> 2 then MsgBox ("Yes")
```

Using Else Statements

Comparisons using `if` can also respond to failures when an `else` clause is included. In this example, the initial `if` test fails, and the `else` clause is executed instead. **Figure 3.41** shows what happens when you run the following script in Script Editor.

Figure 3.41 *The dialog displayed by running a simple comparison script in AppleScript.*

AppleScript
```
set x to 10
if x = 1 then
    display dialog "I'm 1."
else
    display dialog "I'm not 1."
end if
```

Visual Basic
```
Dim x as Integer
x = 10
if x = 1 then
```

```
   MsgBox ("I'm 1.")
else
   MsgBox ("I'm not 1.")
end if
```

Combining Comparisons

To add to the usefulness of comparisons, you can use three logical operators—and, or, and not—to create compound if…then statements. Using these command words, you can create much more elaborate comparisons that test many values at the same time. The following table lists the logical operators and shows how they work.

Using the logical operator here lets you combine two if… then tests into one. Both conditions must be true for the overall test to return true and then beep. Here, the string i would have to equal "yes," and the number inside the variable j would have to be greater than 5 to return true. As in all comparisons, your script goes on to the rest of the statement (and, in this case, beeps) only if the comparisons return true.

AppleScript

```
if i = "yes" and j > 5 then display dialog "OK"
if i <> "no" or j = 1 then display dialog "OK"
```

Visual Basic

```
if i = "yes" and j > 5 then MsgBox ("OK")
if i <> "no" or j = 1 then MsgBox ("OK")
```

Logical/Boolean Operators

OPERATOR	MEANING	SAMPLE
and	Returns true if both tests are successful.	x and y returns true only if x is true and y is true.
or	Returns true if either test succeeds.	x or y returns true as long as either x or y is true.
not	Returns true if test fails; returns false if test is successful.	not x returns false if x is true.

Control Structures

Now that you know AppleScript and Visual Basic both have the smarts provided by comparisons, let's look at the brute force you can add to your scripts with repeat loops and for…next loops. A loop makes a comparison continually over a range of values until it gets a true result. The for…next loop exists only in Visual Basic by name, but its function is mirrored by AppleScript with a special repeat loop.

The repeat loop is one of both AppleScript's and Visual Basic's most essential features, because it lets you do many things over and over in your scripts, saving a great deal of work that would otherwise be done by your own poor fingers. The simplest form of a loop is one that repeats some series of script operations a set number of times.

AppleScript

```
repeat with mycounter from 1 to 20
    display dialog mycounter
end repeat
```

Visual Basic

```
For mycounter = 1 to 20
    MsgBox mycounter
Next
```

In their most exotic form, repeat loops are conditional, much like the `if` statement. This control structure includes conditional logic, so that it loops while or until some condition is true or false.

AppleScript

```
repeat while flag = false
    set flag to (button returned of display dialog "Quit?") = "Cancel"
end repeat


repeat until flag = true
    set flag to (button returned of display dialog "Quit?") = "OK"
end repeat
```

Visual Basic

```
Do While flag = false
    flag = (MsgBox ("Quit?", vbOKCancel)) = vbCancel
loop


Do Until flag = true
    flag = (MsgBox ("Quit?", vbOKCancel)) = vbOK
loop
```

Both AppleScript and Visual Basic have a special loop construction that automates the process of moving through each item in a list or array. In this code, the values of the three items in myList are put individually into the variable myItem, one item for each cycle in the loop. You display the item's value in a dialog box.

AppleScript

```
set myList to {1,2,3}
repeat with myItem in myList
    display dialog myItem
end repeat
```

Visual Basic

```
myList = Array (1,2,3)
For each myItem in myList
    MsgBox myItem
Next
```

Interacting With Users

AppleScript and Visual Basic give us a few simple and similar commands for getting input from the user while your script is running.

You Can Define Up to Three Buttons In a display dialog

In the following example, you tell AppleScript to make the Cancel button the default button, which makes that button show up with a thick border and causes it to be triggered when the user presses the Return or Enter key.

AppleScript

In AppleScript, you can get text data and button choices by using the display dialog command. **Figure 3.42** shows what the dialog box looks like when the script runs.

```
display dialog "Please enter your name" default answer ""
    buttons {"First", "Last", "Cancel"} default button "Cancel"
set x to the button returned of the result
display dialog x
```

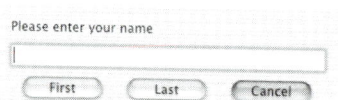

Figure 3.42 The dialog displayed prompts the user to enter text in AppleScript.

The first line of code has AppleScript stop executing and display a dialog box asking the user to supply a name. **Figure 3.43** shows what happens if you enter some text into the field and click the button labeled First. In this example, you also define a default answer, which sets the initial string that appears in the dialog box's editable text field. In this case, you set it to an empty string. If you didn't include the default answer, AppleScript would not show a text field in the dialog box.

```
display dialog "Please enter your name" default answer ""
    buttons {"First", "Last", "Cancel"} default button "Cancel"
```

Here, you access the results of display dialog. When this line is executed, the variable x will equal the string value "First."

```
set x to the button returned of the result
```

Figure 3.43 This dialog is displayed if the user enters some text into the field, then clicks the button labeled "First."

Visual Basic

In Visual Basic, you can get text data by using the InputBox function.

```
Dim x As String
x = InputBox ("Please enter your name", "Question Box", "")
MsgBox (x)
```

The InputBox function stops the execution of your script and displays a dialog box asking the user to supply some text. **Figure 3.44** shows what the dialog box looks like when the script runs. **Figure 3.45** shows what happens if you enter Steve and click the OK button.

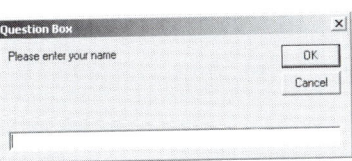

Figure 3.44 *The dialog displayed prompts the user to enter text in Visual Basic.*

Figure 3.45 *This dialog is displayed if the user enters the text "Steve" into the field, then clicks the button labeled "OK."*

Functions and Subroutines

Both AppleScript and Visual Basic make it easy to define a snippet of code as a function. A function is simply a short modular script that performs one specialized task and returns a value. Subroutines do the same kind of thing but don't return a value when they are done. AppleScript often refers to both functions and subroutines as handlers. Some of the scripts you'll create in this book you will use in conjunction with one another as functions or subroutines or create more complex scripts.

Writing simple code contained in functions makes that code especially easy to reuse. As you become a regular scripter, you'll find that many functions you create for one purpose are useful over and over, and you'll soon find yourself with a folder full of reusable function-laden script libraries. Efficient use of functions, like use of straightforward variable names, is an important part of good scripting.

AppleScript

In AppleScript, you simply use the on statement and give your function a name. The example function, named testValue, tests a value passed to it, ensuring that the value is within the range of 1 to 100, and then returns the adjusted value.

```
on testValue(x)
   if x > 100 then set x to 100
     if x < 1 then set x to 1
   return x
end testValue
```

By placing these comparisons within a function, you create a snippet of code you can use whenever you want this comparison made, instead of having to type it every time. You define the function by typing on, followed by the function name. If you want to be able to pass data to the function, you also need to define a variable in the first line of the function to hold that data. This example uses x.

Variables are always placed within parentheses in an on statement:

```
on testValue(x)
```

These two lines are the comparison that works inside the function, setting the value of x, which is the data you passed to the function when you called it:

```
if x > 100 then set x to 100
if x < 1 then set x to 1
```

This important line tells AppleScript to return the value in x to the rest of the script:

```
return x
```

The end tells AppleScript the function is over:

```
end testValue
```

Visual Basic

In Visual Basic, you use the `public function` statement and give your function a name. The sample Visual Basic script below shows the same simple function we wrote for AppleScript above. This function, named testValue, tests a value passed to it, ensuring that the value is within the range of 1 to 100, and then returning the adjusted value.

```
Public Function testValue(x)
   if x > 100 then set x to 100
      if x < 1 then set x to 1
   testValue = x
End Function
```

To pass data to the function, you also need to define a variable in the first line of the function to hold that data. This example uses x.

Variables are always placed within parentheses in a `public function` declaration:

```
Public Function testValue(x)
```

These two lines are the comparison that works inside the handler, setting the value of x, which is the data you passed to the handler when you called it:

```
if x > 100 then set x to 100
if x < 1 then set x to 1
```

This important line tells Visual Basic to return the value in x as the result of this function:

```
testValue = x
```

The end function tells Visual Basic the function is over:

```
End Function
```

Calling Functions and Subroutines

Calling functions is just as easy as defining them. You can pass a function many values of any type, including strings, numbers, and lists. Separate multiple values with commas.

In the following single line of code, you call the function testValue, passing it the value 200. The handler returns its results into the variable z. **Figure 3.46** shows the result of calling our sample function in AppleScript.

AppleScript

```
set z to testValue(200)
display dialog z
```

Visual Basic

```
z = testValue(200)
MsgBox (z)
```

Figure 3.46 The number 100 is displayed by the sample function in AppleScript.

Testing and Troubleshooting Your Scripts

Both scripting environments provide tools for monitoring the progress of your script while it is running, making it easier for you to track down any problems your script might be encountering or causing.

AppleScript

Apple's Script Editor has two very basic debugging tools. The Event Log window allows you to watch the Apple Events sent to other applications and the results those applications return. The Result window shows the most recent evaluated result of an expression. These windows are invaluable tools for debugging scripts in the Script Editor. **Figure 3.47** and **Figure 3.48** show the Event Log and Result windows, respectively.

To use the Script Editor to debug your scripts:

1. Always test your scripts in the Script Editor before saving them. When an error occurs during execution, the Script Editor will conveniently highlight the offending line of code in your script.

2. Leave the Event Log window open at all times when you run scripts from within the Script Editor.

3. Open the Result window to quickly see the results of running a single line of code in the Script Editor.

4. Use AppleScript's special `stop log` and `start log` commands in your script to hide and show selected portions of your code's activity in the Event Log instead of having to look at all the results of your entire script.

5. Insert temporary `display dialog` commands into your script to display the contents of variables during your script's execution. Once your script is debugged, you can easily delete any of these commands.

6. In Mac OS 8.5 and above, you can insert temporary `say` commands into your script to have AppleScript speak the contents of variables during execution instead of using a display dialog.

7. For the best error handling, add complete `try` statements to your scripts that deal intelligently with errors. See the "How to Handle Errors in Your Scripts" section for more information.

Figure 3.47 The Event Log window in Script Editor shows the results of running the sample function.

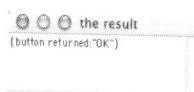

Figure 3.48 The Result window in Script Editor shows the results of running the sample function.

Visual Basic

In the Visual Basic 6.0 IDE, there are many debugging tools available:

1. You can stop your script at any point, or step through your script one line at a time. To stop your script at a particular line, select that line in your script and choose Debug > Toggle Breakpoint. When you run the script, Visual Basic will stop at the breakpoint you have set. Choose Debug > Step Into (or press F8) to execute the next line of your script, or choose Run > Start (or press F5) to continue normal execution of the script. **Figure 3.49** shows the Code window with a breakpoint set.

2. You can also observe the values of variables defined in your script using the Watches window—a very valuable tool for debugging your scripts. To view a variable in the Watches window, select the variable and choose Debug > Quick Watch. Visual Basic displays the Quick Watch dialog box. Click the Add button. Visual Basic displays the Watches window. If you have closed the Watches window, you can display it again by choosing View > Watches Window.

3. You can also add on error resume next statements to your scripts to deal intelligently with errors. See the next section for more information.

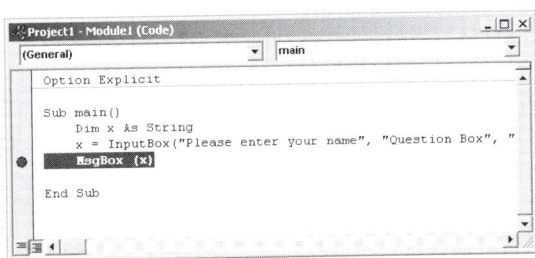

Figure 3.49 The Code window in the Visual Basic editor with a breakpoint set for debugging.

How to Handle Errors in Your Scripts

If you have complete control over the situations in which your script will run, there's no need for you to worry about error handling. If not, however, you'll have to add some error-handling capabilities to your script. Both scripting environments give you a way to intercept execution errors in your scripts with the try statement.

The following examples show how you can stop a script from executing when a specific object cannot be found.

AppleScript

```
tell application "Adobe Illustrator 10"
  activate
  try
    set my2ndObject to page item 2 of current document
  on error
    display dialog "Couldn't locate 2nd page object."
  end try
end tell
```

AppleScript provides the try... on error... end try control statement for intercepting and handling errors in your scripts. The on error portion of the statement is optional.

Visual Basic

```
Option Explicit
Sub Main()
Dim myApp As New Illustrator.Application
  Dim myDoc As Illustrator.Document
  Dim my2ndObject As Illustrator.PageItem
  Set myDoc = myApp.ActiveDocument
  On Error GoTo DisplayError
  Set my2ndObject = myDoc.PageItems(2)
  Exit Sub
  DisplayError:
    MsgBox ("Couldn't locate 2nd page object.")
End Sub
```

In addition to On Error GoTo, Visual Basic also offers the option of using On Error Resume Next, which will cause script execution to move to the immediate next line when any error is encountered.

Ways to Save Your Scripts

There are two primary ways to save your scripts in both AppleScript and Visual Basic. You can choose to save your script as a double-clickable application, or you can save your script as a compiled script file. Both methods have their uses. For example, Illustrator's File > Scripts submenu will display the names of any compiled script files you place in the Illustrator application's Scripts folder. But scripts saved as complete applications will not appear in the Illustrator Scripts submenu.

Saving Your Script As an Application

AppleScript

When you save a script as an application, the main code within the handler executes when a user double-clicks your script's icon. **Figure 3.50** shows the Save dialog box that appears when you choose to save your script as a stand-alone application. Making your script into an application makes it easy for a user to run the script. **Figure 3.51** shows the icon for a script application in the Mac OS X Finder. Double-click it, and it runs.

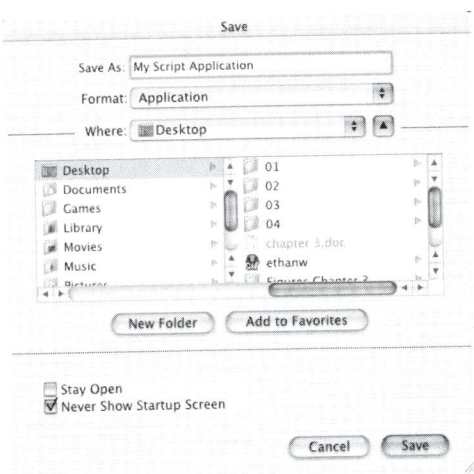

Figure 3.50 *The Save dialog box appears when you choose to save your script as a stand-alone application from the Script Editor in Mac OS.*

Figure 3.51 *The standard icon for a script application as shown by the Mac OS X Finder.*

Visual Basic

To save a Visual Basic script as a Windows application, you must start by creating your code in a Standard .EXE project. When you begin creating a project in the Visual Basic Editor, you're prompted to choose the type of project you want to create. **Figure 3.52** shows the New Project window with a Standard .EXE project selected. When you are ready to save your script as a full Windows application, choose Make Project.exe from the File menu, as shown in **Figure 3.53**. You will be prompted for a location to save the .exe file that contains your double-clickable script.

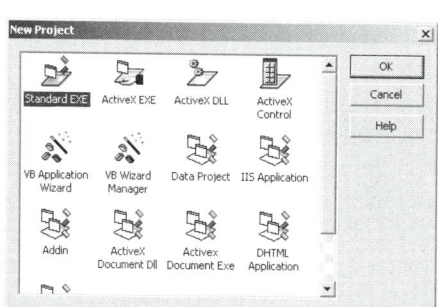

Figure 3.52 *The Visual Basic editor's New Project window with a Standard .EXE project selected.*

Figure 3.53 *When you are ready to save your script as a full Windows application, choose Make Project.exe from the File menu.*

Scripting Illustrator's Object Model

At this point, you should have a good idea of what scripting is and how it works. We are ready to begin looking at scripting Adobe Illustrator. **Figure 3.54** shows the complete scripting object model for Illustrator 10 in AppleScript, while **Figure 3.55** shows the object model for Illustrator in Visual Basic.

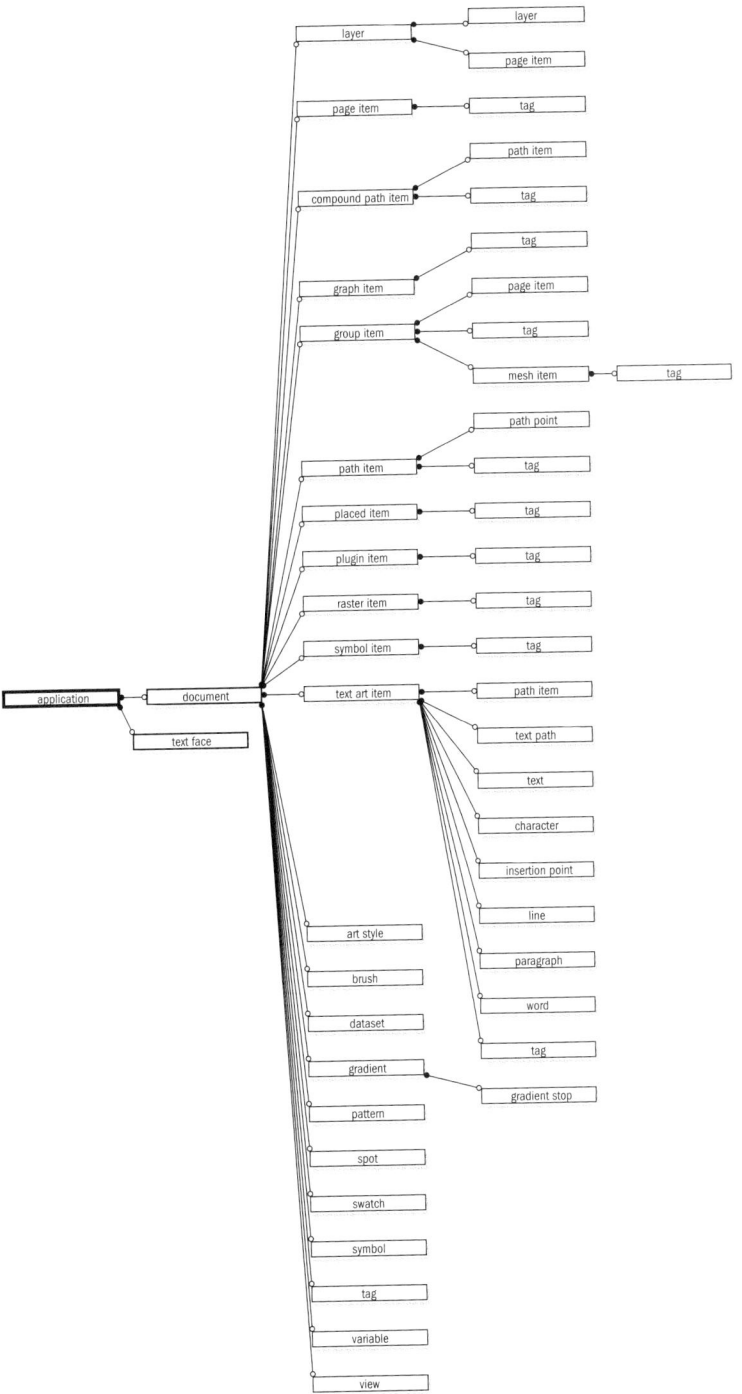

Figure 3.54 *The complete scripting object model for Illustrator 10 in AppleScript.*

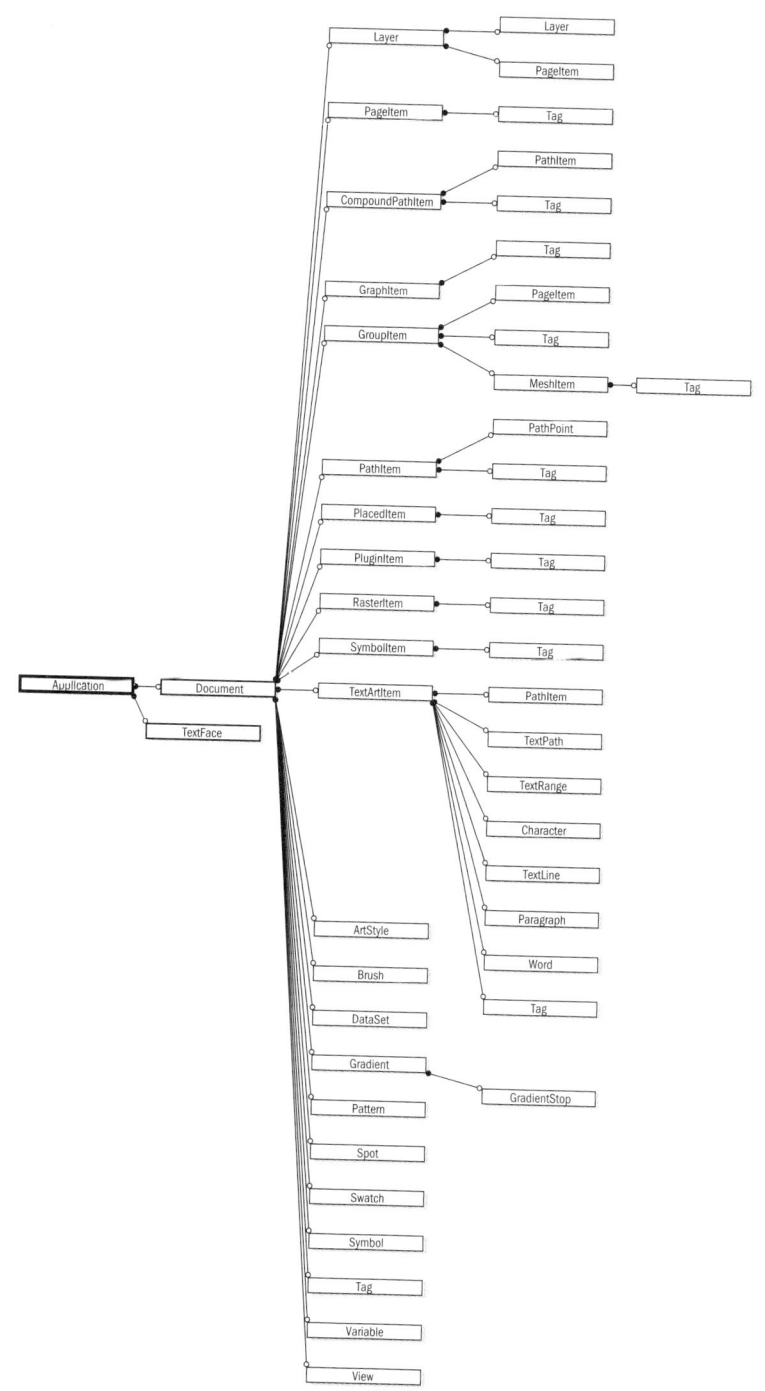

Figure 3.55 The object model for Illustrator in Visual Basic.

Looking at Illustrator's Objects and Commands

While the objects and commands available in Illustrator are all documented in Chapter 5, you can also view them from inside your scripting system.

AppleScript

1. Start Illustrator and then your script editor. Apple's Script Editor comes with all Macintosh systems. If you can't find the Script Editor application, you'll have to reinstall it from your Mac OS system CD.
2. In Script Editor, choose File > Open Dictionary. Script Editor displays an Open File dialog.
3. Find and then select the Illustrator application and click the OK button. Script Editor displays a list of Illustrator's objects and commands. You'll also be able to see the properties and elements associated with each object, as well as the parameters for each command.

Visual Basic

1. In any Visual Basic project, choose Project > References. Visual Basic displays the References dialog box.
2. Turn on the "Adobe Illustrator Type Library" option from the list of available references and click the OK button. If the library does not appear in the list of available references, click the Browse button and locate the file ScriptingSupport.aip in your Illustrator Plug-ins folder. Select the file.
3. Choose View > Object Browser. Visual Basic displays the Object Browser window.
4. Choose "Illustrator" from the list of open libraries shown in the top-left pull-down menu. Visual Basic displays the classes and the members of those classes in the Object Browser window.
5. Click an object class or class member. Visual Basic displays more information about the object in the frame at the bottom of the Object Browser window.

Writing a Script for Illustrator

We'll begin scripting Illustrator by making new things. The most basic activities in Illustrator are the creation of documents and objects—our script will jump right in and do both by making a new document with a text art object in it.

AppleScript

1. Locate and open Script Editor.

2. Enter the following script. As you look through the script, you'll see how we create, then address, each object in turn. The AppleScript command indicates the object that will receive the next message we send.

```
tell application "Adobe Illustrator 10"
    set myDoc to make new document
    set myTextArt to make new text art item in myDoc
        with properties { contents:"I Like Illustrator",
        position:{10, 10} }
end tell
```

3. Run the script. Illustrator will create a new document, add a text art item at position (200, 200), and set the text to "I Like Illustrator". **Figure 3.56** shows the new document created in Illustrator 10 when the script is run.

Figure 3.56 The new document created in Illustrator 10 by running the sample AppleScript script.

Visual Basic

1. Start Visual Basic and create a new project. Add the "Adobe Illustrator Type Library" reference to the project, as shown earlier. If you are using a built-in editor in a VBA application, skip to step 3.

2. Add a code module to the project.

3. Enter the following code. As you look through the script, you'll see how we create, then address, each object in turn. The Visual Basic command GetObject opens a connection between our script and Illustrator.

```
Option Explicit
Sub Main()
    Dim myApp As New Illustrator.Application
    Dim myDoc As Illustrator.Document
    Dim myTextArt As Illustrator.TextArtItem
    Set myDoc = myApp.Documents.Add
    Set myTextArt = myDoc.TextArtItems.Add
    myTextArt.Position = Array(10, 10)
    myTextArt.Contents = "I Like Illustrator"
End Sub
```

5. Save the project.
6. Start Illustrator.
7. Return to Visual Basic and run the program.
8. Run the script. Illustrator will create a new document, add a text art item at the specified position, and set the text to "I Like Illustrator". **Figure 3.57** shows the new document created in Illustrator 10 when the script is run.

Adding Features to Your First Script

Next, let's create a new script that makes changes to the Illustrator document you created with your first script. Don't worry if you've closed the Illustrator document without saving it—just run your script to create a new one.

Our second script will demonstrate how to:

1. Get the active document.
2. Get the width of the active document.
3. Resize the text art item to be half of the document's width.

AppleScript

1. Choose File > New in Script Editor to create a new script.
2. Enter the following code:

```
tell application "Adobe Illustrator 10"
  set myDocWidth to width of document 1
  set width of text art item 1 of document 1 to myDocWidth/2
end tell
```

Figure 3.57 *The new document created in Illustrator 10 by running the sample Visual Basic script.*

3. Save the script.

4. Make sure you have the document created by the original script open, then run the script. **Figure 3.58** shows how the text art object is resized by the script.

Visual Basic

1. Open a new project in the Visual Basic editor.

2. Enter the following code:

```
Sub Main()
    Dim myApp As New Illustrator.Application
    Dim myDoc As Illustrator.Document
    Dim myTextArt As Illustrator.TextArtItem
    Dim myDocWidth As Single
    Set myDoc = myApp.ActiveDocument
    myDocWidth = myDoc.Width
    Set myTextArt = myDoc.TextArtItems(1)
    myTextArt.Width = myDocWidth / 2
End Sub
```

Figure 3.58 The results of the script's resizing of a text art object.

3. Save the project.

4. Open the original document you created using the first script, then return to Visual Basic and run the script.

Using Measurement Units and Coordinates in Scripts

Illustrator always uses points as the unit of distance measurement. One inch is equal to 72 points. Even if you change the current document ruler's units of measurement, Illustrator will still use points when communicating with your scripts.

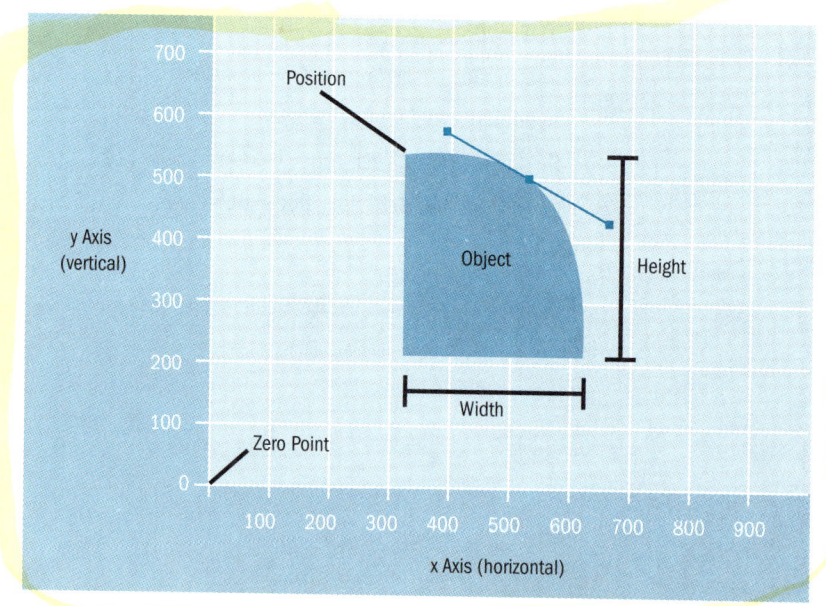

Your scripts will need to perform any unit conversions needed to represent your measurements as points. For example, to move the current selection to a position 2 inches to the right of and 6 inches above its current position, you'd use the following script:

AppleScript

```
tell application "Adobe Illustrator 10"
    translate selection delta x (2*72) delta y (6*72)
end tell
```

Visual Basic

```
Sub Main()
    Dim myApp As New Illustrator.Application
    Dim myDoc As Illustrator.Document
    Dim myObjs As Variant
    Dim myObj As Variant
    Set myDoc = myApp.ActiveDocument
    myObjs = myDoc.Selection
    If TypeName(selectedObjects) = "Variant()" Then
        For Each objectRef In selectedObjects
            objectRef.Translate 2*72, 6*72
        Next
    End If
End Sub
```

If your script depends on adding, subtracting, multiplying, or dividing specific measurement values for units other than points, the script will need to convert between the units numerically. For example, to use English measurements such as inch values for coordinates or measurement units, your script will need to multiply all inch values by 72 to convert to points, since there are 72 points in an inch. To use metric measurements such as centimeters, you will need to multiply all centimeter values by 28.346, since there are 28.346 points in a centimeter.

Unit Conversion to Points

UNIT	CONVERSION FORMULA
centimeters	28.346 points = 1 centimeter
inches	72 points = 1 inch
millimeters	2.835 points = 1 millimeter
picas	12 points = 1 pica
Qs	0.709 point = 1 Q (1 Q equals 0.23 millimeter)

Coordinates

Illustrator uses simple two-dimensional geometry to record the position of objects in a document. The coordinates used in Illustrator are the same as the "traditional" geometric coordinate system you learned about in school.

The horizontal component of a coordinate pair (or "point") is referred to as "x" and the vertical position is denoted by "y." You can see these coordinates in the Info palette when you select or create an object in Illustrator.

Illustrator scripting uses a special class called fixed point to receive and return coordinate data. The fixed point is represented as a list of two items in AppleScript and as a variant array of two elements in Visual Basic. In both cases, the first item is the horizontal or x-coordinate, while the second item is the vertical or y-coordinate. The position (Position in Visual Basic) of objects on a document are described with a fixed point.

AppleScript

In AppleScript, a fixed point with an x-coordinate of 5.0 and a y-coordinate of 10.2 is represented as a list that looks like this:

```
{5.0, 10.2}
```

Visual Basic

In Visual Basic, a fixed point with an x-coordinate of 5.0 and a y-coordinate of 10.2 is represented as a variant array that looks like this:

```
Array (5.0, 10.2)
```

Note that if you declare an array to hold the values of a point, you should pass 1 as the dimension, since Visual Basic uses index position 0 for the first item in an array.

```
Dim aPoint(1) As Single
aPoint(0) = 5.0
aPoint(1) = 10.2
```

The Zero Point

The zero point (0, 0) for coordinate numbering in Illustrator is in the lower-left corner of the document. On the horizontal axis, coordinates to the right of the ruler's zero point are positive numbers, and on the vertical axis, coordinates above the zero point are positive. The page origin (PageOrigin in Visual Basic) of a document defines the lower-left corner of the printable region of the document as a fixed point. **Figure 3.59** shows the zero point of a document in Illustrator.

To work with rectangular coordinates where there is a pair of x and y values, Illustrator uses the special class called a fixed rectangle. This class is composed of a list with four items in AppleScript and a variant array with four elements in Visual Basic. The coordinates of a fixed rectangle in order are: left, top, right, bottom.

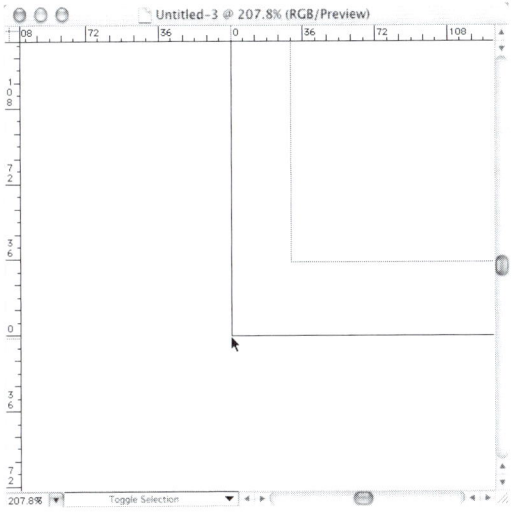

Figure 3.59 *The zero point of a document in Illustrator.*

AppleScript

In AppleScript, a fixed rectangle with a left-top corner of (5.0, 200.0) and a right-bottom corner of (100.0, 20.0) is represented by a list that looks like this:

`{5.0, 200.0, 100.0, 20.0}`

Visual Basic

In Visual Basic, a fixed rectangle with a left-top corner of (5.0, 200.0) and a right-bottom corner of (100.0, 20.0) is represented by a variant array that looks like this:

`Array (5.0, 200.0, 100.0, 20.0)`

Alternatively, you can define your array and assign values to its elements like this:

`Dim boundsRect(3) As Single`

`boundsRect(0) = 5.0`

`boundsRect(1) = 20.0`

`boundsRect(2) = 100.0`

`boundsRect(3) = 200.0`

Position, Width, Height and Bounds

Every object, or page item, in a document has a position (Position in Visual Basic) described by a fixed point and a width and height (Width and Height in VB). The maximum value allowed for the width or height of a page item is 16348 points.

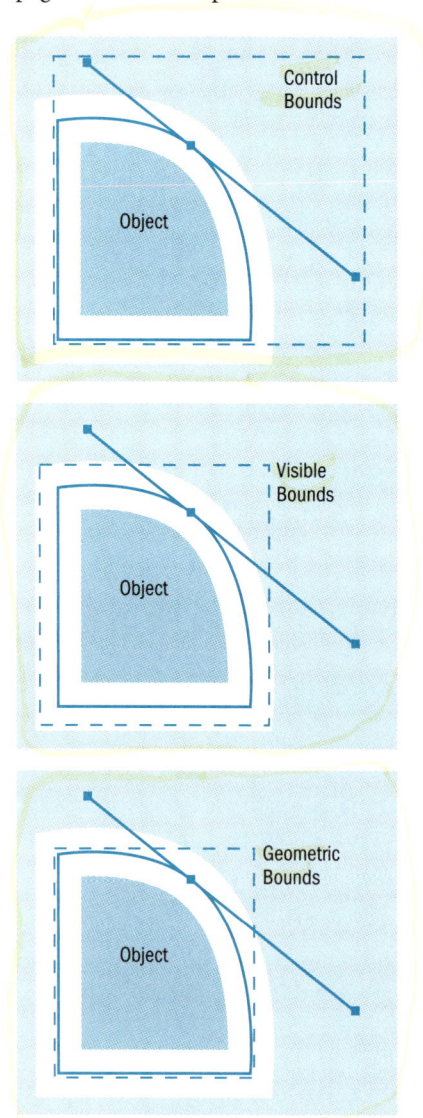

Every page item also has three properties that describe the object's overall extent using fixed rectangles. The `geometric bounds` (GeometricBounds in Visual Basic) of a page item are the rectangular dimensions of the object excluding stroke width. The `visible bounds` (VisibleBounds in Visual Basic) of a page item are the dimensions of the object including any stroke widths. Finally, the `control bounds` (ControlBounds in Visual Basic) define the rectangular dimensions of the object including in- and out-control points. **Figure 3.60** shows a path item selected in a document. The illustration above shows the difference between each kind of bounds.

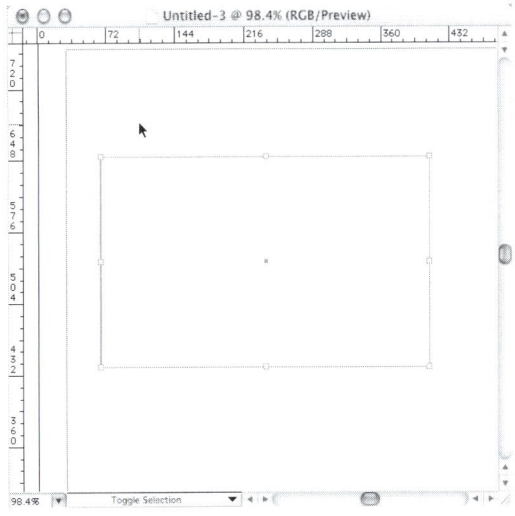

Figure 3.60 *A path item selected in a document.*

Using References to Illustrator Objects

In AppleScript, Illustrator returns object references by index position or name. For example, a reference to the first path in layer 2 would be: path item 1 of layer 2 of document 1. An object's index position may change when other objects are created or deleted. For example, when a new path item is created on layer 2, it will become path item 1 of layer 2 of document 1. This new object displaces our original path item, forcing it to index position 2. Therefore, any references made to path item 1 of layer 2 of document 1 will refer to the new object. Consider the following sample script.

AppleScript

```
tell application "Adobe Illustrator 10"
   set newDocument to make new document
   set rectPath to make new rectangle in newDocument
   set starPath to make new star in newDocument
   set selection of newDocument to {rectPath, starPath}
end tell
```

Figure 3.61 shows the results of running this script. This script will not select both the rectangle and the star. It will select only the star. Why?

Try running the script with the Event Log window open to observe the references returned from Illustrator for each of the consecutive make commands. You will notice that both commands return the same object reference: path item 1 of layer 1 of document 1.

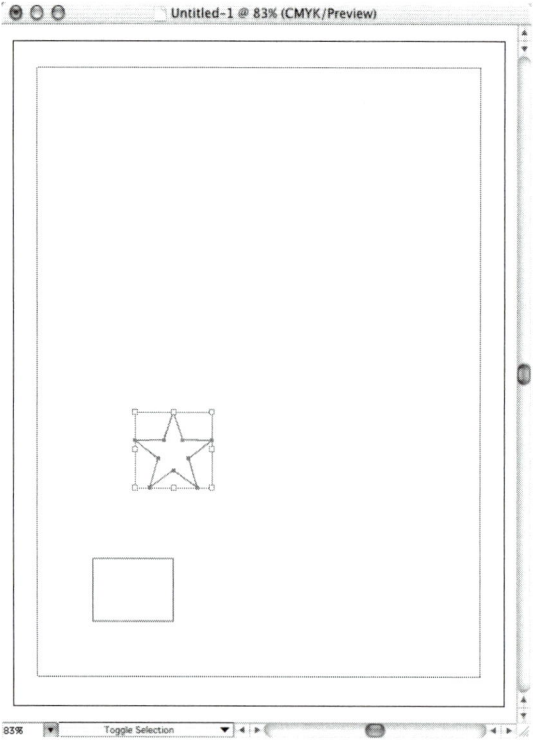

Figure 3.61 *The star selected after running the sample AppleScript.*

Therefore, the script really says:

```
set selection of document 1 to {path item 1 of layer 1 of
   document 1, path item 1 of layer 1 of document 1}
```

Instead, you might try referencing the objects by name, such as:

```
tell application "Adobe Illustrator 10"
   set newDocument to make new document
   make new rectangle in newDocument
      with properties {name:"rectangle"}
   make new star in newDocument with properties {name:"star"}
   set selection of newDocument to
   {path item "rectangle" of newDocument,
   path item "star" of newDocument}
end tell
```

This example illustrates the need to uniquely identify objects. I recommend that you assign names to objects you need to access at a later time, as there's no guarantee you're accessing the objects you expect when accessing them by index.

Visual Basic

Object references in Visual Basic are dynamic and remain valid until disposed.

To create a star and rectangle, and then select them, you could write:

```
Sub Main()
   Dim appRef As New Illustrator.Application
   Dim pathItemsRef As Illustrator.PathItems
   Dim rectPath As Illustrator.PathItem
   Dim starPath As Illustrator.PathItem

   Set pathItemsRef = appRef.ActiveDocument.ActiveLayer.PathItems
   Set rectPath = pathItemsRef.Rectangle(50, 70, 100, 200)
   Set starPath = pathItemsRef.Star(40, 70, 200, 110, 5, False)
```

```
    Dim pathSelection(1) As Variant
    Set pathSelection(0) = rectPath
    Set pathSelection(1) = starPath
    appRef.Selection = pathSelection
End Sub
```

Figure 3.62 shows the results of running the above script.

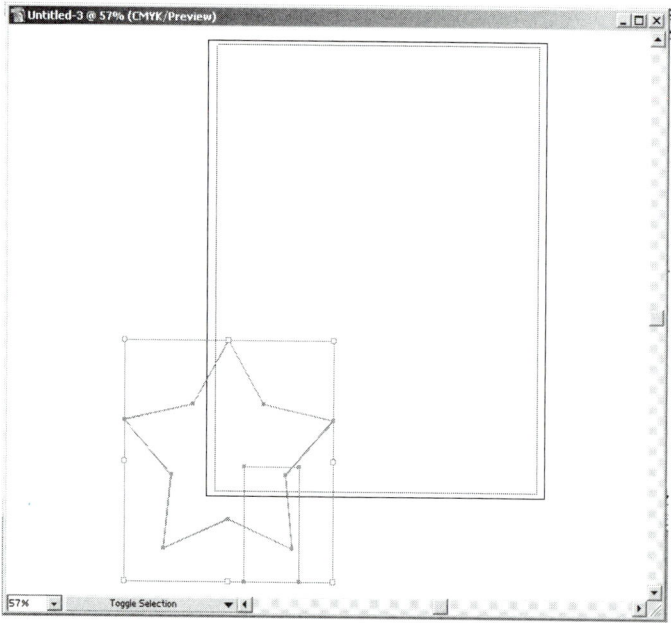

Figure 3.62 *Both the star and rectangle selected after running the sample Visual Basic.*

Working With Objects in Documents and Layers

In Illustrator, all artwork objects are contained in layers, groups, or compound paths that are themselves contained in a document. The index of an object in a layer or group indicates the object's position in the stacking order of the layer or group. This means that page item 1 of layer 1, or Layers(1).PageItems(1) in Visual Basic, is the frontmost object in a document, while page item 2 of layer 1, or Layers(1).PageItems(2) in Visual Basic, lies directly behind in the stacking order.

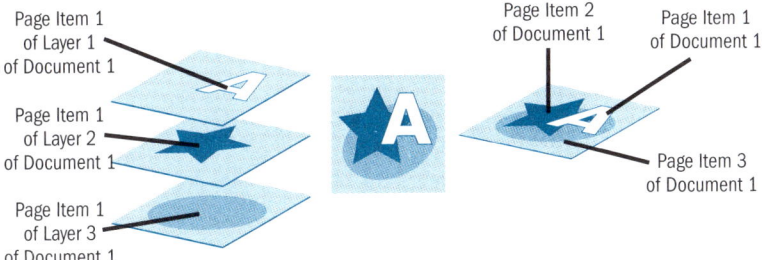

When you refer to an object in your document, you can reference it directly as part of the document or by its complete containment hierarchy, including layers and any group or compound path if valid. When you refer to objects contained by the document directly, you can access the entire flattened contents of the document, without regard to the containment of objects within layers, groups, or compound paths. All objects, whether or not they are contained in groups or compound paths, are returned as individual objects contained by the document. The following script demonstrates how to reference an object as part of a document. **Figure 3.63** shows how a single object can be referenced as either part of a layer or part of the whole document from a script.

AppleScript

```
tell application "Adobe Illustrator 10"
    set pageItemRef to page item 1 of document 1
end tell
```

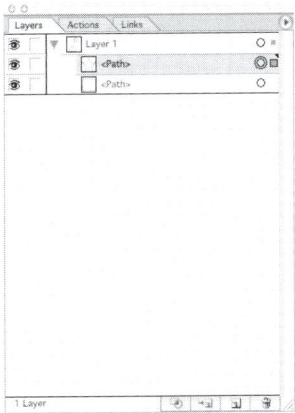

Figure 3.63 *A single object can be referenced as either part of a layer or part of the whole document from a script.*

Visual Basic

```
Sub Main()
    Dim appRef As New Illustrator.Application
    Dim documentRef As Illustrator.Document
    Dim pageItemRef As Illustrator.PageItem
    Set documentRef = appRef.ActiveDocument
    Set pageItemRef = documentRef.PageItems(1)
End Sub
```

In the script below, the variable pageItemRef will not necessarily refer to the same object as the above script since this script includes a reference to a layer.

AppleScript

```
tell application "Adobe Illustrator 10"
    set pageItemRef to page item 1 of layer 1 of document 1
end tell
```

Visual Basic

```
Sub Main()
    Rem Get reference for first page item of document 1
    Dim appRef As New Illustrator.Application
    Dim documentRef As Illustrator.Document
    Dim pageItemRef As Object
    Set documentRef = appRef.ActiveDocument
    Set pageItemRef = documentRef.Layers(1).PageItems(1)
End Sub
```

Working With Selected Objects

There are instances in which you will want to write scripts that act upon the currently selected object(s). For example, you might want to have a script that applies formatting to selected text or changes a selected path's shape. To do this, you need to know the number of selected objects and the type of each object.

The following scripts work with the current selection. They determine what objects are contained in the selection and evaluate what kind of object is selected.

Figure 3.64 shows the result displayed in the Event Log when a script gets the current selection from Illustrator in Script Editor. **Figure 3.65** shows the current selection object as displayed in the Visual Basic IDE's Watches window.

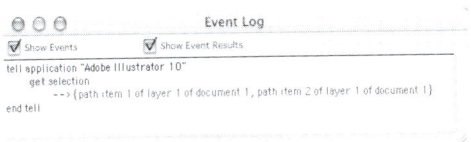

Figure 3.64 The result displayed in the Event Log when a script gets the current selection from Illustrator in Script Editor.

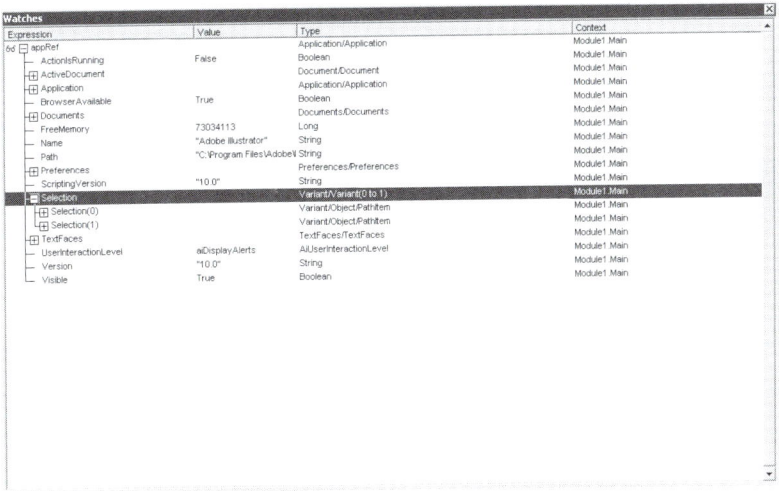

Figure 3.65 The current selection object as displayed in the Visual Basic IDE's Watches window.

AppleScript

```
tell application "Adobe Illustrator 10"
   set mySelection to selection
   try
      if mySelection is {} then
         display dialog "No objects are selected"
      else
```

```
				if class of mySelection = list and
					(count of items in mySelection > 1) then
					--Selection contains more than one object.
				else
					--A single object is selected. What is it?
					set mySelectionClass to class of selectedObjects
					if mySelectionClass= list then
						set mySelectionClass to class of item 1 of
						mySelection
					if mySelectionClass= text then
						-- text is selected
					else
						-- Determine what type of object is selected.
						if mySelectionClass= path item then
							-- object is a path item
						else if mySelectionClass= compound path item then
							-- object is a compound path
						else if mySelectionClass= raster item then
							-- object is a raster image
						else if mySelectionClass= placed item then
							-- object is a placed image
						else if mySelectionClass= mesh item then
							-- object is a mesh
						else if mySelectionClass= text art item then
							-- object is a text art item
						else if mySelectionClass= plugin item then
							-- object is a plugin art item
						else if mySelectionClass= path point then
							-- object is a point of a path
						else if mySelectionClass= group item then
							-- object is a group
						end if
					end if
				end if
			end if
		on error myErrorString
			display dialog myErrorString
		end try
	end tell
```

Visual Basic
```
Sub Main()
   Dim myApp As New Illustrator.Application
   Dim myDocument As Illustrator.Document
   Set myDocument = appRef.ActiveDocument
   mySelection = myDocument.Selection

   If TypeName(mySelection) = "String" Then
      ' text is selected
   Else
   ' Is anything selected?
     If mySelection = Empty Then
        MsgBox "Select an object and try again."
     Else
        mySelectedObject = mySelection(0)
        mySelectionClass = TypeName(mySelectedObject)
        Select Case mySelectionClass
        ' Something is selected, let's find out what it is.
          Case "PathItem"
          ' Object is a path item
          Case "CompoundPathItem"
          ' Object is a compound path
          Case "RasterItem"
          ' Object is a raster image
          Case "PlacedItem"
          ' Object is a placed image
          Case "MeshItem"
          ' Object is a mesh
          Case "TextArtItem"
          ' Object is a text art item
          Case "PluginItem"
          ' Object is a plugin art item
          Case "PathPoint"
          ' Object is a point of a path
          Case "GroupItem"
          ' Object is a group of objects
        End Select
        Next
      End If
End Sub
```

Working With Paths and Points

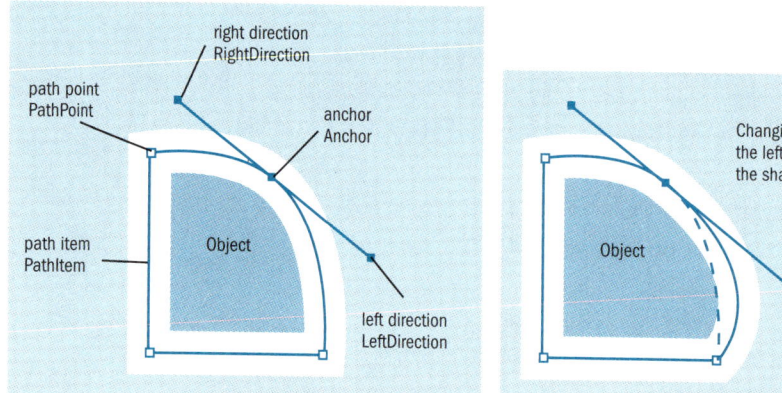

Path items include all artwork that is composed of paths, including rectangles, ellipses, polygons, as well as free-form paths. In Illustrator, every path is composed of Bézier curves that are each defined by a series of four points. Path items, as well as path points, can be created and manipulated from a script.

Every aspect of a path point can be accessed from scripting, including the `anchor point` (AnchorPoint in Visual Basic) and both control points, known as the `left direction` (LeftDirection in Visual Basic) and `right direction` (RightDirection in Visual Basic) properties. **Figure 3.66** shows a basic path item with one of its anchor points selected. Illustration 3.6 shows all of the parts of a path.

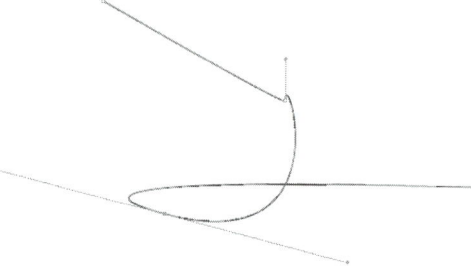

Figure 3.66 *A basic path item with an anchor point selected.*

Refer to the Illustrator Plug-in Software Development Kit Function Reference for more information on working with paths, Bézier curves, and path points. This document is available in Adobe Acrobat Portable Document Format (PDF) as part of the Illustrator Software Development Kit (SDK). The SDK can be downloaded from the Adobe Solutions Network web site (http://partners.adobe.com/asn/developer/sdks.html).

More on Bézier Curves and the Math Behind Them

A Bézier curve, as Illustrator uses them, is defined by four points: two anchor points and two control points. We can call the anchor points (x1, y1) and (x2, y2). The two control points we can call (x3, y3) and (x4, y4).

It turns out to take only two equations to define the points on the curve. Each equation needs to be evaluated in a loop for enough times to fill in points on the curve connecting the two anchor points. A value `t` is varied from 0 to 1 across the loop between the anchor points. One equation generates horizontal x values `x(t)`, the other generates vertical y values, `y(t)`. Put together, points on the curve are plotted by the loop. This is how the equations are defined in Adobe Illustrator:

$$x(t) = (a_x \times t^3) + (b_x \times t^2) + (c_x \times t) + x1$$

$$x2 = x1 + (\frac{c_x}{3})$$

$$x3 = x2 + \frac{(c_x + b_x)}{3}$$

$$x4 = x1 + c_x + b_x + a_x$$

$$y(t) = (a_y \times t^3) + (b_y \times t^2) + (c_y \times t) + y1$$

$$y2 = y1 + (\frac{c_y}{3})$$

$$y3 = y2 + \frac{(c_y + b_y)}{3}$$

$$y4 = y1 + c_y + b_y + a_y$$

These equations can be used to derive the basic equations for the coefficients shown below. So a Bézier curve can be mathematically defined simply by four points.

$$c_x = 3 \times (x2 - x1)$$
$$b_x = 3 \times (x3 - x2) - c_x$$
$$a_x = x4 - x1 - c_x - b_x$$
$$c_y = 3 \times (y2 - y1)$$
$$b_y = 3 \times (y3 - y2) - c_y$$
$$a_y = y4 - y1 - c_y - b_y$$

Working With Color

Swatches can be created and manipulated from your scripts. You can also create new patterns, gradients, and spot colors from scripts. Just as in the user interface, percentages (0.0 through 100.0) are used to specify grayscale, individual CMYK values, and spot tints. **Figure 3.67** shows the Color palette for a defined CMYK color in Illustrator. The range 0.0 to 255.0 is used for the individual RGB color values. A defined RGB color value in Illustrator is shown in **Figure 3.68**.

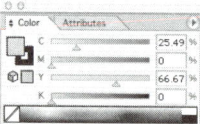

Figure 3.67 The Color palette for a defined CMYK color in Illustrator.

Figure 3.68 A defined RGB color value in Illustrator.

There are two primary groups of objects your scripts will work with when dealing with color: swatch color objects and basic color definition objects. You use basic color definition objects to define the specific colors used for path strokes and fills and most other color specifications. You use swatch color objects to work with the document's collection of color swatches. The tables below help define which objects fall into each of these two basic categories. See Chapter 5 or Chapter 6 for details on each object's definition and use.

AppleScript

Basic Color Definition Objects

OBJECT NAME	SAMPLE USAGE
CMYK color info	set stroke color of path item 1 of document 1 to {cyan: 100.0, magenta: 25.0, yellow: 75.0, black: 10.0}
gradient color info	set fill color of path item 1 of document 1 to {angle: 45.0, gradient: gradient "" of document 1, hilite angle: 75.0, hilite length: 5.0, length: 100.0, matrix: {}, origin: {0.0, 100.0}}
gray color info	set stroke color of path item 1 of document 1 to {gray value: 60.0}
pattern color info	set fill color of path item 1 of document 1 to {matrix: {}, pattern: pattern "" of document 1, reflect: true, reflect angle: 20.0, rotation: 45.0, scale factor: {50.0, 25.0}, shear angle: 120.0, shear axis: 0.0, shift angle: 0.0, shift distance: 0.0}

Basic Color Definition Objects (continued)

OBJECT NAME	SAMPLE USAGE
RGB color info	set stroke color of path item 1 of document 1 to {red: 255.0, green: 64.0, blue: 128.0}
spot color info	set fill color of path item 1 of document 1 to {spot: spot "" of document 1, tint: 40.0}

Swatch Palette Color Objects

OBJECT NAME	SAMPLE USAGE
gradient, gradients	set gradient type of gradient 1 of document 1 to linear
pattern, patterns	set name of pattern 1 of document 1 to "pat"
spot, spots	set name of spot 1 of document 1 to "spotty"
swatch, swatches	delete swatch 1 of document 1

Visual Basic

Basic Color Definition Objects

OBJECT NAME	SAMPLE USAGE
CMYKColor	Dim myColor as New Illustrator.CMYKColor myColor.Cyan = 100# myColor.Magenta = 25# myColor.Yellow = 75# myColor.Black = 10# myApp.Documents(1).PathItems(1).StrokeColor = myColor
GradientColor	Dim myColor as New Illustrator.GradientColor myColor.angle = 45# myColor.Gradient = myApp.Documents(1).Gradients("Black, White Radial") myColor.HiliteAngle = 75# myColor.HiliteLength = 5# myColor.Length = 100# myColor.Origin = Array (0#, 100#) myApp.Documents(1).PathItems(1).FillColor = myColor
GrayColor	Dim myColor as New Illustrator.GrayColor myColor.Gray = 60# myApp.Documents(1).PathItems(1).StrokeColor = myColor
PatternColor	Dim myColor as New Illustrator.PatternColor myColor.Pattern = myApp.Documents(1).Patterns("Honeycomb") myColor.Reflect = True myColor.ReflectAngle = 20# myColor.Rotation = 45# myColor.ScaleFactor = Array (50#, 25#) myColor.ShearAngle = 120# myColor.ShearAxis = 0#

Basic Color Definition Objects (continued)

OBJECT NAME	SAMPLE USAGE
PatternColor	myColor.ShiftAngle = 0# myColor.ShiftDistance = 0# myApp.Documents(1).PathItems(1).FillColor = myColor
RGBColor	Dim myColor as New Illustrator.RGBColor myColor.Red = 255# myColor.Green = 64# myColor.Blue = 128# myApp.Documents(1).PathItems(1).StrokeColor = myColor
SpotColor	Dim myColor as New Illustrator.SpotColor myColor.Pattern = myApp.Documents(1).Spots("[Registration]") myColor.Tint = 100# myApp.Documents(1).PathItems(1).FillColor = myColor

Swatch Palette Color Objects

OBJECT NAME	SAMPLE USAGE
Gradient, Gradients	myApp.Documents(1).Gradients(1).Type = aiLinearGradient
Pattern, Patterns	myApp.Documents(1).Patterns(1).Name = "pat"
Spot, Spots	myApp.Documents(1).Spots(1).Name = "spotty"
Swatch, Swatches	myApp.Documents(1).Swatches.Remove(myApp.Documents(1).Swatches(1))

Pay special attention when working with CMYK and RGB color values. Illustrator supports only a single color model within each document, either CMYK or RGB. **Figure 3.69** shows the New Document window in Illustrator, where a user normally selects the color model for a document. When you specify a CMYK color value in a document that uses the RGB color model, Illustrator will convert the values to RGB and return an RGB color, and vice versa when specifying RGB colors in a CMYK document. However, there is some data loss during this conversion.

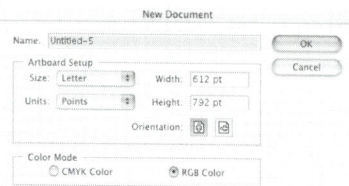

Figure 3.69 *The new document window displayed by Illustrator.*

Scripts have complete control over the creation of gradients as well as other color types. When a new gradient is defined by a script, the colors and midpoint must be defined, as when a user creates a gradient in the user interface. **Figure 3.70** shows the Gradient palette in Illustrator, with the midpoint and color controls identified.

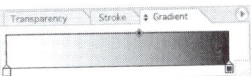

Figure 3.70 *The Gradient palette in Illustrator, with the midpoint and color controls identified.*

Working With Fonts

In both Windows and Mac OS, fonts are a complex and elusive topic. Illustrator's scripting support provides access to the basic information about each font installed on the system you're using. This basic information lets you collect a list of every font name installed in your computer when your script is running.

AppleScript

Without this basic font support from Illustrator, there are no other simple options for AppleScript users to access the system's font information. However, with Illustrator, getting a list of all the font names installed on the system is this easy:

```
tell application "Adobe Illustrator 10" to set myFontNames to
   name of every text face
```

Visual Basic

Getting an array of font names from Illustrator in Visual Basic is best done in a simple loop. The script below demonstrates how to retrieve an array of names of all of the fonts on the current system from Illustrator.

```
Public Function getFontNamesIll()
   Dim myApp As New Illustrator.Application
   Dim myFontCount
   myFontCount = myApp.TextFaces.Count
   Dim myFonts()
   ReDim myFonts(myFontCount)
   For myFontNum = 0 To myFontCount
      myFonts(myFontNum) = myApp.TextFaces(myFontNum).Name
   Next
   getFontNamesIll = myFonts
End Function
```

Visual Basic offers built-in access to system font information in the Screen object of any form. The script below demonstrates how to retrieve an array of names of all of the fonts on the current system using a form's Screen object.

```
Public Function getFontNames()
   Dim myFontNum
   Dim myFontCount
   myFontCount = Screen.FontCount
   Dim myFonts()
   ReDim myFonts(myFontCount)
   For myFontNum = 0 To myFontCount
      myFonts(myFontNum) = Screen.Fonts(myFontNum)
   Next
   getFontNames = myFonts
End Function
```

Figure 3.71 shows the Fonts pull-down menu expanded in the Character palette of Illustrator.

Figure 3.72 shows the main Fonts folder in the Library of a Mac OS X boot volume. This is where you can place font files for fonts that are meant to be shared by all users of a particular computer.

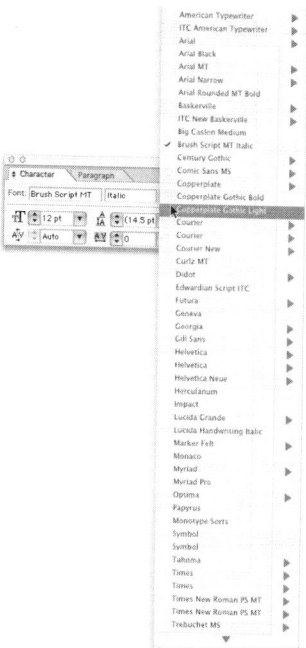

Figure 3.71 The Fonts pull-down menu expanded in the Character palette of Illustrator.

Figure 3.73 shows the main Fonts directory on a Windows 2000 system. This is where all font files for fonts available to the system are placed.

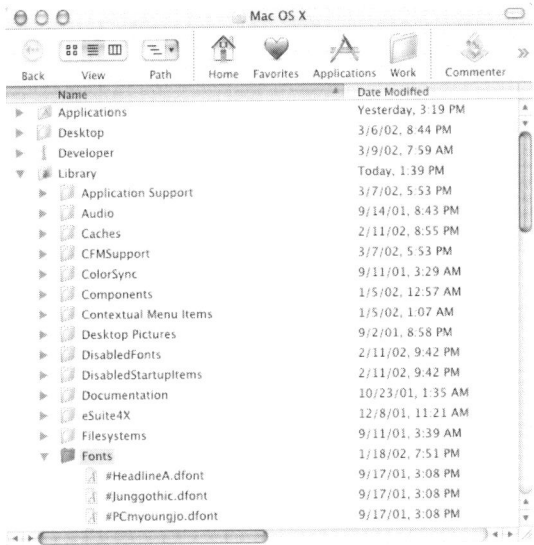

Figure 3.72 The main Fonts folder in the Library of a Mac OS X boot volume.

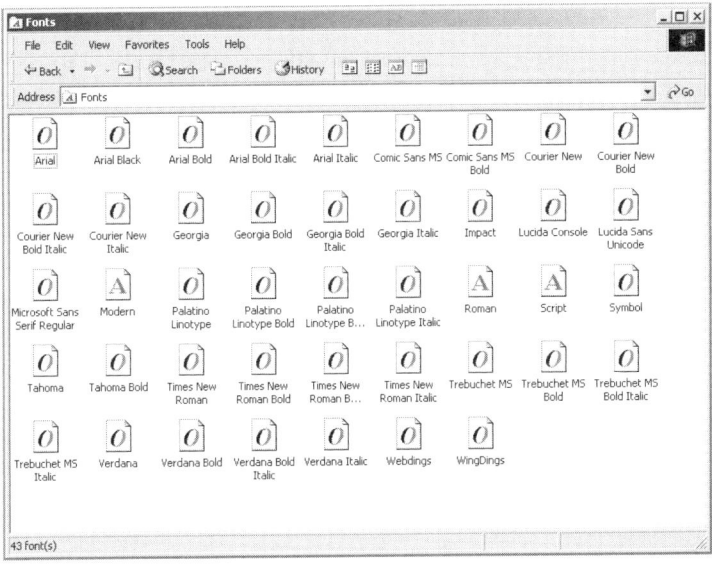

Figure 3.73 The main Fonts directory on a Windows 2000 system.

Working With Text Art Objects

There are three types of text art items in Adobe Illustrator: point text, path text, and area text. **Figure 3.74** shows examples of each kind of text art object in Illustrator. The `kind` property (`Kind` in Visual Basic) of a text art item is used to determine the type of the text art item. While all three kinds of text art have some common characteristics, such as an orientation, each kind of text art also has unique characteristics.

All three kinds of text art have least one text path associated with them. A `text path` (`TextPath` in Visual Basic) is not the same as a path art item, but defines the text art item's position on the artboard and its `orientation` (`Orientation` in VB, horizontal or vertical). Point text is defined completely by the properties of its text art item and associated text path.

For path and area text, text paths are associated with normal path art items. These path art items can be accessed and manipulated to modify the appearance of the associated text art item. If the text art item is path text, it will have a `text path offset` property (`TextPathOffset` in Visual Basic), which indicates where the text begins on the path object.

All text art objects also have at least one line of text depending on the object's geometry. A `line of text` (`TextLine` in Visual Basic) is all of the characters that fit on a single line in the text art item. Text art will have multiple text lines if it contains hard line breaks or its characters flow to a new line because they do not fit in the width of the text art. Unlike characters, paragraphs, and words, lines can be created only by the Illustrator application.

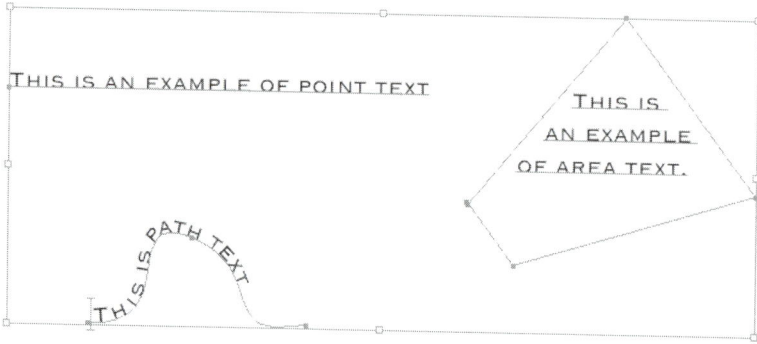

Figure 3.74 *Examples of each kind of text art object in Illustrator.*

Using the Power of Transformation Matrices

Thanks to the matrix class and the many commands that support matrices, you have access to the power of geometric transformation matrices. Transformation matrices are mathematical concepts originating in the field of linear algebra. Geometric manipulations like scaling, rotating, and moving can all be described using transformation matrices.

Matrices are the basis of how Illustrator internally performs a user's request to scale, rotate, or move an object. Using the command set available to create, concatenate, and apply matrices, you can transform objects in documents with super-accurate precision and control. By concatenating a series of rotation, translation, and scaling matrices together and applying the resulting matrix, you can perform a large series of geometric transformations in record speed. The following examples demonstrate how to combine multiple modifications in a single matrix and then apply the matrix to every object in a document. **Figure 3.75** and **Figure 3.76** show the before and after results of running the script on a document containing some rectangles.

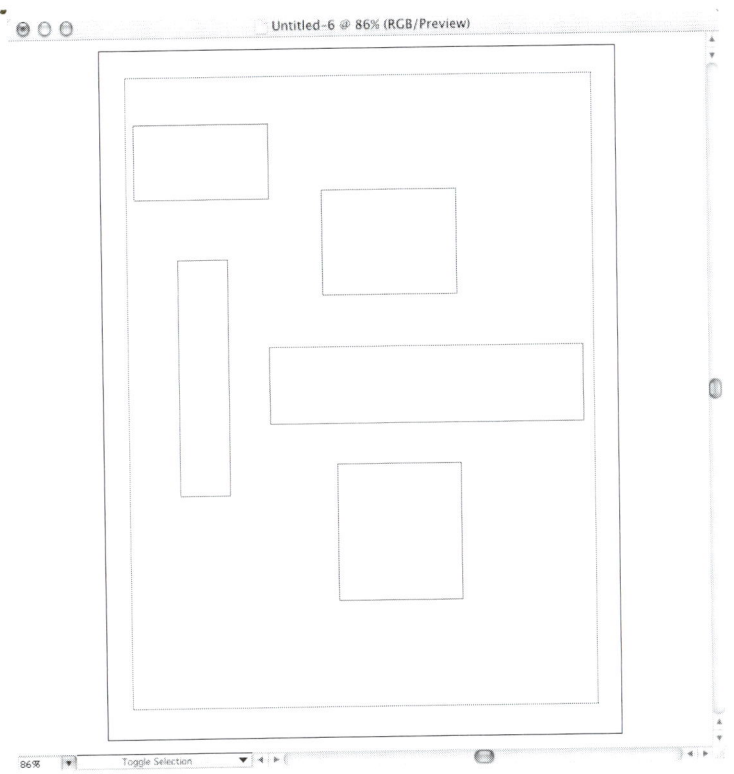

Figure 3.75 *A series of rectangles shown before a transformation script is run on them.*

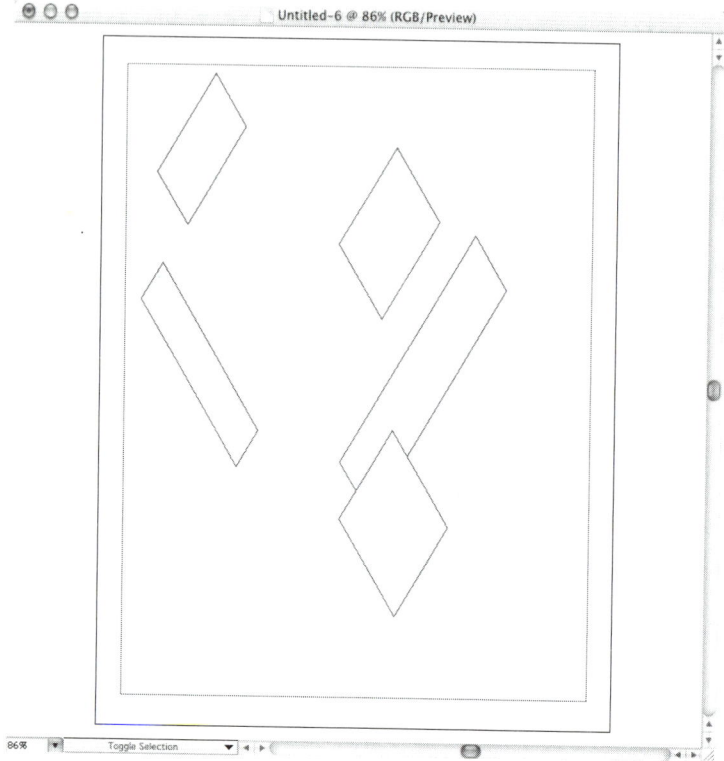

Figure 3.76 *The same series of rectangles shown after the transformation script is run.*

AppleScript

```
tell application "Adobe Illustrator 10"
    set transformationmatrix to get identity matrix
    set transformationmatrix to concatenate rotation matrix transformationmatrix angle 45.0
    set transformationmatrix to concatenate scale matrix transformationmatrix horizontal scale 60
    transform every page item of document 1 using transformationmatrix
end tell
```

Visual Basic

```
Private Sub ApplyMatrix_Click()
    Dim appRef As New Illustrator.Application
    Dim moveMatrix As Illustrator.Matrix
    Dim totalMatrix As Illustrator.Matrix


    Set moveMatrix = appRef.GetTranslationMatrix
    (72# * 0.5, 72# * 1.5)


    Rem Add a rotation to the translation. We rotate 10 degrees
    counter clockwise
    Set totalMatrix =
    appRef.ConcatenateRotationMatrix(moveMatrix, 10)


    Rem apply the transformation to all art in the document
    Dim frontDocument As Illustrator.Document
    Dim artItem As Illustrator.PageItem


    Set frontDocument = appRef.ActiveDocument
    For Each artItem In frontDocument.PageItems
        artItem.Transform totalMatrix
    Next
End Sub
```

A matrix object in Illustrator is composed of six properties. In AppleScript, these properties are mvalue_a, mvalue_b, mvalue_c, mvalue_d, mvalue_tx, and mvalue_ty. In Visual Basic, these properties are MValueA, MValueB, MValueC, MValueD, MValueTX, and MValueTY. By experimenting with the matrix concatenation commands in both AppleScript and Visual Basic, you can figure out how to construct matrices that can be applied to perform movement (also called translation), rotation, scaling, skewing, and other transformations. Adobe's Illustrator Plug-in Software Development Kit Function Reference has more details on working with transformation matrices.

The Math Behind Transformation Matrices

Adobe Illustrator's math-based geometry engine relies on transformation matrices to perform graphical operations on objects in your documents. A transformation matrix defines how to map points from one geometric coordinate space (x1, y1) into another coordinate space (x2, y2). By modifying the contents of a transformation matrix, you can perform object movement, rotation, and scaling. Illustrator provides a set of scripting commands that make it easy to manipulate transformation matrices.

The matrix used to accomplish all kinds of two-dimensional transformations is described mathematically by a 3 number-by-3 number matrix. The matrix below shows a sample 3 number-by-3 number matrix. Some values here will remain constant always, like u = 0.0, v = 0.0, and w= 1.0.

$$\begin{bmatrix} x1 & y1 & 1 \end{bmatrix} \times \begin{bmatrix} a & b & u \\ c & d & v \\ tx & ty & w \end{bmatrix} = \begin{bmatrix} x2 & y2 & 1 \end{bmatrix}$$

During actual transformation operations, Illustrator uses the contents of a 3-by-3 matrix transform a point (x1, y1) into a point (x2, y2) by means of the following equations:

$$x2 = (a \times x1) + (c \times y1) + tx$$
$$y2 = (b \times x1) + (d \times y1) + ty$$

Given these basic equations, it is pretty easy to see that there is one matrix that will copy x1 to x2 and y1 to y2 without any modifications—this is called the identity matrix.

$$\begin{bmatrix} 1 & 0 & 0 \\ 0 & 1 & 0 \\ 0 & 0 & 1 \end{bmatrix}$$

Using the formulas, you can see that this matrix generates a new point (x2, y2) that is the same as the old point (x1, y1):

$$x2 = (1 \times x1) + (0 \times y1) + 0 = x1$$
$$y2 = (0 \times x1) + (1 \times y1) + 0 = y1$$

In order to move an image by a specified horizontal and vertical distance, you can perform a movement transformation. This transformation modifies the x and y coordinates of each point by a specific amount. The matrix shown below consists of a movement operation of tx units horizontally and ty units vertically.

$$\begin{bmatrix} 1 & 0 & 0 \\ 0 & 1 & 0 \\ tx & ty & 1 \end{bmatrix}$$

The Math Behind Transformation Matrices *(continued)*

You can stretch or shrink an image by performing a scaling transformation. This transformation modifies the x and y coordinates by some factor. The magnitude of the x and y factors (sx and sy) governs whether the new image is larger or smaller than the original. In addition, by making a factor negative, you can flip the image about one or both of its axes. The transformation matrix shown below consists of a scaling operation.

$$\begin{bmatrix} sx & 0 & 0 \\ 0 & sy & 0 \\ 0 & 0 & 1 \end{bmatrix}$$

Finally, you can rotate an image by a specified angle by performing a rotation transformation. You specify the magnitude and direction of the rotation by specifying factors for both x and y. The transformation matrix shown below rotates an image counterclockwise by an angle q.

$$\begin{bmatrix} \cos(q) & \sin(q) & 0 \\ -\sin(q) & \cos(q) & 0 \\ 0 & 0 & 1 \end{bmatrix}$$

You can combine multiple transformation matrices into a single matrix. The resulting matrix retains the attributes of all combined transformations. Two matrices are combined by concatenating them. Mathematically, the two matrices are combined using matrix multiplication. The order in which you multiply matrices is important because matrix operations are not commutative, but you don't have to worry about this since Illustrator does the matrix multiplication for you. For example, you can both scale and move an image by defining and combining matrices similar to those shown below.

$$\begin{bmatrix} sx & 0 & 0 \\ 0 & sy & 0 \\ 0 & 0 & 1 \end{bmatrix} \times \begin{bmatrix} 1 & 0 & 0 \\ 0 & 1 & 0 \\ tx & ty & 1 \end{bmatrix} = \begin{bmatrix} sx & 0 & 0 \\ 0 & sy & 0 \\ tx & ty & 1 \end{bmatrix}$$

Launching and Quitting Illustrator

Your scripts can also control the activation and quitting of the Illustrator application. Take note of the particular comments below for your scripting system.

AppleScript

Use the `activate` and `quit` commands to control Illustrator's run state. The `activate` command will bring the Illustrator application to the front if it is not already the frontmost application. Note that if the clipboard contains data at the time of quitting, Illustrator may show a dialog asking if the data on the clipboard should be saved for other applications. You can avoid this dialog by clearing the clipboard with the statement:

```
set the clipboard to {}
```

* must include "the"

Visual Basic

In Visual Basic, the `Activate` method will bring the Illustrator application to the front if it is not already frontmost.

Note that if the clipboard contains data at the time of quitting, Illustrator may show a dialog prompting the user to save the data on the clipboard for other applications. You can avoid this dialog by clearing the clipboard with the command:

```
Clipboard.Clear
```

Limitations of Scripting Illustrator

While Illustrator 10 offers extensive access to the entire set of features in the application via scripting, some functions in Illustrator cannot be scripted. Following are some objects that cannot be created from a script:

- Art styles
- Brushes
- Graphs
- Mesh art
- Plug-in art
- Spirals

4: Script Recipes for Illustrator

The real joy of scripting a program like Adobe Illustrator comes from seeing the results of your successful scripting efforts. Before I spend any more time talking about things, you should get ready to make some useful scripts. If you aren't familiar with the script-editing environment on your platform, review Chapter 3. Otherwise, fire up your editor—either Script Editor in Mac OS, or the Visual Basic development environment editor.

Your approach to scripting Illustrator will be to build reusable pieces of code stored in functions, also known as *handlers* or *subroutines*. If you're not familiar with creating functions in a script, brush up in Chapter 3 before proceeding.

In the first few scripts, I will spend extra time explaining how to get started with the creation of each script in your editing environment. If you're unsure of yourself as you proceed, you may want to review Chapter 3, where you first learned about scripting Illustrator by using editors for AppleScript or Visual Basic.

For new users of Visual Basic, starting a new script project has many more steps than users of AppleScript have to face. I have done my best to provide detailed screen shots and step-by-step explanations of how to get started with a Visual Basic project in Script 4.1 (see Figure 4.2), in Script 4.2 (see Figure 4.4), and in other cases with details that are unique to the setup of your Visual Basic project.

A Modular Approach to Scripting: Using a Cupboard Full of Scriptlets

The scripting effort begins with the creation of some basic reusable scriptlets, much like one prepares basic recipes for combined use in bigger cooking projects. Each of these individual scripts performs simple, often-repetitive tasks. Their power becomes evident when they are combined with additional code in some of the later scripts in the chapter.

How you choose to approach the six scriptlets that follow is up to you. You can study and follow along through the step-by-step creation of each scriptlet to learn some important and useful details about applied Illustrator scripting concepts. Or you can skip ahead to the full scripting "entrées" that follow, where real-world scripting solutions are offered in annotated form. When you find your way to the 14 complete scripts, you'll often encounter one of these scriptlets.

Script 4.1: Batch Processor of Files in Nested Folders

Think of this scriptlet as being the "Puree" button on your Cuisinart. Dump a bunch of folders full of files with extensions that match the ones you tell the script to care about, and you can process each and every document with your own subroutine or handler. Standing alone, **Script 4.1** doesn't do anything but open and close documents in Illustrator. But replace the script lines in doProcessDocument() with some of the later scripts, and you'll see how powerful a folder processor can be.

Because this scriptlet is your first real applied scripting endeavor, I am providing a step-by-step explanation of how to create a new script in AppleScript or project in Visual Basic. **Figure 4.1** shows how easy it is to get started scripting Adobe Illustrator with Script Editor in AppleScript. When you're ready to try your AppleScript script, just click the Run button in your script's window in Script Editor. To save your AppleScript scripts for regular use, save them as applications. You can still reopen them in Script Editor and modify them, even though you've made them applications.

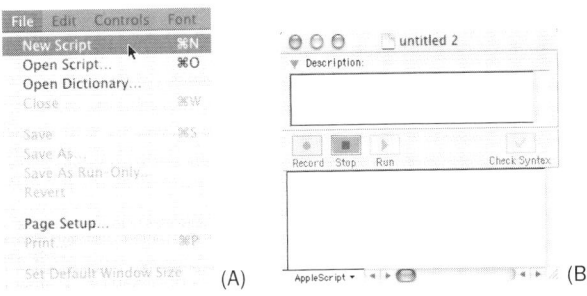

Figure 4.1 *The steps required to prepare to enter your new AppleScript script in Script Editor are identified here. (A) Start by choosing File > New Script. A new untitled script window will appear, as shown in (B). You're ready to AppleScript!*

Figure 4.2 provides, in all its step-by-step glory, a walk-through of everything you need to do in the Visual Basic editor to prepare to enter the scripting code for this effort. When your script is ready to test, click the Run button. It's usually easiest to save your Visual Basic projects as standard executable applications (.exe). You cannot reopen a saved Visual Basic .exe application in the editor to modify it or see its source code, however. Therefore, it's really important to keep all the files that make up your Visual Basic project in an orderly fashion. I recommend giving all the files for one project their own folder.

Try running Script 4.1 in your editor after you've entered it. With Visual Basic's extensive user-interface capabilities, this script's form has a drive list pull-down menu and a directory list to let users choose the folder they want to process. AppleScript, on the other hand, offers almost no user interface. AppleScript does support some very simple and easy-to-use user-interface commands to prompt users for things like folders and files.

AppleScript script applications that contain open handlers also support dragging and dropping items onto the script application to launch it (**Figure 4.3**).

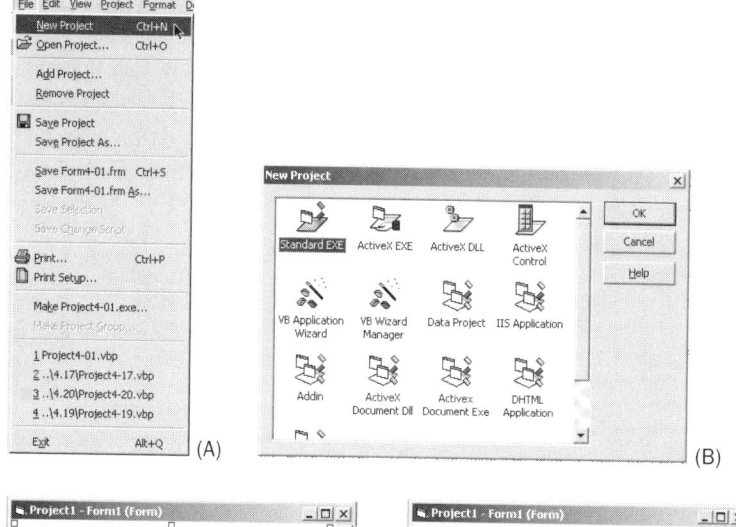

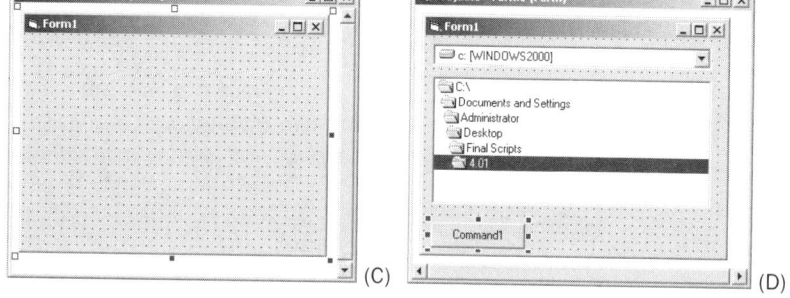

Figures 4.2 A–D *This series of screen shots illustrates the steps necessary to create a new project in the Visual Basic editor with a form in it so you can add Script 4.1's code. (A) Start by choosing File > New Project. (B) Next, select a standard .exe project, and click the OK button. A new project will open, with a new form window showing as in (C). Select the CommandButton tool, and drag out a new button in the open form window. Next, select the DriveListBox tool (looks like a hard disk) and draw a new drive list box. Then select the Folder-ListBox tool (looks like a folder), and draw a new folder list-box control so that the form looks like (D).*

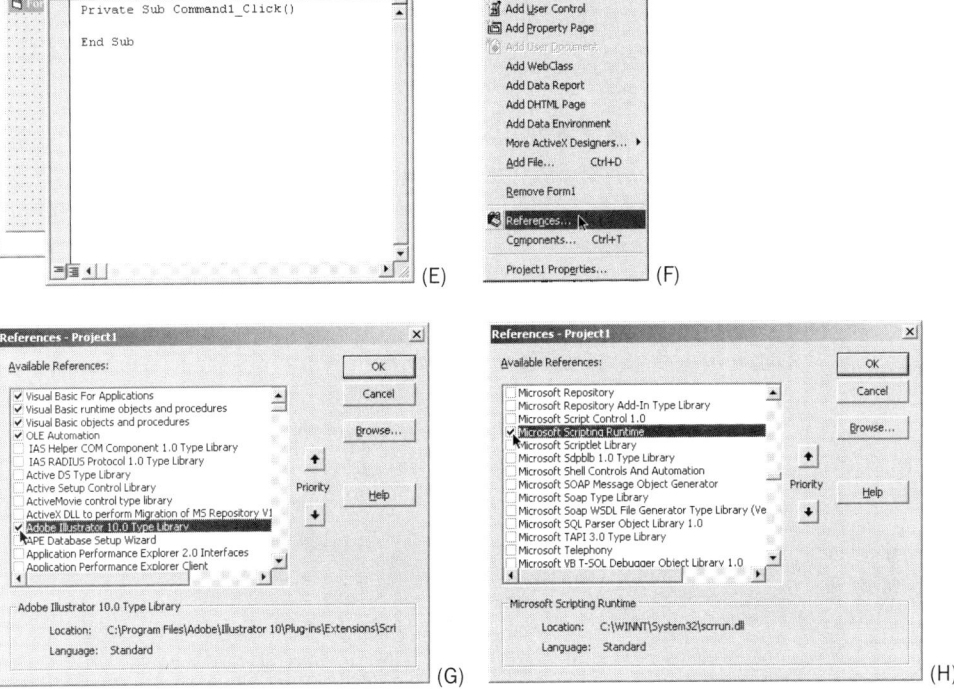

Figures 4.2 E–H Double-click the button in the form to open its code window, shown in (E). This code window is where you will do your script writing. The last step before scripting is attaching a reference to the scripting libraries your project will use so that the project will be able to work with the file system and with Illustrator. To do this, choose Project > References, as shown in (F). Then locate the Adobe Illustrator 10.0 Type Library (G), and activate it by checking the box next to its name. Next, locate the Microsoft Scripting Runtime library, shown in (H), and add it as well. Now you can close the References dialog by clicking the OK button. Time to write Visual Basic!

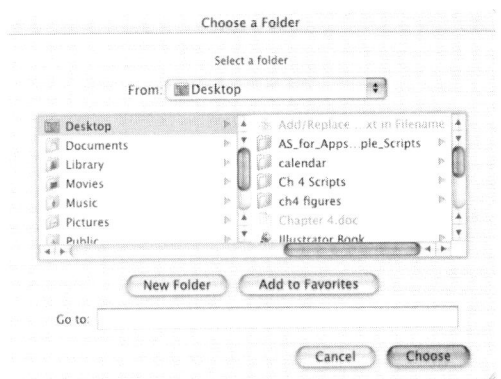

Figure 4.3 Because AppleScript scripts don't have user interfaces to design, the language provides built-in commands to perform drive, folder, and file selection functions. This screen shows the Choose a Folder dialog that appears when the user runs the script without dragging and dropping folders onto it.

AppleScript

Script Tips *If the script is run without any items droppped onto its droplet icon, the run handler will prompt the user to select a folder and then pass that folder reference to the regular open handler as though the folder had been dropped onto the script droplet.*

The open handler is the main bit of code to deal with for now. It looks at every file or folder in the items opened, one at a time. Folders have their contents gathered and passed, recursively, back to the open handler again to process all folders contained. Files have their extensions tested against the list of allowed types.

If the file has a valid extension, the function doProcessDocument() *is called, passing a reference to the file to be processed. Many of the scripts that follow will be fleshed-out* doProcessDocument() *functions that can be used with this main folder-processing script.*

AppleScript
First, define the file extensions to be processed by this script.

```
property myFiletypes : {".ai", ".eps"}
```

The run handler is defined here.

```
on run
    tell me to open {choose folder with prompt "Select a folder"}
end run
```

The open handler is defined here.

```
on open myFinderItems
    repeat with myFinderItem in myFinderItems
        tell application "Finder" to set myItemIsFolder to (kind of myFinderItem = "Folder")
        if myItemIsFolder then
            tell application "Finder" to set myFolderContents to (every item of myFinderItem)
            open myFolderContents
        else
            tell application "Finder" to set myItemExtension to "." & (name extension of myFinderItem) as string
            if myFiletypes contains myItemExtension then
                tell application "Adobe Illustrator 10"
                    open myFinderItem as alias
                    set myDocumentName to name of document 1
```

AS, cont'd.

```
                set current document to document (myDocumentName as
                    string)
                end tell
                doProcessDocument(myDocumentName)
            end if
        end if
    end repeat
end open

on doProcessDocument(myDocumentName)
    tell application "Adobe Illustrator 10" to close document
        myDocumentName saving no
end doProcessDocument
```

doProcessDocument() is the main function that the folder processor script calls to work with the current open document in Illustrator.

Visual Basic

Script Tips *You should start each Visual Basic script with the Option Explicit declaration to ensure that VB makes you declare all your variables explicitly with* `Dim` *statements. It's good VB coding style to do this.*

The `Command1_Click()` subroutine is the main handler for most of the scripts in this book. It is run when the user clicks the button in the form. In this script's `Command1_Click` code, you start by defining the file extensions that should be processed by your script, then call another subroutine to process files. If the button is clicked without any folder being selected, an alert is shown to the user.

The `openFolder` subroutine looks at each file in the folder passed to it. If the file has a valid extension, `doProcessDocument()` is called, passing a reference to the file to be processed. Many of the scripts that follow will be fleshed-out `doProcessDocument()` routines that can be used with this main folder-processing script.

VBScript

Using `Option Explicit` *and* `Dim` *is part of good VB coding style.*

```
Option Explicit
Dim myApp As New Illustrator.Application
Dim myFilesystem As New FileSystemObject
Dim myFiletypes
```

VBS, cont'd.

Whenever the user changes the drive selection in the DriveListBox, this subroutine updates the FolderListBox to show the new drive.

```
Private Sub Drive1_Change()
    Dir1.Path = Left(Drive1.Drive, 1) & ":\"
End Sub
```

This subroutine is the script run when the user clicks your form's button.

```
Private Sub Command1_Click()
    myFiletypes = ".ai,.eps"
    If Dir1.Path = "" Then MsgBox ("Select a folder to process first")
    openFolder Dir1.Path
End Sub
```

The openFolder subroutine processes all files in a folder.

```
Private Sub openFolder(myStartingFolderpath)
    Dim myStartingFolder, myFiles, myFile, myItemExtension, myFolders, myFolder, myDoc
    Set myStartingFolder = myFilesystem.GetFolder(Dir1.Path)
    Set myFiles = myStartingFolder.Files
    For Each myFile In myFiles
        myItemExtension = Mid(myFile.Name, InStrRev(myFile.Name, "."))
        If InStr(myFiletypes, myItemExtension) > 0 Then
            Set myDoc = myApp.Open(myFile.Path)
            doProcessDocument myDoc.Name
        End If
    Next
    Set myFolders = myStartingFolder.SubFolders
    For Each myFolder In myFolders
        openFolder (myFolder)
    Next
End Sub
```

doProcessDocument() is the main subroutine that processes documents in Illustrator. This example closes the document, doing nothing to it.

```
Private Sub doProcessDocument(myDocumentName)
    myApp.Documents(myDocumentName).Close (aiDoNotSaveChanges)
End Sub
```

Script 4.2: Batch Processor of Open Documents in Illustrator

If Script 4.1 is like a Cuisinart, this scriptlet works more like a traditional Osterizer. **Script 4.2** processes every document that is open in Illustrator when the script is run. Standing alone, Script 4.1 doesn't do anything but close all open documents in Illustrator one at a time. Just replace the script lines in doProcessDocument() with some of the later scripts, and you can extend the power of the individual script work across multiple documents.

As the setup for this Visual Basic project differs slightly from the setup for the preceding one, I am providing another step-by-step explanation of how to create a new blank project in Visual Basic. **Figure 4.4** shows each step you have to perform in the Visual Basic editor before you can start entering the script.

This script can be run from Script Editor or the Visual Basic editor, or saved as an application and run from the Desktop or the Scripts menu of Illustrator.

TIP *In an effort to prevent unsightly errors, this script performs extra conditional testing to make sure that a document is open before proceeding. Most of the scripts in this chapter attempt to prevent errors by avoiding assumptions and checking for the existence of objects before addressing them.*

AppleScript

Script Tips *The run handler is the main bit of code to deal with for now. It processes every open document in an expected running copy of Illustrator 10.*

The script requires that each open document have a unique name, because it references documents by their name only. In the main repeat loop, the script goes through each document name in the open documents, making the document frontmost in Illustrator before calling the function.

AppleScript

```
on run
    tell application "Adobe Illustrator 10" to set
    myDocumentNames to name of documents
    if myDocumentNames is {} then
        display dialog "No open documents were found."
    else
        repeat with myDocumentName in myDocumentNames
            tell application "Adobe Illustrator 10" to set current
            document to document (myDocumentName as string)
            doProcessDocument(myDocumentName)
        end repeat
    end if
end run

on doProcessDocument(myDocumentName)
    tell application "Adobe Illustrator 10" to close document
    myDocumentName saving no
end doProcessDocument
```

Time to make sure that some open documents exist in Illustrator.

Here is the main repeat loop.

The function doProcessDocument() is used to process the document whose name is passed to it. For now, it simply closes the document.

Visual Basic

Script Tips *The main* `Command1_Click()` *subroutine first connects to Illustrator and makes sure that there are open documents before proceeding. If there aren't any, the* `MsgBox` *function at the end of the routine will display the dialog shown in Figure 4.5.*

VBScript

```
Option Explicit
Dim myApp As New Illustrator.Application
Dim myCount, myDocumentNames, i

Private Sub Command1_Click()
    Set myApp = New Illustrator.Application
    myCount = myApp.Documents.Count
    If myCount > 0 Then
        ReDim myDocumentNames(myCount)
        For i = 1 To myCount
```

VBS, cont'd.

This loop captures the names of all open documents in an array.

```
        myDocumentNames(i) = myApp.Documents(i).Name
    Next
```

This loop activates each document, passing the document name to doProcessDocument().

```
    For i = 1 To myCount
        myApp.ActiveDocument =
        myApp.Documents(myDocumentNames(i))
        doProcessDocument (myDocumentNames(i))
    Next
  Else
    MsgBox ("No open documents were found.")
  End If
End Sub
```

The document-processing subroutine is just a placeholder for now. It simply closes the document whose name is passed to it.

```
Private Sub doProcessDocument(myDocumentName)
    myApp.Documents(1).Close (aiDoNotSaveChanges)
End Sub
```

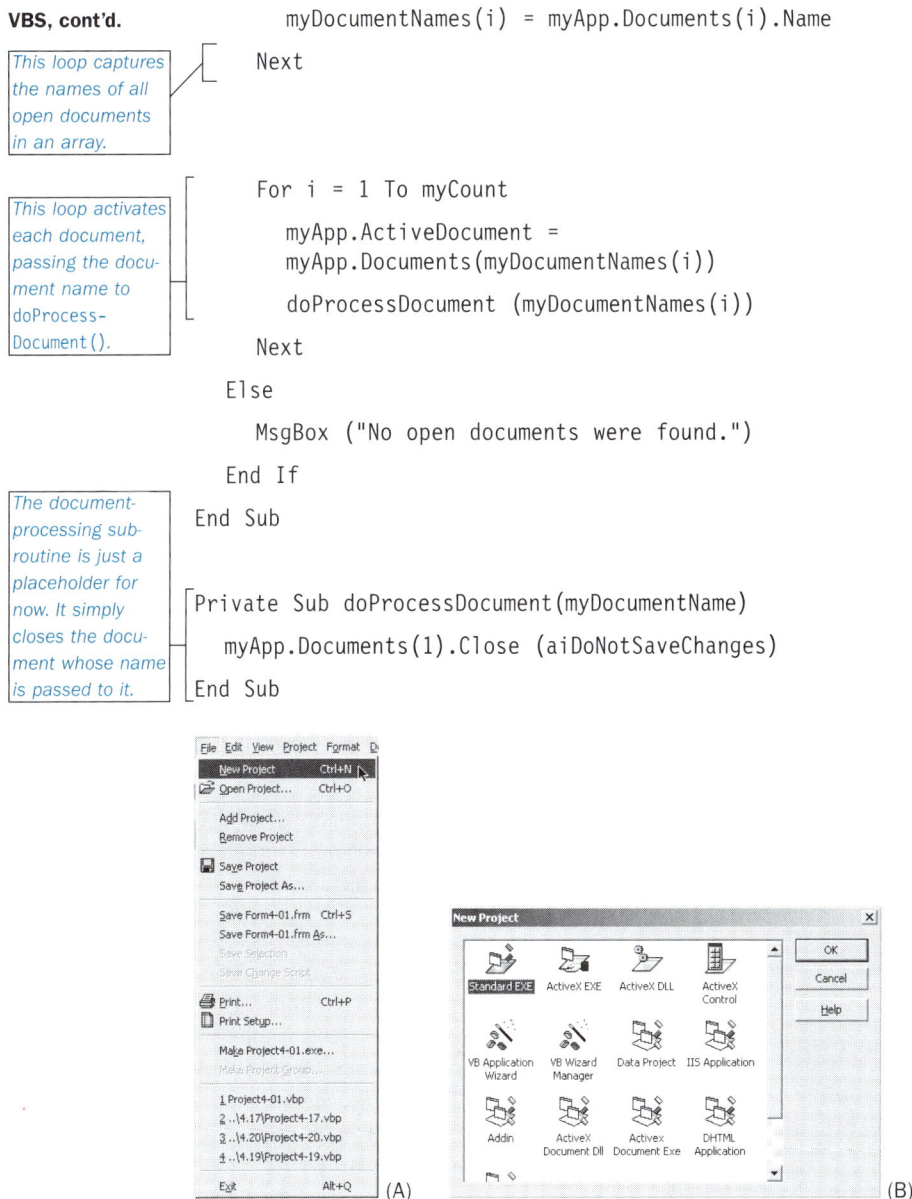

Figure 4.4 A–B   *This series of screen shots illustrates the steps necessary to create a new project with a form so that you can add Script 4.2. (A) Start by choosing File > New Project. (B) Next, select a standard .exe project, and click the OK button. A new project will open, with a new form window showing as in (C).*

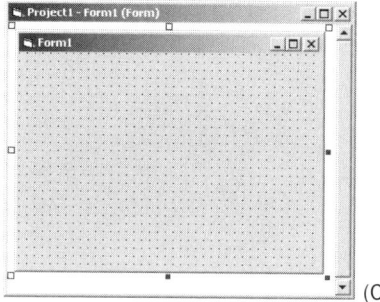 (C)

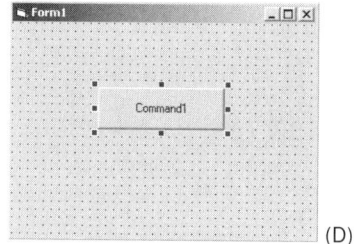 (D)

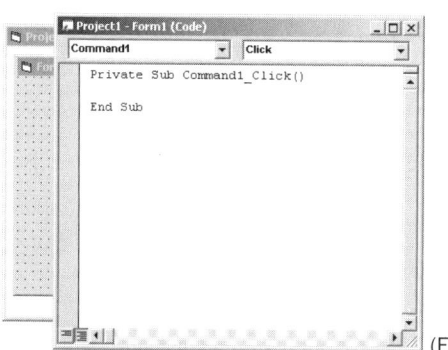 (E)

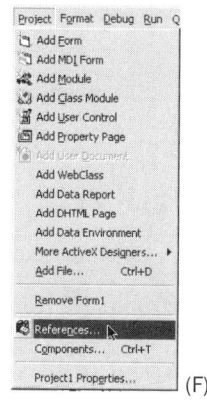 (F)

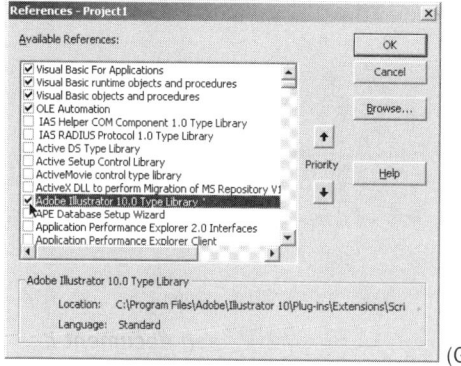 (G)

Figure 4.4 D–G Select the Command-Button tool, and drag out a new button in the open form window so that your form looks like the one shown in (D). Double-click the button in the form to open its code window, shown in (E). This code window is where you will do your script writing. The last step before scripting is attaching a reference to the scripting libraries your project will use so that the project will be able to work with Illustrator. To do this, choose Project > References, as shown in (F). Then locate the Adobe Illustrator 10.0 Type Library (G), and activate it by checking the box next to its name. Now you can close the References dialog by clicking the OK button. Time to write Visual Basic!

Figure 4.5 The Visual Basic script displays this message box when it is run and no documents are open in Illustrator. A similar window is displayed by the AppleScript version of Script 4.2.

Script 4.3: Batch Processor of All Objects in the Current Document

Now things are starting to get interesting. Repetitive as it appears, **Script 4.3** provides a complete framework for building specific handlers or subroutines that can modify or analyze different kinds of page items in the frontmost open document in Illustrator. **Figure 4.6** shows the script's default behavior of displaying each page item's type in a dialog.

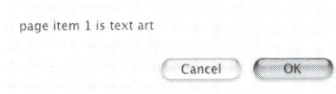

Figure 4.6 In its current form, the script displays each page item's type in a window. Here the AppleScript version of the script shows that the first page item in the document being processed is a text art item.

After you write this script, you can reuse it many times as a shell into which you add specific code for only one or two kinds of page items. Then you can quickly craft a simple text art item or group-item processor, for example, that might suit your needs.

TIP *To create the starting Visual Basic project for this script, follow the steps explained for Script 4.2 in Figure 4.4.*

AppleScript

Script Tips The run handler for this scriptlet is a placeholder. It simply ensures that a document is open in Illustrator before calling the function `doProcessObjects()`.

You can use the `doProcessObjects()` *function in combination with any other code. You could process all objects in every open document by combining this scriptlet with the preceding one, for example.*

The main repeat loop in `doProcessObjects()` *looks at the type of each page item in the current document. Then it calls a different function for each page item type, allowing specific changes to take place within that function.*

Each of the individual object-processing functions receives the index position of the specific page item to process. You can replace the dialog displaying code used here with scripting to modify individual kinds of page items.

AppleScript

```
on run
    tell application "Adobe Illustrator 10" to set
    myDocumentCount to count of documents
    if myDocumentCount > 0 then
        doProcessObjects()
    end if
end run
```

Here is the run handler. → `end run`

doProcessObjects() is the main handler that processes every object in the frontmost document. → `on doProcessObjects()`

```
    tell application "Adobe Illustrator 10" to set myObjectCount
    to count of page items in document 1
    if myObjectCount > 0 then
        repeat with myObjectNum from 1 to myObjectCount
            tell application "Adobe Illustrator 10"
                set myObjectClass to class of page item myObjectNum
                of document 1
                if myObjectClass = compound path item then
                    tell me to doProcessCompoundPath(myObjectNum)
                else if myObjectClass = graph item then
                    tell me to doProcessGraph(myObjectNum)
                else if myObjectClass = group item then
                    tell me to doProcessGroup(myObjectNum)
                else if myObjectClass = mesh item then
                    tell me to doProcessMesh(myObjectNum)
                else if myObjectClass = path item then
                    tell me to doProcessPath(myObjectNum)
                else if myObjectClass = placed item then
                    tell me to doProcessPlaced(myObjectNum)
                else if myObjectClass = plugin item then
                    tell me to doProcessPlugin(myObjectNum)
                else if myObjectClass = raster item then
                    tell me to doProcessRaster(myObjectNum)
```

This main repeat loop calls a function based on object type.

AS, cont'd.

```
                else if myObjectClass = symbol item then
                    tell me to doProcessSymbol(myObjectNum)
                else if myObjectClass = text art item then
                    tell me to doProcessTextArt(myObjectNum)
                end if
            end tell
        end repeat
    end if
end doProcessObjects


on doProcessCompoundPath(myObjectNum)
    display dialog "page item " & myObjectNum & " is a compound
    path"
end doProcessCompoundPath

on doProcessGraph(myObjectNum)
    display dialog "page item " & myObjectNum & " is a graph"
end doProcessGraph

on doProcessGroup(myObjectNum)
    display dialog "page item " & myObjectNum & " is a group"
end doProcessGroup

on doProcessMesh(myObjectNum)
    display dialog "page item " & myObjectNum & " is a mesh"
end doProcessMesh

on doProcessPath(myObjectNum)
    display dialog "page item " & myObjectNum & " is a path"
end doProcessPath

on doProcessPlaced(myObjectNum)
    display dialog "page item " & myObjectNum & " is placed art"
end doProcessPlaced
```

This particular function is passed each graph item found in the document.

AS, cont'd.

```
on doProcessPlugin(myObjectNum)
    display dialog "page item " & myObjectNum & " is plugin art"
end doProcessPlugin


on doProcessRaster(myObjectNum)
    display dialog "page item " & myObjectNum & " is raster art"
end doProcessRaster


on doProcessSymbol(myObjectNum)
    display dialog "page item " & myObjectNum & " is symbol art"
end doProcessSymbol


on doProcessTextArt(myObjectNum)
    display dialog "page item " & myObjectNum & " is text art"
end doProcessTextArt
```

Visual Basic

Script Tips *In this script, the button-click subroutine* `Command1_Click()` *just makes sure that a document is open in Illustrator before calling your* `doProcessObjects()` *subroutine.*

The main `For...Next` *loop in* `doProcessObjects()` *looks at the type of each page item to determine which subroutine to call. Specific changes to individual page items can take place within each subroutine.*

Each of the subroutines provided here to process individual types of page items just shows a message window. You can add custom code to modify page items of a specific type by adding to the appropriate subroutine.

VBScript

```
Option Explicit
Dim myApp As New Illustrator.Application


Private Sub Command1_Click()
    If myApp.Documents.Count > 0 Then
        doProcessObjects
    End If
End Sub
```

VBS, cont'd.

```
Private Sub doProcessObjects()
    Dim myObjectCount, myObjectNum, myObjectClass
    myObjectCount = myApp.Documents(1).PageItems.Count
    If myObjectCount > 0 Then
        For myObjectNum = 1 To myObjectCount
            myObjectClass = myApp.Documents(1).
            PageItems(myObjectNum).PageItemType
            Select Case myObjectClass
                Case aiCompoundPathItem
                    doProcessCompoundPath (myObjectNum)
                Case aiGraphItem
                    doProcessGraph (myObjectNum)
                Case aiGroupItem
                    doProcessGroup (myObjectNum)
                Case aiMeshItem
                    doProcessMesh (myObjectNum)
                Case aiPathItem
                    doProcessPath (myObjectNum)
                Case aiPlacedItem
                    doProcessPlaced (myObjectNum)
                Case aiPluginItem
                    doProcessPlugin (myObjectNum)
                Case aiRasterItem
                    doProcessRaster (myObjectNum)
                Case aiSymbolItem
                    doProcessSymbol (myObjectNum)
                Case aiTextArtItem
                    doProcessTextArt (myObjectNum)
            End Select
        Next
    End If
End Sub
```

This For...Next loop moves through each page item in the frontmost document, calling another subroutine depending on the page item's type.

VBS, cont'd.

```
Private Sub doProcessCompoundPath(myObjectNum)
    MsgBox ("page item " & myObjectNum & " is a compound path")
End Sub


Private Sub doProcessGraph(myObjectNum)
    MsgBox ("page item " & myObjectNum & " is a graph")
End Sub


Private Sub doProcessGroup(myObjectNum)
    MsgBox ("page item " & myObjectNum & " is a group")
End Sub


Private Sub doProcessMesh(myObjectNum)
    MsgBox ("page item " & myObjectNum & " is a mesh")
End Sub


Private Sub doProcessPath(myObjectNum)
    MsgBox ("page item " & myObjectNum & " is a path")
End Sub


Private Sub doProcessPlaced(myObjectNum)
    MsgBox ("page item " & myObjectNum & " is placed art")
End Sub


Private Sub doProcessPlugin(myObjectNum)
    MsgBox ("page item " & myObjectNum & " is plugin art")
End Sub


Private Sub doProcessRaster(myObjectNum)
    MsgBox ("page item " & myObjectNum & " is raster art")
End Sub


Private Sub doProcessSymbol(myObjectNum)
    MsgBox ("page item " & myObjectNum & " is symbol art")
```

This subroutine is passed to each raster item in the document.

VBS, cont'd.

```
End Sub

Private Sub doProcessTextArt(myObjectNum)
    MsgBox ("page item " & myObjectNum & " is text art")
End Sub
```

Script 4.4: Batch Processor of All Objects in the Current Selection

Once you master the art of working with all objects in a document, the next natural step is to deal with all objects actively selected in the frontmost document. This is an invaluable kind of scriptlet for building current-selection-processing scripts that can live in your Illustrator's File > Scripts menu. Script 4.4 picks up from the basic code of Script 4.3, only it processes only the actively selected objects in the frontmost document of Illustrator. **Figure 4.7** shows the current script's behavior of displaying each selected page item's type in a dialog box.

TIP *To create the starting Visual Basic project for this script, follow the steps explained for Script 4.2 in Figure 4.4.*

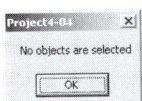

Figure 4.7 *If the selection of the current document is empty, the script will display a message that looks like this one.*

AppleScript

Script Tips *The main script is a placeholder. It simply ensures that a document is open in Illustrator before calling the function* doProcessObjects().

This version of doProcessObjects() *is similar to the preceding script-let, which processed all the objects in the frontmost document. This function processes only those page items in the current selection of the document.*

Each of the object-processing functions receives the index position of the specific page item to process. You can replace the dialog displaying code used here with scripting to modify individual kinds of page items.

AppleScript

```applescript
on run
    tell application "Adobe Illustrator 10" to set myDocumentCount to count of documents
    if myDocumentCount > 0 then
        doProcessObjects()
    end if
end run

on doProcessObjects()
    tell application "Adobe Illustrator 10"
        set mySelection to selection
        set myObjectCount to count of items in mySelection
    end tell
    if myObjectCount > 0 then
        repeat with myObjectNum from 1 to myObjectCount
            tell application "Adobe Illustrator 10"
                set myObjectClass to class of item myObjectNum of mySelection
                if myObjectClass = compound path item then
                    tell me to doProcessCompoundPath(myObjectNum)
                else if myObjectClass = graph item then
                    tell me to doProcessGraph(myObjectNum)
                else if myObjectClass = group item then
                    tell me to doProcessGroup(myObjectNum)
                else if myObjectClass = mesh item then
                    tell me to doProcessMesh(myObjectNum)
                else if myObjectClass = path item then
                    tell me to doProcessPath(myObjectNum)
                else if myObjectClass = placed item then
                    tell me to doProcessPlaced(myObjectNum)
                else if myObjectClass = plugin item then
                    tell me to doProcessPlugin(myObjectNum)
                else if myObjectClass = raster item then
                    tell me to doProcessRaster(myObjectNum)
                else if myObjectClass = symbol item then
```

Here, the script stores the current selection in a variable so that it can evaluate the contents of the selection.

```
                tell me to doProcessSymbol(myObjectNum)
            else if myObjectClass = text art item then
                tell me to doProcessTextArt(myObjectNum)
            end if
          end tell
        end repeat
      else
        display dialog "No objects are selected"
      end if
    end doProcessObjects


    on doProcessCompoundPath(myObjectNum)
      display dialog "item " & myObjectNum & " of the selection is
      a compound path"
    end doProcessCompoundPath


    on doProcessGraph(myObjectNum)
      display dialog "item " & myObjectNum & " of the selection is
      a graph"
    end doProcessGraph


    on doProcessGroup(myObjectNum)
      display dialog "item " & myObjectNum & " of the selection is
      a group"
    end doProcessGroup


    on doProcessMesh(myObjectNum)
      display dialog "item " & myObjectNum & " of the selection is
      a mesh"
    end doProcessMesh


    on doProcessPath(myObjectNum)
      display dialog "item " & myObjectNum & " of the selection is
      a path"
    end doProcessPath
```

AS, cont'd.

```
on doProcessPlaced(myObjectNum)
    display dialog "item " & myObjectNum & " of the selection is placed art"
end doProcessPlaced


on doProcessPlugin(myObjectNum)

    display dialog "item " & myObjectNum & " of the selection is plugin art"
end doProcessPlugin


on doProcessRaster(myObjectNum)
    display dialog "item " & myObjectNum & " of the selection is raster art"
end doProcessRaster


on doProcessSymbol(myObjectNum)
    display dialog "item " & myObjectNum & " of the selection is symbol art"
end doProcessSymbol


on doProcessTextArt(myObjectNum)
    display dialog "item " & myObjectNum & " of the selection is text art"
end doProcessTextArt
```

This function processes each text art item in the document.

Visual Basic

Script Tips *The main* `Command1_Click()` *subroutine ensures that a document is open and that the document's selection is not empty before proceeding to call the* `doProcessSelection()` *subroutine. If the selection is empty, a message is displayed.*

The object-processing subroutines get the index position of the page item they're supposed to process. You can replace the `MsgBox` *function in each subroutine with code to process objects of the specific type.*

VBScript

```vbscript
Option Explicit
Dim myApp As New Illustrator.Application

Private Sub Command1_Click()
   Dim mySelectionType
   If myApp.Documents.Count > 0 Then
      mySelectionType = TypeName(myApp.Selection)
      If mySelectionType <> "Empty" Then
         doProcessSelection
      Else
         MsgBox ("No objects are selected")
      End If
   End If
End Sub

Private Sub doProcessSelection()
   Dim myObjectCount, mySelection, myObject, myObjectNum, myObjectClass
   myObjectCount = UBound(myApp.Selection) + 1
   If myObjectCount > 0 Then
      mySelection = myApp.Selection
      For myObjectNum = 1 To myObjectCount
         Set myObject = mySelection(myObjectNum - 1)
         myObjectClass = myObject.PageItem.PageItemType
         Select Case myObjectClass
            Case aiCompoundPathItem
               doProcessCompoundPath (myObjectNum)
            Case aiGraphItem
               doProcessGraph (myObjectNum)
            Case aiGroupItem
               doProcessGroup (myObjectNum)
            Case aiMeshItem
               doProcessMesh (myObjectNum)
            Case aiPathItem
```

This For...Next loop moves through each object in the current selection, testing its type before calling a specific subroutine to process the page item.

VBS, cont'd.

```
                doProcessPath (myObjectNum)
            Case aiPlacedItem
                doProcessPlaced (myObjectNum)
            Case aiPluginItem
                doProcessPlugin (myObjectNum)
            Case aiRasterItem
                doProcessRaster (myObjectNum)
            Case aiSymbolItem
                doProcessSymbol (myObjectNum)
            Case aiTextArtItem
                doProcessTextArt (myObjectNum)
        End Select
    Next
  End If
End Sub


Private Sub doProcessCompoundPath(myObjectNum)
  MsgBox ("item " & myObjectNum & " of the selection is a
  compound path")
End Sub


Private Sub doProcessGraph(myObjectNum)
  MsgBox ("item " & myObjectNum & " of the selection is a
  graph")
End Sub


Private Sub doProcessGroup(myObjectNum)
  MsgBox ("item " & myObjectNum & " of the selection is a
  group")
End Sub
```

VBS, cont'd.

```
Private Sub doProcessMesh(myObjectNum)
   MsgBox ("item " & myObjectNum & " of the selection is a
   mesh")
End Sub


Private Sub doProcessPath(myObjectNum)
   MsgBox ("item " & myObjectNum & " of the selection is a
   path")
End Sub


Private Sub doProcessPlaced(myObjectNum)
   MsgBox ("item " & myObjectNum & " of the selection is placed
   art")
End Sub


Private Sub doProcessPlugin(myObjectNum)
   MsgBox ("item " & myObjectNum & " of the selection is plugin
   art")
End Sub


Private Sub doProcessRaster(myObjectNum)
   MsgBox ("item " & myObjectNum & " of the selection is raster
   art")
End Sub


Private Sub doProcessSymbol(myObjectNum)
   MsgBox ("item " & myObjectNum & " of the selection is symbol
   art")
End Sub


Private Sub doProcessTextArt(myObjectNum)
   MsgBox ("item " & myObjectNum & " of the selection is text
   art")
End Sub
```

This subroutine handles each symbol art item in the document.

Script 4.5: Creator of New Document with Default Settings

The scriptlet before you, **Script 4.5**, offers a glimpse into the world of perfection. Tired of pressing the five command-key sequences and clicking the palette twice every time you make a new document? OK, maybe you can live with that kind of imperfect reality. For everyone else, this script (with some personalized variations) would make a great addition to the Illustrator Scripts menu.

When this script is running, it creates a new document by calling the useful part, doMakeDocument, which creates a new document of a specified size and color space. The path item default fill and stroke settings are configured. A series of new layers are created, with specific names that you can set in the script (**Figure 4.8**). The document's view is set to 75% zoom, and multiwindow mode is enabled. Illustrator actions just can't touch this handy macro-like script.

TIP *To create the starting Visual Basic project for this script, follow the steps explained for Script 4.2 in Figure 4.4.*

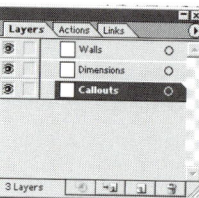

Figure 4.8 The Layers palette for the newly created document shows the three layers created by the script.

AppleScript

Script Tips *The main run handler here simply calls the* doMakeDocument() *function and then brings Illustrator to the front. A script could call* doMakeDocument() *any time to create a document as one step in a multistep workflow.*

The doMakeDocument() *function begins by defining the variable* myDefaults *to hold the properties for a new document to be created shortly. The defaults include dimensions, color space and default stroke and fill properties.*

When the script creates the new document, it adds named layers based on the list myDefaultLayers. *Finally, the script sets the zoom and window mode for the view of the new document.*

AppleScript

This property holds a list of layer names that the doMakeDocument() function will create in every new document it makes.

```applescript
property myDefaultLayers : {"Walls", "Dimensions", "Callouts"}
on run
    doMakeDocument()
    tell application "Adobe Illustrator 10" to activate
end run


on doMakeDocument()
    tell application "Adobe Illustrator 10"
        set myDefaults to {}
        set myDefaults to myDefaults & {color space:CMYK}
        set myDefaults to myDefaults & {width:400.0}
        set myDefaults to myDefaults & {height:800.0}
        set myDefaults to myDefaults & {default filled:true}
        set myDefaults to myDefaults & {default fill color:{cyan:0.0, magenta:50.0, yellow:0.0, black:0.0}}
        set myDefaults to myDefaults & {default fill overprint:false}
        set myDefaults to myDefaults & {default stroked:true}
        set myDefaults to myDefaults & {default stroke color:{cyan:100.0, magenta:0.0, yellow:0.0, black:0.0}}
        set myDefaults to myDefaults & {default stroke width:2.0}
        set myDefaults to myDefaults & {default stroke cap:rounded}
        set myDefaults to myDefaults & {default stroke join:rounded}
        set myDefaults to myDefaults & {default stroke dash offset:0.0}
        set myDefaults to myDefaults & {default stroke dashes:{2.0, 0.5, 2.0, 0.5}}
        set myDefaults to myDefaults & {default stroke overprint:false}
        
        set myDocument to make new document with properties myDefaults
        
        if myDefaultLayers is not {} then
            repeat with myLayer in myDefaultLayers
                make new layer at end of myDocument with properties {name:myLayer}
            end repeat
```

These initial lines specify the color space, height, and width of the new document.

It is time to have Illustrator create a new document, returning a reference to it in a variable.

If myDefaultLayers contains any layer names, a loop creates each new layer, naming it appropriately.

AS, cont'd.

```
        delete layer 1 of myDocument
    end if

    set zoom of view 1 of myDocument to 0.75
    set screen mode of view 1 of myDocument to multiwindow

  end tell
end doMakeDocument
```

Visual Basic

Script Tips *The main script here defines an array of layer names to create before it calls the* doMakeDocument() *subroutine.*

The doMakeDocument() *subroutine begins by declaring variables to hold different properties for the new document with a* Dim *statement. Next, a new document is created with a specified width and height using the values stored in the variables* myWidth *and* myHeight. *We tell the new document's color space to be CMYK by specifying the Illustrator constant* aiDocumentCMYKColor.

VBScript

You declare these variables outside any subroutines so that their values are available to all subroutines.

```
Option Explicit
Dim myApp As New Illustrator.Application
Dim myDefaultLayers

Private Sub Command1_Click()
    myDefaultLayers = Array("Walls", "Dimensions", "Callouts")
    doMakeDocument
End Sub


Private Sub doMakeDocument()
    Dim myDocument, myWidth, myHeight, myCMYKColor, myLayerName, myNewLayer
    myWidth = 400#
    myHeight = 800#
```

VBS, cont'd.

```
Set myDocument = myApp.Documents.Add(aiDocumentCMYKColor, _
myWidth, myHeight)

myDocument.DefaultFilled = True
Set myCMYKColor = New Illustrator.CMYKColor
myCMYKColor.Cyan = 0
myCMYKColor.Magenta = 50
myCMYKColor.Yellow = 0
myCMYKColor.Black = 0
myDocument.DefaultFillColor.CMYK = myCMYKColor
myDocument.DefaultFillOverprint = False
myDocument.DefaultStroked = True
myCMYKColor.Cyan = 100
myCMYKColor.Magenta = 0
myCMYKColor.Yellow = 0
myCMYKColor.Black = 0
myDocument.DefaultStrokeColor.CMYK = myCMYKColor
myDocument.DefaultStrokeWidth = 2#
myDocument.DefaultStrokeCap = aiRoundEndCap
myDocument.DefaultStrokeJoin = aiRoundEndJoin
myDocument.DefaultStrokeDashOffset = 0#
myDocument.DefaultStrokeDashes = Array(2#, 0.5, 2#, 0.5)
myDocument.DefaultStrokeOverprint = False

If UBound(myDefaultLayers) > -1 Then
    For Each myLayerName In myDefaultLayers
        Set myNewLayer = myDocument.Layers.Add()
        myNewLayer.Name = myLayerName
        myNewLayer.MoveToEnd (myDocument)
    Next
    myDocument.Layers.Remove (myDocument.Layers(1))
End If

myDocument.Views(1).Zoom = 0.75
myDocument.Views(1).ScreenMode = aiMultiWindow
End Sub
```

Each color definition in Visual Basic must be created as a new object before its various properties, such as Cyan, can be set.

If myDefaultLayers contains any layer names, a loop creates each new layer, naming it appropriately.

Script 4.6: Exporter of Current Document

This scriptlet is the most important and simple script you could have around. **Script 4.6** is a one-stop shop for exporting and saving any of the file formats that Illustrator can output. It operates on the current document, so it is a perfect companion to Scripts 4.1 and 4.2, in which it can become a batch-processing export machine.

There is a lot of script here, and you don't have to take all of it at once, if you don't want to. Simply leave out any complete `else` or `case` clause and contained lines of code to omit one or more of the file-format outputting sections of the `exportDocument()` function.

The script was written to be versatile, and it is, allowing you to call it to export or save an existing file or an unsaved new document. You can append an additional string to the filename automatically before the file extension that gets added by format type.

In order to run this script, create a simple multi-layered document like the one shown in **Figure 4.9.** Each layer in your test document will be converted into a Flash animation frame in the exported .swf file that will be created when you run the script below as it is. The exported Flash .swf file can be re-imported into Adobe LiveMotion or Macromedia Flash MX, as shown in **Figure 4.10.**

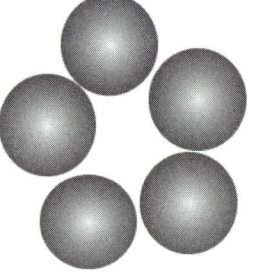
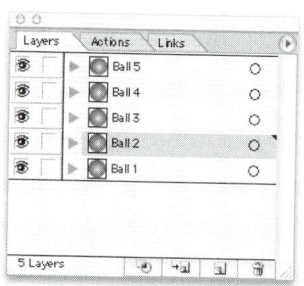

Figure 4.9 *Before you run Script 4.6, create a simple multi-layer document like the one shown in this example. This example has five layers, each with a gradient-filled ellipse located in a different position. These layers will become frames in a Flash .swf file when the script is run.*

TIP *To create the starting Visual Basic project for this script, follow the steps explained for Script 4.2 in Figure 4.4.*

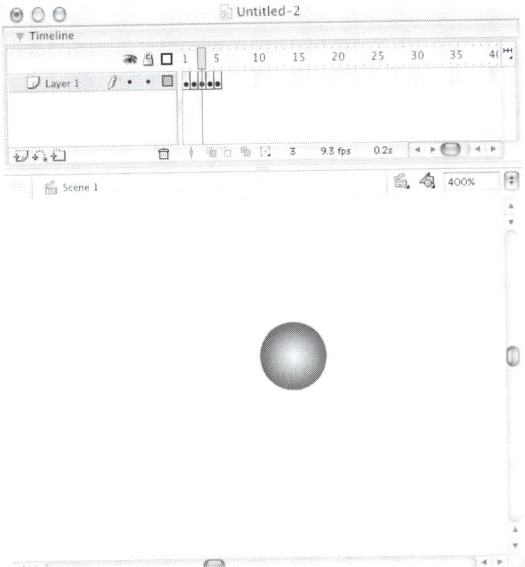

Figure 4.10 *Frame 3 of your script-exported Flash file after the file is imported into a new document in Flash MX.*

AppleScript

Script Tips *This scriptlet starts by defining a property to hold a string that is passed to the* `exportDocument()` *function to determine the file format that it produces. A property is also set that is passed to the function to tell it whether to restore the original file after the new format is saved. This step is necessary because Illustrator switches to the new document when EPS or PDF versions of a document are saved.*

Four parameters are passed to the `exportDocument()` *function, and each deserves an explanation.* `myFormat` *holds a string that tells the function which file format to save or export.* `myNameExtra` *holds a string that is appended to the existing file name before it is saved; it can also be a blank string ("").* `mySaveFolder` *holds the path to the folder to save the new file in or a blank string ("") if the file should be saved in the same folder as the original.* `myRestoreFlag` *holds a Boolean value, true or false. If the value is false, the document is closed after the export. If the value is true, the original document is reopened when necessary.*

Depending on the value of the variable defining the format, `myFormat`, *the script prepares options for the format and then creates the new file. For example, if* `myFormat` *is set to "eps", Illustrator is activated, and an extension is concatenated to the end of the new file's path. Then a variable is created to hold the options for exporting the EPS file. Line after line, parameters are added to the options. Finally, the document is saved in the new file with the EPS file options set. This command changes the current document into the newly saved EPS, so you close the EPS document immediately. If* `myRestoreFlag` *is true, the original file is reopened at the end of the process.*

The `exportDocument()` *function returns a value to the script that has called it that contains the full path to the newly created file.*

AppleScript

```
property myFormat : "flash"
property myRestoreOriginalAfterSave : true
on run
    tell application "Adobe Illustrator 10" to set
        myDocumentCount to count of documents
    if myDocumentCount > 0 then
        set myNewPath to (exportDocument(myFormat, "", "",
            myRestoreOriginalAfterSave))
    end if
end run
on exportDocument(myFormat, myNameExtra, mySaveFolder,
    myRestoreFlag)
    tell application "Adobe Illustrator 10"
        set myOriginalFile to file path of document 1
        if mySaveFolder is not "" then
            set myNewPath to mySaveFolder as string
            if (myOriginalFile as string) contains ":" then set
                myNewPath to myNewPath & (name of document 1)
        else
            set myNewPath to myOriginalFile as string
        end if
        repeat with myCharNum from (count of characters of
            myNewPath) to 1 by -1
            if character myCharNum of myNewPath = "." then
```

The main script just makes sure that a document is open before it calls the `exportDocument()` *function.*

This loop trims off the extension of the current document's file name, if any.

AS, cont'd.

```
            if myCharNum > (count of characters of myNewPath) - 5
            then set myNewPath to (text of characters 1 thru
            (myCharNum - 1) of myNewPath) as string
                exit repeat
            end if
        end repeat
        set myNewPath to myNewPath & myNameExtra
        if myFormat = "eps" then
            activate
            set myNewPath to myNewPath & ".eps"
            set myExportOptions to {}
            set myExportOptions to myExportOptions & {CMYK
            PostScript:true}
            set myExportOptions to myExportOptions &
            {compatibility:Illustrator 10}
            set myExportOptions to myExportOptions & {embed all
            fonts:true}
            set myExportOptions to myExportOptions & {embed linked
            files:true}
            set myExportOptions to myExportOptions & {include
            document thumbnails:true}
            set myExportOptions to myExportOptions &
            {PostScript:level 2}
            set myExportOptions to myExportOptions & {preview:color
            Macintosh}
            set myNewDocument to (save document 1 in file myNewPath
            as eps with options myExportOptions)
            close myNewDocument saving no
            if myRestoreFlag then open myOriginalFile
        else if myFormat = "flash" then
            set myNewPath to myNewPath & ".swf"
            set myExportOptions to {}
            set myExportOptions to myExportOptions & {artboard
            clipping:true}
            set myExportOptions to myExportOptions & {curve
            quality:9}
            set myExportOptions to myExportOptions & {export
            style:layers to frames}
```

This portion of code exports an EPS document.

As with the preceding code, a variable is created to hold the options for exporting the Flash file. If myRestoreFlag is false, the original document is closed.

AS, cont'd.

```applescript
        set myExportOptions to myExportOptions & {frame rate:15.0}
        set myExportOptions to myExportOptions & {generate HTML:false}
        set myExportOptions to myExportOptions & {image format:lossy}
        set myExportOptions to myExportOptions & {JPEG method:optimized}
        set myExportOptions to myExportOptions & {JPEG quality:7}
        set myExportOptions to myExportOptions & {looping:false}
        set myExportOptions to myExportOptions & {read only:false}
        set myExportOptions to myExportOptions & {replacing:yes}
        set myExportOptions to myExportOptions & {resolution:72.0}
        export document 1 to file myNewPath as Flash with options myExportOptions
        if not myRestoreFlag then close document 1 saving no
    else if myFormat = "gif" then
        set myNewPath to myNewPath & ".gif"
        set myExportOptions to {}
        set myExportOptions to myExportOptions & {antialiasing:true}
        set myExportOptions to myExportOptions & {artboard clipping:true}
        set myExportOptions to myExportOptions & {color count:256}
        set myExportOptions to myExportOptions & {color dither:diffusion}
        set myExportOptions to myExportOptions & {color reduction:adaptive}
        set myExportOptions to myExportOptions & {dither percent:50}
        set myExportOptions to myExportOptions & {horizontal scaling:100.0}
        set myExportOptions to myExportOptions & {information loss:0}
```

The GIF export process is the same as the Flash one. Notice how many properties are available for the exported file.

AS, cont'd.

```
        set myExportOptions to myExportOptions &
        {interlaced:true}
        set myExportOptions to myExportOptions & {matte:true}
        set myExportOptions to myExportOptions & {matte
        color:{red:0, green:255, blue:0}}
        set myExportOptions to myExportOptions & {saving as
        HTML:false}
        set myExportOptions to myExportOptions &
        {transparency:false}
        set myExportOptions to myExportOptions & {vertical
        scaling:100.0}
        set myExportOptions to myExportOptions & {web snap:0}
        export document 1 to file myNewPath as GIF with options
        myExportOptions
        if not myRestoreFlag then close document 1 saving no

    else if myFormat = "jpeg" then
        set myNewPath to myNewPath & ".jpg"
        set myExportOptions to {}
        set myExportOptions to myExportOptions &
        {antialiasing:true}
        set myExportOptions to myExportOptions & {artboard
        clipping:true}
        set myExportOptions to myExportOptions & {blur:0.0}
        set myExportOptions to myExportOptions & {horizontal
        scaling:100.0}
        set myExportOptions to myExportOptions & {matte:true}
        set myExportOptions to myExportOptions & {matte
        color:{red:255, green:255, blue:255}}
        set myExportOptions to myExportOptions &
        {optimization:true}
        set myExportOptions to myExportOptions & {quality:70}
        set myExportOptions to myExportOptions & {saving as
        HTML:false}
        set myExportOptions to myExportOptions & {vertical
        scaling:100.0}
        export document 1 to file myNewPath as JPEG with options
        myExportOptions
        if not myRestoreFlag then close document 1 saving no
```

Exporting a JPEG also gives you access to many properties for specifying the JPEG file.

AS, cont'd.

```
    else if myFormat = "pdf" then
        activate
        set myNewPath to myNewPath & ".pdf"
        set myExportOptions to {}
        set myExportOptions to myExportOptions & {color
        compression:JPEG high}
        set myExportOptions to myExportOptions & {color
        downsampling:300.0}
        set myExportOptions to myExportOptions &
        {compatibility:Acrobat 4}
        set myExportOptions to myExportOptions & {compress
        art:true}
        set myExportOptions to myExportOptions & {embed all
        fonts:true}
        set myExportOptions to myExportOptions & {embed ICC
        profile:false}
        set myExportOptions to myExportOptions & {font subset
        threshold:0.0}
        set myExportOptions to myExportOptions & {generate
        thumbnails:true}
        set myExportOptions to myExportOptions & {grayscale
        compression:JPEG high}
        set myExportOptions to myExportOptions & {grayscale
        downsampling:200.0}
        set myExportOptions to myExportOptions & {monochrome
        compression:CCIT3}
        set myExportOptions to myExportOptions & {monochrome
        downsampling:600.0}
        set myExportOptions to myExportOptions & {preserve
        editability:false}
        set myNewDocument to (save document 1 in file myNewPath
        as pdf with options myExportOptions)
        close myNewDocument saving no
        if myRestoreFlag then open myOriginalFile
    else if myFormat = "photoshop" then
        activate
        set myNewPath to myNewPath & ".psd"
        set myExportOptions to {}
```

When a PDF file is saved, the current document becomes the new PDF, so close the document. If myRestoreFlag is true, reopen the original file.

When a Photoshop file is exported, you can export slices, layers, and editable text to the Photoshop file.

AS, cont'd.

```
    set myExportOptions to myExportOptions &
    {antialiasing:true}
    set myExportOptions to myExportOptions & {color
    space:CMYK}
    set myExportOptions to myExportOptions & {compound
    shapes:true}
    set myExportOptions to myExportOptions & {editable
    text:true}
    set myExportOptions to myExportOptions & {embed ICC
    profile:false}
    set myExportOptions to myExportOptions & {hidden
    layers:false}
    set myExportOptions to myExportOptions & {image
    map:true}
    set myExportOptions to myExportOptions & {nested
    layers:true}
    set myExportOptions to myExportOptions &
    {resolution:144.0}
    set myExportOptions to myExportOptions & {slices:true}
    set myExportOptions to myExportOptions &
    {warnings:false}
    set myExportOptions to myExportOptions & {write
    layers:true}
    export document 1 to file myNewPath as Photoshop with
    options myExportOptions
    if not myRestoreFlag then close document 1 saving no

else if myFormat = "png24" then
    set myNewPath to myNewPath & ".png"
    set myExportOptions to {}
    set myExportOptions to myExportOptions &
    {antialiasing:true}
    set myExportOptions to myExportOptions & {artboard
    clipping:true}
    set myExportOptions to myExportOptions & {horizontal
    scaling:100.0}
    set myExportOptions to myExportOptions & {matte:true}
    set myExportOptions to myExportOptions & {matte
    color:{red:255, green:255, blue:255}}
```

The PNG24 export process gives you access to many properties.

AS, cont'd.

```applescript
        set myExportOptions to myExportOptions & {saving as
        HTML:false}
        set myExportOptions to myExportOptions & {vertical
        scaling:100.0}
        export document 1 to file myNewPath as PNG24 with
        options myExportOptions
        if not myRestoreFlag then close document 1 saving no

    else if myFormat = "png8" then
        set myNewPath to myNewPath & ".png"
        set myExportOptions to {}
        set myExportOptions to myExportOptions &
        {antialiasing:true}
        set myExportOptions to myExportOptions & {artboard
        clipping:true}
        set myExportOptions to myExportOptions & {color
        count:256}
        set myExportOptions to myExportOptions & {color
        dither:diffusion}
        set myExportOptions to myExportOptions & {color
        reduction:adaptive}
        set myExportOptions to myExportOptions & {dither
        percent:50}
        set myExportOptions to myExportOptions & {horizontal
        scaling:100.0}
        set myExportOptions to myExportOptions &
        {interlaced:true}
        set myExportOptions to myExportOptions & {matte:true}
        set myExportOptions to myExportOptions & {matte
        color:{red:0, green:255, blue:0}}
        set myExportOptions to myExportOptions & {saving as
        HTML:false}
        set myExportOptions to myExportOptions &
        {transparency:false}
        set myExportOptions to myExportOptions & {vertical
        scaling:100.0}
        set myExportOptions to myExportOptions & {web snap:0}
        export document 1 to file myNewPath as PNG8 with options
        myExportOptions
        if not myRestoreFlag then close document 1 saving no
```

The PNG8 export options closely match the GIF export options.

AS, cont'd.

```
        else if myFormat = "svg" then
            activate
            set myNewPath to myNewPath & ".svg"
            set myExportOptions to {}
            set myExportOptions to myExportOptions & ¬
            {compressed:false} —if set to true, file extension
            becomes .svgz
            set myExportOptions to myExportOptions & {coordinate
            precision:5}
            set myExportOptions to myExportOptions & {CSS
            properties:style attributes}
            set myExportOptions to myExportOptions & {document
            encoding:UTF8}
            set myExportOptions to myExportOptions & {embed all
            fonts:true}
            set myExportOptions to myExportOptions & {embed raster
            images:true}
            set myExportOptions to myExportOptions & {font
            subsetting:all glyphs}
            set myExportOptions to myExportOptions & {include file
            info:true}
            set myExportOptions to myExportOptions & {include
            variables and datasets:false}
            set myExportOptions to myExportOptions & {optimize for
            SVG Viewer:true}
            set myExportOptions to myExportOptions & {preserve
            editability:false}
            set myExportOptions to myExportOptions & {slices:false}
            export document 1 to file myNewPath as SVG with options
            myExportOptions
            close document 1 saving no
            if myRestoreFlag then open myOriginalFile
        end if
    end tell
    return myNewPath
end exportDocument
```

The export command for SVG files changes the current document to the new SVG, so close the document. If myRestoreFlag is true, reopen the original file.

Visual Basic

Script Tips *The main* `Command1_Click()` *subroutine starts by defining variables to hold parameters passed to the* `exportDocument()` *function. Four parameters are passed to the function, and each deserves an explanation.* `myFormat` *holds a string that tells the function which file format to save or export.* `myNameExtra` *holds a string that is appended to the existing file name before it is saved; it can also be a blank string ("").* `mySaveFolder` *holds the path to the folder to save the new file in or a blank string ("") if the file should be saved in the same folder as the original.* `myRestoreFlag` *holds a Boolean value,* `True` *or* `False`*. If the value is* `False`*, the document is closed after the export. If the value is* `True`*, the original document is reopened when necessary.*

Depending on the value of the variable defining the format, `myFormat`*, the script prepares options for the format and then creates the new file. For example, if* `myFormat` *is set to "eps", Illustrator is activated, and an extension is concatenated to the end of the new file's path. Then a variable is created to hold the options for exporting the EPS file. Line after line, parameters are added to the options. Finally, the document is saved in the new file with the EPS file options set. This command changes the current document into the newly saved EPS, so you close the EPS document immediately. If* `myRestoreFlag` *is true, the original file is reopened at the end of the process.*

The `exportDocument()` *function returns a value to the script that has called it that contains the full path of the newly created file.*

VBScript

```
Option Explicit
Dim myApp As New Illustrator.Application

Private Sub Command1_Click()
   Dim myFormat, myNameExtra, mySaveFolder, myRestoreFlag,
   myNewPath
   myFormat = "flash"
   myNameExtra = ""
   mySaveFolder = ""
   myRestoreFlag = True
   If myApp.Documents.Count > 0 Then
      myNewPath = exportDocument(myFormat, myNameExtra,
      mySaveFolder, myRestoreFlag)
```

VBS, cont'd.

```
        End If
    End Sub


    Private Function exportDocument(myFormat, myNameExtra, _
        mySaveFolder, myRestoreFlag)
        Dim myOriginalFile, myNewPath, myCharNum, myExportOptions, _
            myColor
        myOriginalFile = myApp.Documents(1).FullName
        If mySaveFolder <> "" Then
            myNewPath = mySaveFolder & "\"
            If Left(myOriginalFile, 1) <> "\" Then myNewPath = _
                myNewPath & myApp.Documents(1).Name
        Else
            myNewPath = myOriginalFile
        End If
        If InStrRev(myOriginalFile, ".") > Len(myOriginalFile) - 5 _
        Then
            myNewPath = Mid(myOriginalFile, 1, _
                InStrRev(myOriginalFile, ".") - 1)
        End If
        myNewPath = myNewPath & myNameExtra
        Select Case myFormat
            Case "eps"
                myNewPath = myNewPath & ".eps"
                Set myExportOptions = New Illustrator.EPSSaveOptions
                myExportOptions.CMYKPostScript = True
                myExportOptions.Compatibility = aiIllustrator10
                myExportOptions.EmbedAllFonts = True
                myExportOptions.EmbedLinkedFiles = True
                myExportOptions.IncludeDocumentThumbnails = True
                myExportOptions.PostScript = aiLevel2
                myExportOptions.Preview = aiColorTIFF
                myApp.Documents(1).SaveAs myNewPath, myExportOptions
                myApp.Documents(1).Close (aiDoNotSaveChanges)
                If myRestoreFlag Then
                    myApp.Open (myOriginalFile)
                End If
```

This use of the built-in Visual Basic string functions InStrRev(), Len(), *and* Mid() *trims off the extension of the current document's file name, if any.*

This portion of code exports an EPS document.

VBS, cont'd.

```
Case "flash"

    myNewPath = myNewPath & ".swf"

    Set myExportOptions = New Illustrator.
    ExportOptionsFlash

    myExportOptions.ArtBoardClipping = True

    myExportOptions.CurveQuality = 9

    myExportOptions.ExportStyle = aiLayersAsFrames

    myExportOptions.FrameRate = 15#

    myExportOptions.GenerateHTML = False

    myExportOptions.ImageFormat = aiLossy

    myExportOptions.JPEGMethod = aiJPEGOptimized

    myExportOptions.JPEGQuality = 7

    myExportOptions.Looping = False

    myExportOptions.ReadOnly = False

    myExportOptions.Replacing = aiSaveChanges

    myExportOptions.Resolution = 72#

    myApp.Documents(1).Export myNewPath, aiFlash,
    myExportOptions

    If myRestoreFlag = False Then

        myApp.Documents(1).Close (aiDoNotSaveChanges)

    End If

Case "gif"

    myNewPath = myNewPath & ".gif"

    Set myExportOptions = New Illustrator.
    ExportOptionsGIF

    myExportOptions.AntiAliasing = True

    myExportOptions.ArtBoardClipping = True

    myExportOptions.ColorCount = 256

    myExportOptions.ColorDither = aiDiffusion

    myExportOptions.ColorReduction = aiAdaptive

    myExportOptions.DitherPercent = 50

    myExportOptions.HorizontalScale = 100#

    myExportOptions.InfoLossPercent = 0

    myExportOptions.Interlaced = True
```

As with the preceding code, a variable is created to hold the options for exporting the Flash file. If myRestoreFlag is false, the original document is closed.

The GIF export process is the same as the Flash one. Notice how many properties are available for the exported file.

VBS, cont'd.

```
myExportOptions.Matte = True
Set myColor = New Illustrator.RGBColor
myColor.Red = 0#
myColor.Green = 255#
myColor.Blue = 0#
myExportOptions.MatteColor = myColor
myExportOptions.SaveAsHTML = False
myExportOptions.Transparency = False
myExportOptions.VerticalScale = 100#
myExportOptions.WebSnap = 0
myApp.Documents(1).Export myNewPath, aiGIF, myExportOptions
If myRestoreFlag = False Then
    myApp.Documents(1).Close (aiDoNotSaveChanges)
End If

Case "jpeg"
    myNewPath = myNewPath & ".jpg"
    Set myExportOptions = New Illustrator.ExportOptionsJPEG
    myExportOptions.AntiAliasing = True
    myExportOptions.ArtBoardClipping = True
    myExportOptions.BlurAmount = 0#
    myExportOptions.HorizontalScale = 100#
    myExportOptions.Matte = True
    Set myColor = New Illustrator.RGBColor
    myColor.Red = 255#
    myColor.Green = 255#
    myColor.Blue = 255#
    myExportOptions.MatteColor = myColor
    myExportOptions.Optimization = True
    myExportOptions.QualitySetting = 70
    myExportOptions.SaveAsHTML = False
    myExportOptions.VerticalScale = 100#
    myApp.Documents(1).Export myNewPath, aiJPEG, myExportOptions
```

Exporting a JPEG also gives you access to many properties for specifying the JPEG file.

VBS, cont'd.

```
        If myRestoreFlag = False Then
            myApp.Documents(1).Close (aiDoNotSaveChanges)
        End If

    Case "pdf"
        myNewPath = myNewPath & ".pdf"
        Set myExportOptions = New Illustrator.PDFSaveOptions
        myExportOptions.ColorCompression = aiJPEGHigh
        myExportOptions.ColorDownsampling = 300#
        myExportOptions.Compatibility = aiAcrobat4
        myExportOptions.CompressArt = True
        myExportOptions.EmbedAllFonts = True
        myExportOptions.EmbedICCProfile = False
        myExportOptions.FontSubsetThreshold = 0#
        myExportOptions.GenerateThumbnails = True
        myExportOptions.GrayscaleCompression = aiJPEGHigh
        myExportOptions.GrayscaleDownsampling = 200#
        myExportOptions.MonochromeCompression = aiCCIT3
        myExportOptions.MonochromeDownsampling = 600#
        myExportOptions.PreserveEditability = False
        myApp.Documents(1).SaveAs myNewPath, myExportOptions
        myApp.Documents(1).Close (aiDoNotSaveChanges)
        If myRestoreFlag Then
            myApp.Open (myOriginalFile)
        End If

    Case "photoshop"
        myNewPath = myNewPath & ".psd"
        Set myExportOptions = New Illustrator.ExportOptionsPhotoshop
        myExportOptions.AntiAliasing = True
        myExportOptions.CompoundShapes = True
        myExportOptions.EditableText = True
        myExportOptions.EmbedICCProfile = False
```

When a PDF file is saved, the current document becomes the new PDF, so close the document. If myRestoreFlag is true, reopen the original file.

When a Photoshop file is exported, you can export slices, layers, and editable text to the Photoshop file.

VBS, cont'd.

```
        myExportOptions.HiddenLayers = False
        myExportOptions.ImageColorSpace = aiImageCMYK
        myExportOptions.ImageMap = True
        myExportOptions.NestedLayers = True
        myExportOptions.Resolution = 144#
        myExportOptions.Slices = True
        myExportOptions.Warnings = False
        myExportOptions.WriteLayers = True
        myApp.Documents(1).Export myNewPath, aiPhotoshop, 
        myExportOptions
        If myRestoreFlag = False Then
            myApp.Documents(1).Close (aiDoNotSaveChanges)
        End If

    Case "png24"
        myNewPath = myNewPath & ".png"
        Set myExportOptions = New Illustrator.
        ExportOptionsPNG24
        myExportOptions.AntiAliasing = True
        myExportOptions.ArtBoardClipping = True
        myExportOptions.HorizontalScale = 100#
        myExportOptions.Matte = True
        Set myColor = New Illustrator.RGBColor
        myColor.Red = 255#
        myColor.Green = 255#
        myColor.Blue = 255#
        myExportOptions.MatteColor = myColor
        myExportOptions.SaveAsHTML = False
        myExportOptions.Transparency = False
        myExportOptions.VerticalScale = 100#
        myApp.Documents(1).Export myNewPath, aiPNG24, 
        myExportOptions
        If myRestoreFlag = False Then
            myApp.Documents(1).Close (aiDoNotSaveChanges)
        End If
```

The PNG24 export process gives you access to many properties.

VBS, cont'd.

The PNG8 export options closely match the GIF export options.

```
Case "png8"
    myNewPath = myNewPath & ".png"
    Set myExportOptions = New Illustrator.ExportOptionsPNG8
    myExportOptions.AntiAliasing = True
    myExportOptions.ArtBoardClipping = True
    myExportOptions.ColorCount = 256#
    myExportOptions.ColorDither = aiDiffusion
    myExportOptions.ColorReduction = aiAdaptive
    myExportOptions.DitherPercent = 50
    myExportOptions.HorizontalScale = 100#
    myExportOptions.Interlaced = True
    myExportOptions.Matte = True
    Set myColor = New Illustrator.RGBColor
    myColor.Red = 0
    myColor.Green = 255#
    myColor.Blue = 0#
    myExportOptions.MatteColor = myColor
    myExportOptions.SaveAsHTML = False
    myExportOptions.Transparency = False
    myExportOptions.VerticalScale = 100#
    myExportOptions.WebSnap = 0
    myApp.Documents(1).Export myNewPath, aiPNG8, myExportOptions
    If myRestoreFlag = False Then
        myApp.Documents(1).Close (aiDoNotSaveChanges)
    End If
```

VBS, cont'd.

```
            Case "svg"
                myNewPath = myNewPath & ".svg"
                Set myExportOptions = New Illustrator.
                ExportOptionsSVG
                myExportOptions.Compressed = False
                myExportOptions.CoordinatePrecision = 5
                myExportOptions.CSSProperties = aiStyleAttributes
                myExportOptions.DocumentEncoding = aiUTF8
                myExportOptions.EmbedAllFonts = True
                myExportOptions.EmbedRasterImages = True
                myExportOptions.FontSubsetting = aiAllGlyphs
                myExportOptions.IncludeFileInfo = True
                myExportOptions.IncludeVariablesAndDatasets = False
                myExportOptions.OptimizeForSVGViewer = True
                myExportOptions.PreserveEditability = False
                myExportOptions.Slices = True
                myApp.Documents(1).Export myNewPath, aiSVG,
                myExportOptions
                myApp.Documents(1).Close (aiDoNotSaveChanges)
                If myRestoreFlag Then
                   myApp.Open (myOriginalFile)
                End If
        End Select
        exportDocument = myNewPath
    End Function
```

The export command for SVG files changes the current document to the new SVG, so close the document. If myRestoreFlag is true, reopen the original file.

File Saving and Exporting Options

Script 4.6 is a single function that exports the current document in any format that Illustrator can create via scripting. For a clear understanding of how the save and export option properties used in scripting correlate to the options presented in the user interface, see one of the following chapters:

- See Chapter 5 for a detailed AppleScript reference to the save and export option properties for all file formats available.

- See Chapter 6 for a detailed Visual Basic reference to the save and export option properties for all file formats available.

Script 4.7: Remove Unused Swatches, Symbols, and Styles to Reduce File Size

Adobe Illustrator documents can become complicated quickly. If you're like me, you appreciate simplicity, and simplifying your working Illustrator document is what this script is about. **Script 4.7** processes the frontmost document in Illustrator, intelligently deleting unused color swatches and symbols. The script also deletes all the styles in the document on the assumption that you won't be needing them. If this feature is a problem for you, simply comment out the call to the function or subroutine `deleteAllStyles()`.

So why remove these extra unused palette collections from your document? The benefits include saving space and providing coherence in your document. The space you'll save is not insignificant. My tests showed that I saved 148 kilobytes from each document's file size when the swatches, symbols, and styles were removed. Coherence may be the best reason overall. When Illustrator documents are shared among members of a team, for example, it is helpful to keep only the used palette collections in the document. Other users of the document who need to add or modify art objects in the document will have only those swatches and symbols you kept in the document to choose among. This arrangement reduces the likelihood that someone will apply the wrong color or go to town with symbol art items that you don't want in the final document that comes back to you.

To try out this script, consider creating a simple sample document with a few path items, like rectangles, in it. Fill each rectangle with a different kind of color swatch, as in the example shown in **Figure 4.11**. Take a look now one last time at your sample document's Swatches, Symbols and Styles palettes before running the script—they should look similar to the example shown in **Figure 4.12**. Once you've run the script, your palettes are going to look like those in **Figure 4.13**, with only the used swatches and symbols remaining, and all of the styles removed.

TIP To create the starting Visual Basic project for this script, follow the steps explained for Script 4.2 in Figure 4.4.

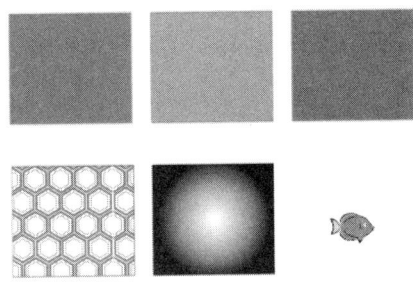

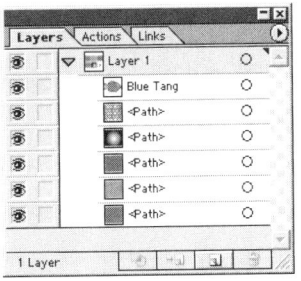

Figure 4.11 A sample document in Illustrator contains five path items filled with different swatch colors, including a gradient, a pattern, and a symbol art item containing a symbol.

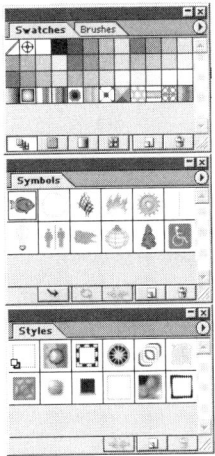

Figure 4.12 The Swatches, Symbols, and Styles palettes for the sample document before the script is run show the complete inventory of items for a typical Illustrator document.

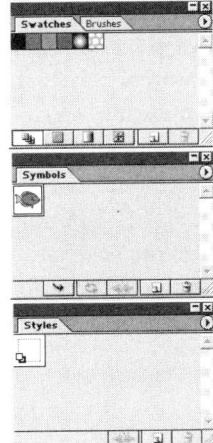

Figure 4.13 After the script runs, the Swatches and Symbols palettes now contain only those swatches and symbols used by page items in the document. All the styles have been deleted, because there is no way to tell from a script whether a style is in use.

AppleScript

Script Tips The run handler just makes sure that a document is open before it calls the `doProcessDocument()` *function. You can delete this part of the script and add the rest of the functions to Scripts 4.1 or 4.2 in order to batch-process documents with the* `doProcessDocument()` *function. Both Script 4.1 and Script 4.2 call the* `doProcessDocument()` *function to do their processing.*

The `doProcessDocument()` *function is the core of the script. It calls each of the other object-purging functions one at a time. If you are interested in disabling part of this script's functionality, you can comment out any line that calls a function you want to skip. If you want to avoid deleting your document's styles, for example, just omit the line that calls* `deleteAllStyles()`. *Each additional function is self-contained and deserves individual attention.*

The `deleteUnusedSwatches()` *function stores a list of references to the swatches in your frontmost document. It loops through all the swatches in the document, starting with the last one first. You do this because AppleScript refers to objects by their index number. If you were to begin deleting swatches from the beginning, the list of swatches immediately gets out of whack; swatch 3 becomes swatch 2, and so on. So you delete from the end, and the index numbers of each swatch stay the same throughout the loop. Delete swatch 28, for example, and the next swatches (27 through 1) to be processed are unaffected. The script attempts to delete the swatch from the document inside of a* `try` *block. If Illustrator generates some kind of error from this attempt, you avoid displaying any error with the* `try... end try` *block.*

The `deleteUnusedSymbols()` *function starts by storing a list of references to the symbols in your frontmost document. The main loop moves through all of the symbols in the document, starting with the last one first. You do this because AppleScript refers to all objects by their index number. If you were to begin deleting symbols from the beginning, the list of symbols immediately gets out-of-whack as* `symbol` 3 *becomes* `symbol` 2 *and so on. Within the loop, store a reference to the current symbol in a variable called* `mysymbol`. *Then simply ask Illustrator for a list of all of the symbol art items that use the current symbol. If the list is empty, you can attempt to delete the symbol from the document. The* `delete` *command is contained in a* `try...end try` *block to avoid displaying any errors to the user.*

DeleteAllStyles() *attempts to delete all styles from the document. If Illustrator generates some kind of error from this attempt, the* try...end try *block prevents any errors from displaying or interrupting the script's execution.*

Finally, to get everything to work, copy the exportDocument() *function from Script 4.6 into this code to enable exporting of the cleaned-up file as an Illustrator-editable PDF file.*

AppleScript

The main run handler calls doProcessDocument().

```
on run
    tell application "Adobe Illustrator 10" to set
    myDocumentNames to name of documents
    if myDocumentNames is not {} then
        doProcessDocument(item 1 of myDocumentNames as string)
    end if
end run
```

The doProcessDocument() function calls each of your other functions one at a time.

```
on doProcessDocument(myDocumentName)
    deleteUnusedSwatches()
    deleteUnusedSymbols()
    deleteAllStyles()
    exportDocument("pdf", "", "", false)
end doProcessDocument
```

This function deletes any swatch color that is not used.

```
on deleteUnusedSwatches()
    tell application "Adobe Illustrator 10"
        if document 1 exists then
            set myswatches to every swatch of document 1
            repeat with myswatchnum from (count of items in
            myswatches) to 1 by -1
                set myswatch to item myswatchnum of myswatches
                set myfilledpaths to (path items of document 1 whose
                fill color = (color of myswatch))
                if myfilledpaths is {} then
                    set mystrokedpaths to (path items of document 1
                    whose stroke color = (color of myswatch))
                    if mystrokedpaths is {} then
```

AS, cont'd.

If no paths use the swatch color, it's time to try to delete the swatch.

```
                    try
                        delete swatch myswatchnum of document 1
                    end try
                end if
            end if
        end repeat
    end if
    end tell
end deleteUnusedSwatches
```

deleteUnused-Symbols() deletes symbols from the palette that aren't referenced in the document.

```
on deleteUnusedSymbols()
    tell application "Adobe Illustrator 10"
        if document 1 exists then
            set mysymbols to every symbol of document 1
            repeat with mysymbolnum from (count of items in mysymbols) to 1 by -1
                set mysymbol to item mysymbolnum of mysymbols
                set mysymbolitems to (symbol items of document 1 whose symbol = mysymbol)
```

If the list of symbol art items using the symbol is empty, you now know the symbol is unused.

```
                if mysymbolitems is {} then
                    try
                        delete symbol mysymbolnum of document 1
                    end try
                end if
            end repeat
        end if
    end tell
end deleteUnusedSymbols
```

This function tries to delete every style in the Styles palette.

```
on deleteAllStyles()
    tell application "Adobe Illustrator 10"
        if document 1 exists then
            try
                delete art styles of document 1
```

AS, cont'd.

```
            end try
         end if
      end tell
   end deleteAllStyles

   on exportDocument(myFormat, myNameExtra, mySaveFolder,
      myRestoreFlag)

   end exportDocument
```

> You need to insert the code here from the scriptlet function exportDocument() of Script 4.6.

Visual Basic

Script Tips The script starts by defining `myApp` as a connection to Illustrator so that the rest of the script can talk to the application.

You can add the `doProcessDocument()` subroutine and the rest of the subroutines to Scripts 4.1 or 4.2 to batch-process documents with doProcessDocument(), because both scriptlets call a Sub of the same name to do their processing. The `doProcessDocument()` subroutine calls each of the other object-purging functions one at a time. Each additional function is explained below.

`deleteUnusedSwatches()` *loops through all the swatches in the document. Within the loop, the script stores a reference to the current swatch in a variable called* `mySwatch`. *Next, the script loops through all the paths in the document, checking for the current color swatch in fill or stroke color. If the script finds that the swatch color is used in the stroke or fill color of the current path, a flag variable is set so that you'll know not to delete the swatch later. You need to test for each possible kind of color and its individual properties to find matches. Much more code is required in Visual Basic to do this, because it lacks the concept of a* `whose` *clause like the one AppleScript has to filter and return only matching objects of a collection.*

The `deleteUnusedSymbols()` *subroutine loops through all the symbol art items in the document, checking for symbol art items that use the current symbol. Unused symbols are deleted from the document's Symbols palette.*

`deleteAllStyles()` *simply deletes every art style in the document.*

Add the code from Script 4.6's `exportDocument()` *function to this script to enable the exporting of the cleaned up document as an editable PDF file.*

VBScript

```
Option Explicit
Dim myApp As New illustrator.Application
```

This subroutine is called when the user clicks the main form's button.

```
Private Sub Command1_Click()
    doProcessDocument
End Sub
```

```
Private Sub doProcessDocument(myDocumentName)
    deleteUnusedSwatches
    deleteUnusedSymbols
    deleteAllStyles
    exportDocument ("pdf", "", "", False)
End Sub
```

This subroutine deletes color swatches not used by page items.

```
Private Sub deleteUnusedSwatches()
    Dim mySwatchNum, mySwatch, myColorUsed, myPathItem
    If myApp.Documents.Count > 0 Then
        For mySwatchNum = myApp.Documents(1).Swatches.Count To 1 Step -1
```

You set up a simple flag variable to keep track of whether you find the color used in the following loop.

```
            Set mySwatch = myApp.Documents(1).Swatches(mySwatchNum)
            myColorUsed = False
            For Each myPathItem In myApp.Documents(1).PathItems
```

This Select statement checks a path's file color for a match against the color in mySwatch.

```
                If myPathItem.FillColor.Color = mySwatch.Color.Color Then
                    Select Case myPathItem.FillColor.Color
                        Case aiColorCMYK
                            If myPathItem.FillColor.CMYK.Black = mySwatch.Color.CMYK.Black
                            And myPathItem.FillColor.CMYK.Cyan = mySwatch.Color.CMYK.Cyan
                            And myPathItem.FillColor.CMYK.Magenta = mySwatch.Color.CMYK.Magenta
                            And myPathItem.FillColor.CMYK.Yellow = mySwatch.Color.CMYK.Yellow Then
                                myColorUsed = True
                            End If
```

VBS, cont'd.

```
        Case aiColorGradient
            If myPathItem.FillColor.Gradient.Gradient.Name
            = mySwatch.Color.Gradient.Gradient.Name Then
                myColorUsed = True
            End If
        Case aiColorGray
            If myPathItem.FillColor.Gray.Gray =
            mySwatch.Color.Gray.Gray Then
                myColorUsed = True
            End If
        Case aiColorPattern
            If myPathItem.FillColor.Pattern.Pattern.Name =
            mySwatch.Color.Pattern.Pattern.Name Then
                myColorUsed = True
            End If
        Case aiColorRGB
            If myPathItem.FillColor.RGB.Blue =
            mySwatch.Color.RGB.Blue
            And myPathItem.FillColor.RGB.Green =
            mySwatch.Color.RGB.Green
            And myPathItem.FillColor.RGB.Red =
            mySwatch.Color.RGB.Red Then
                myColorUsed = True
            End If
        Case aiColorSpot
            If myPathItem.FillColor.Spot.Spot.Name =
            mySwatch.Color.Spot.Spot.Name Then
                myColorUsed = True
            End If
    End Select
End If
If myPathItem.StrokeColor.Color = mySwatch.Color.Color
Then
    Select Case myPathItem.StrokeColor.Color
        Case aiColorCMYK
```

This huge Select statement checks a path's stroke color for a match against mySwatch.

VBS, cont'd.

```
            If myPathItem.StrokeColor.CMYK.Black =
            mySwatch.Color.CMYK.Black
            And myPathItem.StrokeColor.CMYK.Cyan =
            mySwatch.Color.CMYK.Cyan
            And myPathItem.StrokeColor.CMYK.Magenta =
            mySwatch.Color.CMYK.Magenta
            And myPathItem.StrokeColor.CMYK.Yellow =
            mySwatch.Color.CMYK.Yellow Then
                myColorUsed = True
            End If
        Case aiColorGradient
            If myPathItem.StrokeColor.Gradient.Name =
            mySwatch.Color.Gradient.Name Then
                myColorUsed = True
            End If
        Case aiColorGray
            If myPathItem.StrokeColor.Gray.Gray =
            mySwatch.Color.Gray.Gray Then
                myColorUsed = True
            End If
        Case aiColorPattern
            If myPathItem.StrokeColor.Pattern.Name =
            mySwatch.Color.Pattern.Name Then
                myColorUsed = True
            End If
        Case aiColorRGB
            If myPathItem.StrokeColor.RGB.Blue =
            mySwatch.Color.RGB.Blue
            And myPathItem.StrokeColor.RGB.Green =
            mySwatch.Color.RGB.Green
            And myPathItem.StrokeColor.RGB.Red =
            mySwatch.Color.RGB.Red Then
                myColorUsed = True
            End If
        Case aiColorSpot
            If myPathItem.StrokeColor.Spot.Name =
            mySwatch.Color.Spot.Name Then
                myColorUsed = True
            End If
        End Select
    End If
```

VBS, cont'd.

If the flag variable myColorUsed is false, you delete the swatch from the document.

This subroutine deletes all symbols not referenced by objects.

If the flag variable is false, you know that the symbol is unused and can be deleted.

If at least one document is open, this subroutine attempts to delete all styles from the frontmost document.

You need to insert the code here for the exportDocument() function of Script 4.6.

```
            If myColorUsed Then Exit For
            Next
            If myColorUsed = False Then
                myApp.Documents(1).Swatches.Remove (mySwatch)
            End If
        Next
    End If
End Sub

Private Sub deleteUnusedSymbols()
    Dim mmySymbolNum, mySymbol, mySymbolUsed, mySymbolItem
    If myApp.Documents.Count > 0 Then
        For mySymbolNum = myApp.Documents(1).Symbols.Count To 1
          Step -1
            Set mySymbol = myApp.Documents(1).Symbols(mySymbolNum)

            For Each mySymbolItem In myApp.Documents(1).SymbolItems
                If mySymbolItem.Symbol.Name = mySymbol.Name Then
                    mySymbolUsed = True
                    Exit For
                End If
            Next
            If mySymbolUsed = False Then
                myApp.Documents(1).Symbols.Remove (mySymbol)
            End If
        Next
    End If
End Sub

Private Sub deleteAllStyles()
    If myApp.Documents.Count > 0 Then
        myApp.Documents(1).ArtStyles.RemoveAll
    End If
End Sub

Private Function exportDocument(myFormat, myNameExtra, _
    mySaveFolder, myRestoreFlag)

End Function
```

Script 4.8: Make Duplicates of A Selection with Step-and-Repeat

Why isn't there a brilliant tool built into Illustrator that lets you duplicate one or more objects as many times as you like? Such a tool could apply transformations, such as scaling and moving, to each of the newly duplicated objects and save lots of people lots of time. I expect that many Illustrator users, including me, would find this step-and-repeat tool to be a godsend for daily work with the application. Adobe hasn't caught up in its thinking with those of us who know the value of a step-and-repeat function, but it did exceed your expectations with the scripting support in Illustrator 10. So do the Adobe programmers a favor; create your own step-and-repeat tool by using AppleScript or Visual Basic.

Script 4.8 is a simple but really powerful step-and-repeat script. It is a great script to use from Illustrator's File > Scripts menu because it acts on the currently selected objects in the frontmost document. Just select an object or two to duplicate and run the script. You will be prompted for the number of copies you want to make, as shown in **Figure 4.14**. Enter a value, and the script will prompt you sequentially for horizontal and vertical distances to move the duplicates each step, as **Figure 4.15** and **Figure 4.16** show. You'll also be asked to enter the rotation angle, as in **Figure 4.17,** and scale percentage as in **Figure 4.18.** Finally, with all the transformation values gathered, the script will create all the new objects for you quickly, as shown in **Figure 4.19**.

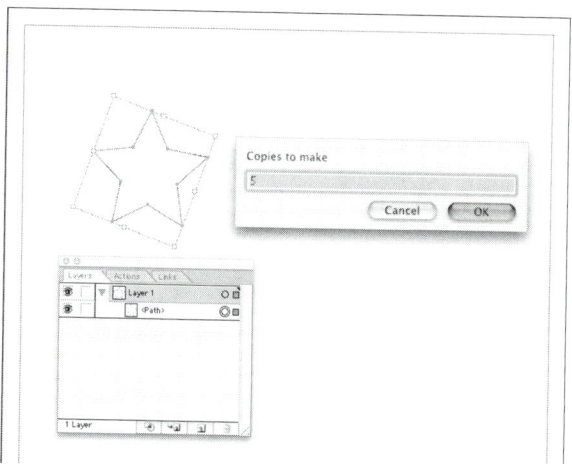

Figure 4.14 *In this view, the user has selected the only object in the document and run the script. Your script creates the dialog prompting the user to enter the number of copies to make.*

Figure 4.15 After the user has entered the desired number of copies to duplicate, a series of screens prompt for transformation values (such as the horizontal distance to move each duplicate).

Figure 4.16 This dialog asks the user for a vertical-movement value.

Figure 4.17 Next, the user is prompted for a rotation value, in degrees.

Figure 4.18 Finally, the user enters a scaling factor, in percentage format.

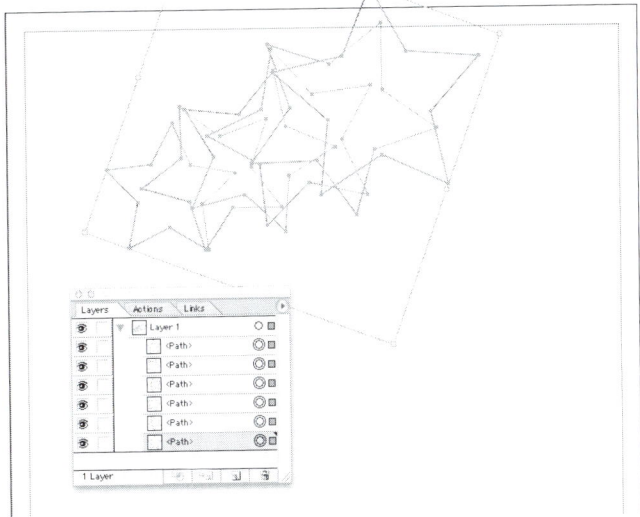

Figure 4.19 This view shows the user's document after the script has run, creating five new copies of the selection and modifying each copy progressively, using the entered transformation values.

TIP To create the starting Visual Basic project for this script, follow the steps explained for Script 4.2 in Figure 4.4.

AppleScript

Script Tips *This script works by using transformation matrices. The script gathers from the user step-and-repeat modification values for moving, rotating, and scaling.*

The script creates a default transformation matrix (an identity matrix) in the variable `myMatrix`. *The script proceeds to combine all the user's requests transformations (moving, rotating, and scaling) into the matrix stored in* `myMatrix`.

Finally, a loop runs the number of times requested by the user, duplicating the current object(s), transforming the new duplicate, and making it the current object(s) by storing a reference in the variable `mySelection` *for use the next time through the loop.*

AppleScript

The script begins by ensuring that a document is open and that the selection is not empty or a range of text in a text art item.

Here's where the matrices are combined together.

```
tell application "Adobe Illustrator 10"
    if (count of documents) > 0 then
        set mySelection to selection
        if class of mySelection is list then
            activate
            set mycopies to text returned of (display dialog "Copies to make" default answer "5") as integer
            if mycopies > 0 then
                set mymoveX to text returned of (display dialog "Move X (pts)" default answer "0.0") as real
                set mymoveY to text returned of (display dialog "Move Y (pts)" default answer "0.0") as real
                set myRotate to text returned of (display dialog "Rotate °" default answer "0.0") as real
                set myScale to text returned of (display dialog "Scale %" default answer "100.0") as real
                set myMatrix to (get identity matrix)
                set myMatrix to concatenate translation matrix myMatrix delta x mymoveX delta y mymoveY
                set myMatrix to concatenate rotation matrix myMatrix angle myRotate
                set myMatrix to concatenate scale matrix myMatrix horizontal scale myScale vertical scale myScale
                repeat with myNum from 1 to mycopies
```

AS, cont'd.

```
            set myNewObjects to (duplicate mySelection to
               beginning of document 1)
            transform myNewObjects using myMatrix about center
            set mySelection to myNewObjects
         end repeat
      end if
   end if
 end if
end tell
```

Visual Basic

Script Tips *This script works by using transformation matrices. The script gathers from the user step-and-repeat modification values for moving, rotating, and scaling.*

The script creates a default transformation matrix (an identity matrix) in the variable myMatrix. *The script proceeds to combine all the user's requests transformations (moving, rotating, and scaling) into the matrix stored in* myMatrix.

Finally, a loop runs the number of times requested by the user, duplicating the current object(s), transforming the new duplicate, and making it the current object(s) by storing a reference in the variable mySelection *for use the next time through the loop.*

VBScript

```
Option Explicit
Private Sub Command1_Click()
   Dim myApp As New Illustrator.Application
   Dim mySelection, mycopies, mymoveX, mymoveY, myRotate, myScale
   Dim myMatrix, myNum, myPageItem, myNewObject
   If myApp.Documents.Count > 0 Then
      mySelection = myApp.Documents(1).Selection
      If TypeName(mySelection) <> "Empty" Then
         mycopies = InputBox("Copies to make", , "5")
         If IsNumeric(mycopies) Then
            mycopies = CInt(mycopies)
```

The script begins by ensuring that a document is open and that the selection is not empty or a range of text in a text art item.

VBS, cont'd.

```
            If mycopies > 0 Then
                mymoveX = InputBox("Move X (pts)", , "0.0")
                mymoveY = InputBox("Move Y (pts)", , "0.0")
                myRotate = InputBox("Rotate °", , "0.0")
                myScale = InputBox("Scale %", , "100.0")
                If IsNumeric(mymoveX) And IsNumeric(mymoveY) And
                IsNumeric(myRotate) And IsNumeric(myScale) Then
                    mymoveX = CLng(mymoveX)
                    mymoveY = CLng(mymoveY)
                    myRotate = CLng(myRotate)
                    myScale = CLng(myScale)
                    Set myMatrix = myApp.GetIdentityMatrix()
                    Set myMatrix = myApp.ConcatenateTranslationMatrix
                    (myMatrix, mymoveX, mymoveY)
                    Set myMatrix = myApp.ConcatenateRotationMatrix
                    (myMatrix, myRotate)
                    Set myMatrix = myApp.ConcatenateScaleMatrix
                    (myMatrix, myScale, myScale)
                    For myNum = 1 To mycopies
                        myApp.Documents(1).Selection = Empty
                        For Each myPageItem In mySelection
                            Set myNewObject = myPageItem.Duplicate()
                            myNewObject.Transform myMatrix, , , , ,
                            aiTransformCenter
                            myNewObject.Selected = True
                        Next
                        mySelection = myApp.Documents(1).Selection
                    Next
                End If
            End If
        End If
    End If
End If
End Sub
```

If the values entered by the user are numbers, the script converts each value to a long integer.

The script combines the moving, rotating, and scaling transformations in the matrix stored in myMatrix.

Script 4.9: Collect Files for Prepress Output and Generate Font Report

Professional users of Adobe Illustrator often need to send their electronic files out to service bureaus or other vendors to generate output. The process of preparing your files to send away for final printing can be harrowing if you haven't done a good job of keeping track of all your placed linked art and fonts used in text art. Why? If you don't send the service bureau all the external linked files and all the font files used, your output will look horrible. Your beautiful linked art will print will low-resolution preview images, if at all. Your text art will print with fonts such as Courier and Helvetica instead of the gorgeous type you planned to use.

If you also use desktop design and layout software such as QuarkXPress, you've probably gotten used to the process of *collecting for output*. This cool term has a simple meaning. In applications like Quark, when you are ready to ship your files off to the service bureau, you just choose File > Collect for Output, and voila—you have a folder filled with all linked files and all the fonts you used.

Script 4.9 brings the collect-for-output function to Illustrator by way of your scripting talent. The Visual Basic version has a considerable number of form controls to set up, as **Figure 4.20** shows. Because the script operates on the frontmost open document, it's a good candidate to use from the Scripts menu in Illustrator. When you are ready to ship your files off, run this script. It will prompt you for the location in which to save a copy of the Illustrator document as in **Figure 4.21,** all linked files, and a text file listing of all used fonts, as **Figure 4.22** shows. Because Illustrator's scripting model doesn't provide any information about fonts other than their names, your script can't locate the font files and copy them to the collection folder. That task is left for you to perform manually after the script has run. To see which fonts are used, just open the font-report text file in a text editor, as **Figure 4.23** shows.

TIP To create the starting Visual Basic project for this script, follow the steps explained for Script 4.1 in Figure 4.2.

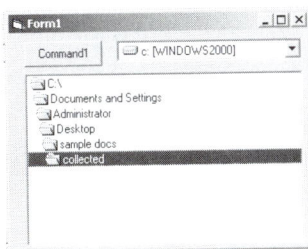

Figure 4.20 This screen shows the Visual Basic version of the script with its form controls set by the user to collect for output into the folder called collected.

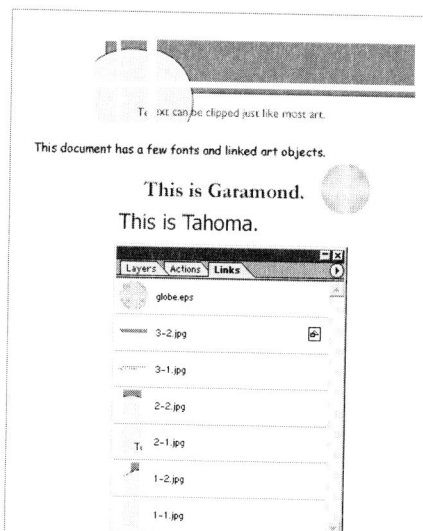

Figure 4.21 Here is the sample document filled with linked raster art, a placed EPS, and some text art in various fonts.

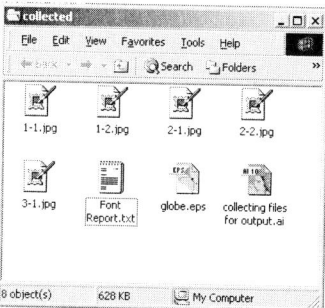

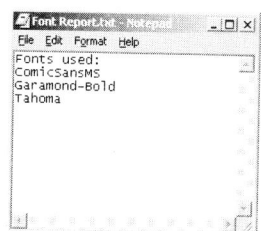

Figure 4.22 After the script has run, the collection folder—in this case named collected—should be filled with the collected linked art, the font-report text file, and a copy of the Illustrator file itself, as shown here.

Figure 4.23 If you open the font-report text file in an editor, each used font's name appears on a separate line.

AppleScript

Script Tips *The script begins by defining a global variable that the script and all functions will be able to access. Then it prompts the user to select a folder as the collection folder and stores the user selection in the new global variable for use later.*

The first repeat loop block of code checks to see whether there are any raster art objects in the document. If so, it loops through each raster item, copying the file linked to the raster item into the collection folder if the raster item is not embedded.

The second repeat loop block of code is much like the preceding one. It checks to see whether there are any placed art objects in the document. If so, it loops through each item, copying the linked art file to the collection folder.

Once the linked files have been collected, it is time to create a text file that contains the names of all fonts used by the document's text art items. This portion of the script creates a text file named Font Report.txt *in the collection folder and then methodically loops through each available text face, checking to see whether any text art item's text uses the text face. If so, the font name is written to the text file. Finally, the file is closed.*

AppleScript

```
global myFolder
set myFolder to (choose folder with prompt "Select folder to
    collect files into")

tell application "Adobe Illustrator 10"
    if (count of documents) > 0 then
        activate
        set myRasterItems to raster items of document 1
        if myRasterItems is not {} then
            repeat with myRasterItem in myRasterItems
                if embedded of myRasterItem is false then
                    tell me to doCopyFile(file path of myRasterItem as
                        string)
                end if
            end repeat
        end if
```

If there is at least one open document in Illustrator, the script proceeds.

Here is the first repeat loop—it processes raster items.

AS, cont'd.

```
        set myPlacedItems to placed items of document 1
        if myPlacedItems is not {} then
```

> The second repeat loop processes placed art items.

```
            repeat with myPlacedItem in myPlacedItems
                tell me to doCopyFile(file path of myPlacedItem as
                    string)
            end repeat
        end if


        set myFileRef to open for access (myFolder & "Font
            Report.txt" as string) with write permission
        write "Fonts used:" & return to myFileRef
        try
            repeat with myFont in text faces
                set myFontName to name of myFont as string
                repeat with myTextArtItem in text art items of
                    document 1
```

> The font report file is written and closed.

```
                    set myText to (characters of myTextArtItem whose
                        font = myFontName)
                    if myText is not {} then
                        write myFontName & return to myFileRef
                        exit repeat
                    end if
                end repeat
            end repeat
        end try
        close access myFileRef
```

> The last bit of work is to save the Illustrator document in the collection folder and display a message to the user.

```
        set myNewFile to myFolder & name of document 1 as string
        save document 1 in file myNewFile as Illustrator
        display dialog "Collect for output complete."
    end if
end tell
```

> This function uses the Finder to attempt to duplicate a linked art file to the folder path specified in myFilePath.

```
on doCopyFile(myFilePath)
    tell application "Finder"
```

AS, cont'd.

```
        try
            duplicate item myFilePath to myFolder
        end try
    end tell
end doCopyFile
```

Visual Basic

Script Tips *The script begins by creating new object variables to open a connection to Illustrator and allow access to the file system. It also declares the variable* myFolder *globally so that the script and all functions will be able to access its value.*

The first For *loop checks to see whether there are any raster art objects in the document. If so, it loops through each raster item, copying the linked art file to the collection folder if it is not embedded.*

The second For *loop is much like the preceding one. It checks to see whether there are any placed art objects in the document. If so, it loops through each item, copying the linked art file to the collection folder.*

Now that the linked files have been collected, it is time to create a text file that contains the names of all fonts used by the document's text art items. This portion of the script creates a text file named Font Report.txt *in the collection folder and then methodically loops through each available text face, checking to see whether any text art item's paragraphs use the text face. If so, the font name is written to the text file. Finally, the file is closed.*

VBScript

```
Option Explicit
Dim myApp As New Illustrator.Application
Dim myFileSysObject As New FileSystemObject
Dim myFolder

Private Sub Drive1_Change()
    Dir1.Path = Drive1.Drive & ":\"
End Sub
```

This subroutine copies the new drive path to the directory list box whenever the drive list is changed.

VBS, cont'd.

```
Private Sub Command1_Click()

    Dim myNum, myTextFile, myFont, myFontName, myTextArtItem,
    myFound, myChar

    Dim myNewFile, mySaveOptions

    If Dir1.Path <> "" Then

        myFolder = Dir1.Path

        If myApp.Documents.Count > 0 Then

            If myApp.Documents(1).RasterItems.Count > 0 Then

                For myNum = 1 To myApp.Documents(1).RasterItems.Count

                    If myApp.Documents(1).RasterItems(myNum).Embedded = False Then

                        doCopyFile (myApp.Documents(1).
                        RasterItems(myNum).File)

                    End If

                Next

            End If


            If myApp.Documents(1).PlacedItems.Count > 0 Then

                For myNum = 1 To myApp.Documents(1).PlacedItems.Count

                    doCopyFile (myApp.Documents(1).
                    PlacedItems(myNum).File)

                Next

            End If


            Set myTextFile = myFileSysObject.OpenTextFile(myFolder &
            "\Font Report.txt", ForWriting, True)

            myTextFile.Write ("Fonts used:" & vbCrLf)

            For Each myFont In myApp.TextFaces

                myFontName = myFont.Name

                For Each myTextArtItem In
                myApp.Documents(1).TextArtItems

                    myFound = False
```

This loop deals with all raster objects.

This loop deals with all placed art objects.

To make the font search more exhaustive (but slower), you can change Paragraphs to Characters to look for font matches in each character.

VBS, cont'd.

```
              For Each myChar In myTextArtItem.TextRange().
              Paragraphs
                'use Characters for exhaustive font search
                If myChar.Font = myFontName Then
                  myFound = True
                  Exit For
                End If
              Next
              If myFound = True Then
                myTextFile.Write (myFontName & vbCrLf)
                Exit For
              End If
            Next
          Next
          myTextFile.Close

          myNewFile = myFolder & "\" & myApp.Documents(1).Name
          Set mySaveOptions = New Illustrator.
          IllustratorSaveOptions
          myApp.Documents(1).SaveAs myNewFile, mySaveOptions
          MsgBox ("Collect for output complete.")
        End If
      End If
    End Sub

    Private Sub doCopyFile(myFilePath)
      Dim myFileName
      myFileName = myFileSysObject.GetFileName(myFilePath)
      myFileSysObject.CopyFile myFilePath, myFolder & "\" &
      myFileName, True
    End Sub
```

This Sub uses the Microsoft Scripting Runtime type library to copy a file to the folder path in `myFilePath`.

Script 4.10: Autocomplete a Title Block with File and User Information

The world of professional illustration has long embraced Illustrator for its capabilities and ease of use. This same world often places standards requirements on electronic documents, mandating that key information be stored inside the document itself, often in the form of a title block. Document title blocks are used by advertising agencies, graphic-design shops, and architecture firms, among others. In my office, we use a standard document stationery template for all new Illustrator documents which includes a blank title block. The typical title block usually contains information about the project to which the document belongs, as well as information about the document's version, creator, and file path.

Script 4.10 demonstrates how scripting support in Illustrator breathes new life into the title-block concept. No longer does a user in Illustrator have to complete each of the fields in the title block by hand every time he or she changes something. This script will enter most of the basic information about the document automatically into the text art items of a sample title block. The information entered includes the system's user name, the file path and name of the document, and its creation and last-modification dates.

Visual Basic scripters should follow the multiple steps shown in **Figure 4.24** to get started. When you're ready to enter the script code, open the code module's Code window by double-clicking its entry in the Project window, as shown in **Figure 4.25**.

To prepare your own title block art for use with this script, follow these steps:

1. Create an Illustrator document that you will use in the future as a template for all documents that contain the title block.

2. Copy your title-block art into the new document.

3. Name each text art item in the title block so your script will find the text art and replace its contents with the appropriate values.

   To do this, open the Layers palette, expand the layer your title block is in. and double-click any object's entry in the hierarchical Layers palette to access the object Options window, where you can assign a name to the selected object.

4. Double-click the Layers-palette entry for the text art object that represents the document's creation date, as shown in **Figure 4.26**.

5. Enter the following name in the field provided in the Options window: **titleblock-date**.

6. Double-click the Layers-palette entry for the text art object that represents the document's revised or modified date, as shown in **Figure 4.27**.

7. Give the object the following name: **titleblock-revised**.

8. Double-click the Layers-palette entry for the text art object that represents the document's editor (the current system's user), as shown in **Figure 4.28**.

9. Give the object the name **titleblock-editor**.

10. Double-click the Layers-palette entry for the text art object that represents the document's file name, as shown in **Figure 4.29**.

11. Give the object the name **titleblock-file**.

12. Double-click the Layers-palette entry for the text art object that represents the document's full file path, as shown in **Figure 4.30**.

13. Give the object the name **titleblock-path**.

    You're done naming the text art objects in your title-block template document.

14. Save the document somewhere and then try running Script 4.10 to see what it does (**Figure 4.31**).

TIP *To create the starting Visual Basic project for this script, follow the steps explained in Figure 4.24 below.*

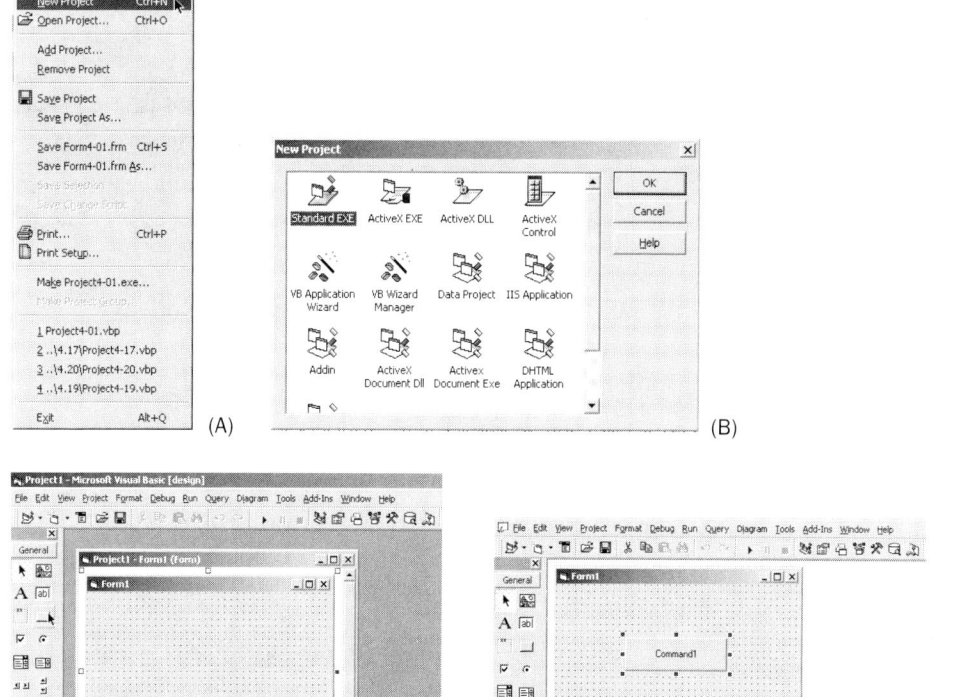

Figure 4.24 *This series of screen shots illustrates the steps necessary to create a new project in the Visual Basic editor with a form in it so that you can add Script 4.10's code. (A) Start by choosing File > New Project. (B) Next, select a standard .exe project and click the OK button. A new project will open, with a new form window showing as in (C). Select the CommandButton tool, and drag out a new button in the open form window so that the form looks like (D). Double-click the button in the form to open its code window, shown in (E). This code window is where you will do your script writing. Next, choose Project > References, as shown in (F). Then locate the Adobe Illustrator 10.0 Type Library (G), and activate it by checking the box next to its name. Next, locate the Microsoft Scripting Runtime library, shown in (H), and add it as well. Now you can close the References dialog by clicking the OK button. You also have to add a code module to your project to store a special declaration and function that will let you call a Windows system function to get the user name. So choose Project > Add Module, as shown in (I). Last, select the module (J), and click the Open button to add a code module. Now we can write Visual Basic!*

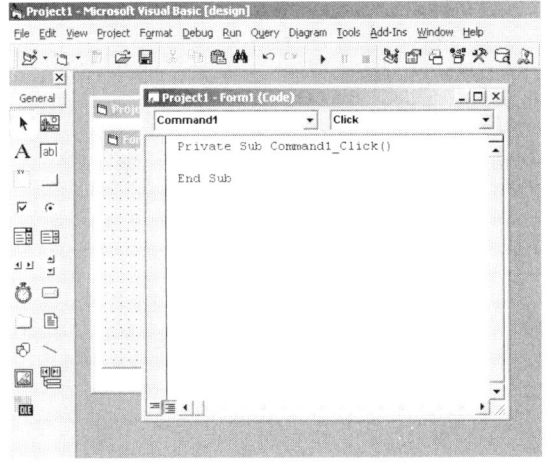
(E)

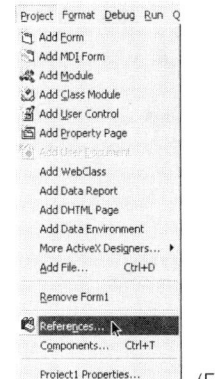
(F)

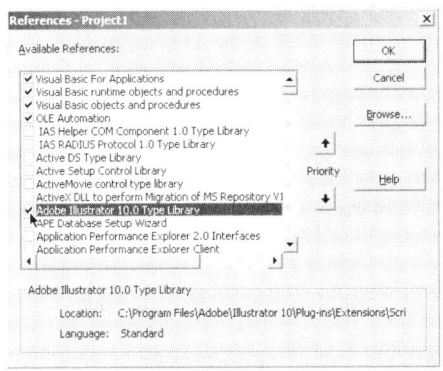
(G)

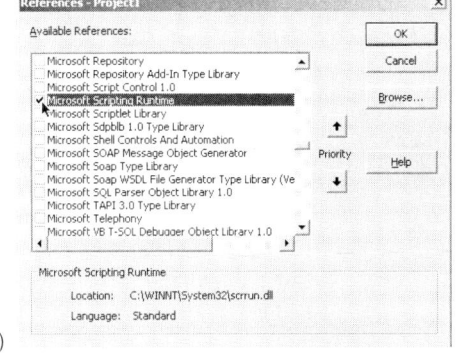
(H)

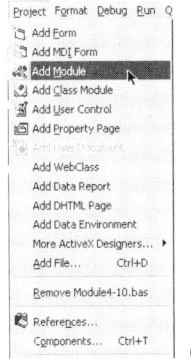
(I)

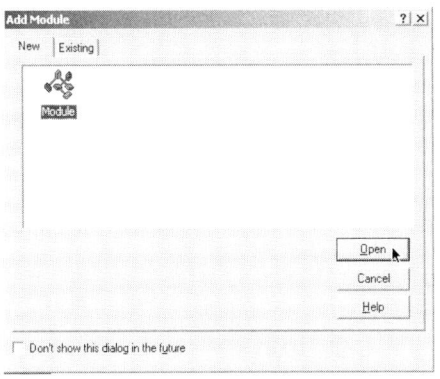
(J)

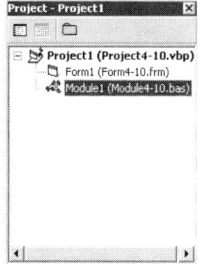

Figure 4.25 The Project window in the Visual Basic editor provides quick access to the code window of the module when you double-click the module entry in the window.

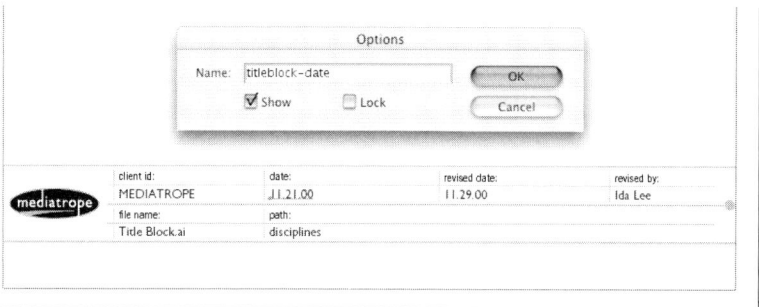

Figure 4.26 Each text art item in the title block needs to be named so that your script can reference it. By double-clicking the object's entry in the hierarchical Layers palette, you can access the object Options window in Illustrator, where you can assign a name to the selected object. Here, you've selected the text art item that holds the creation date and named it so that your script will find it.

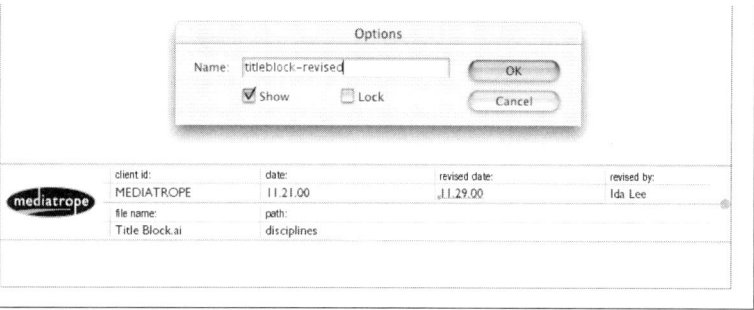

Figure 4.27 You have selected the text art item that holds the revised date and named it so that your script will find it.

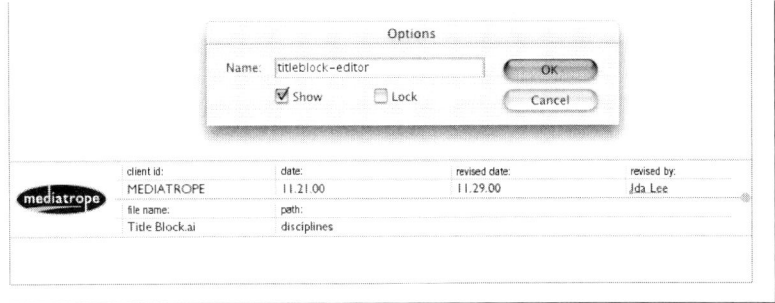

Figure 4.28 *You have selected the text art item that holds the editor (really, the system user name) and named it so that your script will find it.*

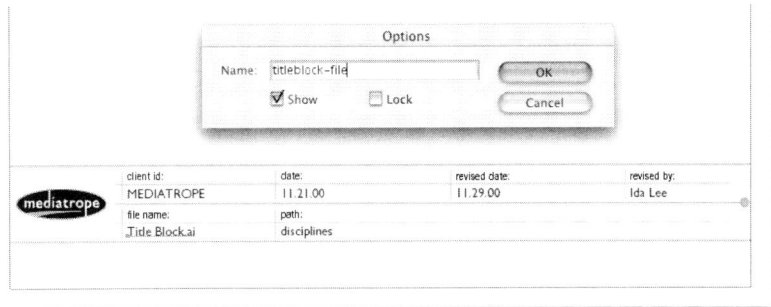

Figure 4.29 *You have selected the text art item that holds the file name and named it so that your script will find it.*

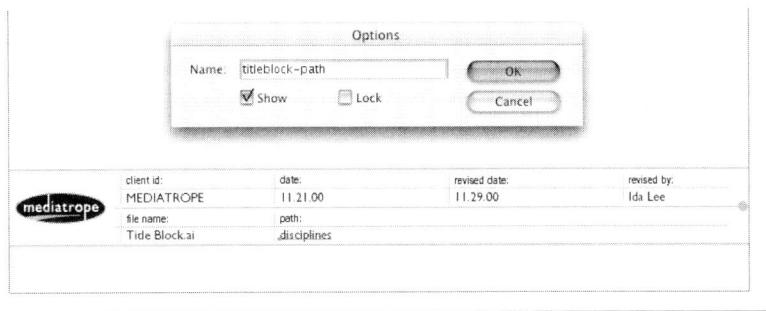

Figure 4.30 *You have selected the text art item that holds the full file path and named it so that your script will find it.*

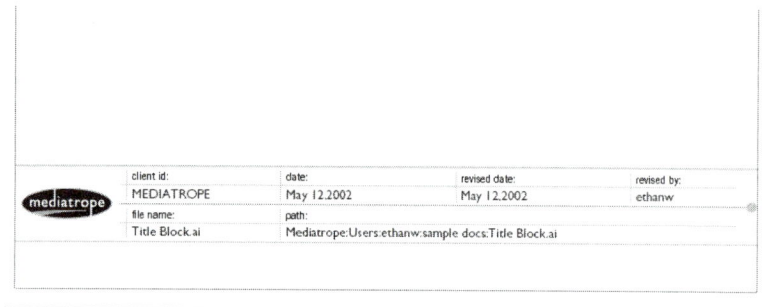

Figure 4.31 *An updated title block in a document after the script has run.*

AppleScript

Script Tips *The script starts by ensuring that at least one document is open in Illustrator before proceeding. Next, the file name and full path for the frontmost document are stored in variables so that they can be inserted into the text of your Illustrator document's title block later. The creation and modification dates for the document's file, as well as the current user's name, are retrived from the Finder and stored in variables so that they can be inserted into the title block.*

Finally, the script cautiously attempts to assign the text contents of each named text art item in the title block to the appropriate value stored in one of the variables.

AppleScript

```
tell application "Adobe Illustrator 10" to set myDocCount to
  count of documents
if myDocCount > 0 then
  tell application "Adobe Illustrator 10"
    set myFile to name of document 1
    set myPath to file path of document 1
  end tell

  tell application "Finder"
    set myDate to creation date of myPath as string
    set myRevised to modification date of myPath as string
```

AS, cont'd.

```
            set myEditor to owner of home as string
        end tell
```

The date values are modified in strings that list the month, day, and year for each date.

```
        set myDate to (word 2 of myDate) & " " & (word 3 of myDate) &
        "," & (word 4 of myDate) as string
        set myRevised to (word 2 of myRevised) & " " & (word 3 of
        myRevised) & "," & (word 4 of myRevised) as string
```

Each text art item's contents are updated here.

```
        tell application "Adobe Illustrator 10"
            if exists (text art item "titleblock-file" of document 1)
            then
                set contents of text art item "titleblock-file" of
                document 1 to myFile
            end if
            if exists (text art item "titleblock-path" of document 1)
            then
                set contents of text art item "titleblock-path" of
                document 1 to myPath as string
            end if
            if exists (text art item "titleblock-date" of document 1)
            then
                set contents of text art item "titleblock-date" of
                document 1 to myDate
            end if
            if exists (text art item "titleblock-revised" of document 1)
            then
                set contents of text art item "titleblock-revised" of
                document 1 to myRevised
            end if
            if exists (text art item "titleblock-editor" of document 1)
            then
                set contents of text art item "titleblock-editor" of
                document 1 to myEditor
            end if
        end tell
    end if
```

Visual Basic

Script Tips *The main* `Command1_Click()` *subroutine starts by ensuring that at least one document is open in Illustrator before proceeding. Next, the file name and full path for the frontmost document are stored in variables so that they can be inserted into the text of your Illustrator document's title block later. The creation and modification dates for the document's file are gathered from the file system object, formatted, and stored in variables so that they can be inserted into the title block later.*

Finally, the script cautiously assigns the text contents of each named text art item in the title block to the appropriate value stored in one of the variables. If an error occurs, Visual Basic will continue to the next line after the error, thanks to `On Error Resume Next`.

TIP *The main code module portion of your script defines a function,* `GetUserName()`, *that makes a system call to a special function built into the Windows system file* `mpr.dll` *to return the current user's login name. The function has to convert the value returned by removing the null character that terminates it. Strings in C are null-terminated. Strings in Visual Basic are not null-terminated. The null character must be removed from the C strings to be used in Visual Basic. Finally, the function returns the name of the person who's logged onto the machine.*

The following code goes into the code window of the project's form:

VBScript

```vb
Option Explicit

Private Sub Command1_Click()
    Dim myApp As New Illustrator.Application
    Dim myFileSysObject As New FileSystemObject
    Dim myFileName, myPath, myFile, myDate, myRevised, myEditor
    If myApp.Documents.Count > 0 Then
      myFileName = myApp.Documents(1).Name
      myPath = myApp.Documents(1).Path
      
      Set myFile = myFileSysObject.GetFile(myPath)
      myDate = MonthName(Month(myFile.DateCreated))
      myDate = myDate & " " & Day(myFile.DateCreated)
      myDate = myDate & ", " & Year(myFile.DateCreated)
      myRevised = MonthName(Month(myFile.DateLastModified))
      myRevised = myRevised & " " & Day(myFile.DateLastModified)
```

VBS, cont'd.

Your script calls the special GetUserName() function, which you'll write in the main code module later.

The text art items' contents are updated here.

```
        myRevised = myRevised & ", " & 
        Year(myFile.DateLastModified)


        myEditor = GetUserName()


        On Error Resume Next
        myApp.Documents(1).TextArtItems("titleblock-file").Contents
        = myFile
        myApp.Documents(1).TextArtItems("titleblock-path").Contents
        = myPath
        myApp.Documents(1).TextArtItems("titleblock-date").Contents
        = myDate
        myApp.Documents(1).TextArtItems("titleblock-revised").
        Contents = myRevised
        myApp.Documents(1).TextArtItems("titleblock-editor").
        Contents = myEditor
    End If
End Sub
```

The following code goes into the project's module-code window. You can open this window by double-clicking the module entry in the Project window, as shown in **Figure 4.24**.

This line removes the null character terminating the C string returned by the system.

```
Declare Function WNetGetUser Lib "mpr.dll" _
    Alias "WNetGetUserA" (ByVal lpName As String, _ByVal
    lpUserName As String, lpnLength As Long) As Long Function
    GetUserName()
    Const lpnLength As Integer = 255
    Dim status As Integer
    Dim lpName, lpUserName As String
    lpUserName = Space$(lpnLength + 1)
    status = WNetGetUser(lpName, lpUserName, lpnLength)
    If status = 0 Then
        lpUserName = Left$(lpUserName,
        InStr(lpUserName, Chr(0)) - 1)
    Else
        lpUserName = "<ERROR>"
    End If
    GetUserName = lpUserName
End Function
```

Script 4.11: Create and Export Animations Based on Math and Physics

You probably already know that graphics programs such as Adobe Illustrator rely heavily on math—especially geometry—to pull off amazing feats of visual beauty. Now that scripting has opened the internal geometry engine that powers Illustrator, you can leverage these capabilities to create objects and animations that are built on math. Especially exciting is the prospect of being able to create animated movement that uses the principles of physics.

Script 4.11 is a simple example of how you can use the power of physics and the mathematical formulas that physicists have developed to simulate the real-world movement of a ball. This ball will appear at a random position in a new document created by your script. Then the script proceeds to create a whole series of animated frames of movement by applying speed, friction, and bounce factors to the variables that control your ball's motion. Each new frame is represented by a new layer created by the script, in which it makes a copy of the bouncing ball and updates its coordinates, as shown

Hungry for More Information on Using Real-World Physics in Your Animation Scripting?

Several academic books cover various aspects of physics for real-world simulation. The best book I have found for learning a great deal about using physics in animation simulations is *Physics for Game Developers*, by David M. Bourg (O'Reilly & Associates Inc.), which includes code examples.

The Web is an even more incredible resource than you might imagine for finding examples of physics-based animation code and conceptual explanations for various audiences. Try searching in an engine such as Google (**www.google.com**) for descriptive phrases such as *bouncing-ball code example*, *collision detection*, or *game physics*.

The long-used multimedia development environment Macromedia Director has a large Web user base, and many Director resource sites provide code examples for physics-based animations. The examples are in Lingo (Director's scripting language), but often, it is easy to translate the formula and math-heavy code used for physics scripting from one language to another. JavaScript and DHTML example sites often have code samples demonstrating how to implement basic physics properties into your animations.

Take advantage of Illustrator's capability to create rich and complex vector art that's completely under script control. You'll break new ground in animation techniques!

in **Figure 4.32**. Once done, the script uses your `exportDocument()` function from Script 4.6 to export a Flash .swf file that contains all of the frames of animation for the ball. This exported file can be opened and manipulated in Adobe LiveMotion or Macromedia Flash MX like you do in **Figure 4.33**. You can experiment with this script by changing the basic variables that control the ball's radius, speed, friction, bounce and the total number of frames to create.

TIP *To create the starting Visual Basic project for this script, follow the steps explained for Script 4.2 in Figure 4.4.*

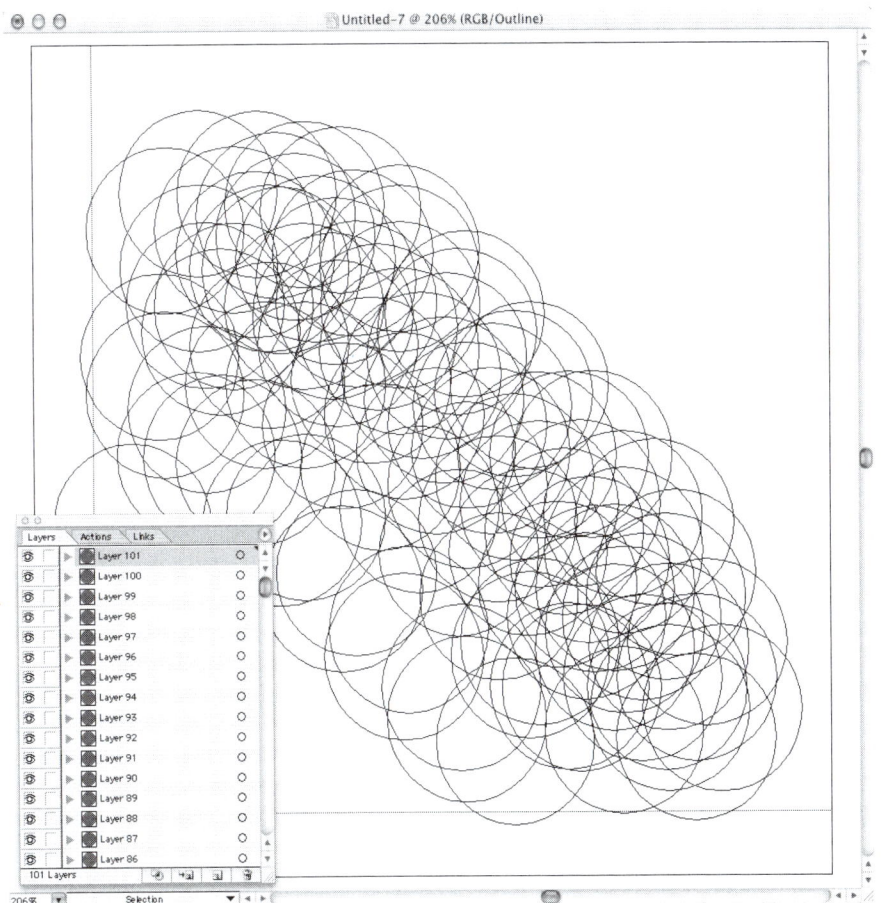

Figure 4.32 *After the script has finished creating all the layers, your new Illustrator document will look something like this screen shot, shown in outline view to make it easier to see all the different positions of the 100 ball objects in the 100 layers.*

185

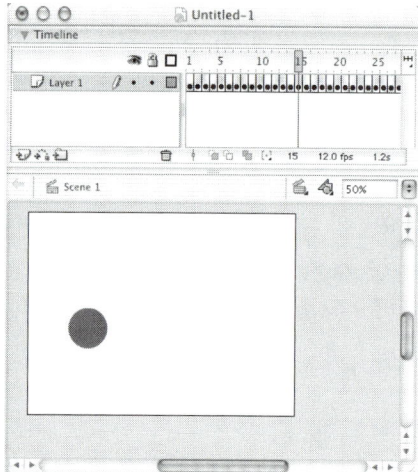

Figure 4.33 *The exported Flash .swf file from this script can be imported into Adobe LiveMotion or Flash MX and integrated into an existing animation sequence.*

AppleScript

Script Tips The script begins by defining some properties and setting their values. These properties determine most of the behavior of the bouncing-ball animation that the script creates. Experiment with different values. The number of frames to generate is set by the `myFrameCount` property.

The new document created by the script is a 400-by-400-point RGB color document. The script also initializes some variables to keep track of the ball's position and its maximum X and Y values before starting the main loop.

In the main loop the ball is drawn and the script updates the variable that holds the ball's horizontal X coordinate. If the X coordindate has gone out of range, the horizontal veolcity of the ball is reversed and augmented with the constant value stored in `myWallBounce` to give it a little zip. Just as the variable representing the horizontal coordinate gets updated, so does the variable for the vertical Y coordinate of the ball.

Finally, the speed factors for both the X and Y directions are modified with a friction coefficient stored in the variable `myFriction`. *The loop completed, the script uses the* `exportDocument()` *function from Script 4.6 to create a Flash file with the new ball animation.*

AppleScript

The folder in which to save the resulting Flash file is set to the current user's home directory.

In the loop to create a new frame of the ball animation, you start by creating a new layer for the ball path item to be placed in.

```
property myBallRadius : 40
property myBallSpeedX : 30
property myBallSpeedY : 35
property myMaxSpeed : 200
property myFriction : 0.2
property myWallBounce : 1.1
property myFrameCount : 100

set mySaveFolder to path to current user folder as string

tell application "Adobe Illustrator 10"
    activate
    set myDocument to make new document with properties {color space:RGB, width:400, height:400}
    set default fill color of myDocument to {red:127, green:0, blue:255}
    set myXMax to width of myDocument
    set myXPos to myXMax / (random number from 2 to 6)
    set myYMax to height of myDocument
    set myYPos to myYMax / (random number from 2 to 6)
    repeat with myNum from 1 to myFrameCount
        set myLayer to make new layer at beginning of myDocument
        
        set myXPos to myXPos + myBallSpeedX
        if myXPos ≤ (myBallSpeedX + (myBallRadius * 2)) or myXPos ≥ (myXMax - myBallSpeedX - myBallRadius) then
            set myXPos to myXPos - (myBallSpeedX * 2)
            set myBallSpeedX to -myBallSpeedX * myWallBounce
        end if
        
        set myYPos to myYPos + myBallSpeedY
        if myYPos ≤ (myBallSpeedY + (myBallRadius * 2)) or myYPos ≥ (myYMax - myBallSpeedY - myBallRadius) then
            set myYPos to myYPos - (myBallSpeedY * 2)
```

AS, cont'd.

```
        set myBallSpeedY to -myBallSpeedY * myWallBounce
    end if
```

Now the script draws a new ball object in the new layer at the current position.

```
    set myBall to make new ellipse at beginning of myLayer
        with properties {filled:true, stroked:false, bounds:
        {myXPos - myBallRadius, myYPos - myBallRadius, myXPos +
        myBallRadius, myYPos + myBallRadius}}

    set myBallSpeedX to myBallSpeedX * (1 - myFriction)
    set myBallSpeedY to myBallSpeedY * (1 - myFriction)
end repeat

exportDocument("flash", "ball", mySaveFolder, false)
end tell
```

You need to insert the code here from the scriptlet function exportDocument() of Script 4.6.

```
on exportDocument(myFormat, myNameExtra, mySaveFolder,
    myRestoreFlag)
end exportDocument
```

Visual Basic

Script Tips The script begins by defining some variables and setting their values. These variables determine most of the behavior of the bouncing-ball animation that the script creates. Experiment with different values. The number of frames to generate is set by the `myFrameCount` variable.

The script creates a new document—it is a 400-by-400-point RGB color document. The script also initializes some varaibles to keep track of the ball's position and its maximum X and Y values befoe starting its main loop.

In the main loop, the ball is drawn for the current frame on a new layer. The script also updates the variable that holds the ball's horizontal X coordinate. If the X coordindate has gone out of range, the horizontal veolcity of the ball is reversed and augmented with the constant value stored in `myWallBounce` to give it a little zip. Just as the variable representing the horizontal coordinate gets updated, so does the variable for the vertical Y coordinate of the ball.

Finally, the speed factors for both the X and Y directions are modified with a friction coefficient stored in the variable myFriction.

Once the loop is over, the script uses the exportDocument() *function from Script 4.6 to create a Flash file with the new ball animation.*

VBScript

```
Option Explicit
Dim myApp As New Illustrator.Application

Private Sub Command1_Click()
    Dim myBallRadius, myBallSpeedX, myBallSpeedY
    Dim myMaxSpeed, myFriction, myWallBounce, myFrameCount
    Dim mySaveFolder, myDocument
    Dim myXMax, myXPos, myYMax, myYPos, myNum, myLayer

    myBallRadius = 40
    myBallSpeedX = 30
    myBallSpeedY = 35
    myMaxSpeed = 200
    myFriction = 0.02
    myWallBounce = 1.1
    myFrameCount = 100

    mySaveFolder = "C:\"

    Set myDocument = myApp.Documents.Add(aiDocumentRGBColor, 400#, 400#)
    Dim myColor As New Illustrator.RGBColor
    myColor.Red = 127#
    myColor.Green = 0#
    myColor.Blue = 255#
    myDocument.DefaultFillColor.RGB = myColor
    myXMax = myDocument.Width
    myXPos = myXMax / Int((6 - 2 + 1) * Rnd + 2)
    myYMax = myDocument.Height
    myYPos = myYMax / Int((6 - 2 + 1) * Rnd + 2)
```

The folder in which to save the resulting Flash file is set to the top level of the C drive.

VBS, cont'd.

A new layer is added for this frame of animation.

```
For myNum = 1 To myFrameCount
    Set myLayer = myDocument.Layers.Add
    myLayer.MoveToBeginning (myDocument)

    myXPos = myXPos + myBallSpeedX
    If myXPos <= (myBallSpeedX + (myBallRadius * 2)) _
    Or myXPos >= (myXMax - myBallSpeedX - myBallRadius) Then
        myXPos = myXPos - (myBallSpeedX * 2)
        myBallSpeedX = -myBallSpeedX * myWallBounce
    End If

    myYPos = myYPos + myBallSpeedY
    If myYPos <= (myBallSpeedY + (myBallRadius * 2)) _
    Or myYPos >= (myYMax - myBallSpeedY - myBallRadius) Then
        myYPos = myYPos - (myBallSpeedY * 2)
        myBallSpeedY = -myBallSpeedY * myWallBounce
    End If
```

Now the script draws a new ball object in the new layer at the current position.

```
    myDocument.PathItems.Ellipse myYPos + myBallRadius, _
    myXPos - myBallRadius, myBallRadius * 2, myBallRadius * 2

    myBallSpeedX = myBallSpeedX * (1 - myFriction)
    myBallSpeedY = myBallSpeedY * (1 - myFriction)
Next

exportDocument "flash", "ball", mySaveFolder, False
End Sub
```

You need to insert the code here from the scriptlet function exportDocument() of Script 4.6.

```
Private Function exportDocument(myFormat, myNameExtra, _
    mySaveFolder, myRestoreFlag)
End Function
```

Script 4.12: Convert Multipage PDFs to Multiple Illustrator Files

How frustrating is it that Illustrator 10 cannot open more than one page of a PDF at a time? If you've encountered this restriction of the application, you probably work with multipage PDFs in Illustrator regularly. I can only speculate about how you've tackled the challenge of working with more than one page. Perhaps you have that look of intense concentration on your face as you go into autopilot mode, opening the file from the menu bar (**Figure 4.34**) and then choosing the page number in the dialog Illustrator shows every time you open a multipage PDF (**Figure 4.35**). Next, you'd have to choose File > Save As and then name the Illustrator file you want to create that contains the current page of the PDF. And then you repeat this process for each page. Ouch!

Script 4.12 takes over for you after you've opened one page of the PDF in Illustrator, as shown in **Figure 4.36**. It figures out where the PDF file lives on your hard drive and proceeds to perform all the steps discussed in the preceding paragraph—automatically! What a relief scripting can be. **Figure 4.37** shows the results of your script after it has saved an Illustrator file for each page of the sample three-page PDF.

TIP To create the starting Visual Basic project for this script, follow the steps explained for Script 4.2 in Figure 4.4.

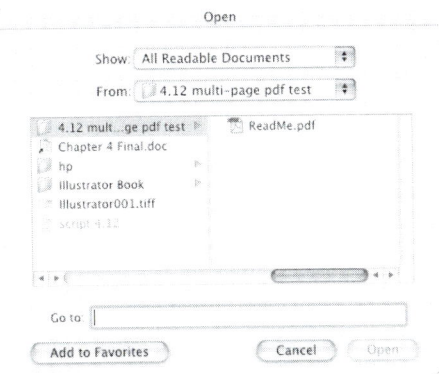

Figure 4.34 Select a PDF file to open before running this script. In your example, the Open dialog shows the PDF that you're about to open.

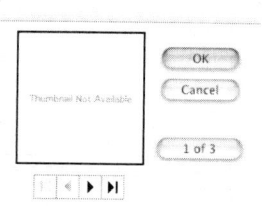

Figure 4.35 *Illustrator only opens one page of a PDF at a time. This dialog appears every time a user tries to open a multipage PDF in Illustrator, asking which page to open. Your script bypasses this dialog.*

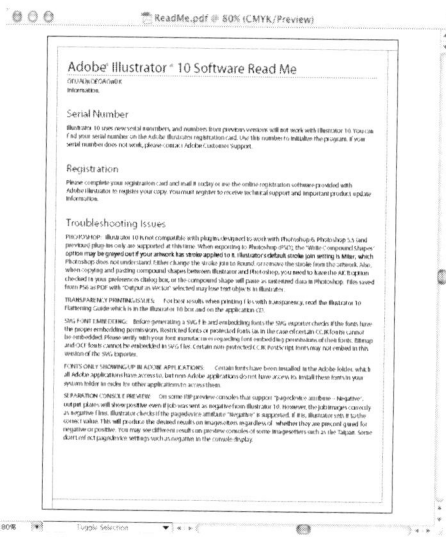

Figure 4.36 *Page 1 of the sample PDF used (the three-page Illustrator Read Me PDF document), shown in Illustrator.*

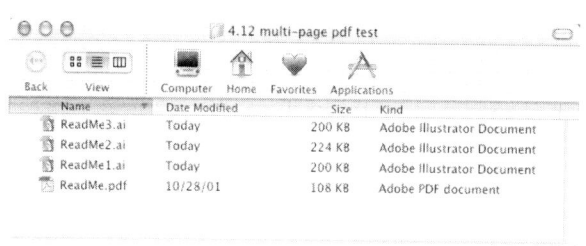

Figure 4.37 *After your script has run, the original folder containing the PDF holds a separate Illustrator file containing each PDF page. In this case, you have three documents corresponding to the three pages of the original PDF.*

AppleScript

Script Tips This script starts with a series of preparatory steps, like confirming the existence of at least one open document in Illustrator. Next, the Illustrator application's current user-interaction-level property is stored in a variable so that it can be restored later. Then the interaction level is changed to prevent any dialogs from appearing while the script opens the different pages of the PDF document. The script gets the full path to the frontmost Illustrator document and confirms that the file is a PDF by checking its file extension.

The main portion of the script is a `repeat` loop, which is contained in a `try` statement. Because you don't know how many pages exist in your PDF, the loop places the numbers 1 through 1000 sequentially in the variable `myPage`. It attempts to open the PDF with the current page number in the loop. When the variable `myPage` exceeds the actual number of pages in the PDF, Illustrator will generate an error. The error will trigger the `try` statement and move execution of the script to the line after `end try`.

Last but not least, the script resets Illustrator's user-interaction level to whatever it was set to before you ran the script.

AppleScript

Here we save and change the user interaction level for Illustrator.

The main repeat loop tries to open each page of the PDF file, up to page 1000.

```
tell application "Adobe Illustrator 10"
    if (count of documents) > 0 then
        set myInteractLevel to user interaction level
        set user interaction level to never interact
        set myPath to file path of document 1 as string
        if myPath ends with ".pdf" then
            try
                repeat with myPage from 1 to 1000
                    open alias myPath with options {page:myPage}
                    set myNewPath to myPath
                    repeat with myCharNum from (count of characters of myNewPath) to 1 by -1
                        if character myCharNum of myNewPath = "." then
                            if myCharNum > (count of characters of myNewPath) - 5 then set myNewPath to (text of characters 1 thru (myCharNum - 1) of myNewPath) as string
                            exit repeat
                        end if
                    end repeat
```

AS, cont'd.

```
            set myNewPath to myNewPath & myPage & ".ai"
            save document 1 in file myNewPath as Illustrator
            close document 1 saving no
        end repeat
    end try
            end if
        set user interaction level to myInteractLevel
    end if
end tell
```

Visual Basic

Script Tips *This main* `Command1_Click()` *subroutine starts with a series of preparatory steps, like declaring variables and confirming the existence of an open document in Illustrator. Next, the Illustrator application's current user-interaction-level property is stored in a variable so that it can be restored later. Then the interaction level is changed to prevent any dialogs from appearing while the script opens the different pages of the PDF document. The script gets the full path to the frontmost Illustrator document and confirms that the file is a PDF by checking its file extension.*

The main portion of this script is a `For...Next` *loop, which is contained after an* `On Error GoTo` *statement. The* `On Error` *statement causes the script go to* `AllDone` *in the script when an error occurs. This error-handling helps you, since you don't know how many pages exist in the PDF, the loop places the numbers 1 through 1000 sequentially in the variable* `myPage`. *It attempts to open the PDF with the current page number in the loop. When the variable* `myPage` *exceeds the actual number of pages in the PDF, Illustrator will generate an error. The error will trigger the* `On Error GoTo` *statement and movse execution of the script to the line after the label* `AllDone`.

VBScript

```
Option Explicit


Private Sub Command1_Click()
    Dim myApp As New Illustrator.Application
    Dim myPDFOptions As New Illustrator.PDFOpenOptions
```

VBS, cont'd.

```
        Dim myInteractLevel, myPath, myPage, myNewPath
        If myApp.Documents.Count > 0 Then

            myInteractLevel = myApp.UserInteractionLevel
            myApp.UserInteractionLevel = aiDontDisplayAlerts


            myPath = myApp.Documents(1).FullName
            If Right(myPath, 4) = ".pdf" Then
              On Error GoTo AllDone
                For myPage = 1 To 1000
                    myPDFOptions.PageToOpen = myPage
                    myApp.Open myPath, , myPDFOptions
                    myNewPath = myPath
                    If InStrRev(myPath, ".") > Len(myPath) - 5 Then
                        myNewPath = Mid(myPath, 1, InStrRev(myPath, ".")
                          - 1)
                    End If
                    myNewPath = myNewPath & myPage & ".ai"
                    myApp.Documents(1).SaveAs myNewPath
                    myApp.Documents(1).Close (aiDoNotSaveChanges)
                Next
              AllDone:
            End If
            myApp.UserInteractionLevel = myInteractLevel
        End If
    End Sub
```

Now the script gets the full path to the frontmost Illustrator document and confirms that the file is a PDF by checking its file extension.

The main loop tries to open each page of the PDF file, up to page 1000.

Time to reset Illustrator's user-interaction level to whatever it was before you ran the script.

Script 4.13: Resize and Embed All Raster Art for a Specific Resolution

Working with placed raster art can be a slow and tedious process when you've got externally linked source files that contain too much data for your purposes. Save and reopen your document filled with such files, and you might find the need for a nap while you're waiting for Illustrator to check each of the huge external files you've linked to. Downsampling high-resolution raster images to a resolution of your choosing is the answer to this time-consuming problem, especially if you embed the resized raster art in your Illustrator document. Working with documents that do not have any external links to big files, you'll find that's everything faster and more responsive in Illustrator.

Script 4.13 does the trick of resizing and embedding each of the raster art items in the frontmost open Illustrator document. It uses the powerful raster-file-opening capabilities of Illustrator 10 to open and resize each of the placed raster files directly. This script expects a file to be open when it is run, so have a sample file, like the one in **Figure 4.38,** open before launching the script. After the script is launched, the user is prompted to choose a target resolution for final output in points per inch, as **Figure 4.39** shows. When the art is resized, the script needs to reset the placed art's boundaries to maintain the exact position and scale of the art. Then, in a final flourish, the script embeds the placed art inside the Illustrator document, freeing it from any connection to the original source art file.

TIP To create the starting Visual Basic project for this script, follow the steps explained for Script 4.2 in Figure 4.4.

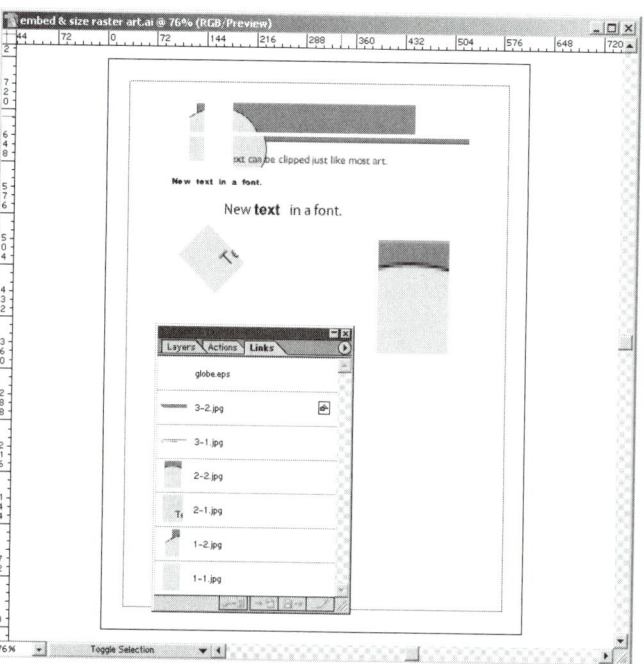

Figure 4.38 A sample document, shown along with its Links palette, shows several linked raster art objects contained in the document, as well as a single embedded art item.

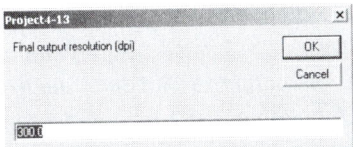

Figure 4.39 *When the script is run, the user is prompted for a target resolution for each raster item before the script embeds it in the Illustrator document.*

AppleScript

Script Tips If at least one document is open, the script prompts the user for the target resolution for all raster art in the document.

Within a loop that traverses each raster art item in the document, the current raster item's width, height, and position are stored in variables—this is so that the script can restore these values after the source art has been resized. Then the raster art is copied to the Clipboard so that the art can be pasted into a new document as part of the process of resizing.

Now it is time to create a new letter-size document with its color space matching that of your existing document. The document size really doesn't matter, because Illustrator will not clip the raster art to the artboard unless you ask it to (and you won't). With the document open, paste the raster art.

To work with the raster art in its original untransformed state, you reset the transformations of the raster art to none by applying the identity matrix to the raster art. An identity matrix is a transformation matrix that does not change the object at all.

Next, the script gets the new dimensions of the unaltered raster art and calculates the resizing percentage to apply to the art so that it ends up being the right resolution in the original document. Then it moves the art to the center of the document for tidiness.

Now it is time to export the modified raster art as a Photoshop .psd file with its resolution set appropriately. The temporary document you created to hold the raster art will be closed without saving by the `exportPSDDocument()` function you are calling.

Back in your original document filled with placed raster items, you relink the current raster art item to the new Photoshop file you have exported. After relinking, the height, width, and position of the raster art will shift. You reset these properties so that the new art ends up matching the old art's dimensions, but with a resolution that will result in the file's being output at the desired resolution.

The `exportPSDDocument()` *function is based on a portion of Script 4.6. You don't use Script 4.6's* `exportDocument()` *function verbatim here, because you want to set the output resolution of the exported Photoshop file, which the original function doesn't let you do. Notice that the first big difference in this function is that you pass the desired export resolution to the function in* `myResolution`.

AppleScript

```
tell application "Adobe Illustrator 10" to set myDocCount to
    count of documents

if myDocCount > 0 then
    set myDesiredResolution to text returned of (display dialog
    "Final output resolution (dpi)" default answer "300")
    tell application "Adobe Illustrator 10" to set myFilePath to
    file path of document 1
    if (myFilePath as string) contains ":" then
        tell application "Finder" to set myFolder to container of
        myFilePath as string
        tell application "Adobe Illustrator 10"
            activate
            set myInteractionLevel to user interaction level
            set user interaction level to never interact
            if (count of raster items of document 1) > 0 then
                repeat with myNum from 1 to count of raster items in
                document 1
                    set selection of document 1 to {}
                    set selected of raster item myNum of document 1 to
                    true
                    set myWidth to width of raster item myNum of
                    document 1
                    set myHeight to height of raster item myNum of
                    document 1
                    set myPosition to position of raster item myNum of
                    document 1
                    copy
                    set myDefaults to {}
                    set myDefaults to myDefaults & {color space:color
                    space of document 1}
                    set myDefaults to myDefaults & {width:8.5 * 72.0}
```

This test ensures that the frontmost Illustrator document has been saved before.

AS, cont'd.

```
        if mySaveFolder is not "" then
            set myNewPath to mySaveFolder as string
            if (myOriginalFile as string) contains ":" then set
            myNewPath to myNewPath & (name of document 1)
        else
            set myNewPath to myOriginalFile as string
        end if
        repeat with myCharNum from (count of characters of
        myNewPath) to 1 by -1
            if character myCharNum of myNewPath = "." then
                if myCharNum > (count of characters of myNewPath) - 5
                then set myNewPath to (text of characters 1 thru
                (myCharNum - 1) of myNewPath) as string
                exit repeat
            end if
        end repeat
        set myNewPath to myNewPath & myNameExtra
        if myFormat = "photoshop" then
            activate
            set myNewPath to myNewPath & ".psd"
            set myExportOptions to {}
            set myExportOptions to myExportOptions &
            {antialiasing:true}
            set myExportOptions to myExportOptions & {color
            space:CMYK}
            set myExportOptions to myExportOptions & {compound
            shapes:true}
            set myExportOptions to myExportOptions & {editable
            text:true}
            set myExportOptions to myExportOptions & {embed ICC
            profile:false}
            set myExportOptions to myExportOptions & {hidden
            layers:false}
            set myExportOptions to myExportOptions & {image
            map:true}
            set myExportOptions to myExportOptions & {nested
            layers:true}
            set myExportOptions to myExportOptions & {resolution:
            myResolution}
```

> To keep things simple, omit all the other format export options that Script 4.6 has except Photoshop.

> The only big difference from Script 4.6 is here. Instead of hard-wiring the output resolution, set it to the value passed to the function.

AS, cont'd.	`set myDefaults to myDefaults & {height:11 * 72.0}`
With the new document open, paste the raster art.	`set myTempDoc to (make new document with properties myDefaults)`
	`paste`
	`set matrix of raster item 1 of myTempDoc to (get identity matrix)`
	`set myNewWidth to width of raster item 1 of myTempDoc`
	`set myNewheight to height of raster item 1 of myTempDoc`
Calculate new width, height, resolution and position.	`set myNewResolution to myDesiredResolution * ((myWidth + myHeight) / (myNewWidth + myNewheight))`
	`set position of raster item 1 of myTempDoc to {((width of myTempDoc) / 2) - (myNewWidth / 2), ((height of myTempDoc) / 2) - (myNewheight / 2)}`
	`tell me to set myNewPath to (exportPSDDocument (myNewResolution, myNum, myFolder, false))`
	`set file path of raster item myNum of document 1 to alias myNewPath`
Relink original placed item to new file, update dimensions and embed.	`set width of raster item myNum of document 1 to myWidth`
	`set height of raster item myNum of document 1 to myHeight`
	`set position of raster item myNum of document 1 to myPosition`
	`set embedded of raster item myNum of document 1 to true`
	`end repeat`
	`end if`
	`set user interaction level to myInteractionLevel`
	`end tell`
	`end if`
	`end if`
This function is based on a portion of Script 4.6.	`on exportPSDDocument(myResolution, myNameExtra, mySaveFolder, myRestoreFlag)`
	`set myFormat to "photoshop"`
	`tell application "Adobe Illustrator 10"`
	`set myOriginalFile to file path of document 1`

AS, cont'd.

```
        set myExportOptions to myExportOptions & {slices:true}
        set myExportOptions to myExportOptions &
        {warnings:false}
        set myExportOptions to myExportOptions & {write
        layers:true}
        export document 1 to file myNewPath as Photoshop with
        options myExportOptions
        if not myRestoreFlag then close document 1 saving no
      end if
    end tell
    return myNewPath
end exportPSDDocument
```

Visual Basic

Script Tips If at least one document is open, the script prompts the user for the target resolution for all raster art in the document.

Within a loop that traverses each raster art item in the document, the current raster item's width, height, and position are stored in variables—this is so that the script can restore these values after the source art has been resized. Then the raster art is copied to the Clipboard so that the art can be pasted into a new document as part of the process of resizing.

Now it is time to create a new letter-size document with its color space matching that of your existing document. The document size really doesn't matter, because Illustrator will not clip the raster art to the artboard unless you ask it to (and you won't). With the document open, paste the raster art.

To work with the raster art in its original untransformed state, you reset the transformations of the raster art to none by applying the identity matrix to the raster art. An identity matrix is a transformation matrix that does not change the object at all.

Next, the script gets the new dimensions of the unaltered raster art and calculates the resizing percentage to apply to the art so that it ends up being the right resolution in the original document. Then it moves the art to the center of the document for tidiness.

Now it is time to export the modified raster art as a Photoshop .psd file with its resolution set appropriately. The temporary document you created to hold the raster art will be closed without saving by the `exportPSDDocument()` function you are calling.

Back in your original document filled with placed raster items, you relink the current raster art item to the new Photoshop file you have exported. After relinking, the height, width, and position of the raster art will shift. You reset these properties so that the new art ends up matching the old art's dimensions, but with a resolution that will result in the file's being output at the desired resolution.

TIP The `exportPSDDocument()` function is based on a portion of Script 4.6. You don't use Script 4.6's `exportDocument()` function verbatim here, because you want to set the output resolution of the exported Photoshop file, which the original function doesn't let you do. Notice that the first big difference in this function is that you pass the desired export resolution to the function in `myResolution`.

VBScript

```
Option Explicit
Dim myApp As New Illustrator.Application
Dim myFileSysObject As New FileSystemObject


Private Sub Command1_Click()
    Dim myDesiredResolution, myFilePath, myFolder, _
        myInteractionLevel
    Dim myNum, myWidth, myHeight, myPosition, myTempDoc
    Dim myNewWidth, myNewHeight, myNewResolution, myNewPath
    Dim myRasterItem, myNewRasterItem
    If myApp.Documents.Count > 0 Then
        myDesiredResolution = InputBox("Final output resolution _
            (dpi)", , "300.0")

        myFilePath = myApp.Documents(1).FullName
        If Left(myFilePath, 1) <> "\" Then
            myFolder = myFileSysObject.GetParentFolderName _
                (myFilePath)
            myInteractionLevel = myApp.UserInteractionLevel
            myApp.UserInteractionLevel = aiDontDisplayAlerts
            If myApp.Documents(1).RasterItems.Count > 0 Then
```

This test ensures that the frontmost Illustrator document has been saved before.

VBS, cont'd.

```
myNum = 1
For Each myRasterItem In myApp.Documents(1).
RasterItems
   myApp.Documents(1).Selection = Empty
   myRasterItem.Selected = True
   myWidth = myRasterItem.Width
   myHeight = myRasterItem.Height
   myPosition = myRasterItem.Position
   myApp.Documents(1).Copy
```

With the new document open, paste the raster art.

```
   Set myTempDoc = myApp.Documents.Add(myApp.
   Documents(1).DocumentColorSpace, myWidth, myHeight)
   myTempDoc.Paste

   myTempDoc.RasterItems(1).Matrix =
   myApp.GetIdentityMatrix()
```

Calculate new width, height, resolution and position.

```
   myNewWidth = myTempDoc.RasterItems(1).Width
   myNewHeight = myTempDoc.RasterItems(1).Height
   myNewResolution = myDesiredResolution * ((myWidth +
   myHeight) / (myNewWidth + myNewHeight))
   myTempDoc.RasterItems(1).Position =
   Array(((myTempDoc.Width) / 2) - (myNewWidth / 2),
   ((myTempDoc.Height) / 2) - (myNewHeight / 2))
   myNewPath = exportPSDDocument(myNewResolution,
   myNum, myFolder, False)

   myApp.Documents(1).RasterItems.Remove
   (myRasterItem)
   Set myNewRasterItem = myApp.Documents(1).
   RasterItems.Add
   myNewRasterItem.File = myNewPath
   'Link existing raster item to new Photoshop file.
```

Relink original placed item to new file, update dimensions and embed.

```
   myNewRasterItem.Width = myWidth
   myNewRasterItem.Height = myHeight
   myNewRasterItem.Position = myPosition
   myNewRasterItem.Embedded = True
```

VBS, cont'd.

```
                Next
              End If
              myApp.UserInteractionLevel = myInteractionLevel
            End If
          End If
        End Sub
```

This function is based on a portion of Script 4.6.

```
        Private Function exportPSDDocument(myResolution, myNameExtra, _
          mySaveFolder, myRestoreFlag)
          Dim myFormat, myOriginalFile, myNewPath, myExportOptions
          myFormat = "photoshop"
          myOriginalFile = myApp.Documents(1).FullName
          If mySaveFolder <> "" Then
            myNewPath = mySaveFolder & "\"
            If Left(myOriginalFile, 1) <> "\" Then myNewPath = _
              myNewPath & myApp.Documents(1).Name
          Else
            myNewPath = myOriginalFile
          End If
          If InStrRev(myOriginalFile, ".") > Len(myOriginalFile) - 5 _
          Then
            myNewPath = Mid(myOriginalFile, 1, _
              InStrRev(myOriginalFile, ".") - 1)
          End If
          myNewPath = myNewPath & myNameExtra
          Select Case myFormat
```

To keep things simple, omit all the other format export options that Script 4.6 has except Photoshop.

```
            Case "photoshop"
              myNewPath = myNewPath & ".psd"
              Set myExportOptions = New Illustrator. _
                ExportOptionsPhotoshop
              myExportOptions.AntiAliasing = True
              myExportOptions.CompoundShapes = True
              myExportOptions.EditableText = True
              myExportOptions.EmbedICCProfile = False
              myExportOptions.HiddenLayers = False
```

VBS, cont'd.

The only big difference from Script 4.6 is here. Instead of hardwiring the output resolution, set it to the value passed to the function.

```
        myExportOptions.ImageColorSpace = aiImageCMYK
        myExportOptions.ImageMap = True
        myExportOptions.NestedLayers = True
        myExportOptions.Resolution = myResolution

        myExportOptions.Slices = True
        myExportOptions.Warnings = False
        myExportOptions.WriteLayers = True
        myApp.Documents(1).Export myNewPath, aiPhotoshop, 
        myExportOptions
        If myRestoreFlag = False Then
            myApp.Documents(1).Close (aiDoNotSaveChanges)
        End If

    End Select
    exportPSDDocument = myNewPath
End Function
```

Script 4.14: Create and Work with Parametric Shapes in Documents

Parametric shapes are geometric shapes that have their dimensional properties defined by variables, which means that a parametric shape remembers its basic size and geometry and then applies variable factors to each of its properties that have been parameterized or assigned to a variable. Simply put, variables can be assigned to a series of objects in a document, and whenever you change the values associated with the variables, all the objects whose geometry is associated with the variables change automatically. Computer-aided-design applications such as Autodesk's AutoCAD and Ashlar's Vellum offer built-in support for creating parametric shapes, because designers of complex geometries in mechanical and architectural engineering have been relying on parametric geometry for a long time to rescale and reuse existing drawings of objects when requirements or conditions change. **Figure 4.40** shows a parametric shape whose horizontal- and vertical-scale values have been assigned variables.

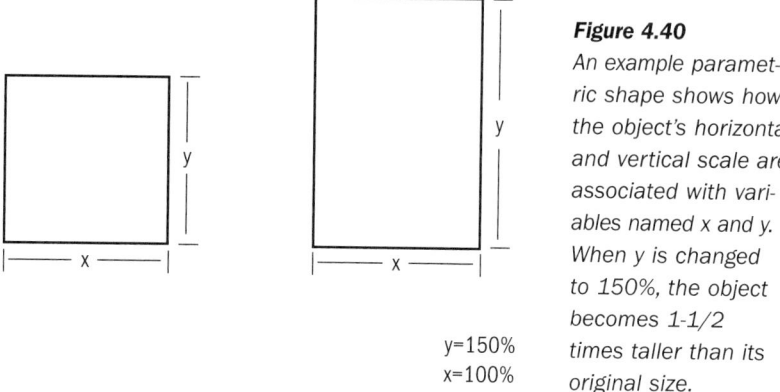

Figure 4.40
An example parametric shape shows how the object's horizontal and vertical scale are associated with variables named x and y. When y is changed to 150%, the object becomes 1-1/2 times taller than its original size.

Adobe Illustrator offers no native support for making objects parametric. But with a little help from scripting, you can achieve this amazing feat on your own. In **Script 4.14**, you take on the simple challenge of parameterizing the horizontal and vertical scale of all objects in a new document to get a feel for how easy this concept is to apply.

Follow these steps to prepare the sample document used with Script 4.14:

1. Create a new document in Illustrator.

    The document can be any size and can use either color space.

2. Create two text art items in the document, and set their contents as shown in **Figure 4.41**.

3. Open the Layers palette, expand the layer containing the two text art items, and double-click the entry for each text art item.

4. In the object Options dialog, name one of the text art items **Xscale**, and name the other text art item **Yscale**.

5. Now go ahead and create some paths and other objects in your document.

    Make at least a couple of shapes so that you can get a feel for how the script works later.

6. Save your document.

7. Enter Script 4.14 in your script editor and then run the script. You should see results like those shown in **Figure 4.42**.

8. Try changing the values contained in the two text art items and running the script a few times.

The first time you run the script, it will store the original dimensions of each page item in a tag to remember the original dimension of the object. Every time you run the script, it should resize each of the objects dynamically, depending on the values you place in the two special text art items. You can "test" your object's memory by setting the text art item contents both to 100 and running the script to switch everything back to its original size, as shown in **Figure 4.43**.

TIP *To create the starting Visual Basic project for this script, follow the steps explained for Script 4.2 in Figure 4.4.*

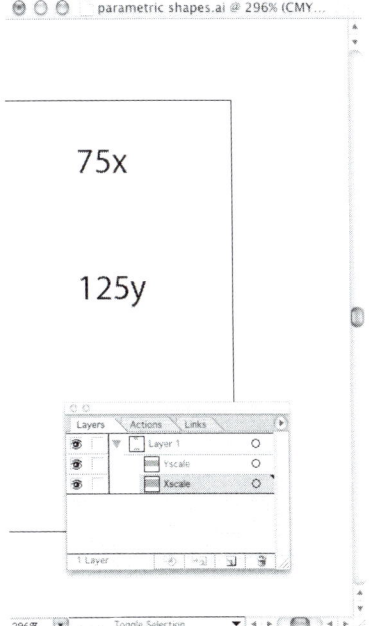

Figure 4.41 *The two specially named text art items are shown along with the Layers palette, demonstrating that each text art item has been named appropriately to work with the script.*

Parametric Shapes Have "Memory"

Note that the scale values you use are always in relation to the objects' original size, because each parametric object remembers its original dimensions and uses them as the starting point each time it resizes.

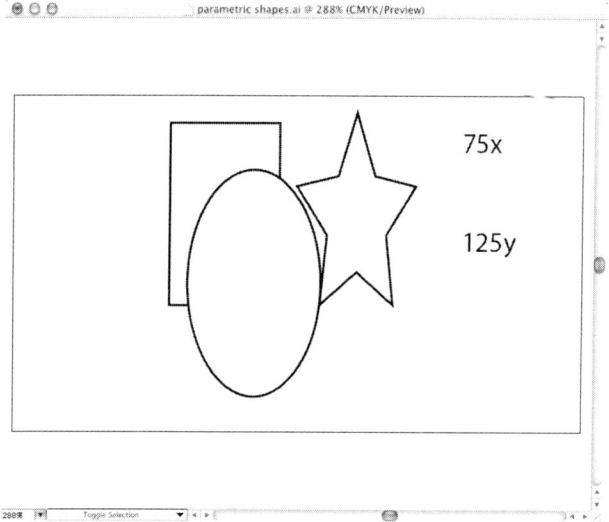

Figure 4.42 *The sample document shown has three page items that are affected by the script. When you run your script, the page items in the document reflect a 75% horizontal scaling and a 125% vertical scaling from their original sizes.*

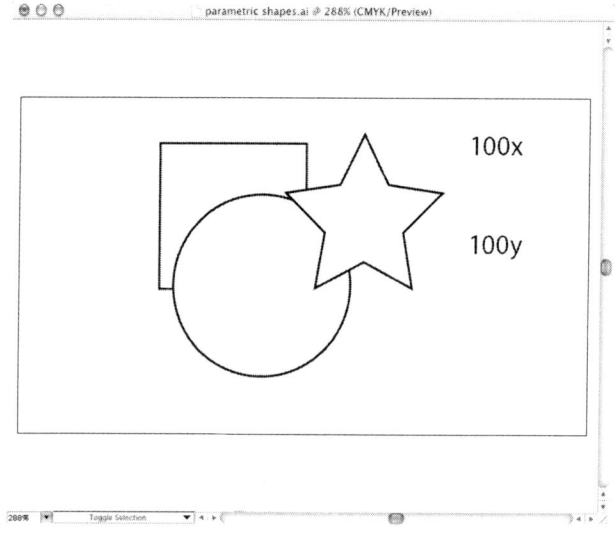

Figure 4.43 *Change both the scaling values to 100. Don't forget to leave the letters x and y in the contents of the respective text art items. Now run the script again, and you should see something like this screen shot. All page items' sizes are reset to their original sizes, regardless of all other modifications you may have made in the meantime.*

AppleScript

Script Tips *The script starts by ensuring that an open document exists in Illustrator. It proceeds to gather the new horizontal- and vertical-scaling values from the contents of the two specially named text art items that you created in steps 2 and 3 above. The values are tested to make sure that they are in the range 1% to 200%.*

Within the main loop that looks at each page item in the document, the script gets the name of the current page item and checks to make sure that it doesn't match one of the specially named text art items you use to hold your scale values.

Next, it's time to see whether the object at hand has already had its original dimensions and position saved in a tag named "OriginalBounds". If this tag exists, the script calls the function `getBounds()`*, passing the index order of the current page item so that the function can reference it. The original dimensions of the object will be returned from the function in the variable* `myBounds`*. You use the four items in the list returned in* `myBounds` *to set the position, width, and height of the current page item.*

If the tag named "OriginalBounds" does not exist, it is time to call your function `setBounds()` *to create the tag and store the page item's dimensions in the tag's value.*

When it is certain that the current page item's dimensions have been reset to their original values, the script rescales the page item to the new values.

The `setBounds()` *function receives the index order of the page item for which it needs to create a tag. Then it gathers the position, width, and height of the page item in question. These values are combined into a string with commas separating them so that you can break the values apart easily in* `getBounds()`*. Finally, a new tag is created for the page item, and its name and value are set.*

The `getBounds()` *function does the work of retrieving the string value from the page item's tag. It uses the power of AppleScript's text item delimiters to convert the comma-delimited string value of the tag to a four-item list of values. Finally, the list is returned to the script calling the function.*

AppleScript

```
tell application "Adobe Illustrator 10"
    if (count of documents) > 0 then
        set myXscale to contents of text art item "Xscale" of
            document 1
        set myYscale to contents of text art item "Yscale" of
            document 1
        set myXscale to (characters 1 thru -2 of myXscale as
            string) as real
        if myXscale < 1.0 then myXscale = 1.0
        if myXscale > 200.0 then myXscale = 200.0
        set myYscale to (characters 1 thru -2 of myYscale as
            string) as real
        if myYscale < 1.0 then myYscale = 1.0
        if myYscale > 200.0 then myYscale = 200.0
        repeat with myNum from 1 to count of page items of
            document 1
            set myItemName to name of page item myNum of document 1
            if myItemName is not "Xscale" and myItemName is not
                "Yscale" then
                if exists (tag "OriginalBounds" of page item myNum of
                    document 1) then
                    tell me to set myBounds to getBounds(myNum)
                    set position of page item myNum of document 1 to
                        {item 1 of myBounds, item 2 of myBounds}
                    set width of page item myNum of document 1 to item
                        3 of myBounds
                    set height of page item myNum of document 1 to
                        item 4 of myBounds
                else
                    tell me to setBounds(myNum)
                end if
                scale page item myNum of document 1 horizontal scale
                    myXscale vertical scale myYscale about center
```

This main repeat loop moves through each page item in the front-most document.

Reset the current page item's dimensions if the tag "OriginalBounds" exists.

Resize the current page item to its new size.

AS, cont'd.

```
            end if
         end repeat
      end if
   end tell

on setBounds(myNum)
    tell application "Adobe Illustrator 10"
        set myPosition to position of page item myNum of
           document 1
        set myWidth to width of page item myNum of document 1
        set myHeight to height of page item myNum of document 1
        set myBoundsString to ((item 1 of myPosition) & "," &
           (item 2 of myPosition) as string) & ","
        set myBoundsString to myBoundsString & myWidth & "," &
           myHeight as string
        set mytag to (make new tag at (page item myNum of
           document 1))
        set name of mytag to "OriginalBounds"
        set value of mytag to myBoundsString
    end tell
end setBounds
```

setBounds()
stores a page item's dimensions in a tag.

```
on getBounds(myNum)
    tell application "Adobe Illustrator 10"
        set myValue to value of tag "OriginalBounds" of page item
           myNum of document 1
    end tell
    set myDelimiters to text item delimiters
    set text item delimiters to {","}
    set mylist to text items of myValue as list
    set text item delimiters to myDelimiters
    return mylist
end getBounds
```

getBounds()
returns a list of page item dimensions based on the value in a tag.

Visual Basic

Script Tips *The script starts by ensuring that an open document exists in Illustrator. It proceeds to gather the new horizontal- and vertical-scaling values from the contents of the two specially named text art items that you created in steps 2 and 3. The values are tested to make sure that they are in the range 1% to 200%.*

Within the main loop that looks at each page item in the document, the script gets the name of the current page item and checks to make sure that it doesn't match one of the specially named text art items you use to hold your scale values.

Next, it's time to see whether the object at hand has already had its original dimensions and position saved in a tag named "OriginalBounds". If this tag exists, the script calls the function `getBounds()`, *passing the index order of the current page item so that the function can reference it. The original dimensions of the object will be returned from the function in the variable* `myBounds`. *You use the four elements in the array returned in* `myBounds` *to set the position, width, and height of the current page item.*

If the tag named "OriginalBounds" does not exist, it is time to call your function `setBounds()` *to create the tag and store the page item's dimensions in the tag's value.*

When it is certain that the current page item's dimensions have been reset to their original values, the script rescales the page item to the new values.

The `setBounds()` *function receives the index order of the page item for which it needs to create a tag. Then it gathers the position, width, and height of the page item in question. These values are combined into a string with commas separating them so that you can break the values apart easily in* `getBounds()`. *Finally, a new tag is created for the page item, and its name and value are set.*

The `getBounds()` *function does the work of retrieving the string value from the page item's tag. It uses Visual Basic's* `Split` *function to convert the comma-delimited string value of the tag to a four-element array of values. Finally, the array is returned to the script calling the function.*

VBScript

```vbscript
Option Explicit
Dim myApp As New Illustrator.Application

Private Sub Command1_Click()
    Dim myXscale, myYscale, myNum, myItemName, myTagExists, myBounds, myTag
    If myApp.Documents.Count > 0 Then
        myXscale = myApp.Documents(1).TextArtItems("Xscale").Contents
        myYscale = myApp.Documents(1).TextArtItems("Yscale").Contents
        myXscale = CSng(Left(myXscale, Len(myXscale) - 1))
        myYscale = CSng(Left(myYscale, Len(myYscale) - 1))
        If myXscale < 1# Then myXscale = 1#
        If myXscale > 200# Then myXscale = 200#
        If myYscale < 1# Then myYscale = 1#
        If myYscale > 200# Then myYscale = 200#
        
        For myNum = 1 To myApp.Documents(1).PageItems.Count
            myItemName = myApp.Documents(1).PageItems(myNum).Name
            If myItemName <> "Xscale" And myItemName <> "Yscale" Then
            
                myTagExists = False
                For Each myTag In myApp.Documents(1).PageItems(myNum).Tags
                    If myTag.Name = "OriginalBounds" Then
                        myTagExists = True
                        Exit For
                    End If
                Next
                If myTagExists Then
                
                    myBounds = getBounds(myNum)
                    myApp.Documents(1).PageItems(myNum).Position = Array(myBounds(0), myBounds(1))
```

The main For...Next loop moves through each page item in the frontmost document.

Reset the current page item's dimensions if the tag "OriginalBounds" exists.

VBS, cont'd.

```
                    myApp.Documents(1).PageItems(myNum).Width
                    = myBounds(2)
                    myApp.Documents(1).PageItems(myNum).Height
                    = myBounds(3)

                Else
                    setBounds myNum

                End If
                myApp.Documents(1).PageItems(myNum).Resize myXscale,
                myYscale, , , , , aiTransformCenter
```
Resize the current page item to its new size.

```
            End If
        Next
    End If
End Sub


Private Sub setBounds(myNum)
    Dim myPosition, myWidth, myHeight, myBoundsString, myTag
    myPosition = myApp.Documents(1).PageItems(myNum).Position
    myWidth = myApp.Documents(1).PageItems(myNum).Width
    myHeight = myApp.Documents(1).PageItems(myNum).Height
    myBoundsString = myPosition(0) & "," & myPosition(1) & ","
    myBoundsString = myBoundsString & myWidth & "," & myHeight
    Set myTag = myApp.Documents(1).PageItems(myNum).Tags.Add
    myTag.Name = "OriginalBounds"
    myTag.Value = myBoundsString
End Sub
```
setBounds() stores a page item's dimensions in a tag.

```
Private Function getBounds(myNum)
    Dim myValue, myList
    myValue = myApp.Documents(1).PageItems(myNum).Tag("OriginalBounds")
    myList = Split(myValue, ",")
    getBounds = myList
End Function
```
getBounds() returns an array of page item dimensions based on the value in a tag.

Script 4.15: Use Tags to Attach Searchable Data to Objects

Adobe Illustrator contains a built-in database. Did you know that? Most people don't. In fact, Adobe has never really promoted the fact that every page item in a document can have data values associated with it. Each associated data value also has a name, and these name-value pairs are called *tags*. To you and me, this means that any object in a document can be tagged with as many named values as you want. This feature of Illustrator is incredibly cool—so cool that only the Adobe programmers ever had access to it until Illustrator 9 and 10 arrived on the scene. The Adobe Illustrator programmers have used tags to hold special data associated with objects for a long time now. Take, for instance, the Note that you can create for some page items. Notes are nothing more than tags exposed through the user interface.

The power of tagging page items has never really been tapped until now. **Script 4.15** gives you total control of the tags in your documents. It lets you attach tags with names and values to any page item. It also lets you search the values stored in those tags. When a match is found, the page item associated with the tag is selected. The uses for this script are numerous: attach street addresses to objects representing houses on a street, like in the sample document shown in **Figure 4.45** through **Figure 4.51**, and then search them; attach inventory and SKU data to images representing products so that they can be selected by SKU; save descriptive comments about art objects in a document; and so on. The options are pretty much endless, and I leave it up to you to discover a use for this powerful script. Watch for special object tags created and used by Illustrator, like BBAccumRotation shown in **Figure 4.46**—these tag values can be changed, sometimes for noticeable results, but be careful. Everything stored in a tag by Illustrator is there for good reason.

The example I've chosen to illustrate this is, in essence, a very simple GIS usage of Illustrator. In the strictest sense, a geographic information system (GIS) is a computer system capable of assembling, storing, manipulating, and displaying geographically referenced information, like data identified according to its location or relationship to a visual object representing a place.

Create a simple document, like the one shown in Figure 4.45, and then run the script. Try to add a new tag to one of your document's objects as in **Figure 4.47**. The script will prompt you for a name for the tag—enter a name without spaces. Once you enter a valid name, you'll be prompted to enter an associated value for the newly named tag, as in **Figure 4.48**. Try the script again after adding a few tags and you'll be able to choose from existing tags when you run the script again, as in **Figure 4.49**. The script's final ability is to search tags and select associated page items with matches. You can search through all of the existing tags' values for a matching substring, as in **Figure 4.50**. Matches are displayed to allow a user selection of a value. The chosen value's associated tag is matched to its object and the object is selected in Illustrator, as in **Figure 4.51**.

TIP *To create the starting Visual Basic project for this script, follow the steps explained in Figure 4.44.*

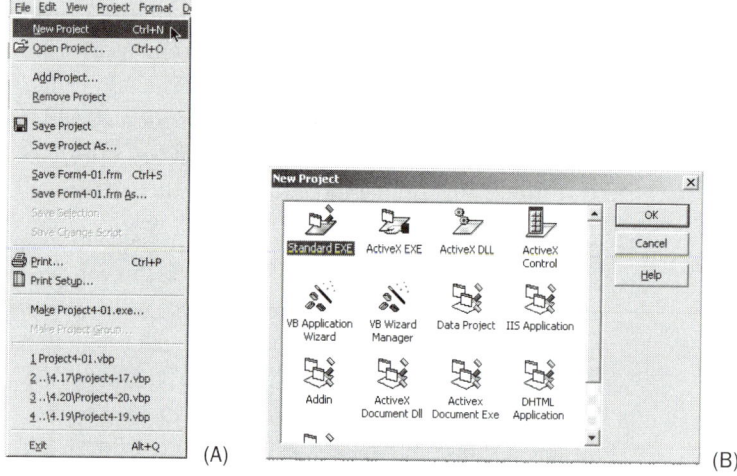

Figure 4.44 *This series of screen shots illustrates the steps necessary to create a new project in the Visual Basic editor with a form in it so that you can add Script 4.15's code. (A) Start by choosing File > New Project. (B) Next, select a standard .exe project, and click the OK button. A new project will open, with a new form window showing as in (C). Select the CommandButton tool, and drag out a new button in the open form window. Next, select the ComboBox tool (looks like a scrolling list with a pull-down menu on top), and draw a new combo box. Then select the ListBox tool (looks like a scrolling list), and draw a list-box control so that the form looks like (D). Double-click the button in the form to open its code window, shown in (E). This code window is where you will do your script writing. Next, choose Project > References. as shown in (F). Then locate the Adobe Illustrator 10.0 Type Library (G), and activate it by checking the box next to its name. Now you can close the References dialog by clicking the OK button. It is finally time to write Visual Basic!*

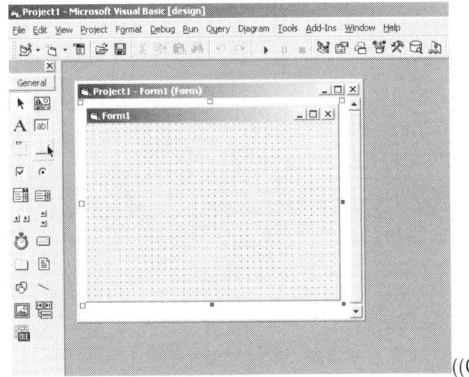
(C)

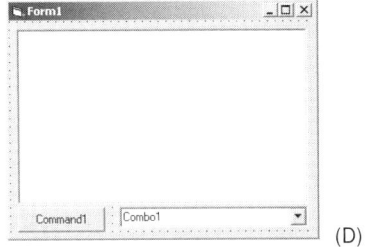
(D)

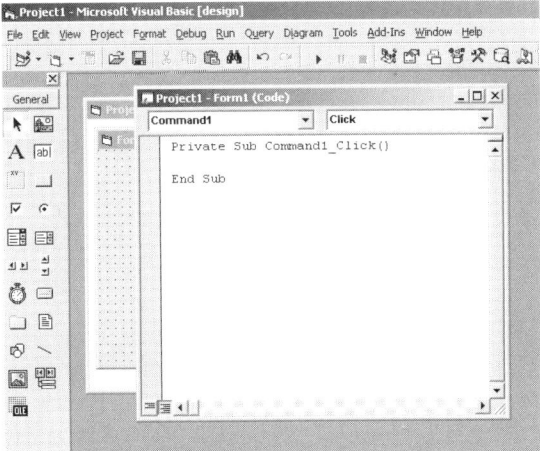
(E)

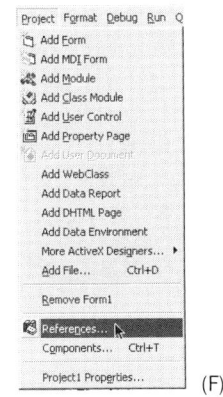
(F)

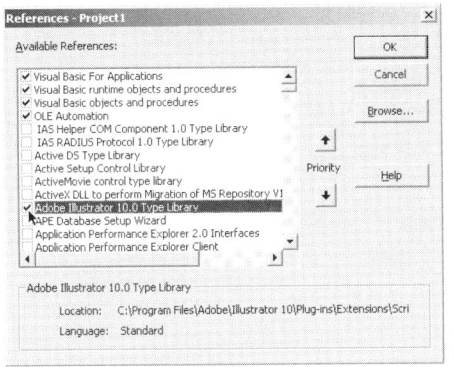
(G)

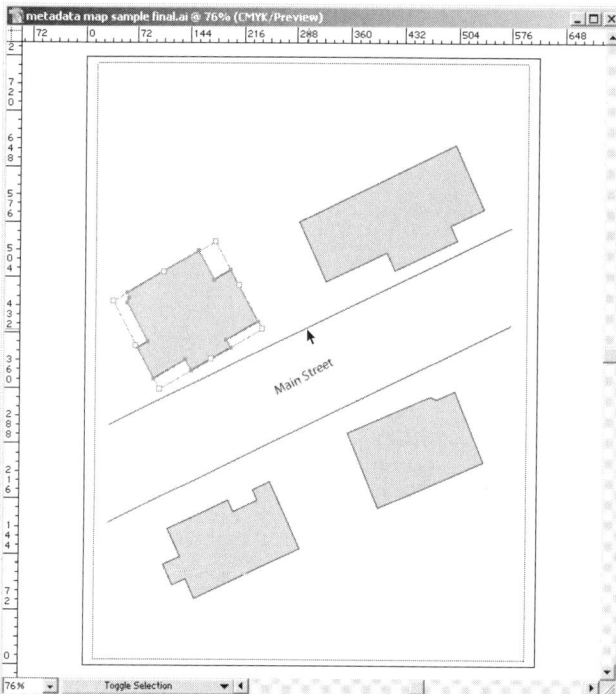

Figure 4.45 A sample map document in Illustrator shows four houses on a street. One house is selected before the script runs.

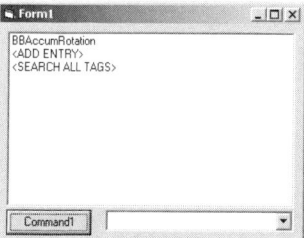

Figure 4.46 The form is displayed while the script is running. It shows that the selected page item in Illustrator contains a single tag, named *"BBAccumRotation"*. Illustrator uses this tag internally to keep track of an object's rotation value, as compared with its original state. For now, you'll leave this tag alone. Later, you can try modifying its value to see its effect, if any, on the object.

Figure 4.47 When the user chooses to add a new tag to the selected object, the script first displays this dialog, prompting for a name for the new tag.

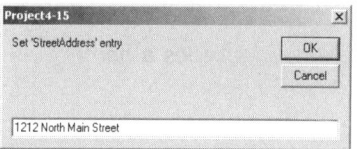

Figure 4.48 The second dialog shown when the script is adding a new tag, asking for a value for the newly named tag.

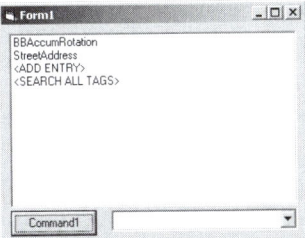

Figure 4.49 *If you run the script again after adding the new tag, the form displayed should look like this.*

Figure 4.50 *Choosing to search for a tag value displays this dialog.*

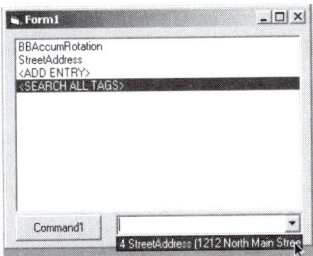

Figure 4.51 *Any matches found are shown in the combo box's pull-down menu. Choosing one of these entries will select the tagged page item in the Illustrator document.*

AppleScript

Script Tips *The script begins with a series of tests to make sure that a document is open and only one page item is selected.*

Next, a check is performed to see whether the selected page item has any tags associated with it. If there are tags, their names are stored in the variable myTagNames. *If no tags exist for this page item, the variable* myTagNames *is set to an empty list.*

Two additional items, "<ADD ENTRY>" and "<SEARCH ALL TAGS>", are appended to the list in myTagNames. *These items will represent special choices for the user when the list is displayed via choose from list.*

If the user selects the choice to add a new tag to the page item, they are prompted to name the new tag. If the user supplies a name with spaces, which is not allowed by Illustrator, the script repeats the prompt until the user provides a name that does not contain spaces. If the name provided isn't blank, the user is prompted to provide a value to associate with the new tag. Finally, the tag is created for the page item, and its name and value are set.

If the user chooses to search the existing tags in the document, he or she is prompted for some text to search for in the tag values. The script then loops through each tag in the document, checking to see whether the value of the current tag in the loop contains the search text. If so, the name of the tag is added to a list that will be displayed later. If the list of matching tag names is empty, the script knows that no matches were found and alerts the user. If matches were found, the user is prompted to make a choice from the list of matching tag names. If the user chooses a tag, everything else is unselected, and the page item that is associated with the tag is selected in the Illustrator document.

If the user chooses to edit an existing tag, the existing tag value is retrieved and stored in myTagValue. Then the user is prompted to enter a new value, with the existing tag value shown as a default. If the user entered anything, the tag's value is updated to the new data. If the user entered a blank empty string, the tag is deleted.

AppleScript

```
tell application "Adobe Illustrator 10"
    activate
    if (count of documents) > 0 then
        if selection is not {} then
            set mySelection to selection
            if class of mySelection is list then
                if (count of items in mySelection) = 1 then
                    set myPageItem to item 1 of mySelection
                    if (count of tags of myPageItem) > 0 then
                        set myTagNames to name of tags of myPageItem
                    else
                        set myTagNames to {}
                    end if
                    set myTagNames to myTagNames & "<ADD ENTRY>"
                    set myTagNames to myTagNames & "<SEARCH ALL TAGS>"
                    set myChoices to (choose from list myTagNames with prompt "Select entry to edit")
                    if class of myChoices is list then
                        set myTagName to item 1 of myChoices as string
                        if myTagName is "<ADD ENTRY>" then
                            set myNewName to " "
```

Is one page item selected?

If the user has selected something from the list, the choice is stored in myTagName.

AS, cont'd.

```
    repeat until myNewName does not contain " "
        set myNewName to text returned of (display
        dialog "Name new entry" default answer "")
        if myNewName contains " " then display
        dialog "Entry names cannot contain spaces."
    end repeat
    if myNewName is not "" then
        set myNewValue to text returned of (display
        dialog "Set '" & myNewName & "' entry"
        default answer "")
        set myNewTag to (make new tag at
        myPageItem)
        set name of myNewTag to myNewName
        set value of myNewTag to myNewValue
    end if
else if myTagName is "<SEARCH ALL TAGS>" then
    set mySearchValue to text returned of (display
    dialog "Search entries for what" default
    answer "")
    set myTagNames to {}
    repeat with myNum from 1 to count of tags in
    document 1
        if value of tag myNum of document 1
        contains mySearchValue then
            set myEntry to myNum & " " & (name of
            tag myNum of document 1) as string
            set myEntry to myEntry & " (" & (value
            of tag myNum of document 1) & ")" as
            string
            set myTagNames to myTagNames & myEntry
            as list
        end if
    end repeat
    if myTagNames = {} then
        display dialog "No matches found for '" &
        mySearchValue & "'."
    else
```

If the user chose to search the existing tags in the document, he or she is prompted for some text to search for in the tag values.

If the list of matching tag names is empty, the script knows that no matches were found and alerts the user.

AS, cont'd.

```
            set myChoices to (choose from list
            myTagNames with prompt "Choose match to
            select")
            if class of myChoices is list then
                set selection of document 1 to {}
                set myTagName to item 1 of myChoices as
                string
                set myTagNumber to word 1 of myTagName
                as integer
                set myItemSelect to container of tag
                myTagNumber of document 1
                set selected of myItemSelect to true
            end if
        end if
    else
        set myTagValue to value of tag myTagName of
        myPageItem
        set myNewValue to text returned of (display
        dialog "Change '" & myTagName & "' entry"
        default answer myTagValue)
        if myNewValue is not "" then
            set value of tag myTagName of myPageItem to
            myNewValue
        else
            delete tag myTagName of myPageItem
        end if
    end if
                end if
            end if
        end if
    end if
end tell
```

> The final else handles editing of an existing tag.

Visual Basic

Script Tips *This script is made up of a series of specialized subroutines.*

The `doRefreshControls()` *subroutine is responsible for preparing the form's list box and combo box. It begins with a series of tests to make sure that a document is open and only one page item is selected. If these criteria are met, a reference to the page item is stored in* `myPageItem`, *and the list box in the form is cleared of all values to prepare for the script's populating of the list box. Next, a check is performed to see whether the selected page item has any tags associated with it. If so, their names are appended to the values contained in the form's list box. Two additional items are appended to the list box's values. These items represent special choices for the user. Next, the combo box's pull-down menu is cleared of any values. It will be populated by the script when the user searches tags with all matching results.*

The `Command1_Click()` *subroutine is run when a user clicks the form's button. When this happens, it is time to make sure that the user has selected an entry in the list box and also that an object is still selected in the Illustrator document. If these criteria are met, a reference to the page item is stored in* `myPageItem`, *and the selected item in the list box is stored in* `myTagName`.

If the user chose to add a new tag to the page item, they are prompted to name the new tag. If the user supplies a name with spaces, which is not allowed by Illustrator, the script repeats the prompt until the user provides a name that does not contain spaces. If the name provided isn't blank, the user is prompted to provide a value to associate with the new tag. Finally, the tag is created for the page item, its name and value are set, and the `doRefreshControls()` *subroutine is called to repopulate the list box and combo box.*

If the user chose to search the existing tags in the document, he or she is prompted for some text to search for in the tag values. The combo box's values are also cleared from any previous search that may have been conducted. The script loops through each tag in the document, checking to see whether the value of the current tag in the loop contains the search text. If so, the name of the tag is appended as an entry in the combo box pull-down menu.

If the user has chosen to edit an existing tag, this part of the script will be run. The existing tag value is retrieved and stored in myTagValue. *Then the user is prompted to enter a new value, with the existing tag value shown as a default. If the user entered anything, the tag's value is updated to the new data. If the user entered a blank empty string, the tag is deleted.*

The Combo1_Click() *subroutine is run when the user clicked the combo box's pull-down menu to change its value. The combo box holds values only after a successful search is completed.*

If the user has chosen an entry from the combo box, everything else is unselected in the Illustrator document, and the page item that is associated with the tag is selected.

VBScript

```
Option Explicit
Dim myApp As New illustrator.Application
```

This subroutine is run whenever the script is started, before the form is displayed to the user.

```
Private Sub Form_Load()
    doRefreshControls
End Sub
```

This subroutine is responsible for preparing the form's list box and combo box.

```
Private Sub doRefreshControls()
Dim mySelectionType, mySelection, myTagNames, myTag, myPageItem
    If myApp.Documents.Count > 0 Then
        mySelectionType = TypeName(myApp.Documents(1).Selection)
        If mySelectionType <> "Empty" Then
            mySelection = myApp.Documents(1).Selection
            Set myPageItem = mySelection(0)
            List1.Clear
        If myPageItem.Tags.Count > 0 Then
            ReDim myTagNames(myPageItem.Tags.Count + 2)
            For Each myTag In myPageItem.Tags
                List1.AddItem myTag.Name
            Next
        End If
        
        End If
```

VBS, cont'd.

```vbs
            List1.AddItem "<ADD ENTRY>"
            List1.AddItem "<SEARCH ALL TAGS>"
            Combo1.Clear

      End If
   End Sub
```

This subroutine is run whenever the user clicks the form's button.

```vbs
   Private Sub Command1_Click()
      Dim mySelectionType, mySelection, myTagName, myPageItem
      Dim myNewName, myNewValue, myNewTag, mySearchValue, myNum
      Dim myEntry, myTagValue
      If List1.ListIndex > -1 Then
         mySelectionType = TypeName(myApp.Documents(1).Selection)
         If mySelectionType <> "Empty" Then
            mySelection = myApp.Documents(1).Selection
            Set myPageItem = mySelection(0)
            myTagName = List1.List(List1.ListIndex)
            Select Case myTagName
               Case "<ADD ENTRY>"
                  myNewName = " "
                  Do While InStr(myNewName, " ") > 0
                     myNewName = InputBox("Name new entry", , "")
                     If InStr(myNewName, " ") > 0 Then
                        MsgBox ("Entry names cannot contain spaces.")
                     End If
                  Loop
                  If myNewName <> "" Then
                     myNewValue = InputBox("Set '" & myNewName & "' entry", , "")
                     Set myNewTag = myPageItem.Tags.Add
                     myNewTag.Name = myNewName
                     myNewTag.Value = myNewValue
                     doRefreshControls
                  End If
```

If the user chose to add a new tag to the page item, these lines of code are executed.

VBS, cont'd.

```
              Case "<SEARCH ALL TAGS>"
                mySearchValue = InputBox("Search entries for
                what", "")
                Combo1.Clear

                For myNum = 1 To myApp.Documents(1).Tags.Count
                  If InStr(myApp.Documents(1).Tags(myNum).Value,
                  mySearchValue) > 0 Then
                    myEntry = myNum & " " & myApp.Documents(1).
                    Tags(myNum).Name
                    myEntry = myEntry & " (" & myApp.Documents(1).
                    Tags(myNum).Value & ")"
                    Combo1.AddItem myEntry
                  End If
                Next

                If Combo1.ListCount = 0 Then
                  MsgBox ("No matches found for '" & mySearchValue
                  & "'.")
                End If
              Case Else
                myTagValue = myPageItem.Tags(myTagName).Value
                myNewValue = InputBox("Change '" & myTagName & "'
                entry", , myTagValue)
                If myNewValue <> "" Then
                  myPageItem.Tags(myTagName).Value = myNewValue
                Else
                  myPageItem.Tags.Remove
                  (myPageItem.Tags(myTagName))
                End If
            End Select
          End If
        End If
      End Sub

      Private Sub Combo1_Click()
```

If the combo box's list of entries is empty, the script knows that no matches were found and alerts the user.

The Case Else handles editing of an existing tag.

This subroutine runs when the combo box changes.

VBS, cont'd.

```
        Dim myTagName, myTagNumber, myItemSelect
        If Combo1.ListIndex > -1 Then
          myApp.Documents(1).Selection = Empty
          myTagName = Combo1.List(Combo1.ListIndex)
          myTagNumber = Left(myTagName, InStr(myTagName, " ") - 1)
          myTagNumber = CInt(myTagNumber)
          Set myItemSelect = myApp.Documents(1).Tags(myTagNumber).
          Parent
          myItemSelect.Selected = True
        End If
      End Sub
```

Script 4.16: Use a Web Service to Translate Text in a Document

The world of Web services is burgeoning. You've probably heard about these newfangled Internet tools that let your scripts and applications use the capabilities of remote systems via the Web. My favorite Web service to date is the great Babelfish translation-engine service provided by the Web services portal XMethods.com. It provides language-translation services via the Web from English to several other languages, including Spanish, French, and German.

Script 4.16 uses this cool Web service to translate all the text in the frontmost Illustrator document from English to Spanish. You need an active Internet connection to use this script, as well as a special SOAP type library, shown in **Figure 4.52** and explained in the sidebar, if you're using Visual Basic.

The provider of this free Web service is XMethods—their Web site has access and details for many Web services now available on the Internet. Each Web service is documented online, including Babelfish, shown in **Figure 4.54**. See **Table 4.1** for a complete list of language-translation options and the corresponding code to send to the service.

When you're ready to run the script, have an open document with some text art containing English words in it, like in **Figure 4.55**. After you run the script, the text art contents should be translated into Spanish, like in **Figure 4.56**.

TIP *To create the starting Visual Basic project for this script, follow the steps explained in Figure 4.53.*

Figure 4.52
The initial screen displayed by Microsoft's SOAP Toolkit 2.0 SP2 installer. You need to install the toolkit before starting Script 4.16 in Visual Basic.

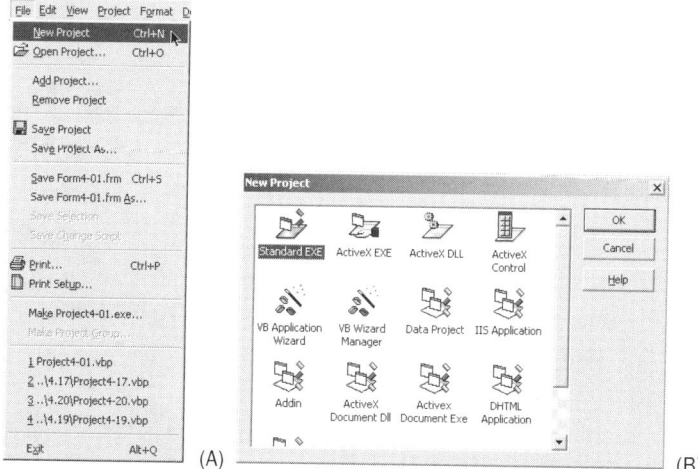

Figure 4.53 This series of screen shots illustrates the steps necessary to create a new project in the Visual Basic editor with a form in it so that you can add Script 4.16's code. (A) Start by choosing File > New Project. (B) Next, select a standard .exe project, and click the OK button. A new project will open, with a new form window showing as in (C). Select the CommandButton tool, and drag out a new button in the open form window so that the form looks like (D). Double-click the button in the form to open its code window, shown in (E). This code window is where you will do your script writing. Next, choose Project > References, as shown in (F). Then locate the Adobe Illustrator 10.0 Type Library (G), and activate it by checking the box next to its name. Next, locate the Microsoft Soap Type Library, shown in (H), and add it as well. Now you can close the References dialog by clicking the OK button. It is finally time to write Visual Basic!

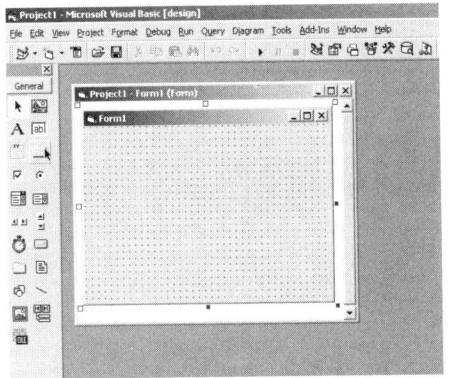
(C)

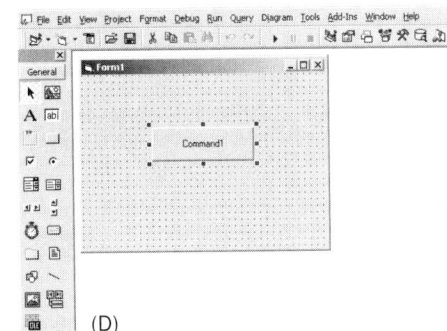
(D)

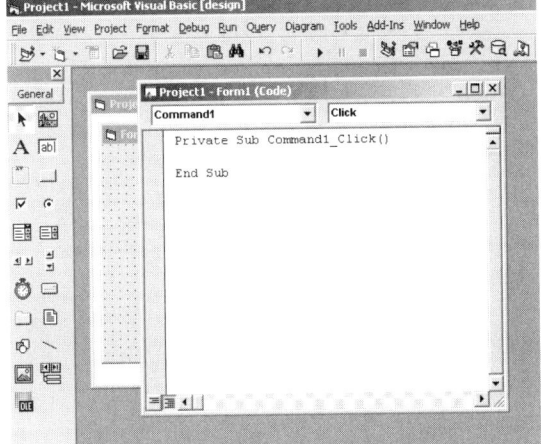
(E)

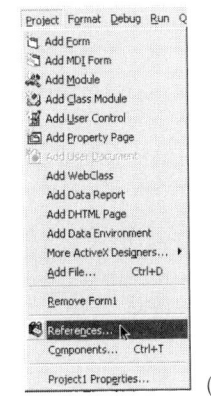
(F)

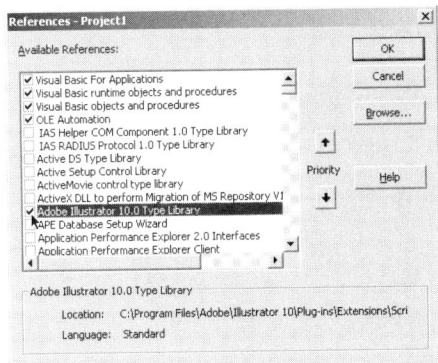
(G)

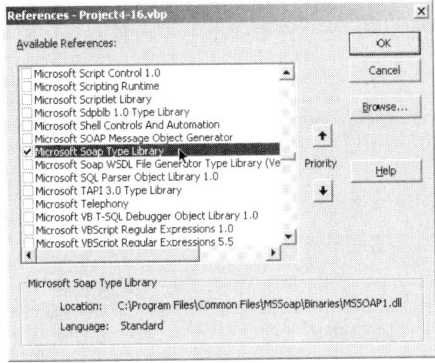
(H)

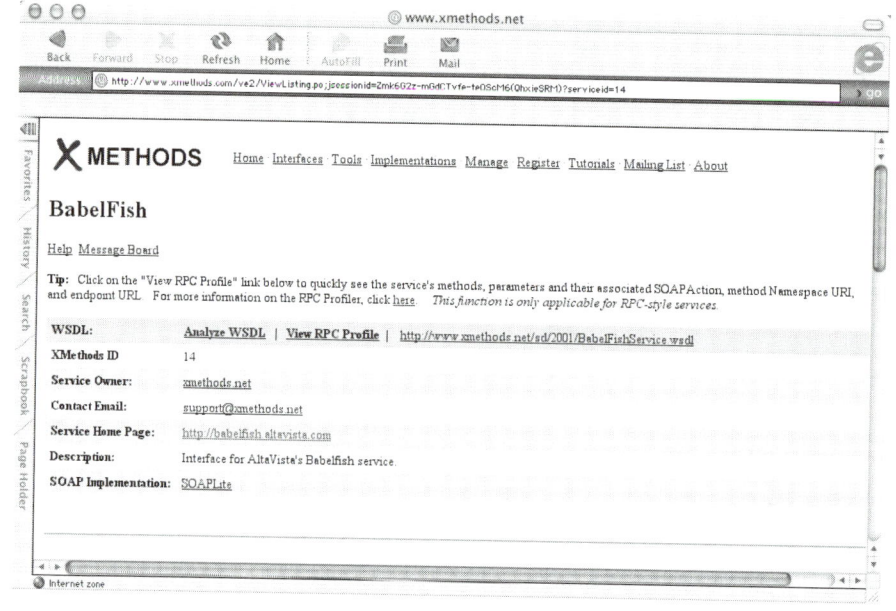

Figure 4.54 The provider of the Babelfish Web service is XMethods. The Web site provides details about the Web service and many others that XMethods provides. This Web page shows the Babelfish service's definition page at **www.xmethods.com**.

Table 4.1 Language-translation modes supported by the XMethods Babelfish translation engine. You may substitute any of the translation-mode strings in place of "en_es" in your script to change the translation languages.

Babelfish Translation Engine Options

TRANSLATION DESIRED	TRANSLATION-MODE STRING
English -> French	"en_fr"
English -> German	"en_de"
English -> Italian	"en_it"
English -> Portuguese	"en_pt"
English -> Spanish	"en_es"
French -> English	"fr_en"
German -> English	"de_en"
Italian -> English	"it_en"
Portuguese -> English	"pt_en"
Russian -> English	"ru_en"
Spanish -> English	"es_en"

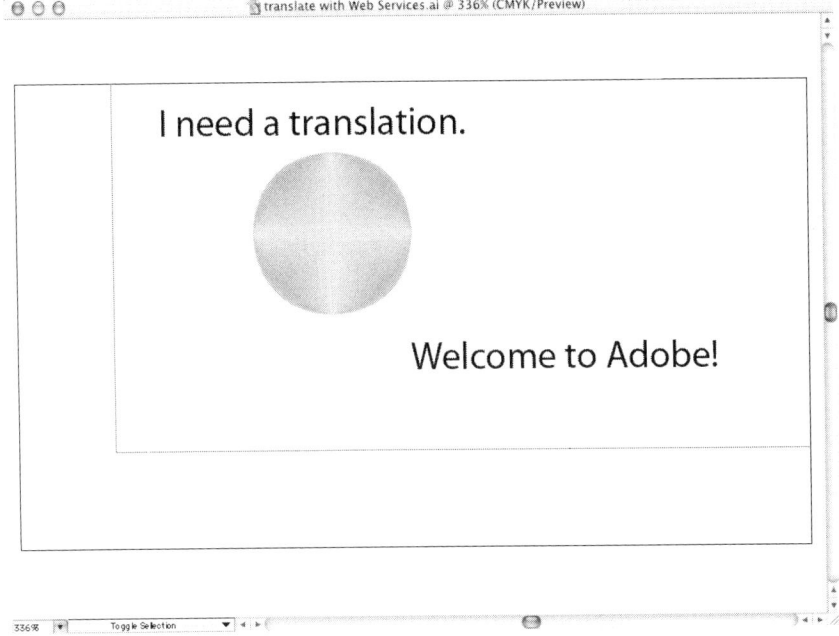

Figure 4.55 *A sample document with two text art items in English is shown before the translation script has run.*

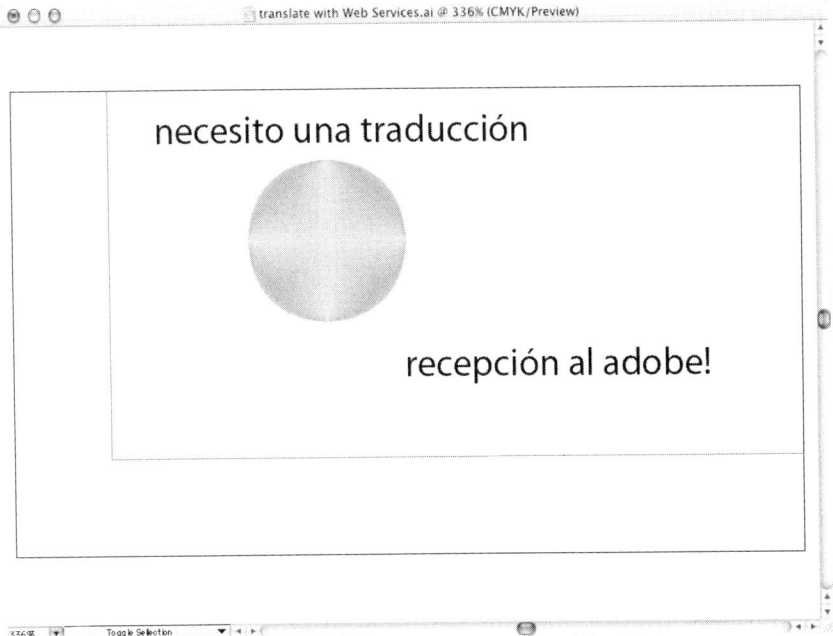

Figure 4.56 *The same sample document, after the script has run, shows off its new Spanish text.*

Installing SOAP Toolkit 2.0 for Windows to Access Web Services from Visual Basic

Although Apple has given AppleScript the capability to support accessing remote Web-based services via XML-RPC and SOAP protocols, Microsoft has yet to catch up to the curve by including built-in support for Web services in Visual Basic. This situation is a bit peculiar, because Microsoft has made "Web services" its newest mantra, but you're used to adding additional capabilities to your Visual Basic projects by choosing Project > References, and you can do it again for Web-services support in VB.

First, you'll need the installer that adds the required Visual Basic type library to your computer. This installer is called the SOAP Toolkit 2.0 SP2 (for Service Pack 2), and it's available from Microsoft's MSDN Web site at **http://msdn.microsoft.com/downloads**. Just search for *SOAP Toolkit* on the downloads page to find a link to a direct download page.

After you've downloaded the installer, named SOAPToolkit20.exe, just double-click its icon and follow any prompts to complete the installation.

AppleScript

Script Tips *The script starts by defining the kind of translation desired and storing the associated translation mode in a property named* myTranslationMode. *The other properties contain constant values required for the Babelfish Web service (at http://services.xmethods.net) to function properly.*

The main portion of the script is simple, because the more-complex Web service call has been isolated in the function doTranslate(). *The main script simply ensures that at least one document is open in Illustrator and that it contains some text art before the script begins a loop. This loop moves through each text art item in the document, calling the translation function* doTranslate() *each time. The returned translation text string is used to replace the existing contents of the text art item.*

The doTranslate() *function starts by setting up an error-flag variable,* errFlag, *for later testing to see if all went well. In a* try *block to intercept errors, the script talks to the remote Perl CGI at services.xmethods.net with the built-in AppleScript function* call soap. *The* call soap *function requires a* method name, method namespace uri, *parameters unique to each Web application, and a* SOAPaction. *If an error happens, the script checks the error number. If a connection error took place, the number matches -916, and a special message is returned. If no error happened, the translated phrase is returned.*

AppleScript

This script uses properties to store the values used for the SOAP call.

```
property myTranslationMode : "en_es"
property mySOAPmethod : "BabelFish"
property mySOAPnamespace : "urn:xmethodsBabelFish"
property mySOAPaction : "urn:xmethodsBabelFish#BabelFish"
tell application "Adobe Illustrator 10"
    activate
    if (count of documents) > 0 then
        if (count of text art items of document 1) > 0 then
            repeat with myNum from 1 to count of text art items in document 1
                set myText to contents of text art item myNum of document 1 as string
                tell me to set myText to doTranslate(myText)
                set contents of text art item myNum of document 1 to myText
            end repeat
        end if
    end if
end tell
```

This function makes a SOAP call to translate a passed string, returning the translated text.

```
on doTranslate(myTranslationText)
    set errFlag to false
    try
        tell application "http://services.xmethods.net:80/perl/soaplite.cgi"
            set mySOAPresult to call soap {method name:mySOAPmethod,
                method namespace uri:mySOAPnamespace,
                parameters:{translationmode:myTranslationMode,
                sourcedata:myTranslationText}, SOAPAction:mySOAPaction}
        end tell
    on error errMessage number errNumber
        set errFlag to true
        if errNumber is -916 then
            set mySOAPresult to "[Service Connection Error]"
```

AS, cont'd.

```
        else
            set mySOAPresult to ""
        end if
    end try
    return mySOAPresult
end doTranslate
```

Visual Basic

Script Tips *The* `Command1_Click()` *subroutine is simple, because the more-complex Web service call has been isolated in the function* `doTranslate()`. *The main script simply ensures that at least one document is open in Illustrator and that it contains some text art before the script begins a loop. This loop moves through each text art item in the document, calling the translation function* `doTranslate()` *each time. The returned translation text string is used to replace the existing contents of the text art item.*

The first step in the translation function `doTranslate()` *creates a new variable that contains a SOAP client object. You use this SOAP client object's built-in* `mssoapinit` *method to open a connection to the Babelfish service, located at www.xmethods.net. The connection's parameters are defined by the Web Service Definition Language document at that URL. Finally, the Babelfish function of the remote Web service is called, passing it your translation mode and text to translate. The returned translation is passed back by the* `doTranslate()` *function.*

VBScript

```
Option Explicit


Private Sub Command1_Click()
    Dim myTextArt, myText
    Dim myApp As New Illustrator.Application
    If myApp.Documents.Count > 0 Then
        If myApp.Documents(1).TextArtItems.Count > 0 Then
            For Each myTextArt In myApp.Documents(1).TextArtItems
                myText = myTextArt.Contents
```

VBS, cont'd.

```
            myText = doTranslate(myText)
            myTextArt.Contents = myText
        Next
    End If
  End If
End Sub
```

This function makes a SOAP call to translate a passed string.

```
Private Function doTranslate(myText)
    Dim mySOAPClient As New SoapClient

    mySOAPClient.mssoapinit
    "http://www.xmethods.net/sd/2001/BabelFishService.wsdl",
    "BabelFishService", "", ""
```

BabelFish is called with the translation mode and text.

```
    doTranslate = mySOAPClient.BabelFish("en_es", myText)
End Function
```

What Are Web Services?

Web services are really fairly simple, if you avoid the hype and jargon generally associated with them. For a big dose of this jargon and numerous links to white papers and online resources for Web services, visit **www.webservices.org** to learn more about this emerging technology standard.

The simple definition is that a *Web service* is any computer application on any computer that can communicate over the World Wide Web. This means that a human or software entity can send a request via the Web to a server that houses an application. That application can process the request, which might be a command or request for data. Then the remote application can send results back via the Web. This process works just like a human user's going to a specific Web address to see a page, but instead of an HTML page being returned by the server, the results of the remote application queried are sent back.

Currently, you have two primary ways to access Web services. One way uses a protocol named XML-RPC (eXtensible Markup Language-Remote Procedure Call), and the other uses SOAP (Simple Object Access Protocol). For the most part, these two protocols provide similar capabilities. Which one you use really depends on what protocol the Web service you want to access is designed to use. If you are hungry for more information, do visit the Web site mentioned in this sidebar.

Script 4.17: Slice by Guides and Export for Web Use

This script demonstrates how amazing things can get, thanks to Illustrator's advanced scripting support. It compiles the vertices where each horizontal and vertical guide intersect in your current Illustrator document; then it creates clipping masks for each of the rectangular slices created by the intersections of all those guides. The script moves the individually clipped rectangular regions one by one into new temporary documents and then exports each one, using the `exportDocument()` function from Script 4.6. This functionality essentially gives you scripted capabilities similar to slices, which aren't really accessible from your script. You use this script in your office to prepare sliced graphics ready for Web use directly from your Illustrator documents. The added benefits of doing this under script control include automatic rescaling of art before export, intelligent naming of each slice, and whatever else you can think to do to each slice before you export it. The sky really is the limit with how far you can push the functionality of **Script 4.17**.

Try out the capabilities of this script by placing guides onto an existing document that contains some art. Place all your guides so that the rectangular regions defined by them are each defining a separate graphic to export, as in **Figure 4.58**. After you run the script, open an exported file and see how it has cropped the image to fit one of the guide-defined rectangles in your source document, as in **Figure 4.59**.

TIP To create the starting Visual Basic project for this script, follow the steps explained in Figure 4.57.

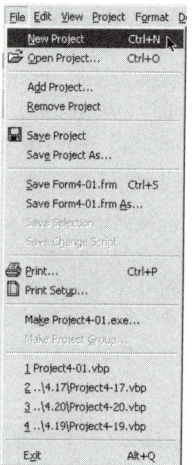

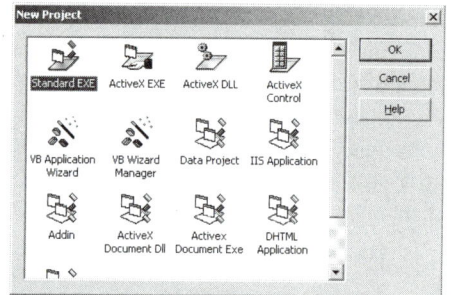

Figure 4.57 A-B This series of screen shots illustrates the steps necessary to create a new project in the Visual Basic editor with a form in it so that you can add Script 4.17's code. (A) Start by choosing File > New Project. (B) Next, select a standard .exe project, and click the OK button.

(A)   (B)

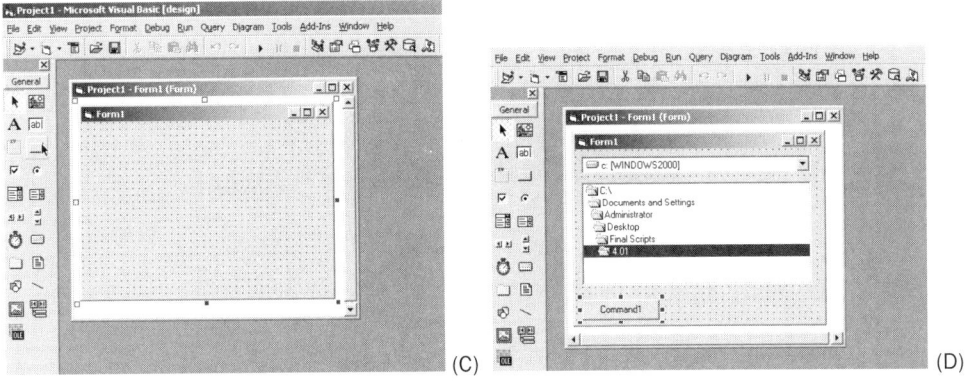

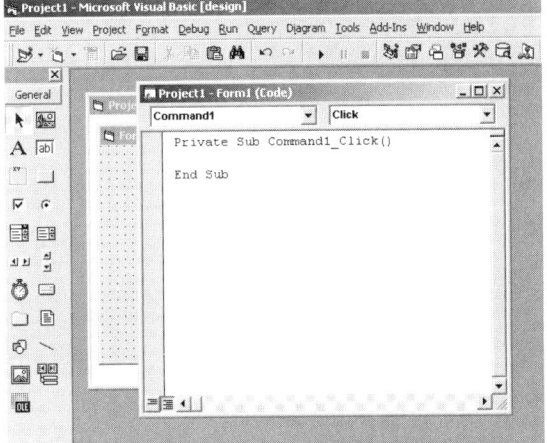

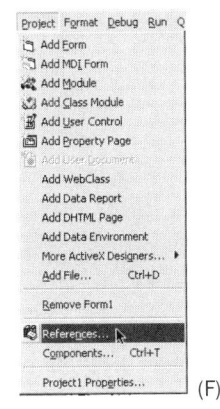

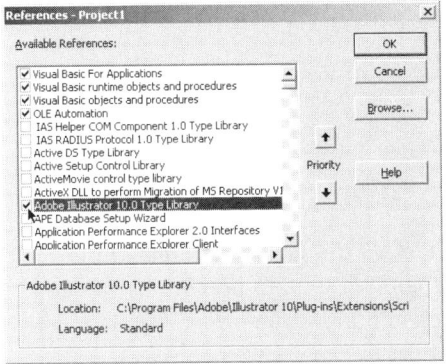

Figure 4.57 C-G *A new project will open, with a new form window showing as in (C). Select the CommandButton tool, and drag out a new button in the open form window. Next, select the DriveListBox tool (looks like a hard disk), and draw a new drive list box. Now select the FolderListBox tool (looks like a folder), and draw a new folder list box control so that the form looks like (D). Double-click the button in the form to open its code window, shown in (E). This code window is where you will do your script writing. The last step before scripting is attaching a reference to the scripting libraries your project will use so that it will be able to work with Illustrator. To do this, choose Project > References, as shown in (F). Then locate the Adobe Illustrator 10.0 Type Library (G), and activate it by checking the box next to its name. Now you can close the References dialog by clicking the OK button. Time to write Visual Basic!*

237

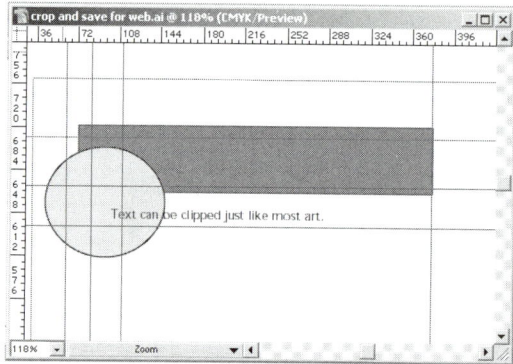

Figure 4.58 *A sample document containing some art ready to be chopped up into Web graphics.*

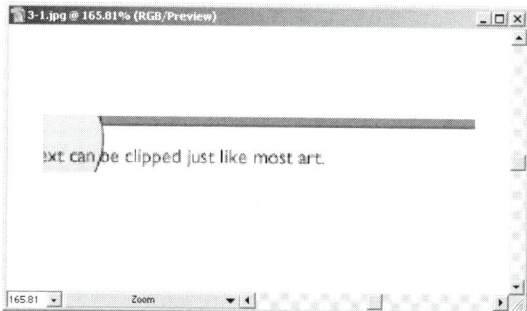

Figure 4.59 *One of the slices created by the script when it is run on the sample document has been reopened in Adobe Illustrator to demonstrate how the script slices the individual graphics precisely along the guides.*

AppleScript

Script Tips First, the script gathers all the guide positions in the frontmost document into a list. Then it is time to prepare a list of all the horizontal locations for guides in the document, as well as a list of the vertical locations.

A `repeat` *loop starts so that the script can look at each guide position's X (or horizontal) and Y (or vertical) coordinates. The horizontal and vertical coordinates for the current guide position are stored in individual variables* (`myGuideX` *and* `myGuideY`) *so that it's easier to work with them later.*

You want only one instance of each X and Y coordinate so that you can make rectangles using the unique coordinates later. So the script makes sure that the list of guide positions doesn't already contain the current coordinate. If the guide is on the document then it is time to add it to the list.

You use a simple function, `OrderValues()`, *covered later in this section, to make sure that your list of coordinates stays sorted in order. The coordinates must stay sorted so rectangles can be created based on them.*

Once the first repeat loop is done, the script prepares to output cropped rectangular regions by looping through horizontal guide positions and vertical guide positions in a pair of nested `repeat` *loops. In the first loop, the current and next X coordinates are stored in variables for easy use later. The next loop goes through the vertical guide positions to gather Y coordinates for your cropping rectangle. The current and next Y coordinates are stored in variables to use later.*

For each set of rectangular coordinates, a new path is created to use as a clipping mask on the document's contents. A new group is also created in preparation for setting up the clipping mask. All clipping masks in Illustrator are built from a group with its `clipping` *property set to* `true`. *The script moves all the art in the document, except guides, into the group so that it will get clipped. The clipping mask is enabled for the group and it is selected and copied to the Clipboard.*

Now it is time to make a new document with the dimensions of the clipping mask and using the RGB color space. Set the document's color space to RGB so it will be working in the native color space of JPEGs and GIFs on the Web.

Paste in the clipped art from your source document and move the whole clipped group to the new document's `page origin`. *Now calculate the difference between the clipped groups' current position and the clipping path (which is* `page item 2`*) inside* `page item 1` *(which is the group). You add in the offset of the height, because Illustrator's* `page origin` *is in the bottom-left corner, not the top-left corner.*

It is important to set the position of the clipped group accurately so that the artboard lines up with the clipped art. This step lets you use the export options to ensure that your exported file for the Web is cropped to the right size. And don't forget to export the file using `exportDocument()`.

Once the clipped document has been exported and closed, the script removes the group and clipping path in preparation for the next iteration of the repeat loop to create another clipping rectangle.

The `OrderValues()` *function receives an existing ordered list and a new item to insert into it. It proceeds to figure out where the new item should be inserted into the existing list so that the entire list will remain in order, smallest values first to largest values last.*

For the `exportDocument()` *function, you'll need to insert the code from Script 4.6.*

AppleScript

```
set mySaveFolder to (choose folder with prompt "Select folder
    to save Web art")
set myFormat to "jpeg"

tell application "Adobe Illustrator 10"
    activate
    set myGuidePositions to position of path items of document 1
        whose guides = true
    set myDocWidth to width of document 1
    set myDocHeight to height of document 1
end tell
set myHorizontals to {}
set myVerticals to {}
repeat with myGuidePosition in myGuidePositions
    set myGuideX to item 1 of myGuidePosition
    set myGuideY to item 2 of myGuidePosition
```

Gather all guide positions into a list.

This loop creates a unique ordered list of X and Y coordinates.

AS, cont'd.

```
            if myHorizontals does not contain myGuideX then
                if myGuideX ≥ 0 and myGuideX ≤ myDocWidth then
                    set myHorizontals to OrderValues(myHorizontals,
                      myGuideX)
                end if
            end if
            if myVerticals does not contain myGuideY then
                if myGuideY ≥ 0 and myGuideY ≤ myDocHeight then
                    set myVerticals to OrderValues(myVerticals, myGuideY)
                end if
            end if
        end repeat
```

This first of a pair of loops moves through X coordinates.

```
        repeat with myXnum from 1 to
           (count of items in myHorizontals) - 1
            set myX1 to item myXnum of myHorizontals
            set myX2 to item (myXnum + 1) of myHorizontals
            repeat with myYnum from 1 to
            (count of items in myVerticals) - 1
                set myY1 to item myYnum of myVerticals
                set myY2 to item (myYnum + 1) of myVerticals
                tell application "Adobe Illustrator 10"
```

Create a clipping path and group.

```
                    set myCropPath to (make new path item at beginning of
                      document 1
                      with properties {stroked:false, filled:false, entire
                      path:{{anchor:{myX1, myY1}, point type:corner},
                      {anchor:{myX2, myY1}, point type:corner},
                      {anchor:{myX2, myY2}, point type:corner},
                      {anchor:{myX1, myY2}, point type:corner},
                      {anchor:{myX1, myY1}, point type:corner}}})
                    set myImageWidth to width of myCropPath
                    set myImageHeight to height of myCropPath
                    set myGroupItem to (make new group item at end of
                      document 1)
                    repeat with myNum from
                    (count of page items of document 1) - 1 to 1 by -1
                        set myClass to class of page item myNum of document 1
```

AS, cont'd.

```
        if myClass = path item then
            if guides of page item myNum of document 1 is
            false then
                move page item myNum of document 1 to beginning
                of myGroupItem
            end if
        else
            move page item myNum of document 1 to beginning of
            myGroupItem
        end if
    end repeat
    set clipped of myGroupItem to true
    set selected of myGroupItem to true
    copy
```

Create a new document, paste the clipped art and position it.

```
    set myTempDoc to (make new document with properties
    {width:myImageWidth, height:myImageHeight, color
    space:RGB})
    paste
    set position of page item 1 of myTempDoc to {0.0, 0.0}
    set myCropPosition to position of page item 2 of
    myTempDoc
    set item 1 of myCropPosition to -(item 1 of
    myCropPosition as real)
    set item 2 of myCropPosition to -(item 2 of
    myCropPosition as real)
    set item 2 of myCropPosition to (item 2 of
    myCropPosition as real) + myImageHeight
    set position of page item 1 of myTempDoc to
    myCropPosition
end tell
exportDocument(myFormat, myXnum & "-" & myYnum,
mySaveFolder, false)
tell application "Adobe Illustrator 10"
    repeat with myNum from 2 to (count of page items of
    group item 1 of document 1)
        move page item 2 of group item 1 of document 1 to end
        of document 1
    end repeat
```

AS, cont'd.

Remove clipping path from original art before continuing loop.

This function adds a new value to a list in order.

You need to insert the code here exportDocument() in Script 4.6.

```
            delete group item 1 of document 1
        end tell
      
     end repeat
   end repeat

on OrderValues(myCurrentList, myInsert)
   set mylastItem to -1
   set myInserted to false
   repeat with myNum from 1 to count of items in myCurrentList
      set myItem to item myNum of myCurrentList
      if myInsert > mylastItem and myInsert ≤ myItem then
         if myNum = 1 then
            set myCurrentList to myInsert & myCurrentList
         else
            set myFrontHalf to items 1 thru (myNum - 1) of
              myCurrentList
            set myBackHalf to items myNum thru -1 of
              myCurrentList
            set myCurrentList to myFrontHalf & myInsert &
              myBackHalf
         end if
         set myInserted to true
         exit repeat
      end if
      set mylastItem to myItem
   end repeat
   if myInserted is false then
      set myCurrentList to myCurrentList & myInsert
   end if
   return myCurrentList
end OrderValues

on exportDocument(myFormat, myNameExtra, mySaveFolder,
   myRestoreFlag)
end exportDocument
```

Visual Basic

Script Tips You start the script with `Option Explicit` to let Visual Basic know that you will declare all variables explicitly with `Dim` statements. `Option Base 1` tells Visual Basic that you want any arrays created to start with element number 1 instead of the default of starting with 0. You also open a connection to the active running version of Illustrator.

The `Drive1_Change()` subroutine is triggered whenever the drive list box is changed. It sets the directory list box's root drive path to the newly selected drive.

The `Command1_Click()` subroutine is the main show here. It is triggered whenever the button in the form is clicked. First, the script gathers all the guide positions in the frontmost document into an array. Next it is time to prepare to create an array of all the horizontal locations for guides in the document, as well as an array of the vertical locations.

A `For...Next` loop starts so that the script can look at each guide position's X (horizontal) and Y (vertical) coordinates. The horizontal and vertical coordinates for the current guide position get stored in individual variables (`myGuideX` and `myGuideY`) so that it's easier to work with them later. If the guide is in the document, it is time to add it to the list.

You want only one instance of each X and Y coordinate so that you can make rectangles using the unique coordinates later. So the script makes sure that the list of guide positions doesn't already contain the current coordinate. If the guide is on the document then it is time to add it to the list.

You use a simple function, `OrderValues()`, to make sure that your array of coordinates stays sorted in order. This function is necessary for the code to make rectangles based on the guides later.

Once the first repeat loop is done, the script prepares to output cropped rectangular regions by looping through horizontal guide positions and vertical guide positions in a pair of nested `repeat` loops. In the first loop, the current and next X coordinates are stored in variables for easy use later. The next loop goes through the vertical guide positions to gather Y coordinates for your cropping rectangle. The current and next Y coordinates are stored in variables to use later.

For each set of rectangular coordinates, a new path is created to use as a clipping mask on the document's contents. A new group is also created in preparation for setting up the clipping mask. All clipping masks in Illustrator are built from a group with its `Clipping` property set to `True`. The script moves all the art in the document, except guides, into the group so that it will get clipped. The clipping mask is enabled for the group and it is selected and copied to the Clipboard.

Next the script makes a new document with the dimensions of the clipping mask and sets the document's color space to RGB by specifying the enumeration `aiDocumentRGBColor`. RGB is used as the standard color space for the files we'll export—JPEGs and GIFs for the Web.

Paste in the clipped art from your source document and move the whole clipped group to the new document's `PageOrigin`. Now calculate the difference between the clipped groups' current position and the clipping path (which is `PageItem 2`) inside `PageItem 1` (which is the group). You add in the offset of the height, because Illustrator's `PageOrigin` is in the bottom-left corner, not the top-left corner.

It is important to set the position of the clipped group accurately so that the artboard lines up with the clipped art. This step lets you use the export options to ensure that your exported file for the Web is cropped to the right size. And don't forget to export the file using `exportDocument()`.

Once the clipped document has been exported and closed, the script removes the group and clipping path in preparation for the next iteration of the `For...Next` loop to create another clipping rectangle.

The `OrderValues()` function receives an existing ordered array and a new value to insert into it. It proceeds to figure out where the new value should be inserted into the existing array so that the entire array will remain in sorted order, smallest values first to largest values last.

For the `exportDocument()` function, you'll need to insert the code from the Script 4.6.

VBScript

`Drive1_Change()` is executed when the drive list box changes.

```
Option Explicit
Option Base 1
Dim myApp As New Illustrator.Application
Private Sub Drive1_Change()
    Dir1.Path = Drive1.Drive & ":\"
End Sub
Private Sub Command1_Click()
```

VBS, cont'd.

```vbs
Dim mySaveFolder, myFormat, myGuidePositions(), myNum
Dim myPathItem, myDocWidth, myDocHeight, myFirstX, myFirstY
Dim myHorizontals(), myVerticals()
Dim myGuidePosition, myGuideX, myGuideY, myXnum, myYnum, _
myX1, myX2, myY1, myY2
Dim myCropPath, myPathPoint, myImageWidth, myImageHeight, _
myGroupItem
Dim myTempDoc, myCropPosition
If Dir1.Path <> "" Then
   mySaveFolder = Dir1.Path
   myFormat = "jpeg"
   If myApp.Documents.Count > 0 Then
      myNum = 1
      For Each myPathItem In myApp.Documents(1).PathItems
         If myPathItem.Guides = True Then
            ReDim Preserve myGuidePositions(myNum)
            myGuidePositions(myNum) = myPathItem.Position
            myNum = myNum + 1
         End If
      Next

      myDocWidth = myApp.Documents(1).Width
      myDocHeight = myApp.Documents(1).Height
      myFirstX = True
      myFirstY = True

      For Each myGuidePosition In myGuidePositions
         myGuideX = myGuidePosition(0)
         myGuideY = myGuidePosition(1)

         If myGuideX > 0 And myGuideX <= myDocWidth Then
```

Gather all guide positions into an array.

This loop creates a unique ordered list of X and Y coordinates.

VBS, cont'd.

This first of a pair of loops moves through X coordinates.

```
            If myFirstX Then
                ReDim myHorizontals(1)
                myHorizontals(1) = myGuideX
                myFirstX = False
            Else
                If UBound(Filter(myHorizontals, myGuideX)) = -1 
                Then

                    myHorizontals = OrderValues(myHorizontals, 
                    myGuideX)

                End If
            End If
        End If
        If myGuideY > 0 And myGuideY <= myDocHeight Then

            If myFirstY Then
                ReDim myVerticals(1)
                myVerticals(1) = myGuideY
                myFirstY = False
            Else
                If UBound(Filter(myVerticals, myGuideY)) = -1 
                Then

                    myVerticals = OrderValues(myVerticals, 
                    myGuideY)

                End If
            End If
        End If
    Next
```

VBS, cont'd.

```
                    For myXnum = 1 To UBound(myHorizontals) - 1
                        myX1 = myHorizontals(myXnum)
                        myX2 = myHorizontals(myXnum + 1)

                        For myYnum = 1 To UBound(myVerticals) - 1

                            myY1 = myVerticals(myYnum)
                            myY2 = myVerticals(myYnum + 1)

                            Set myCropPath = myApp.Documents(1).PathItems.Add
                            myCropPath.Stroked = True
                            myCropPath.Filled = False
                            Set myPathPoint = myCropPath.PathPoints.Add
                            myPathPoint.PointType = aiCorner
                            myPathPoint.LeftDirection = Array(myX1, myY1)
                            myPathPoint.RightDirection = Array(myX1, myY1)
                            myPathPoint.Anchor = Array(myX1, myY1)
                            Set myPathPoint = myCropPath.PathPoints.Add
                            myPathPoint.PointType = aiCorner
                            myPathPoint.LeftDirection = Array(myX2, myY1)
                            myPathPoint.RightDirection = Array(myX2, myY1)
                            myPathPoint.Anchor = Array(myX2, myY1)
                            Set myPathPoint = myCropPath.PathPoints.Add
                            myPathPoint.PointType = aiCorner
                            myPathPoint.LeftDirection = Array(myX2, myY2)
                            myPathPoint.RightDirection = Array(myX2, myY2)
                            myPathPoint.Anchor = Array(myX2, myY2)
                            Set myPathPoint = myCropPath.PathPoints.Add
                            myPathPoint.PointType = aiCorner
                            myPathPoint.LeftDirection = Array(myX1, myY2)
                            myPathPoint.RightDirection = Array(myX1, myY2)
                            myPathPoint.Anchor = Array(myX1, myY2)
                            Set myPathPoint = myCropPath.PathPoints.Add
```

Create a clipping path and group.

VBS, cont'd.

```
myPathPoint.PointType = aiCorner
myPathPoint.LeftDirection = Array(myX1, myY1)
myPathPoint.RightDirection = Array(myX1, myY1)
myPathPoint.Anchor = Array(myX1, myY1)
myImageWidth = myCropPath.Width
myImageHeight = myCropPath.Height
Set myGroupItem = myApp.Documents(1).GroupItems.Add
myGroupItem.MoveToEnd (myApp.Documents(1))


For myNum = myApp.Documents(1).PageItems.Count - 1 
To 1 Step -1
  If myApp.Documents(1).PageItems(myNum).
  PageItemType = aiPathItem Then
    If myApp.Documents(1).PageItems(myNum).
    PathItem.Guides = False Then
      myApp.Documents(1).PageItems(myNum).
      MoveToBeginning (myGroupItem)
    End If
  Else
    myApp.Documents(1).PageItems(myNum).
    MoveToBeginning (myGroupItem)
  End If
Next
```

Create a new document, paste the clipped art and position it.

```
myGroupItem.Clipped = True
myGroupItem.Selected = True
myApp.Documents(1).Copy
Set myTempDoc = myApp.Documents.Add
(aiDocumentRGBColor, myImageWidth, myImageHeight)
myTempDoc.Paste
myTempDoc.PageItems(1).Position = Array(0#, 0#)


myCropPosition = myTempDoc.PageItems(2).Position
myCropPosition(0) = -myCropPosition(0)
myCropPosition(1) = -myCropPosition(1)
```

VBS, cont'd.

```
                    myCropPosition(1) = myCropPosition(1) + 
                    myImageHeight
                    
                    
                    myTempDoc.PageItems(1).Position = myCropPosition
                    
                    
                    exportDocument myFormat, myXnum & "-" & myYnum, 
                    mySaveFolder, False
                    For myNum = myApp.Documents(1).GroupItems(1).
                    PageItems.Count To 2 Step -1
                        myApp.Documents(1).GroupItems(1).PageItems
                        (myNum).MoveToBeginning (myApp.Documents(1))
                    Next
```

Remove clipping path from original art before continuing loop.

```
                    myApp.Documents(1).GroupItems.Remove 
                    (myApp.Documents(1).GroupItems(1))
                    

                Next
            Next
        End If
    End If
End Sub
```

This function adds a new value to an array in order.

```
Public Function OrderValues(myCurrentList, myInsert)
    Dim myLastItem, myInserted, myNum, myBackNum
    myLastItem = -1
    myInserted = False
    For myNum = 1 To UBound(myCurrentList)
        If myInsert > myLastItem And myInsert <= 
        myCurrentList(myNum) Then
            If myNum = 1 Then
                ReDim Preserve myCurrentList(UBound(myCurrentList) 
                + 1)
```

VBS, cont'd.

```
            For myBackNum = UBound(myCurrentList) - 1 
            To 1 Step -1
                myCurrentList(myBackNum + 1) = 
                myCurrentList(myBackNum)
            Next
            myCurrentList(1) = myInsert
         Else
            ReDim Preserve myCurrentList(UBound(myCurrentList) 
            + 1)
            For myBackNum = UBound(myCurrentList) To myNum Step 
            -1
                myCurrentList(myBackNum) = myCurrentList(myBackNum 
                - 1)
            Next
            myCurrentList(myNum) = myInsert
         End If
         myInserted = True
         Exit For
      End If
      myLastItem = myCurrentList(myNum)
   Next
   If myInserted = False Then
      ReDim Preserve myCurrentList(UBound(myCurrentList) + 1)
      myCurrentList(UBound(myCurrentList)) = myInsert
   End If
   OrderValues = myCurrentList
End Function

Private Function exportDocument(myFormat, myNameExtra, 
   mySaveFolder, myRestoreFlag)
End Function
```

You need to insert the code here from the function exportDocument() in Script 4.6.

Script 4.18: Create a Two-up Booklet Imposition

Imposing pages for final printing has always been the job of experienced prepress operators. There is good reason for this assignment of duty: The art and science of imposition is not a simple thing, especially for large multiple-signature books. But there is good reason to want to be able to perform imposition tasks yourself. Suppose that you're creating a short-run booklet that you want to print directly from a laser printer. Wouldn't it be nice to have all the pages in this booklet laid out for you for two-up printing onto something like tabloid paper? No need to call your local printer or prepress shop for this simple task. **Script 4.18** provides all you need to create 8-, 16-, and 32-page booklets that are laid out two pages to a sheet side, for a total of four pages per double-sided sheet. All the page-sequencing information has been built into the script, so you don't have to remember a thing. Just choose an Illustrator document for each page as the script prompts you, as in **Figure 4.61,** and the script will create separate laid-out documents for each side of each sheet that you need to print for your booklet. All the adjacent page pairings will be performed, and you'll end up with a folder full of PDF files ready to print, just like the sample output folder shown in **Figure 4.62!**

TIP *To create the starting Visual Basic project for this script, follow the steps explained in Figure 4.60.*

What Is Imposition?

Pages often need to be printed out of sequential order so that they can be bound together to create a sequentially numbered booklet. *Imposition*, or the act of creating printer's spreads, is the process of printing multiple pages on a piece of paper in such a way that when they are folded and bound together, they end up in the right order.

Take a simple four-page booklet that's comprised of four letter-size pages. To print these four pages on a double-size tabloid-size sheet of paper, you'll need to lay out the front of the sheet with pages 2 and 3 and the back with pages 1 and 4.

For a great deal of information on page imposition for printing, visit About.com's topic site on imposition at **http://desktoppub.about.com/cs/imposition/**.

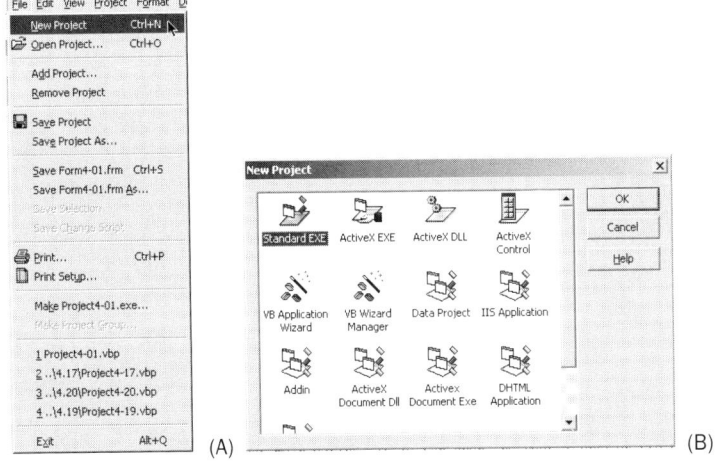
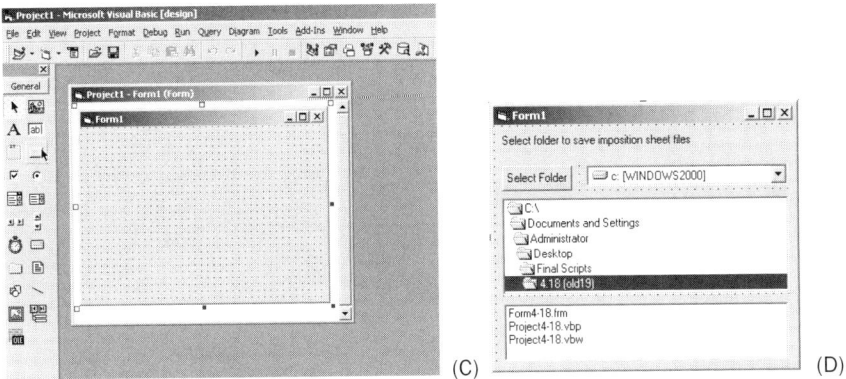

Figure 4.60 A-D *This series of screen shots illustrates the steps necessary to create a new project in the Visual Basic editor with a form in it so that you can add Script 4.18's code. (A) Start by choosing File > New Project. (B) Next, select a standard .exe project, and click the OK button. A new project will open, with a new form window showing as in (C). Select the CommandButton tool, and drag out a new button in the open form window. Set its caption to "Select Folder". Next, select the DriveListBox tool (looks like a hard disk), and draw a new drive list box. Select the FolderListBox tool (looks like a folder), and draw a new folder list box control. Now select the FileListBox tool (looks like a dog-eared document), and draw a new file list box. Finally, select the Label tool (looks like a capital letter A), add a label, and set its caption so that the form looks like (D).*

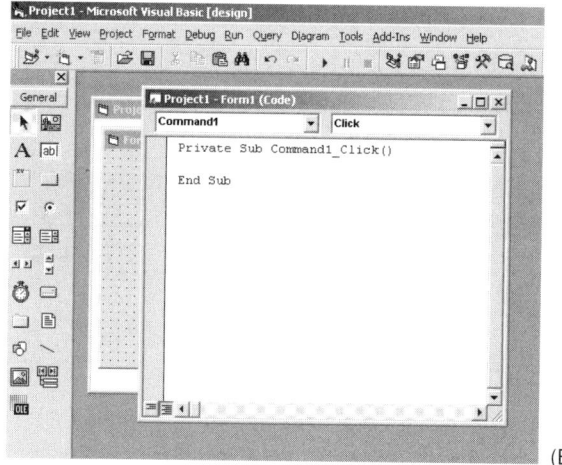
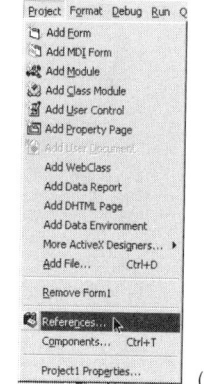

(E) (F)

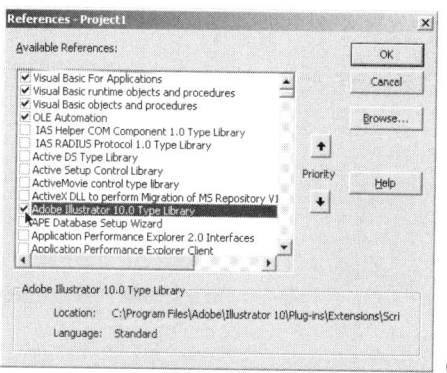

(G)

Figure 4.60 E-G *Double-click the button in the form to open its code window, shown in (E). This code window is where you will do your script writing. The last step before scripting is attaching a reference to the scripting libraries your project will use so that it will be able to work with Illustrator. To do this, choose Project > References, as shown in (F). Then locate the Adobe Illustrator 10.0 Type Library (G), and activate it by checking the box next to its name. Now you can close the References dialog by clicking the OK button. Time to write Visual Basic!*

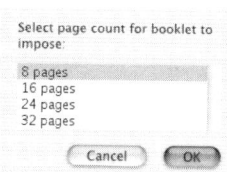

Figure 4.61 *A dialog displayed by the script, prompting the user to choose a page count for the imposition.*

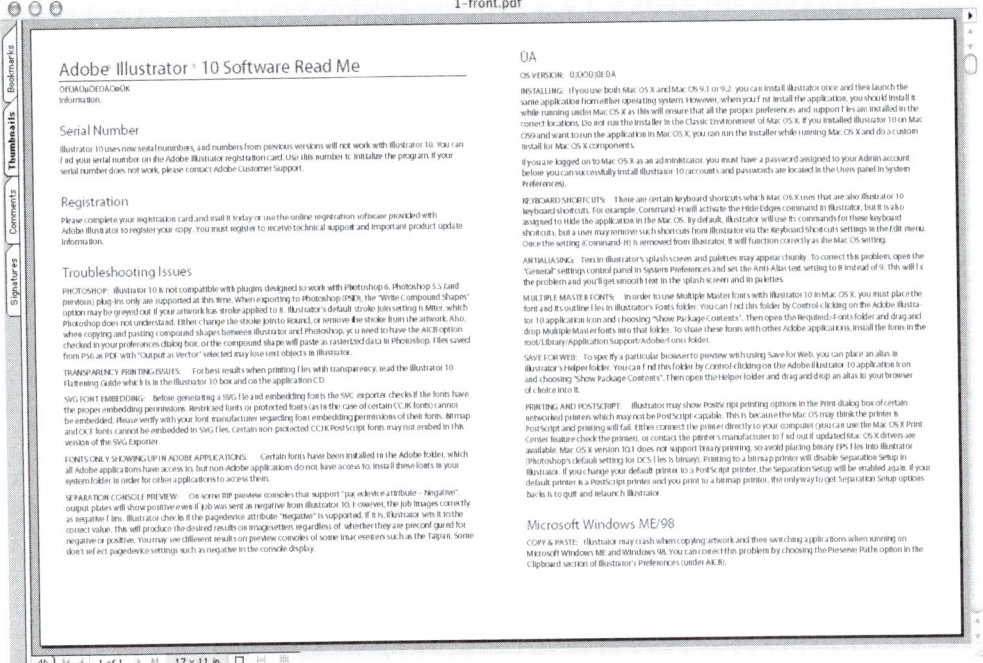

Figure 4.62 *A sample imposition spread shown in Adobe Acrobat after the script has created it as a PDF file.*

AppleScript

Script Tips This script supports impositions of 8, 16, 24, and 32 pages.

The script starts by prompting the user for the page count of the booklet to impose. If the user has made a choice, initialize lists of page pairs for the front and back of each sheet of the imposition layout. In a loop, the script gathers the page pairs for the front and back of the current sheet. The user is prompted for the four files that comprise the front-page pair and the back-page pair for an imposition sheet.

The script opens the left page for the front of the sheet in Illustrator. You get the document size to calculate the imposition-sheet size, which is the same height as and twice the width of a single page, because this is a two-up imposition. Now it is time to create an invisible rectangular path to bound the sheet size. Now export the current file as EPS to place in the imposition sheet. The document ends up being closed by the exportDocument() *function*.

Now the script opens the right page for the front of the sheet in Illustrator. Create an invisible rectangular path to bound the sheet size. Again, export the current file as EPS to place in the imposition sheet. The document ends up being closed by the exportDocument() *function*.

Now you can make the front-sheet imposition file. The script places each page's EPS file in a new sized document. It positions it so that the pages face on the imposed sheet. Then it exports the imposed sheet as a PDF with a file name that will make it easy to identify later when you want to print the booklet from Acrobat.

The script repeats each of the steps it performed for the front imposition sheet for the back sheet, converting the two pages to EPS files, creating a new document, placing and positioning each EPS, and saving a PDF for use later.

AppleScript

```
set myPageCount to (choose from list {"8 pages", "16 pages",
    "24 pages", "32 pages"} with prompt "Select page count for
    booklet to impose:")
set myFolder to (choose folder with prompt "Select folder to
    save imposition sheet files") as string
if class of myPageCount is list then
    set myPageCount to myPageCount as string
    if myPageCount = "8 pages" then
        set myFrontPagePairs to {{8, 1}, {6, 3}}
        set myBackPagePairs to {{2, 7}, {4, 5}}
    else if myPageCount = "16 pages" then
        set myFrontPagePairs to {{16, 1}, {14, 3}, {12, 5},
            {10, 7}}
        set myBackPagePairs to {{2, 15}, {4, 13}, {6, 11}, {8, 9}}
    else if myPageCount = "24 pages" then
        set myFrontPagePairs to {{24, 1}, {22, 3}, {20, 5},
            {18, 7}, {16, 8}, {14, 11}}
```

AS, cont'd.

```
        set myBackPagePairs to {{2, 23}, {4, 21}, {6, 19},
        {8, 17}, {10, 15}, {12, 13}}
    else if myPageCount = "32 pages" then
        set myFrontPagePairs to {{32, 1}, {30, 3}, {28, 5},
        {26, 7}, {24, 9}, {22, 11}, {20, 13}, {18, 15}}
        set myBackPagePairs to {{2, 31}, {4, 29}, {6, 27},
        {8, 25}, {10, 23}, {12, 21}, {14, 19}, {16, 17}}
    end if
    repeat with myNum from 1 to count of items in
    myFrontPagePairs
```

Gather page pairs for current sheet in loop.

```
        set myFrontPagePair to item myNum of myFrontPagePairs
        set myBackPagePair to item myNum of myBackPagePairs
        tell application "Adobe Illustrator 10"
            activate
            set myFrontPageLeft to (choose file with prompt "Sheet "
            & myNum & return & "Step 1 of 4" & return & "Select
            page # " & item 1 of myFrontPagePair as string)
            set myFrontPageRight to (choose file with prompt "Sheet "
            & myNum & return & "Step 2 of 4" & return & "Select
            page # " & item 2 of myFrontPagePair as string)
            set myBackPageLeft to (choose file with prompt "Sheet "
            & myNum & return & "Step 3 of 4" & return & "Select
            page # " & item 1 of myBackPagePair as string)
            set myBackPageRight to (choose file with prompt "Sheet "
            & myNum & return & "Step 4 of 4" & return & "Select
            page # " & item 2 of myBackPagePair as string)
```

Open left front page.

```
            open myFrontPageLeft
            set myPageWidth to width of document 1
            set myPageHeight to height of document 1
            set myPageColorSpace to color space of document 1
            set mySheetHeight to myPageHeight
            set mySheetWidth to myPageWidth * 2
            make new path item at beginning of document 1
                with properties {stroked:false, filled:false, entire
                path:{{anchor:{0, 0}, point type:corner},
                {anchor:{myPageWidth, 0}, point type:corner},
                {anchor:{myPageWidth, myPageHeight}, point
                type:corner}, {anchor:{0, myPageHeight}, point
                type:corner}, {anchor:{0, 0}, point type:corner}}}
```

AS, cont'd.

Open right front page.

Place left and right front pages in new document and export as PDF.

Open back left page.

Open back right page.

```
tell me to set myLeftFilePath to exportDocument("eps",
"", "", false)

open myFrontPageRight

make new path item at beginning of document 1
    with properties {stroked:false, filled:false, entire
    path:{{anchor:{0, 0}, point type:corner},
    {anchor:{myPageWidth, 0}, point type:corner},
    {anchor:{myPageWidth, myPageHeight}, point
    type:corner}, {anchor:{0, myPageHeight}, point
    type:corner}, {anchor:{0, 0}, point type:corner}}}

tell me to set myRightFilePath to exportDocument("eps",
"", "", false)

set myFrontDoc to (make new document with properties
{color space:myPageColorSpace, width:mySheetWidth,
height:mySheetHeight})

set myPlacedArt to (make new placed item at beginning
of myFrontDoc with properties {file path:alias
myLeftFilePath})

set position of myPlacedArt to {0, myPageHeight}

set myPlacedArt to (make new placed item at beginning
of myFrontDoc with properties {file path:alias
myRightFilePath})

set position of myPlacedArt to {myPageWidth,
myPageHeight}

tell me to set mySheetFilePath to exportDocument("pdf",
myNum & "-front", myFolder, false)

open myBackPageLeft

make new path item at beginning of document 1
    with properties {stroked:false, filled:false, entire
    path:{{anchor:{0, 0}, point type:corner},
    {anchor:{myPageWidth, 0}, point type:corner},
    {anchor:{myPageWidth, myPageHeight}, point
    type:corner}, {anchor:{0, myPageHeight}, point
    type:corner}, {anchor:{0, 0}, point type:corner}}}

tell me to set myLeftFilePath to exportDocument("eps",
"", "", false)

open myBackPageRight

make new path item at beginning of document 1
```

AS, cont'd.

```
        with properties {stroked:false, filled:false, entire
        path:{{anchor:{0, 0}, point type:corner},
        {anchor:{myPageWidth, 0}, point type:corner},
        {anchor:{myPageWidth, myPageHeight}, point
        type:corner}, {anchor:{0, myPageHeight}, point
        type:corner}, {anchor:{0, 0}, point type:corner}}}
    tell me to set myRightFilePath to exportDocument
    ("eps", "", "", false)
    set myBackDoc to (make new document with properties
    {color space:myPageColorSpace, width:mySheetWidth,
    height:mySheetHeight})
    set myPlacedArt to (make new placed item at beginning
    of myBackDoc with properties {file path:alias
    myLeftFilePath})
    set position of myPlacedArt to {0, myPageHeight}
    set myPlacedArt to (make new placed item at beginning
    of myBackDoc with properties {file path:alias
    myRightFilePath})
    set position of myPlacedArt to {myPageWidth,
    myPageHeight}
    tell me to set mySheetFilePath to exportDocument("pdf",
    myNum & "-back", myFolder, false)
        end tell
    end repeat
end if
on exportDocument(myFormat, myNameExtra, mySaveFolder,
    myRestoreFlag)
end exportDocument
```

> Place left and right back pages in new document and export as PDF.

> You need to insert the code here from the function exportDocument() in Script 4.6.

Visual Basic

Script Tips *The* `Drive1_Change()` *subroutine is called whenever the user changes the drive in the drive list box. It updates the paths of the directory list box and the file list box to the new drive selected.*

The `Dir1_Change()` *subroutine is called whenever the user changes the directory in the directory list box. It updates just the path of the file list box to the new directory selected.*

The main `Command1_Click()` subroutine is called whenever the user clicks the form's button. This script does a number of different things, depending on what the label caption on the button reads, allowing one form and set of controls to be used for multiple activities as the script runs. The script itself changes the captions of both the button and the label as it proceeds.

When the button reads "Select Folder", the first `Case` block of code will execute. If the directory list box has a directory selected, the user is prompted to choose the number of pages for the imposition. Next, based on the choice entered by the user, the script initializes arrays of page pairs for the front and back of each sheet of the imposition layout. Finally, it sets up the captions on the button and label for the next step in the process.

If the user clicked the button, and it reads "Step 1", the file list box is tested to make sure that a file has been selected. If so, the front-left page's file path is collected from the file list box's path.

If the user clicked the button, and it reads "Step 2", the file list box is tested to make sure that a file has been selected. If so, the front-right page's file path is collected from the file list box's path.

If the user clicked the button, and it reads "Step 3", the file list box is tested to make sure that a file has been selected. If so, the back-left page's file path is collected from the file list box's path.

If the user clicked the button, and it reads "Step 4", the file list box is tested to make sure that a file has been selected. If so, the back-right page's file path is collected from the file list box's path. Now you are ready to create impositions for the current sheet!

Immediately after the back-right page's file path is collected, the script opens the left page for the front of the sheet in Illustrator. It gets the document size to calculate the imposition-sheet size, which is the same height as and twice the width of a single page, because this is a two-up imposition. Now it is time to create an invisible rectangular path to bound the sheet size. Export the current file as EPS to place in the imposition sheet. The document will end up being closed by the `exportDocument()` *function.*

Now the right page for the front of the sheet is opened in Illustrator. The script creates an invisible rectangular path to bound the sheet size. And it exports the current file as EPS to place in the imposition sheet. The document will end up being closed by the `exportDocument()` *function.*

Now the script can make the front-sheet imposition file. The script places each page's EPS file and positions it so the pages face on the imposed sheet. Then it exports the imposed sheet as a PDF with a file name that will make it easy to identify later when you want to print the booklet from Acrobat.

TIPS The script repeats each of the steps it performed for the front imposition sheet for the back sheet, converting the two pages to EPS files, creating a new document, placing and positioning each EPS, and saving a PDF for use later.

Next, if there are more page-imposition sheets to create, the captions for the button and label are set. Otherwise, you're finished, so the button and label captions get set back to their original state.

VBScript

```
Option Explicit
Dim myApp As New Illustrator.Application
Dim myFolder, myFrontPageLeft, myFrontPageRight, myBackPageLeft,
    myBackPageRight
Dim myFrontPagePairs, myBackPagePairs, myNum
```

> *This Sub executes when the drive list box changes.*

```
Private Sub Drive1_Change()
    If Drive1.Drive <> "" Then
        Dir1.Path = Left(Drive1.Drive, 1) & ":\"
        File1.Path = Dir1.Path
    End If
End Sub
```

> *This Sub executes when the directory list box changes.*

```
Private Sub Dir1_Change()
    If File1.Path <> "" Then
        File1.Path = Dir1.Path
    End If
End Sub
```

> *This Sub executes when the button is clicked.*

```
Private Sub Command1_Click()
    Dim myPageCount, myValidPageCount, myPageWidth, myPageHeight,
        myPageColorSpace
    Dim mySheetHeight, mySheetWidth, myPath, myPathPoint
```

VBS, cont'd.

This Select decides what code gets run depending on the button's Caption text.

```
Dim myLeftFilePath, myRightFilePath, myFrontDoc, myBackDoc
Dim myPlacedArt, mySheetFilePath
If TypeName(myNum) = "Empty" Then myNum = 0
Select Case Command1.Caption

    Case "Select Folder"
        If Dir1.Path <> "" Then
            myFolder = Dir1.Path
            myPageCount = InputBox("Enter page
            count(8,16,24,32):", , "8")
            Select Case myPageCount
                Case "8"
                    myFrontPagePairs = Array(Array(8, 1),
                    Array(6, 3))
                    myBackPagePairs = Array(Array(2, 7),
                    Array(4, 5))
                    myValidPageCount = True
                Case "16"
                    myFrontPagePairs = Array(Array(16, 1),
                    Array(14, 3), Array(12, 5), Array(10, 7))
                    myBackPagePairs = Array(Array(2, 15),
                    Array(4, 13), Array(6, 11), Array(8, 9))
                    myValidPageCount = True
                Case "24"
                    myFrontPagePairs = Array(Array(24, 1),
                    Array(22, 3), Array(20, 5), Array(18, 7),
                    Array(16, 8), Array(14, 1))
                    myBackPagePairs = Array(Array(2, 23),
                    Array(4, 21), Array(6, 19), Array(8, 17),
                    Array(10, 15), Array(12, 13))
                    myValidPageCount = True
                Case "32"
                    myFrontPagePairs = Array(Array(32, 1),
                    Array(30, 3), Array(28, 5), Array(26, 7),
                    Array(24, 9), Array(22, 11), Array(20, 13),
                    Array(18, 15))
```

VBS, cont'd.

```
            myBackPagePairs = Array(Array(2, 31),
            Array(4, 29), Array(6, 27), Array(8, 25),
            Array(10, 23), Array(12, 21), Array(14, 19),
            Array(16, 17))
            myValidPageCount = True
          Case Else
            myValidPageCount = False
        End Select
        If myValidPageCount = True Then
          myNum = 0
          Command1.Caption = "Step 1"
          Label1.Caption = "Select page # " &
          myFrontPagePairs(myNum)(0)
        End If
      End If

    Case "Step 1"
      If File1.FileName <> "" Then
        myFrontPageLeft = File1.Path & "\" & File1.FileName
        Command1.Caption = "Step 2"
        Label1.Caption = "Select page # " &
        myFrontPagePairs(myNum)(1)
      End If

    Case "Step 2"
      If File1.FileName <> "" Then
        myFrontPageRight = File1.Path & "\" & File1.FileName
        Command1.Caption = "Step 3"
        Label1.Caption = "Select page # " &
        myBackPagePairs(myNum)(0)
      End If

    Case "Step 3"
      If File1.FileName <> "" Then
        myBackPageLeft = File1.Path & "\" & File1.FileName
```

VBS, cont'd.

```
            Command1.Caption = "Step 4"
            Label1.Caption = "Select page # " & _
                myBackPagePairs(myNum)(1)
        End If
```

> Once all page file paths are stored in variables, its time to create impositions for the sheet.

```
    Case "Step 4"
        If File1.FileName <> "" Then
            myBackPageRight = File1.Path & "\" & File1.FileName
            Set myApp = New illustrator.Application
```

> Open left front page.

```
            myApp.Open (myFrontPageLeft)
            myPageWidth = myApp.Documents(1).Width
            myPageHeight = myApp.Documents(1).Height
            myPageColorSpace = myApp.Documents(1).
                DocumentColorSpace
            mySheetHeight = myPageHeight
            mySheetWidth = myPageWidth * 2

            Set myPath = myApp.Documents(1).PathItems.Add
            myPath.Stroked = True
            myPath.Filled = False
            Set myPathPoint = myPath.PathPoints.Add
            myPathPoint.PointType = aiCorner
            myPathPoint.LeftDirection = Array(0, 0)
            myPathPoint.RightDirection = Array(0, 0)
            myPathPoint.Anchor = Array(0, 0)
            Set myPathPoint = myPath.PathPoints.Add
            myPathPoint.PointType = aiCorner
            myPathPoint.LeftDirection = Array(myPageWidth, 0)
            myPathPoint.RightDirection = Array(myPageWidth, 0)
            myPathPoint.Anchor = Array(myPageWidth, 0)
            Set myPathPoint = myPath.PathPoints.Add
            myPathPoint.PointType = aiCorner
            myPathPoint.LeftDirection = Array(myPageWidth,
                myPageHeight)
```

VBS, cont'd.

```
myPathPoint.RightDirection = Array(myPageWidth, myPageHeight)
myPathPoint.Anchor = Array(myPageWidth, myPageHeight)
Set myPathPoint = myPath.PathPoints.Add
myPathPoint.PointType = aiCorner
myPathPoint.LeftDirection = Array(0, myPageHeight)
myPathPoint.RightDirection = Array(0, myPageHeight)
myPathPoint.Anchor = Array(0, myPageHeight)
Set myPathPoint = myPath.PathPoints.Add
myPathPoint.PointType = aiCorner
myPathPoint.LeftDirection = Array(0, 0)
myPathPoint.RightDirection = Array(0, 0)
myPathPoint.Anchor = Array(0, 0)

myLeftFilePath = exportDocument("eps", "", "", False)
```

Open right front page.

```
myApp.Open (myFrontPageRight)
Set myPath = myApp.Documents(1).PathItems.Add
myPath.Stroked = True
myPath.Filled = False
Set myPathPoint = myPath.PathPoints.Add
myPathPoint.PointType = aiCorner
myPathPoint.LeftDirection = Array(0, 0)
myPathPoint.RightDirection = Array(0, 0)
myPathPoint.Anchor = Array(0, 0)
Set myPathPoint = myPath.PathPoints.Add
myPathPoint.PointType = aiCorner
myPathPoint.LeftDirection = Array(myPageWidth, 0)
myPathPoint.RightDirection = Array(myPageWidth, 0)
myPathPoint.Anchor = Array(myPageWidth, 0)
Set myPathPoint = myPath.PathPoints.Add
myPathPoint.PointType = aiCorner
myPathPoint.LeftDirection = Array(myPageWidth, myPageHeight)
```

VBS, cont'd.

```
myPathPoint.RightDirection = Array(myPageWidth, myPageHeight)
myPathPoint.Anchor = Array(myPageWidth, myPageHeight)
Set myPathPoint = myPath.PathPoints.Add
myPathPoint.PointType = aiCorner
myPathPoint.LeftDirection = Array(0, myPageHeight)
myPathPoint.RightDirection = Array(0, myPageHeight)
myPathPoint.Anchor = Array(0, myPageHeight)
Set myPathPoint = myPath.PathPoints.Add
myPathPoint.PointType = aiCorner
myPathPoint.LeftDirection = Array(0, 0)
myPathPoint.RightDirection = Array(0, 0)
myPathPoint.Anchor = Array(0, 0)

myRightFilePath = exportDocument("eps", "", "", False)

Set myFrontDoc = myApp.Documents.Add(myPageColorSpace, mySheetWidth, mySheetHeight)

Set myPlacedArt = myApp.Documents(1).PlacedItems.Add
myPlacedArt.MoveToBeginning (myFrontDoc)
myPlacedArt.File = myLeftFilePath
myPlacedArt.Position = Array(0, myPageHeight)
Set myPlacedArt = myApp.Documents(1).PlacedItems.Add
myPlacedArt.MoveToBeginning (myFrontDoc)
myPlacedArt.File = myRightFilePath
myPlacedArt.Position = Array(myPageWidth, myPageHeight)
mySheetFilePath = exportDocument
("pdf", (myNum + 1) & "-front", myFolder, False)
myApp.Open (myBackPageLeft)
Set myPath = myApp.Documents(1).PathItems.Add
myPath.Stroked = True
myPath.Filled = False
Set myPathPoint = myPath.PathPoints.Add
```

Place left and right front pages in new document and export as PDF.

Open back left page.

VBS, cont'd.

```
myPathPoint.PointType = aiCorner
myPathPoint.LeftDirection = Array(0, 0)
myPathPoint.RightDirection = Array(0, 0)
myPathPoint.Anchor = Array(0, 0)
Set myPathPoint = myPath.PathPoints.Add
myPathPoint.PointType = aiCorner
myPathPoint.LeftDirection = Array(myPageWidth, 0)
myPathPoint.RightDirection = Array(myPageWidth, 0)
myPathPoint.Anchor = Array(myPageWidth, 0)
Set myPathPoint = myPath.PathPoints.Add
myPathPoint.PointType = aiCorner
myPathPoint.LeftDirection = Array(myPageWidth, 
    myPageHeight)
myPathPoint.RightDirection = Array(myPageWidth, 
    myPageHeight)
myPathPoint.Anchor = Array(myPageWidth, myPageHeight)
Set myPathPoint = myPath.PathPoints.Add
myPathPoint.PointType = aiCorner
myPathPoint.LeftDirection = Array(0, myPageHeight)
myPathPoint.RightDirection = Array(0, myPageHeight)
myPathPoint.Anchor = Array(0, myPageHeight)
Set myPathPoint = myPath.PathPoints.Add
myPathPoint.PointType = aiCorner
myPathPoint.LeftDirection = Array(0, 0)
myPathPoint.RightDirection = Array(0, 0)
myPathPoint.Anchor = Array(0, 0)
myLeftFilePath = exportDocument("eps", "", "", False)
```

Open back right page.

```
myApp.Open (myBackPageRight)
Set myPath = myApp.Documents(1).PathItems.Add
myPath.Stroked = True
myPath.Filled = False
Set myPathPoint = myPath.PathPoints.Add
myPathPoint.PointType = aiCorner
myPathPoint.LeftDirection = Array(0, 0)
```

VBS, cont'd.

```
myPathPoint.RightDirection = Array(0, 0)
myPathPoint.Anchor = Array(0, 0)
Set myPathPoint = myPath.PathPoints.Add
myPathPoint.PointType = aiCorner
myPathPoint.LeftDirection = Array(myPageWidth, 0)
myPathPoint.RightDirection = Array(myPageWidth, 0)
myPathPoint.Anchor = Array(myPageWidth, 0)
Set myPathPoint = myPath.PathPoints.Add
myPathPoint.PointType = aiCorner
myPathPoint.LeftDirection = Array(myPageWidth,
myPageHeight)
myPathPoint.RightDirection = Array(myPageWidth,
myPageHeight)
myPathPoint.Anchor = Array(myPageWidth, myPageHeight)
Set myPathPoint = myPath.PathPoints.Add
myPathPoint.PointType = aiCorner
myPathPoint.LeftDirection = Array(0, myPageHeight)
myPathPoint.RightDirection = Array(0, myPageHeight)
myPathPoint.Anchor = Array(0, myPageHeight)
Set myPathPoint = myPath.PathPoints.Add
myPathPoint.PointType = aiCorner
myPathPoint.LeftDirection = Array(0, 0)
myPathPoint.RightDirection = Array(0, 0)
myPathPoint.Anchor = Array(0, 0)
myRightFilePath = exportDocument("eps", "", "", False)

Set myBackDoc = myApp.Documents.Add(myPageColorSpace,
mySheetWidth, mySheetHeight)
Set myPlacedArt = myApp.Documents(1).PlacedItems.Add
myPlacedArt.MoveToBeginning (myBackDoc)
myPlacedArt.File = myLeftFilePath
myPlacedArt.Position = Array(0, myPageHeight)
Set myPlacedArt = myApp.Documents(1).PlacedItems.Add
myPlacedArt.MoveToBeginning (myBackDoc)
myPlacedArt.File = myRightFilePath
```

Place left and right back pages in new document and export as PDF.

VBS, cont'd.

```vbs
            myPlacedArt.Position = Array(myPageWidth, _
                myPageHeight)
            mySheetFilePath = exportDocument("pdf", (myNum + 1) & _
                "-back", myFolder, False)
            If myNum <= UBound(myFrontPagePairs) Then
                myNum = myNum + 1
                Command1.Caption = "Step 1"
                Label1.Caption = "Select page # " & _
                    myFrontPagePairs(myNum)(0)
                
            Else
                Command1.Caption = "Select Folder"
                Label1.Caption = "Select folder to save imposition sheet files"
                
            End If
        End If
    End Select
End Sub
```

> *You need to insert the code here from the function exportDocument() in Script 4.6.*

```vbs
Private Function exportDocument(myFormat, myNameExtra, _
    mySaveFolder, myRestoreFlag)
End Function
```

Script 4.19: Merge Database Text with Template to Create Custom Documents

One of the most typical needs that production-oriented Illustrator users have is to mass-produce customized documents based on a template. For example, you may have a document that you want to mail-merge with a database, replacing placeholder text in the template with actual data from various fields in a database. Illustrator 10 provides some automatic support for templates and data with its Variables palette and datasets. But exporting and reformatting your database data to work with the fixed XML format required for importing datasets is no simple task.

Script 4.19 shows you how to do database text merging in a template without having to figure out how to export your data in an XML format that is compatible with Illustrator's datasets. The script replaces many placeholders in a document as you create, using a simple formula for the placeholder text of a hash mark (or number sign) on either side of the field name you want to insert. If you wanted to insert data into your document from a field named email, for example, you'd just type **#email#** in some portion of a text art item in the document.

Before you begin Script 4.19, you must have a database source from which to get your data. Perhaps you already have a database ready to go in one of the two database applications you're using: FileMaker Pro or Microsoft Access. If not, follow along with the steps that correspond to the database application you're using to create a sample database.

To create a sample database in FileMaker Pro 5.5, follow these steps:

1. Choose File > New to open the New Database dialog.

2. Choose Create a New Empty File, as shown in **Figure 4.63**, and click the OK button.

3. Save the new database document with the name Personalize, as shown in **Figure 4.64**.

Now you are ready to define some fields in your database.

4. Add two text fields named email and name, respectively, as shown in **Figure 4.65**; then click the Done button.

Finally, you can add some data to the database.

5. Create two new records, and populate them with some sample data, as in **Figure 4.66**.

Leave the database open, and you're ready to AppleScript.

To create a sample database in Microsoft Access and prepare it for script access, follow these steps:

1. Choose File > New to open the New dialog.

2. Select the database icon and click the OK button, as shown in **Figure 4.67**.

3. Save the new database document with the name Personalize.mdb, as shown in **Figure 4.68**.

4. Create a new table in your database by double-clicking the Create Table in Design View option in the database's main window, as shown in **Figure 4.69**.

Now you are ready to define some fields in your database.

5. Add two Memo fields named email and name, respectively, as shown in **Figure 4.70**; then click the close button in the top-right corner of the window.

6. When Access asks whether you want to save changes to the table, click Yes button.

7. Name the new table data, and click the OK button, as shown in **Figure 4.71**.

   Access will ask whether you want to add a primary key to the table. This choice is your call; your script doesn't care whether a key exists in the table or not. Generally speaking, it's a good idea to have a primary key defined in every table you make in Access.

   At this point, you should be back at the main database window, which now displays the newly added data table, as **Figure 4.72** shows.

8. Double-click the table's entry to add some records of data to the table.

   Enter a couple of records like the ones shown in **Figure 4.73** before you close the table (by clicking its window's close button).

   Now you are ready to connect the database to the ODBC Data Sources control panel, granting scripts access to the database.

9. Locate and open the control panel in your Control Panels folder or inside one of the folders it contains, depending on your version of Windows.

   In my case, I'm using Windows 2000 Professional, which places the control panel in the Administrative Tools folder inside Control Panels, as shown in **Figure 4.74**.

10. When the control panel opens, switch to the System DSN tab, and click the Add button, as shown in **Figure 4.75**.

11. Choose the English version of the Access driver to let your computer know that you're connecting an Access database to the ODBC drivers, as shown in **Figure 4.76**.

    ODBC, by the way, stands for *Open Data Base Connectivity*, and it is the protocol that many systems use to access shared databases.

    Now it is time to specify your ODBC Data Source Name (DSN). You will use this name to refer to your database in the Visual Basic script.

12. Name your DSN **personalize**, as shown in **Figure 4.77**.

13. Click the Select button, and navigate to find your Access database wherever you saved it, as shown in **Figure 4.78**.

14. Click the OK button in each of the screens left open in the control panel until it is closed.

Now you can write your Visual Basic script to access the database.

TIP To create the starting Visual Basic project for this script, follow the steps explained in **Figure 4.79**.

When you're ready to test the script with an Illustrator document, start with something simple like the basic business card example shown in **Figure 4.80** with its two dynamic placeholders for name and email set. The exported PDF documents created by script with the sample data in your database and the placeholder template will look something like the samples in **Figure 4.81**.

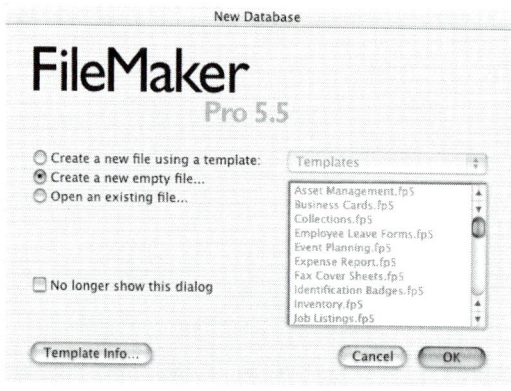

Figure 4.63 FileMaker Pro's New Database dialog.

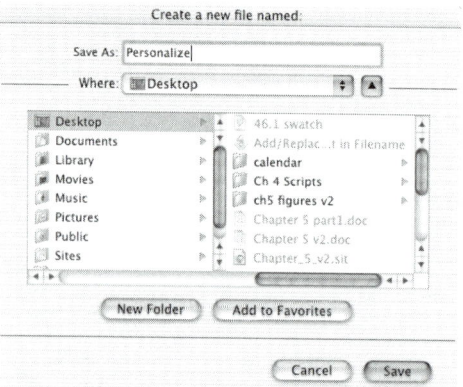

Figure 4.64 The Create a New File Named dialog of FileMaker Pro, with the new database about to be saved as the file named Personalize.

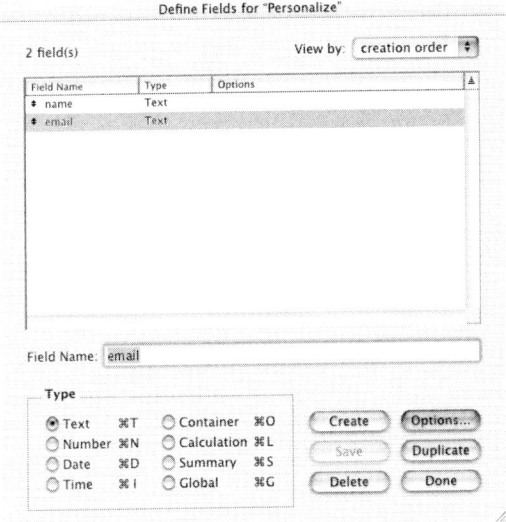

Figure 4.65 *FileMaker Pro's Define Fields dialog, with two fields already defined.*

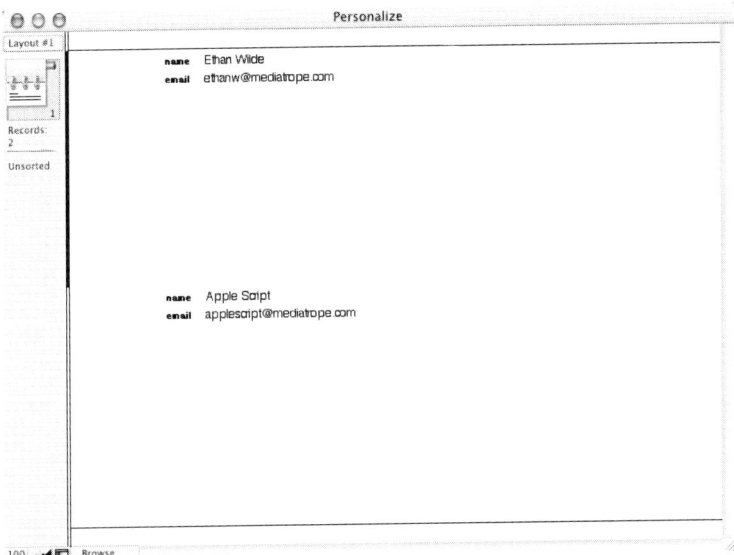

Figure 4.66 *The Browse mode of FileMaker allows you to enter data in records and create new records easily.*

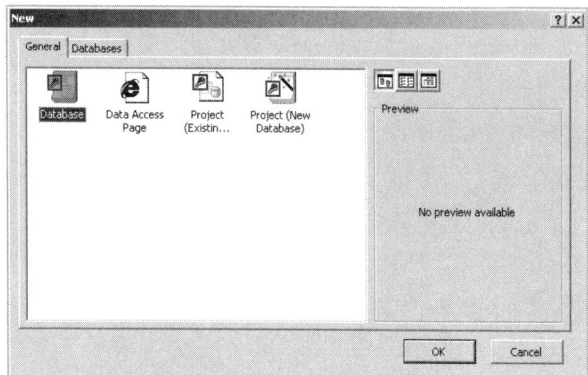

Figure 4.67 Microsoft Access's New dialog, ready to allow you to create a new database.

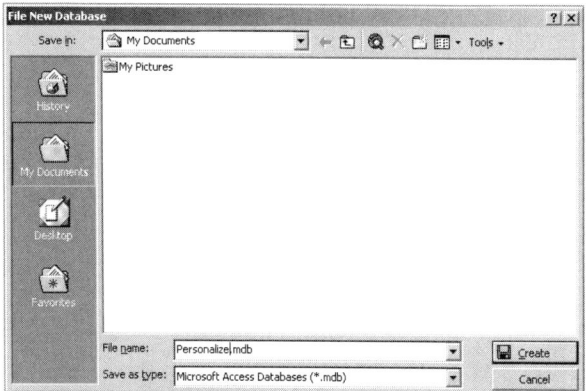

Figure 4.68 The File New Database dialog of Access is where you choose the location to save your new database.

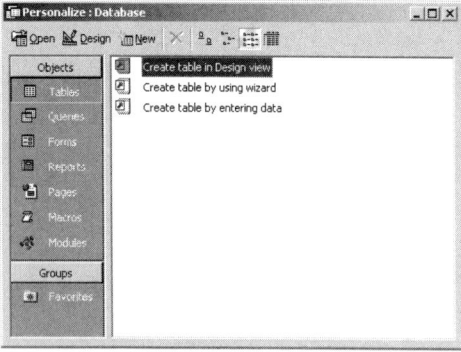

Figure 4.69 Access's main database window, providing options for working with all the objects that can stored inside an Access database.

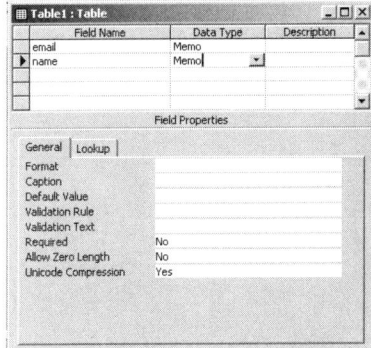

Figure 4.70 The Design view of Microsoft Access lets you create and edit new database tables.

Figure 4.71 Access displays the Save As dialog when you are ready to save your new database table.

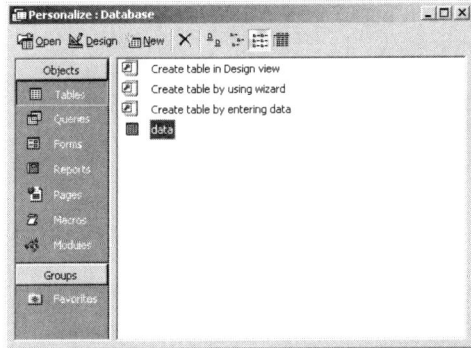

Figure 4.72 The main database window of the sample database shows a new table named data.

Figure 4.73 The data table window of the sample database shows two records that have been entered.

Figure 4.74 The ODBC Data Sources control panel is a required—yet less than obvious—part of working with databases from Visual Basic.

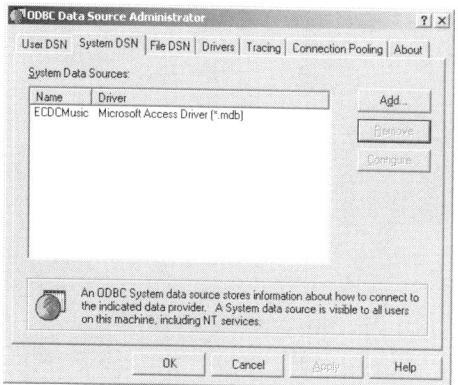

Figure 4.75 The System DSN tab of the control panel lets you link various kinds of databases to ODBC drivers so that your scripts can access the databases.

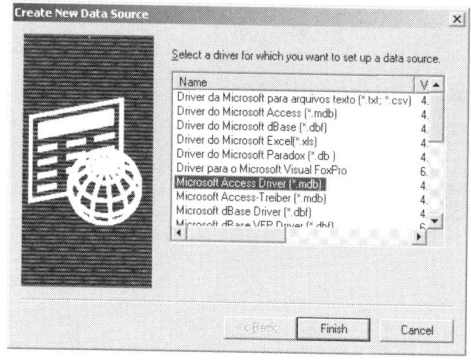

Figure 4.76 You need to select the kind of ODBC driver you want to use with your database. This choice depends solely on the kind of database you have.

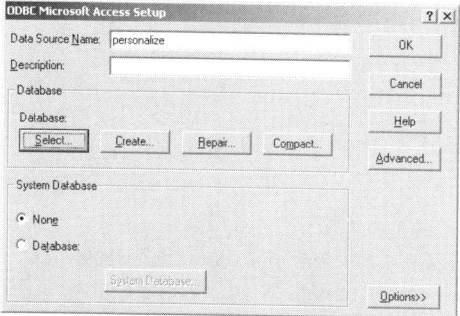

Figure 4.77 The name you assign to your DSN is the name you will use to access the database from your script.

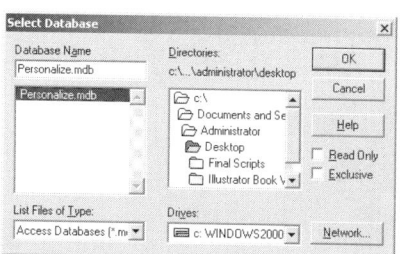

Figure 4.78 Last but not least, you need to select the database file to connect to the DSN. In this case, choose your sample database, Personalize.mdb.

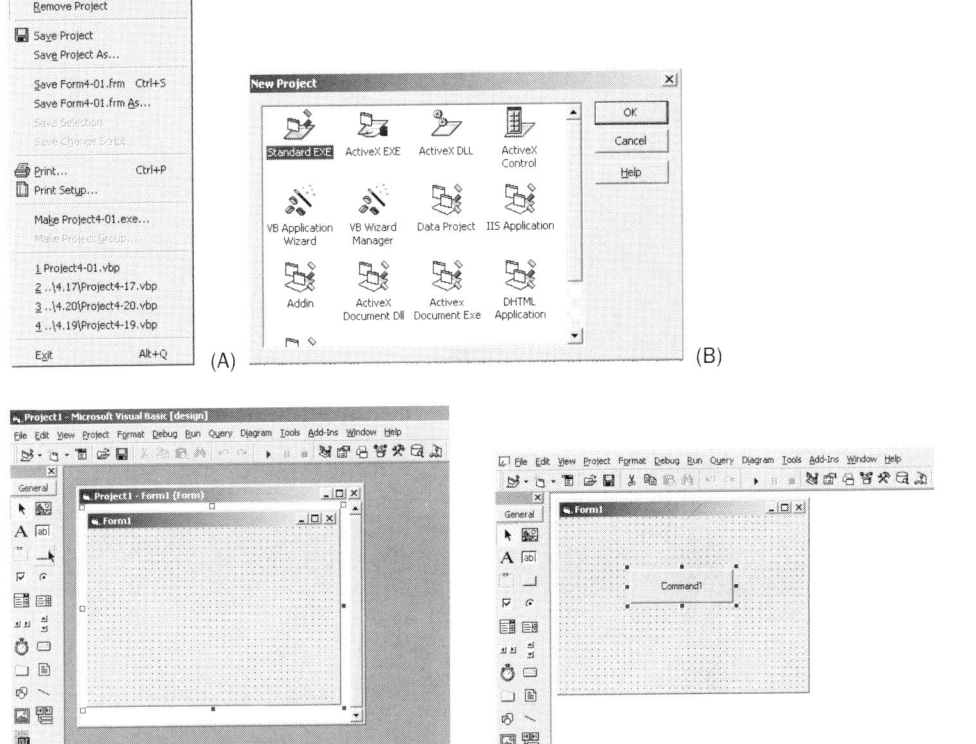

Figure 4.79 A-D *This series of screen shots illustrates the steps necessary to create a new project in the Visual Basic editor with a form in it so that you can add Script 4.19's code. (A) Start by choosing File > New Project. (B) Next, select a standard .exe project, and click the OK button. A new project will open, with a new form window showing as in (C). Select the CommandButton tool, and drag out a new button in the open form window so that the form looks like (D).*

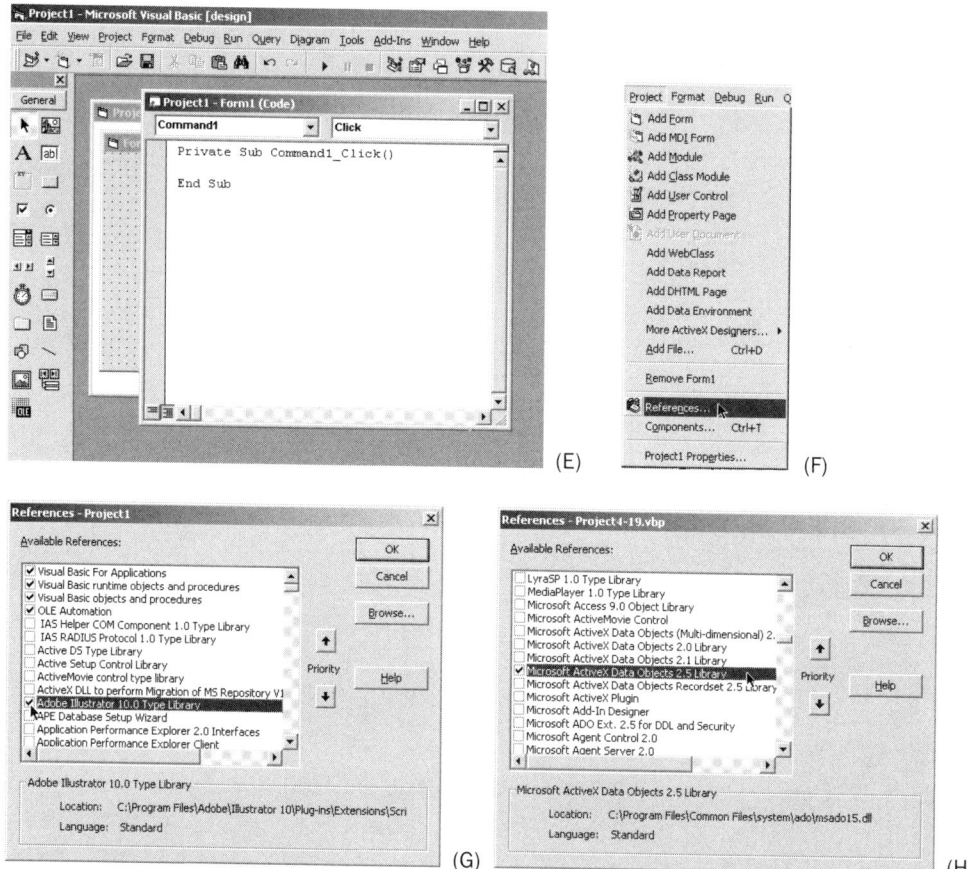

Figure 4.79 E-H *Double-click the button in the form to open its code window, shown in (E). This code window is where you will do your script writing. Next, choose Project > References, as shown in (F). Then locate the Adobe Illustrator 10.0 Type Library (G), and activate it by checking the box next to its name. Next, locate the Microsoft ActiveX Data Objects Library 2.5, shown in (H), and add it as well. Now you can close the References dialog by clicking the OK button. It is finally time to write Visual Basic!*

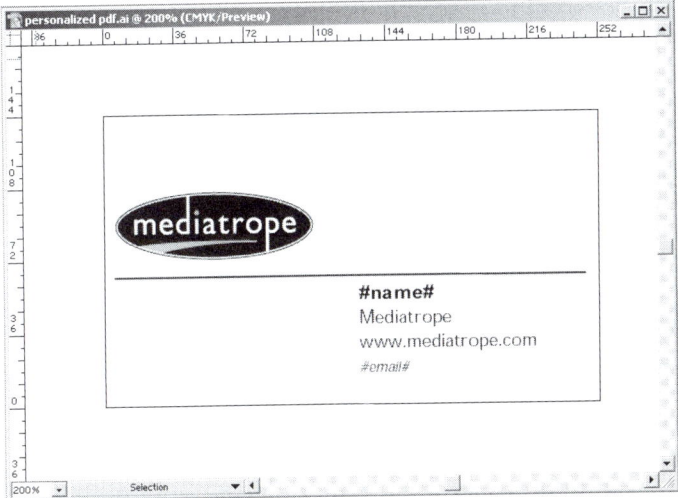

Figure 4.80 The sample template document is a simple business card. It contains placeholder text for two database fields: email and name.

Figure 4.81 The two customized PDF documents are reopened by hand in Illustrator after the script has run to check them out. Notice that the placeholder text has been swapped with data from fields in each of the two sample database records you created earlier.

AppleScript

Script Tips If at least one document is open in Illustrator, and one or more records exist in the frontmost open FileMaker database, the script proceeds.

A repeat *loop is started that will move through all the records in the database. The field names and their values for the current record are stored in variables for later use. Next, a nested loop runs through each of the items in the list variable* myFieldNames *holding all the field names. This loop will allow the script to insert values from any named field into the document.*

The final nested loop traverses all text art items in the document so that the script can look at the contents of each, searching and replacing any matches found for the current field name with the value from that field in the current record. The text replacing is performed by a simple function, doReplace(), *explained later.*

The last step to perform before moving to the next record in the database is exporting the customized document as a PDF, using the exportDocument() *function that you've used so many times before.*

The doReplace() *function receives three parameters: the source string to search, the string to find, and the string with which to replace any found instances. The function loops for as long as any matches of the search string are found in the source, replacing each with the new replacement string. Finally, it returns the updated string to the script that called it.*

AppleScript

```
tell application "Adobe Illustrator 10" to set mycount to count
    of documents
if mycount > 0 then
    tell application "FileMaker Pro" to set myrecordcount to
        count of records of document 1
```

This loop moves through records in the database.

```
    if myrecordcount > 0 then
        repeat with myNum from 1 to myrecordcount
            tell application "FileMaker Pro"
                set myFieldNames to name of cells of record myNum of
                    document 1
                set myFieldValues to cellValue of cells of record
                    myNum of document 1
            end tell
```

This loop moves through fields in the current record.

```
            repeat with myFieldNum from 1 to count of items in
                myFieldNames
                tell application "Adobe Illustrator 10"
```

The final loop moves through text art items in the front document.

```
                    repeat with myTextNum from 1 to count of text art
                        items in document 1
                        set myDynamicText to contents of text art item
                            myTextNum of document 1 as string
```

AS, cont'd.

```applescript
                    tell me to set myDynamicText to
                        doReplace(myDynamicText, "#" & item myFieldNum
                        of myFieldNames & "#", item myFieldNum of
                        myFieldValues)
                    set contents of text art item myTextNum of
                        document 1 to myDynamicText
                end repeat
            end tell
        end repeat
        exportDocument("pdf", myNum, "", true)
    end repeat
end if
end if
```

This function replaces all instances of a substring with another substring.

```applescript
on doReplace(mySource, myFind, myReplace)
    repeat while (offset of myFind in mySource) > 0
        set myOffset to offset of myFind in mySource
        if myOffset > 1 then
            set myStartChars to text of characters 1 thru
                (myOffset - 1) of mySource as string
        else
            set myStartChars to ""
        end if
        if myOffset + (count of characters in myFind) ≤ (count of
            characters in mySource) then
            set myEndChars to text of characters (myOffset + (count
                of characters in myFind)) thru (count of characters in
                mySource) of mySource as string
        else
            set myEndChars to ""
        end if
        set mySource to myStartChars & myReplace & myEndChars as
            string
    end repeat
    return mySource
end doReplace
```

You need to insert the code here from the function exportDocument() in Script 4.6.

```applescript
on exportDocument(myFormat, myNameExtra, mySaveFolder,
    myRestoreFlag)

end exportDocument
```

Visual Basic

Script Tips *If at least one document is open in Illustrator, the script proceeds. The next step is opening a connection to your database via ODBC, using your Data Source Name (DSN). Now the script can create a new empty recordset to hold the results of a query of the database. You use SQL to talk to the database and ask it to return all fields for all records contained in the data table you created and populated.*

If any records exist in the database table, the script begins a loop of all the records in the database. Next, a loop runs through each field in the current recordset. This loop allows the script to insert values from any named field into the document.

The final nested loop traverses all text art items in the document so that the script can look at the contents of each, searching and replacing any matches found for the current field name with the value from that field in the current record. The text replacing is performed by Visual Basic's built-in Replace() *function.*

The last step to perform before moving to the next record in the database is exporting the customized document as a PDF, using the exportDocument() *function that you've used so many times before.*

VBScript

```
Option Explicit
Dim myApp As New Illustrator.Application


Private Sub Command1_Click()
    Dim myDBConnection, myFoundRecords, mySQLStatement, myRecordCount, myNum
    Dim myField, myTextNum, myDynamicText, myNewPath
    If myApp.Documents.Count > 0 Then

        Set myDBConnection = New ADODB.Connection
        myDBConnection.Open "personalize", "", ""

        Set myFoundRecords = New ADODB.Recordset
        mySQLStatement = "SELECT * FROM [data]"
        myFoundRecords.Open mySQLStatement, myDBConnection, 3, 3
```

VBS, cont'd.

This loop moves through records in the database.

This loop moves through fields in the current record.

The final loop moves through text art items in the front document.

```
        myRecordCount = myFoundRecords.RecordCount
        If myRecordCount > 0 Then
            myNum = 1
            Do While Not myFoundRecords.EOF

                For Each myField In myFoundRecords.Fields
                    For myTextNum = 1 To myApp.Documents(1).
                    TextArtItems.Count
                        myDynamicText = myApp.Documents(1).TextArtItems
                        (myTextNum).Contents
                        myDynamicText = Replace(myDynamicText, "#" &
                        myField.Name & "#", myField.Value)
                        myApp.Documents(1).TextArtItems(myTextNum).
                        Contents = myDynamicText

                    Next
                Next
                myNewPath = exportDocument("pdf", myNum, "", True)

                myNum = myNum + 1
                myFoundRecords.MoveNext
            Loop
        End If
        myFoundRecords.Close
        Set myFoundRecords = Nothing
        myDBConnection.Close
        Set myDBConnection = Nothing
    End If
End Sub
```

You need to insert the code here from the function exportDocument() in Script 4.6.

```
Private Function exportDocument(myFormat, myNameExtra,
    mySaveFolder, myRestoreFlag)
End Function
```

Script 4.20: Import Database Data into a Document as Datasets

Working with database data and the Variables palette can be a challenge if you have to write out the complete XML file necessary to import datasets into an existing Illustrator document. **Script 4.20** shows a novel and more compelling way to get your data into datasets in Illustrator. The approach taken here is pretty much 180 degrees from building your own dataset XML file for import. This script creates datasets in an existing document simply by applying the data from a database record's fields to the page items that have variables bound to them. Then the script takes a dataset snapshot to create a new dataset before moving to the next record in the database. To keep things simple, you'll start by using the database you created in Script 4.19. If you haven't already created this database, using FileMaker Pro or Microsoft Access, skip back to the steps in the preceding section to prepare the database.

Before starting this scripting endeavor, you'll need to bind a variable to each of the text art items that you used in Script 4.19—namely, the ones with **#name#** and **#email#** as their contents. Follow these steps:

1. Select the first text art item and then choose Make Text Dynamic from the Variables palette's pop-out menu, as shown in **Figure 4.82**.

2. Repeat Step 1 for the second text art item.

   When you're done with the binding steps, the Variables palette should look something like **Figure 4.83**.

   Now it is time to rename each of the variables to match your database field names. You do this because the script copies data over to variable's page items only when the variable name matches the database field name. This arrangement keeps the script very flexible and adaptable to any document and database without any recoding.

3. To rename the first variable, double-click its entry in the Variables palette.

   The Variable Options dialog appears, as shown in **Figure 4.84**.

4. Enter **name** in the Name field, and click the OK button.

5. Repeat steps 3 and 4 for the second variable, naming this one email.

   When you're done, the Variables palette should look like **Figure 4.85**.

Once you run the script in import data, you'll have a number of datasets added to the Variables palette, like the example shown in **Figure 4.86**.

TIPS *Graph variables are not handled by this script, because graph data cannot be updated from a script.*

To create the starting Visual Basic project for this script, follow the steps explained for Script 4.19 in Figure 4.79.

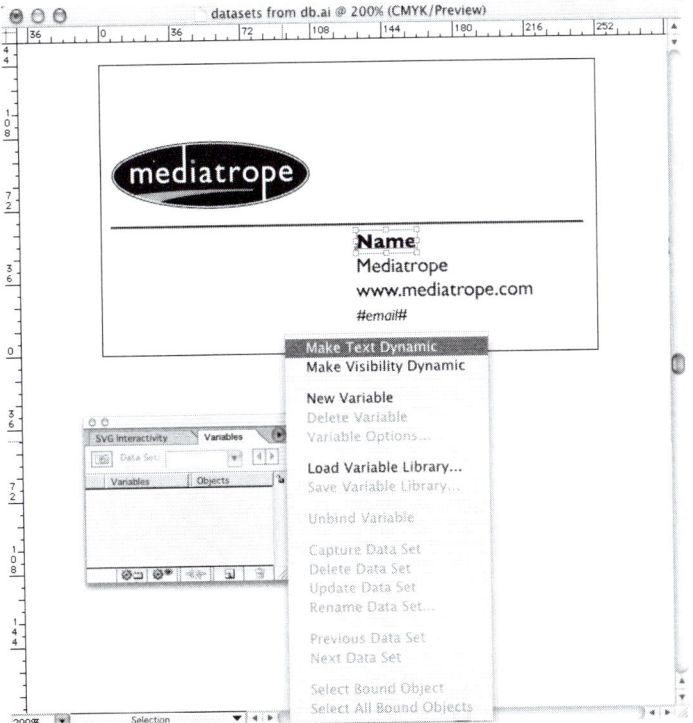

Figure 4.82 *The variable-binding process starts when you select a page item (text art, in this case) and choose Make Text Dynamic from the Variables palette's pop-out menu.*

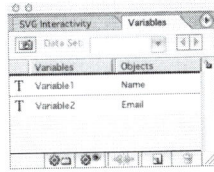

Figure 4.83 *The Variables palette shows two variables in this document, each bound to one page item.*

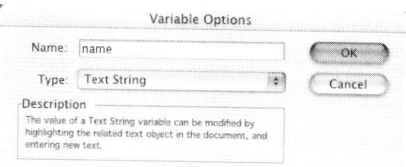

Figure 4.84 The Variable Options dialog lets you assign specific names to each of your document's variables.

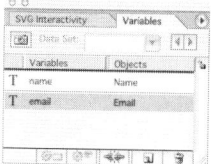

Figure 4.85 When all the variables have unique assigned names, the Variables palette will look like this screen shot.

Figure 4.86 The sample document is shown along with its Variables palette after Script 4.20 has run. Notice that there are two datasets in the palette and that the text art contents of the two bound text art items reflect the last database record's values.

AppleScript

Script Tips *If at least one document is open in Illustrator, and one or more records exist in the frontmost open FileMaker database, the script proceeds. A loop is started that will move through all the records in the database. The field names and their values for the current record are stored in variables for later use.*

Next, two nested loops run through all the field names and all Illustrator document variables, respectively. These loops will allow the script to associate field data with a matching-named variable's page items.

The final nested loop inside all the others moves through each of the page items bound to the current variable in the next-outermost loop. In this loop, the type of variable is checked and the appropriate page item property is set: the file path for placed and raster items bound to image variables, contents for text art items bound to textual variables, and visibility for page items of any kind bound to visibility variables. Notice that the visiblity test looks to see whether the field data equals true or yes when the script decides whether to show or hide the page item.

Finally, after the script loops though all the page items bound to all the variables that have names that match your database field names, you create a new dataset that will capture all the page-item properties you set in the innermost loop.

AppleScript

```
tell application "Adobe Illustrator 10" to set mycount to count
    of documents
if mycount > 0 then
    tell application "FileMaker Pro" to set myrecordcount to
        count of records of document 1
    if myrecordcount > 0 then
        repeat with myNum from 1 to myrecordcount
            tell application "FileMaker Pro"
                set myFieldNames to name of cells of record myNum of
                    document 1
                set myFieldValues to cellValue of cells of record
                    myNum of document 1
            end tell
            tell application "Adobe Illustrator 10"
                repeat with myNum from 1 to count of items in
                    myFieldNames
                    repeat with myVarNum from 1 to count of variables
                        in document 1
```

> This loop moves through records in the database.

> These two nested loops move through database fields and Illustrator document variables, respectively.

AS, cont'd.

```
                    if name of variable myVarNum of document 1 is
                        (item myNum of myFieldNames as string) then
                        repeat with myItemCount from 1 to count of
                            page items of variable myVarNum of document 1
                            if kind of variable myVarNum of document 1
                                is image then
                                try
                                    set file path of page item myItemCount
                                        of variable myVarNum of document 1 to
                                        (item myNum of myFieldValues as alias)
                                end try
                            else if kind of variable myVarNum of
                                document 1 is textual then
                                set contents of page item myItemCount of
                                    variable myVarNum of document 1 to (item
                                    myNum of myFieldValues as string)
                            else if kind of variable myVarNum of
                                document 1 is visibility then
                                if (item myNum of myFieldValues as
                                    string) is "true" or "yes" then
                                    set visibility of page item
                                        myItemCount of variable myVarNum of
                                        document 1 to true
                                else
                                    set visibility of page item
                                        myItemCount of variable myVarNum of
                                        document 1 to false
                                end if
                            end if
                        end repeat
                    end if
                end repeat
            end repeat
            make new dataset at document 1
        end tell
    end repeat
    end if
end if
```

A new dataset is created after page items bound to variables are updated with the current record's field data.

Visual Basic

Script Tips If at least one document is open in Illustrator, the script proceeds. The next step is opening a connection to your database via ODBC, using your Data Source Name (DSN). Now the script can create a new empty recordset to hold the results of a query of the database. You use SQL to talk to the database and ask it to return all fields for all records contained in the data table you created and populated.

If any records exist in the database table, the script begins a loop of all the records in the database. Next, two nested loops run through all the field names and all Illustrator document variables, respectively. These loops will allow the script to associate field data with a matching-named variable's page items.

The final nested loop inside all the others moves through each of the page items bound to the current variable in the next-outermost loop. In this loop, the type of variable is checked and the appropriate page item property is set: file path for placed and raster items bound to image variables, contents for text art items bound to textual variables, and hidden for page items of any kind bound to visibility variables. Notice that the visiblity test looks to see whether the field data equals true or yes when the script decides whether to show or hide the page item.

Finally, after the script loops though all the page items bound to all the variables that have names that match your database field names, it is time to create a new dataset that will capture all the page-item properties you set in the innermost loop. And of course, you move to the next record in the found records of your database.

VBScript

```vb
Option Explicit
Dim myApp As New Illustrator.Application

Private Sub Command1_Click()
    Dim myDBConnection, myFoundRecords, mySQLStatement, myRecordCount, myNum
    Dim myField, myVarNum, myItemCount
    If myApp.Documents.Count > 0 Then
    
        Set myDBConnection = New ADODB.Connection
        myDBConnection.Open "personalize", "", ""
```

VBS, cont'd.

```
Set myFoundRecords = New ADODB.Recordset
mySQLStatement = "SELECT * FROM [data]"
myFoundRecords.Open mySQLStatement, myDBConnection, 3, 3

myRecordCount = myFoundRecords.RecordCount
If myRecordCount > 0 Then
   myNum = 1
   Do While Not myFoundRecords.EOF
```
This loop moves through records in the database.

```
      For Each myField In myFoundRecords.Fields
         For myVarNum = 1 To myApp.Documents(1).Variables.
         Count
```
These two nested loops move through database fields and Illustrator document variables, respectively.

```
            If myApp.Documents(1).Variables(myVarNum).Name =
            myField.Name Then
               For myItemCount = 1 To myApp.Documents(1).
               Variables(myVarNum).PageItems.Count
                  Select Case myApp.Documents(1).Variables
                  (myVarNum).Kind
                     Case aiImage
                        Select Case myApp.Documents(1).
                        Variables(myVarNum).PageItems
                        (myItemCount).PageItemType
                     Case aiPlacedItem
                        myApp.Documents(1).Variables
                        (myVarNum).PageItems(myItemCount).
                        PlacedItem.File = myField.Value
                     Case aiRasterItem
                        myApp.Documents(1).Variables
                        (myVarNum).PageItems(myItemCount).
                        RasterItem.File = myField.Value
                     End Select
                     Case aiTextual
                        myApp.Documents(1).Variables
                        (myVarNum).PageItems(myItemCount).
                        TextArtItem.Contents = myField.Value
```

VBS, cont'd.

```
                    Case aiVisibility
                        If myField.Value = "yes" Or
                        myField.Value = "true" Then
                            myApp.Documents(1).Variables
                            (myVarNum).PageItems(myItemCount).
                            Hidden = False
                        Else
                            myApp.Documents(1).Variables
                            (myVarNum).PageItems(myItemCount).
                            Hidden = True
                        End If
                    End Select

                Next
            End If
        Next
    Next
    myApp.Documents(1).DataSets.Add
    myFoundRecords.MoveNext

    Loop
End If
myFoundRecords.Close
Set myFoundRecords = Nothing
myDBConnection.Close
Set myDBConnection = Nothing

    End If
End Sub
```

A new dataset is created after page items bound to variables are updated with the current record's field data.

5: AppleScript Reference

This reference section illustrates and defines the objects and commands in Illustrator's AppleScript dictionary. All of the objects in the dictionary are presented by their importance in the object model.

Each object listing includes the following:

- Illustrated screenshots of the user interface elements that give users access to the object's properties with callouts showing the scripting term you can use to access the same properties from your script.

- Elements that are contained within the object. For example, layers are contained in documents, and page items are contained in layers. The ways you can ask for or refer to elements are also listed: by index number, by name, before or after another element, part of a range (such as 1 through 5), or by a comparison test (such as documents whose width equals 560).

- Properties of the object, including the value type for the property, an explanation, and whether the property is read-only or not (read-only is indicated by an asterisk*).

- Valid commands you can use with the object in your script.

- Notes to explain special issues that might be of interest to you.

Throughout this chapter, when an object inherits properties or commands from another object, I reference the superclass object and list all properties or commands inherited.

AppleScript Language Reference

Illustrator's Object Model

A good understanding of Illustrator's object model will improve your scripting abilities. These diagrams show the containment hierarchy of the object model, starting with the application object. Note that the layer, group item, and all text classes can contain additional objects of the same class, which can in turn contain additional nested objects.

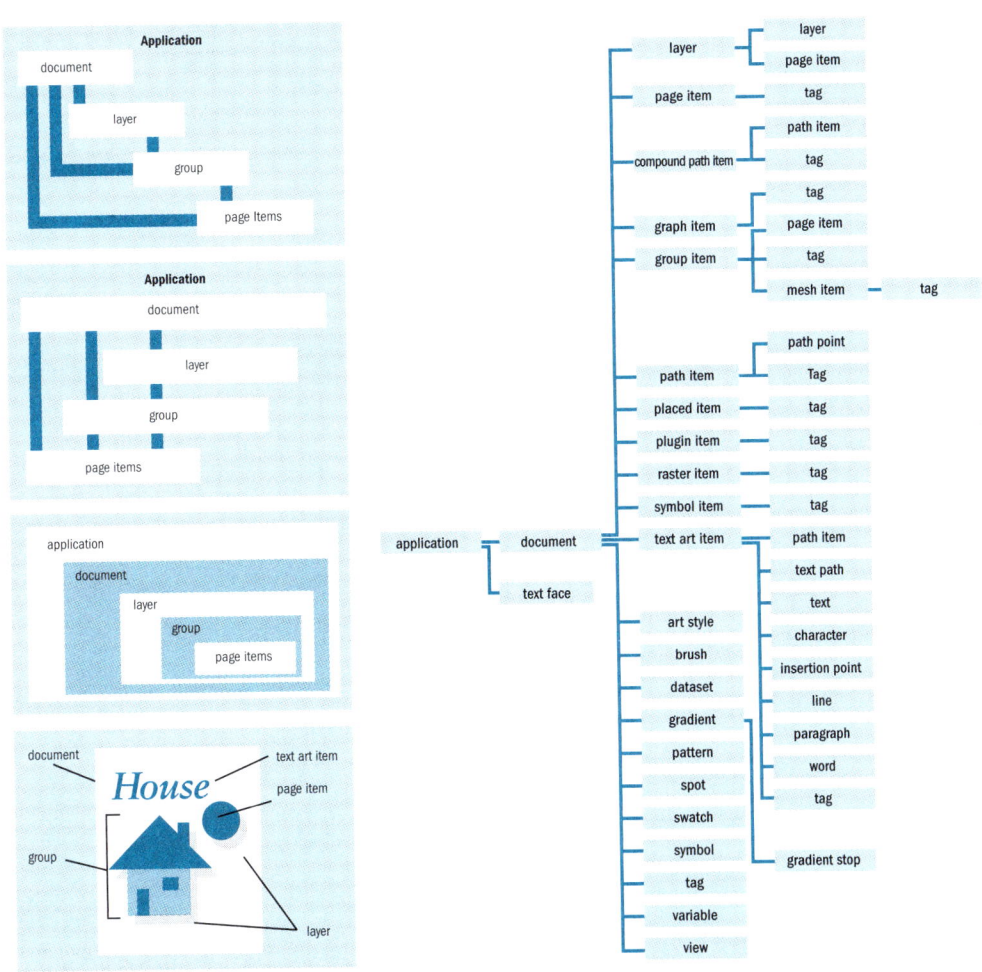

Primary Objects

application

The Adobe Illustrator application object, which contains all other Illustrator objects.

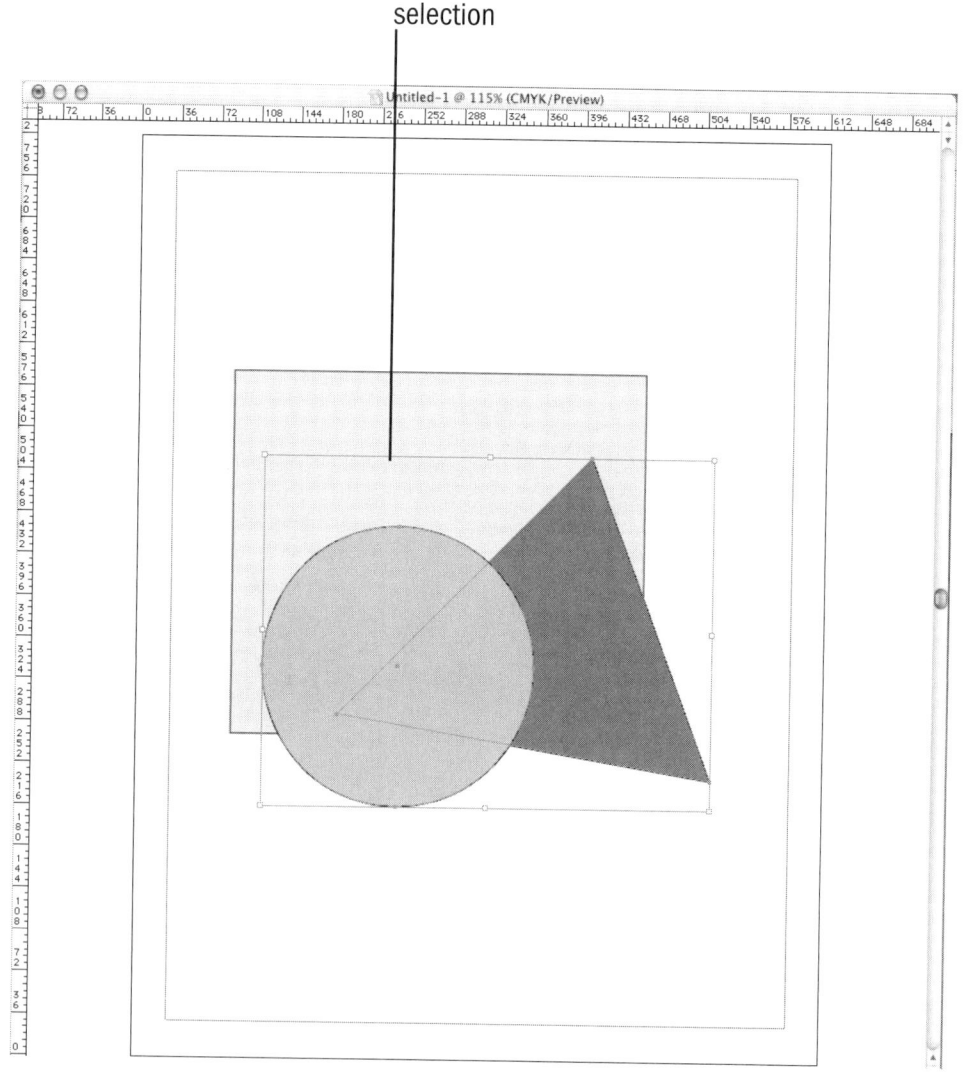

Figure 5.1 *The application object's selection property holds an array of references to the currently selected objects in the current document. Each document also has a selection property that contains references to any selected page items if there are any. The selection is an empty list, {}, when no page items are highlighted.*

Elements

ELEMENT	CAN BE REFERENCED BY
document	name, index, before/after, range, test
text face	name, index, before/after, range, test

Properties

PROPERTY	VALUE TYPE	EXPLANATION
best type*	class	The best type for the application object's value. Always returns reference.
browser available*	boolean	Is a Web browser available?
class*	class	The application object's class, which is application.
current document	object reference	The active (frontmost) document in Illustrator.
default type*	class	The default type for the application object's value. Always returns reference.
free memory*	integer	The amount of unused memory (in bytes) within the Adobe Illustrator partition.
frontmost*	boolean	Is this the frontmost (active) application?
name*	string	The application's name (not related to the filename of the application file). Always returns "Adobe Illustrator".
properties	record	All of the application's properties returned in a single record (properties that are individually read-only remain so in this record).
scripting version*	string	The version of the Scripting plug-in.
selection	list (of object references)	All of the currently selected objects in the active (frontmost) document. See the "Notes" for more information.
settings*	Illustrator preferences	A record of the preferences for Illustrator, including Photoshop file option defaults used for opening Photoshop files.
user interaction level	interact with all/interact with local/interact with self/never interact	The level of interaction with the user that should be allowed when handling script commands. Use this property carefully—in Illustrator 10 not all application dialogs are aware of this property.
version*	string	The version of the Adobe Illustrator application.

Valid Commands

COMMAND	RETURN VALUE	EXPLANATION
activate	nothing	Brings Illustrator application to front.
copy	nothing	Copies current selection to clipboard.
cut	nothing	Cuts current selection to clipboard.
do javascript "javascriptcode-or-filepath"	string-result	Executes JavaScript literal code or from source at filepath specified.
do script "scriptname" from "actionsetname" [dialogs boolean]	nothing	Executes an action from an existing action set.
launch	nothing	Starts Illustrator application.
paste	nothing	Pastes current selection from clipboard.
print list-of-document-or-file-references [dialog boolean]		Prints each document or file in list to current printer.
quit	nothing	Attempts to quit Illustrator application.
redraw	nothing	Refreshes screen by redrawing.

Commands that operate on matrix objects, covered in detail in the entry for the matrix object:

concatenate matrix, concatenate rotation matrix, concatenate scale matrix, concatenate translation matrix, equal matrices, get identity matrix, get rotation matrix, get scale matrix, get translation matrix, invert matrix, singular matrix

TIP *In Illustrator, the application's selection can be accessed as well as modified. The selection will contain an empty list, {}, when there are no selected objects. To deselect all objects in the current document, simply set the selection to an empty list. A reference to an insertion point is returned when there is an active insertion point in the contents of a text art item. Similarly, a reference to a range of text is returned when characters are selected in the contents of a text art item. Set the selection to change the application's current selection.*

document, documents

An Illustrator document or a list of documents. Documents are contained in the application object.

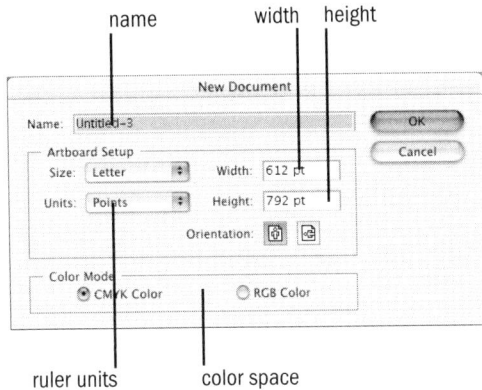

Figure 5.2 Some of a document object's most basic properties are accessed from the user interface in the New Document dialog box. In a script, you can set a document's width, height, and color space only when you are creating a new document.

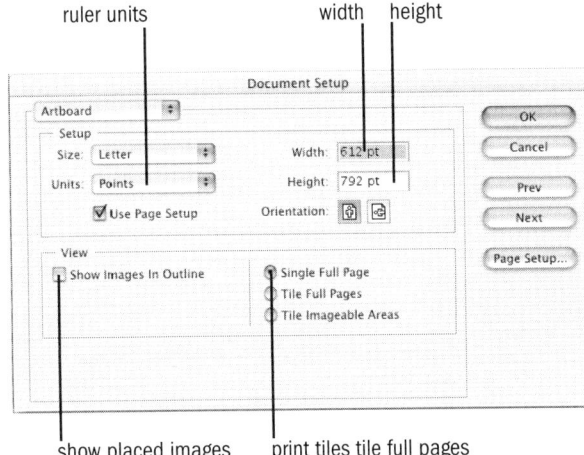

Figure 5.3 You can access the additional properties to show placed images, print tiles, and tile full pages of the document object from the Document Setup dialog box in the user interface.

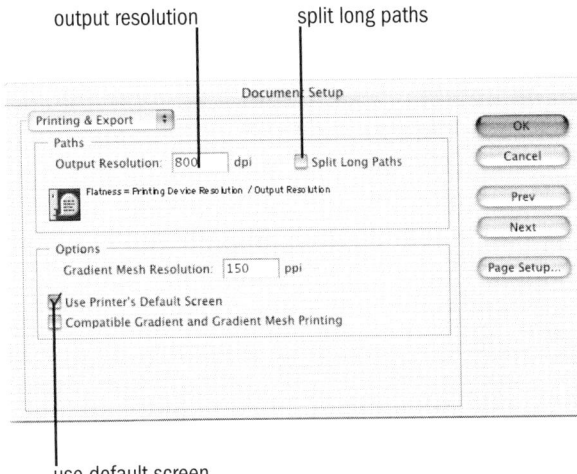

Figure 5.4 The Printing & Export panel of the Document Setup dialog box provides access to yet more document object properties. All of these properties are read-only from your scripts, which means you cannot change their values, but only look at them.

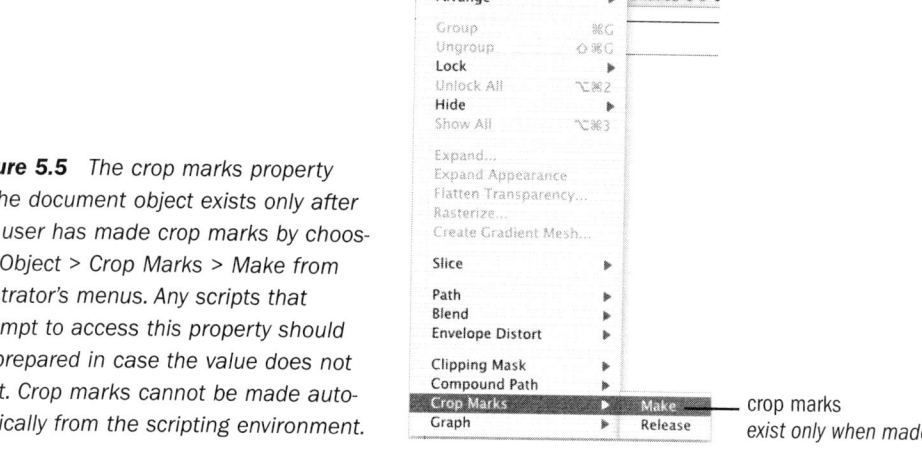

Figure 5.5 The crop marks property of the document object exists only after the user has made crop marks by choosing Object > Crop Marks > Make from Illustrator's menus. Any scripts that attempt to access this property should be prepared in case the value does not exist. Crop marks cannot be made automatically from the scripting environment.

crop marks exist only when made

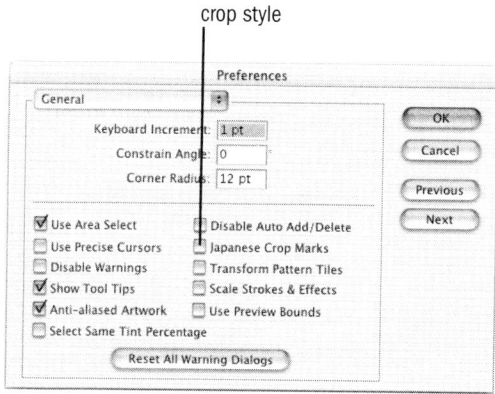

crop style

Figure 5.6 The General panel of the Preferences dialog box provides access to the rare and mysterious crop style property of the document object, which is called Japanese Crop Marks in the user interface.

current layer

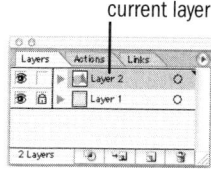

Figure 5.7 A document object's current layer property is simply an object reference to the currently selected layer in the document, as shown in the Layers palette of the user interface.

every view, views provide script access to all views of a document

current view provides access to view in use

Figure 5.8 A document's views are a list that contains an object reference to each of the document's views, which are listed at the bottom of the user interface's View menu. The current view property provides a reference to the view being used in the user interface.

default fill color
default stroke color

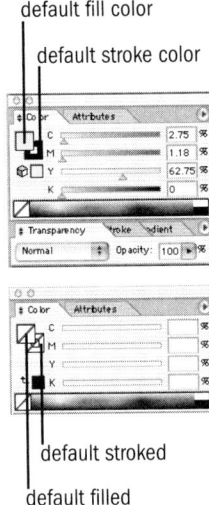

default stroked
default filled

Figure 5.9 All of the properties of the document object that start with the word "default" define the settings used for new path items created in the document, such as the fill and stroke colors and states. The default properties default fill color, default filled, default stroke color, and default stroked are also accessible from the Color palette of the user interface. If you set either default filled or default stroked to false, the value of their corresponding color property is ignored by the application.

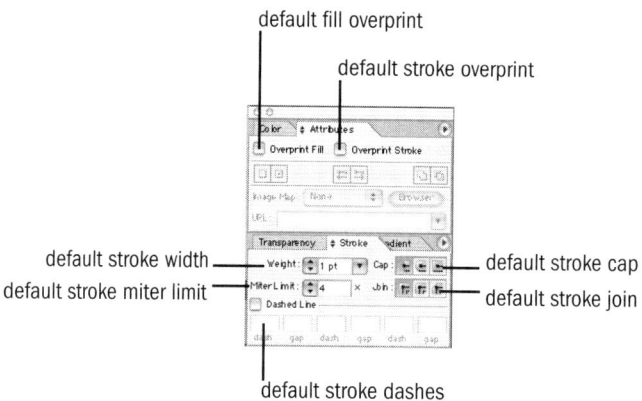

Figure 5.10 *The Attributes palette is another place in the user interface where many of the document object's default path item properties are found. Scripters get access to an additional property for dashed lines with default stroke dash offset, which lets you specify where the dash pattern should start in relation to the beginning of a path to which it is applied.*

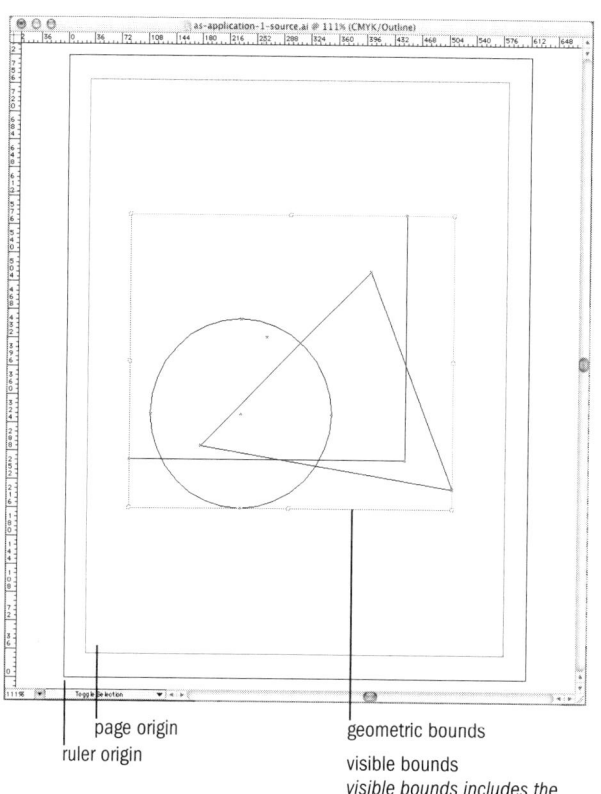

Figure 5.11 *The basic geometric properties of a document object are things we take for granted in the user interface of Illustrator. But having access to basic orientation information such as page origin and ruler origin enable your scripts to know all about the positioning geometry details of a document and its contents. Your script can figure out where the zero-point of a document's coordinate system (ruler origin) is in relation to its artboard (page origin). A more curious, but potentially useful pair of properties are geometric bounds and visible bounds. The geometric bounds property provides the overall rectangle that contains all objects in a document, based on the object's actual coordinates. The visible bounds property is the same, except it adds in the thicknesses of any strokes applied and accounts for any object clipping.*

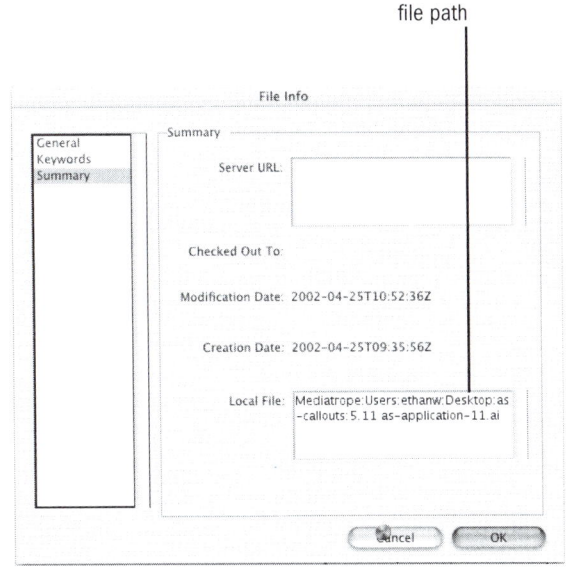

file path

Figure 5.12 *Hidden from users in the user interface under the Summary panel of the File Info dialog box, the document's file path property is fundamentally important to scripts that want to know where a document is saved in the file system.*

Elements

ELEMENT	CAN BE REFERENCED BY
art style	name, index, before/after, range, test
brush	name, index, before/after, range, test
compound path item	name, index, before/after, range, test
dataset	name, index, before/after, range, test
gradient	name, index, before/after, range, test
graph item	name, index, before/after, range, test
group item	name, index, before/after, range, test
layer	name, index, before/after, range, test
mesh item	name, index, before/after, range, test
page item	name, index, before/after, range, test
path item	name, index, before/after, range, test
pattern	name, index, before/after, range, test
placed item	name, index, before/after, range, test
plugin item	name, index, before/after, range, test
raster item	name, index, before/after, range, test
spot	name, index, before/after, range, test
swatch	name, index, before/after, range, test

Elements (continued)

ELEMENT	CAN BE REFERENCED BY
symbol	name, index, before/after, range, test
symbol item	name, index, before/after, range, test
tag	name, index, before/after, range, test
text art item	name, index, before/after, range, test
variable	name, index, before/after, range, test
view	index, before/after, range, test

Properties

PROPERTY	VALUE TYPE	EXPLANATION
best type*	class	The best type for the document object's value. Always returns reference.
class*	class	The document object's class, which is document.
color space*	RGB/CMYK	The color specification system to use for this document's color space.
crop marks	fixed rectangle	The boundary of the document's cropping box for output. This value exists only after the Object > Crop Marks > Make menu item has been selected to add crop marks to the document.
crop style	standard/japanese	The style of the document's cropping box, either standard or Japanese.
current dataset	object reference	The active dataset in the document.
current layer	object reference	The active layer in the document.
current view*	object reference	The document's current view.
default fill color	CMYK color info/gray color info/RGB color info/spot color info/pattern color info/gradient color info	The color to fill new paths if default filled is true.
default fill overprint	boolean	Will art beneath a filled object be overprinted by default?
default filled	boolean	Should a new path be filled?
default stroke cap	butted/rounded/projecting	Default type of line capping for paths created.

Properties (continued)

PROPERTY	VALUE TYPE	EXPLANATION
default stroke color	CMYK color info/gray color info/RGB color info/spot color info/pattern color info/gradient color info	The stroke color for new paths if default stroked is true.
default stroke dash offset	real	The default distance into the dash pattern at which the pattern should be started for new paths.
default stroke dashes	list (of real numbers)	Default lengths for dashes and gaps in dashed lines, starting with the first dash length, followed by the first gap length, and so on. Set to an empty list, {}, for a solid line.
default stroke join	mitered/rounded/beveled	Default type of joints in new paths.
default stroke miter limit	real	Specifies when a join is mitered (pointed) or beveled (squared-off) by default, when default stroke join is set to mitered.
default stroke overprint	boolean	Will art beneath a stroked object be overprinted by default?
default stroke width	real	Default width of stroke for new paths.
default stroked	boolean	Should a new path be stroked?
default type*	class	The default type for the document object's value. Always returns reference.
file path*	file specification	The file associated with the document, which includes the complete path to the file.
geometric bounds*	fixed rectangle	The bounds of the illustration excluding the stroke width of any objects in the document.
height*	real	The height of the document.
index*	integer	The position of this document in the stacking order of all open documents. The current (frontmost) document is always document 1.
modified	boolean	Has the document been modified since the last save?
name*	string	The document's name (not the complete file path to the document).

Properties (continued)

PROPERTY	VALUE TYPE	EXPLANATION
output resolution*	real	The current output resolution for the document in dots per inch (dpi).
page origin	fixed point	The zero-point of the page in the document without margins, relative to the overall height and width.
print tiles*	boolean	Does this document print as tiled output?
properties	record	All of the document's properties returned in a single record (properties that are individually read-only remain so in this record).
ruler origin	fixed point	The zero-point of the rulers in the document relative to the bottom left of the document.
ruler units*	unknown/inches/ centimeters/points/picas/ millimeters/qs	The default units for the rulers in the document.
selection	list (of object references)	The list of references to the objects in this document's current selection.
show placed images*	boolean	Are placed images displayed in the document?
split long paths*	boolean	Are long paths to be split when printing?
stationery*	boolean	Is the document saved as a stationery file?
tile full pages*	boolean	Should full pages be tiled when printing this document?
use default screen*	boolean	Should the printer's default screen be used when printing this document?
variables locked	boolean	Are the variables in this document locked?
visible bounds*	fixed rectangle	The visible bounds of the document, including stroke width of any objects in the illustration.
width*	real	The width of this document.

Valid Commands

COMMAND	RETURN VALUE	EXPLANATION
close document index-or-name [saving ask/no/yes]	nothing	Closes document with or without prompting and saving.
count of documents [whose match-criteria]	integer	Returns number of open documents.
exists document index-or-name [whose match-criteria]	boolean	Returns existence of specific document.
export document index-or-name to file-specification as Flash/GIF/JPEG/PNG24/PNG8/Photoshop/SVG [with options export-related-options]		Exports document as specified file type with options specified.
make new document [with data {data-list}] [with properties {document-properties}]	document-reference	Creates new document as frontmost document with properties specified.
open file-specification [forcing CMYK/RGB] [with options open-related-options]		Opens document at specified file.
print document index-or-name [dialog boolean]		Prints document to current printer.
save document index-or-name in file-specification [as eps/Illustrator/pdf] [with options save-related-options]	document-reference	Saves document in file as file type specified.

TIPS Illustrator's default document settings—those properties starting with the word "default"—are global settings that affect the current document. Be sure to modify these default properties only when a document is open. Note that if you set default properties to desired values before creating new objects, you can streamline your scripts, eliminating the need to specify properties such as fill color and stroke that have analogous default properties.

A document's color space, height, and width can be set only when the document is created. Once a document is created, these properties cannot be changed.

The frontmost document can be referred to as either current document or document 1.

layer, layers

A layer or list of layers. Layers may contain nested layers, which are called sublayers in the user interface.

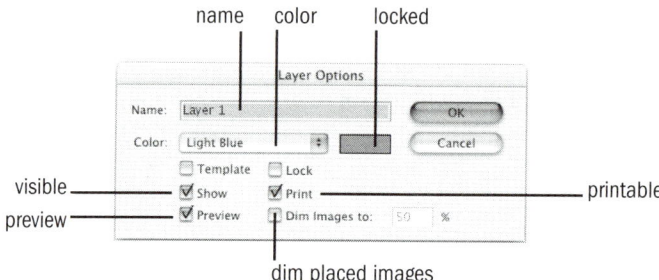

Figure 5.13 Double-click on any layer in the Layers palette of Illustrator and you get access to a plethora of properties. This illustration maps the property names to the controls in the Layer Options dialog box of the user interface.

Elements

ELEMENT	CAN BE REFERENCED BY
compound path item	name, index, before/after, range, test
graph item	name, index, before/after, range, test
group item	name, index, before/after, range, test
layer	name, index, before/after, range, test
mesh item	name, index, before/after, range, test
page item	name, index, before/after, range, test
path item	name, index, before/after, range, test
placed item	name, index, before/after, range, test
plugin item	name, index, before/after, range, test
raster item	name, index, before/after, range, test
symbol item	name, index, before/after, range, test
text art item	name, index, before/after, range, test

Properties

PROPERTY	VALUE TYPE	EXPLANATION
best type*	class	The best type for the layer object's value. Always returns reference.
blend mode	normal/multiply/screen/overlay/soft light/hard light/color dodge/color burn/darken/lighten/difference/exclusion/hue/saturation/color blend/luminosity/numeric	The mode to use when compositing this layer. A layer is considered composited when its opacity is set to less than 100.0 (or 100%).
class*	class	The layer object's class, which is layer.
color	RGB color info	The layer's selection mark color.
container*	object reference	A reference to the document that contains this layer.
default type*	class	The default type for the layer object's value. Always returns reference.
dim placed images	boolean	Are placed images to be rendered as dimmed in this layer?
has selected artwork	boolean	Is any object in this layer selected? Setting this property to false deselects all objects in the layer.
index*	integer	The position of this layer in the current stacking order of layers in this document, where layer 1 is always the topmost layer in the stacking order.
isolated	boolean	Is this layer isolated?
knockout	unknown/disabled/enabled/inherited	Is this layer used to create a knockout?
locked	boolean	Is this layer editable? Setting this property to false locks the layer.
name	string	The name of this layer.
opacity	real	The opacity of this layer, where 100.0 is completely opaque and 0.0 is completely transparent.
preview	boolean	Is this layer displayed using preview mode?
printable	boolean	Is this layer printed when printing the document?

Properties (continued)

PROPERTY	VALUE TYPE	EXPLANATION
properties	record	All of the layer's properties returned in a single record (properties which are individually read-only remain so in this record).
sliced	boolean	Does this layer contain slices?
visible	boolean	Is this layer visible?

Valid Commands

COMMAND	RETURN VALUE	EXPLANATION
count of layers [in object-reference/whose match-criteria]	integer	Returns number of layers in containing object or found by whose criteria.
delete layer index-or-name [in object-reference/whose match-criteria]	nothing	Deletes object specified.
duplicate layer index-or-name [to location-reference]	layer-reference	Duplicates object specified, returning a reference to the new object.
exists layer index-or-name [in object-reference/whose match-criteria]	boolean	Tests for the existence of the specified object, returning true or false.
make new layer at location-reference [with properties {layer-properties}]	layer-reference	Creates new object at location specified within containing object using optional properties.
move layer index-or-name [in object-reference/whose match-criteria] to location-reference	layer-reference	Move object to location specified within containing object.

TIP *Illustrator's layer object contains all of the page items in the specific layer as elements. Your script can access page items as elements of either the layer object or as elements of the document object. When accessing page items as elements of a layer, only objects in that layer can be accessed. To access page items throughout the entire document, be sure to refer to them as elements of the document.*

Page Item Superclass of Objects

page item, page items

Any art object or list of art objects. Every art object and group in a document is a page item. Page items may be referenced as an element of a document, layer(s), or group(s).

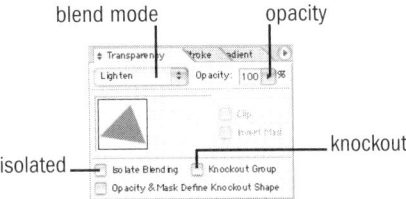

Figure 5.14 *A page item object is the meat and potatoes of any good Illustrator document. The Transparency palette is where some of the more powerful visual properties of a page item can be changed from the user interface. Most of these properties are available to scripts as well.*

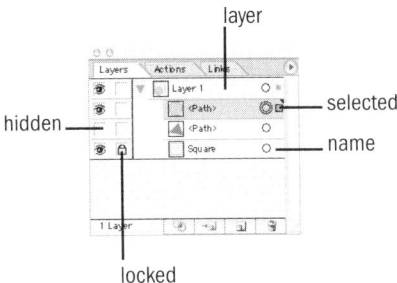

Figure 5.15 *Many of a page item object's fundamental properties are viewed in the user interface from the hierarchical Layers palette. All of the page item properties shown are directly editable from a script, except the read-only layer property, which must be changed using the move command.*

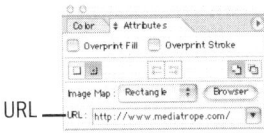

Figure 5.16 *The URL property of a page item can be set from a script, enabling you to create scripts that export images and HTML complete with hyperlinks.*

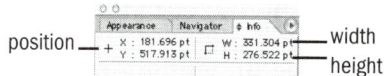

Figure 5.17 *The three most basic properties—position, width, and height—are visible in the Info palette of the user interface.*

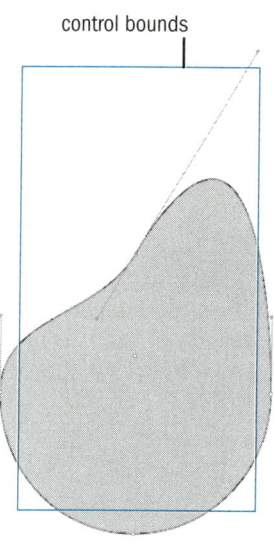

Figure 5.18 *Script access to geometric bounding properties is abundant in Illustrator. In addition to geometric bounds and visible bounds, there are also control bounds, which, believe me or not, actually provide the rectangular bounds created by the extent of all control handles (left direction and right direction) of any path points in the object.*

Elements

ELEMENT	CAN BE REFERENCED BY
tag	name, index, before/after, range, test

Properties

PROPERTY	VALUE TYPE	EXPLANATION
best type*	class	The best type for the page item object's value. Always returns reference.
blend mode	normal/multiply/screen/overlay/soft light/hard light/color dodge/color burn/darken/lighten/difference/exclusion/hue/saturation/color blend/luminosity/numeric	The mode to use when compositing this object. An object is considered composited when its opacity is set to less than 100.0 (or 100%).
class*	class	The page item object's class, which can be any one of the specific classes that are children of the page item class, including compound path item, group item, mesh item, path item, placed item, plugin item, raster item, and text art item.

Properties (continued)

PROPERTY	VALUE TYPE	EXPLANATION
container*	object reference	A reference to the layer that contains this page item.
control bounds*	fixed rectangle	The bounds of the object, including stroke width and controls.
default type*	class	The default type for the path item object's value. Always returns reference.
editable*	boolean	Can this page item be modified?
geometric bounds*	fixed rectangle	The bounds of the object excluding stroke width.
height	real	The height of the page item.
hidden	boolean	Is this page item hidden?
index*	integer	The position of this page item in the current stacking order of the containing layer, where page item 1 is always topmost.
isolated	boolean	Is this object isolated?
knockout	unknown/disabled/ enabled/inherited	Is this object used to create a knockout?
layer*	object reference	The layer to which this page item belongs.
locked	boolean	Is this page item locked?
name	string	The name of this page item.
opacity	real	The opacity of this object, where 100.0 is completely opaque and 0.0 is completely transparent.
position	fixed point	The position of the top-left corner of the page item.
properties	record	All of the page item's properties returned in a single record (properties that are individually read-only remain so in this record).
selected	boolean	Is this object selected?
sliced	boolean	Is the page item sliced?
URL	string	The value of the Adobe URL tag assigned to this page item.
visibility variable	variable object reference	The visibility variable bound to this page item
visible bounds*	fixed rectangle	The visible bounds of the page item, including stroke width.
width	real	The width of the page item.

Valid Commands

COMMAND	RETURN VALUE	EXPLANATION
count of page items [in object-reference/whose match-criteria]	integer	Returns number of page items in containing object or found by whose criteria.
delete page item index-or-name [in object-reference/whose match-criteria]	nothing	Deletes object specified.
duplicate page item index-or-name [in object-reference/whose match-criteria]	page-item-reference	Duplicates object specified, returning a reference to the new object.
exists page item index-or-name [in object-reference/whose match-criteria]	boolean	Tests for the existence of the specified object, returning true or false.
move page item index-or-name [in object-reference/whose match-criteria] to location-reference	page-item-reference	Move object to location specified within containing object.
translate page item index-or-name [in object-reference/whose match-criteria] [delta x real-number] [delta y real-number] [transforming objects boolean] [transforming fill patterns boolean] [transforming fill gradients boolean] [transforming stroke patterns boolean]	nothing	Repositions object specified in x-y-coordinate system.
rotate page item index-or-name [in object-reference/whose match-criteria] angle real-number [transforming objects boolean] [transforming fill patterns boolean] [transforming fill gradients boolean] [transforming stroke patterns boolean] [about bottom/bottom left/bottom right/center/document origin/left/right/top/top left/top right]	nothing	Rotates object specified number of degrees.
scale page item index-or-name [in object-reference/whose match-criteria] horizontal scale real-number vertical scale real-number [transforming objects boolean] [transforming fill patterns boolean] [transforming fill gradients boolean] [transforming stroke patterns boolean] [about bottom/bottom left/bottom right/center/document origin/left/right/top/top left/top right]	nothing	Scales object specified to separate horizontal and vertical scales.

Valid Commands (commands)

COMMAND	RETURN VALUE	EXPLANATION
transform page item index-or-name [in object-reference/whose match-criteria] using matrix [transforming objects boolean] [transforming fill patterns boolean] [transforming fill gradients boolean] [transforming stroke patterns boolean] [line scale real-number] [about bottom/bottom left/bottom right/center/document origin/left/right/top/top left/top right]	nothing	Applies transformation matrix specified to object, changing object geometry.

TIPS *The page item class gives you complete access to every art object contained in an Illustrator document. The page item class is the superclass of all artwork objects in a document. The classes compound path item, group item, mesh item, path item, placed item, plugin item, raster item, and text art item each inherit a set of properties from the page item class.*

You cannot create a page item directly. You must use create one of the specific page item subclasses, such as path item.

compound path item, compound path items

A compound path or list of compound paths. Compound paths are objects composed of multiple intersecting paths, resulting in transparent interior spaces where the original paths overlapped.

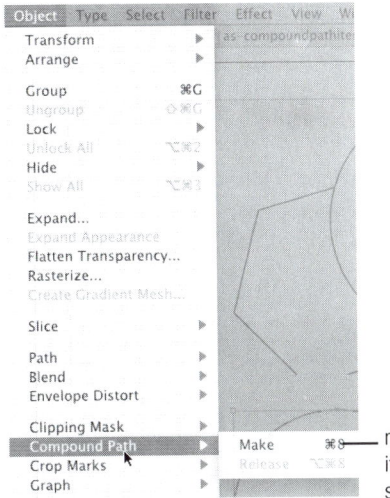

Figure 5.19 *Making compound paths in the user interface is a multistep process: Select two or more objects, choose Object > Compound Path > Make from the menus. As soon as you do this, your selected objects appear as one in the user interface. But from the script perspective, you have added an additional object to the document—a compound path item—that now contains all of the path items you had selected.*

— make a compound path item from two or more selected objects

Elements

ELEMENT	CAN BE REFERENCED BY
path item	name, index, before/after, range, test
tag	name, index, before/after, range, test

Properties

PROPERTY	VALUE TYPE	EXPLANATION
inheritance*	class	The class that is the parent for this class. Always returns page item.

Properties inherited from the superclass page item:
best type*, blend mode, class*, container*, control bounds*, default type*, editable*, geometric bounds*, height, hidden, index*, isolated, knockout, layer*, locked, name, opacity, position, properties, selected, sliced, URL, visible bounds*, visibility variable, width

Valid Commands

COMMAND	RETURN VALUE	EXPLANATION
make new compound path item at location-reference [with data {data-list}] [with properties {compound-path-item-properties}]	compound-path-item-reference	Creates new object at location specified within containing object using optional properties.

Commands inherited from the superclass page item:
count, delete, duplicate, exists, move, rotate, scale, transform, translate

TIPS Paths contained within a compound path or group in a document will be returned as individual paths when a script asks for the paths contained in the document. However, paths contained in a compound path or group will not be returned when a script asks for the paths in a layer that contains the compound path or group.

All paths inside of a compound path share property values. Therefore, if you set the value of a property of any one of the paths in the compound path, all other path's matching property will be updated to the new value.

graph item, graph items

A graph object or objects.

Elements

ELEMENT	CAN BE REFERENCED BY
tag	name, index, before/after, range, test

Properties

PROPERTY	VALUE TYPE	EXPLANATION
content variable	variable object reference	The content variable bound to this graph item.

Properties inherited from the superclass page item:
best type*, blend mode, class*, container*, control bounds*, default type*, editable*, geometric bounds*, height, hidden, index*, isolated, knockout, layer*, locked, name, opacity, position, properties, selected, sliced, URL, visible bounds*, visibility variable, width

Valid Commands

Commands inherited from the superclass page item:
count, delete, duplicate, exists, move, rotate, scale, transform, translate

> **TIP** Graph items cannot be created from a script. Existing graph objects may be modified from a script by using a technique of binding a variable to the graph object and then importing datasets under script control to update the values in the graph object. See Chapter 4, "Script Recipes for Illustrator," for an example of this technique.

group item, group items

A grouped set of art objects.

Elements

ELEMENT	CAN BE REFERENCED BY
compound path item	name, index, before/after, range, test
graph item	name, index, before/after, range, test
group item	name, index, before/after, range, test
mesh item	name, index, before/after, range, test
page item	name, index, before/after, range, test
path item	name, index, before/after, range, test
placed item	name, index, before/after, range, test
plugin item	name, index, before/after, range, test
raster item	name, index, before/after, range, test
symbol item	name, index, before/after, range, test
tag	name, index, before/after, range, test
text art item	name, index, before/after, range, test

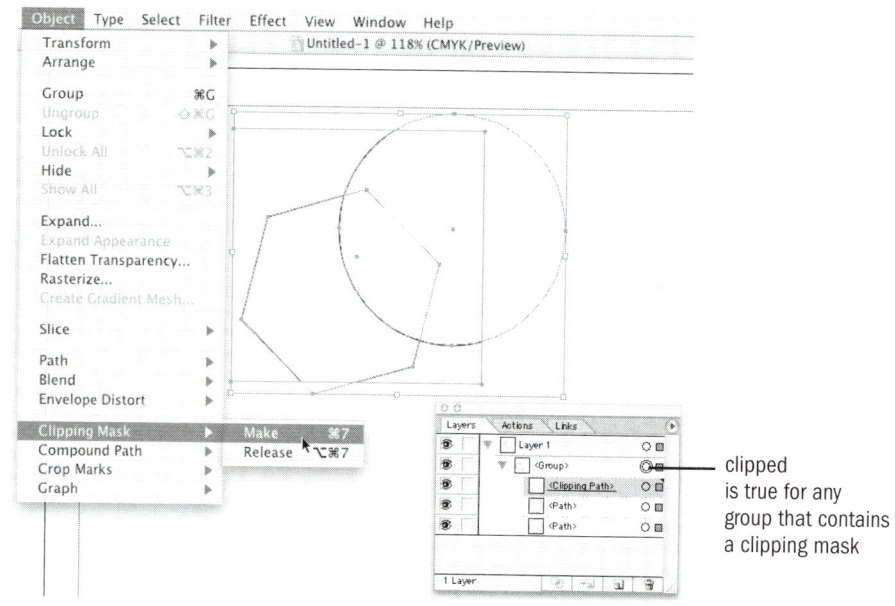

Figure 5.20 *A clipping mask can be made from the user interface by selecting the objects you want to mask as well as the masking path itself, making sure it is frontmost, and choosing Object > Clipping Mask > Make from the menus. The result is that the objects get grouped, and the group object's clipped property is set to true. A script can make a clipping mask simply by doing the same: create a group object, add page items to it, and set the clipped property to true for the group object. Or you can set the clipping property of the first path item in the group to true. This property is also editable and in turn changes the group's clipped property value automatically.*

Properties

PROPERTY	VALUE TYPE	EXPLANATION
clipped	boolean	Is the group clipped to its first path item?
inheritance*	class	The class that is the parent for this class. Always returns page item.

Properties inherited from the superclass page item:
 best type*, blend mode, class*, container*, control bounds*, default type*, editable*, geometric bounds*, height, hidden, index*, isolated, knockout, layer*, locked, name, opacity, position, properties, selected, sliced, URL, visible bounds*, visibility variable, width

Valid Commands

COMMAND	RETURN VALUE	EXPLANATION
make new group item at location-reference [with data {data-list}] [with properties {group-item-properties}]	group-item-reference	Creates new object at location specified within containing object using optional properties.

Commands inherited from the superclass page item:
 count, delete, duplicate, exists, move, rotate, scale, transform, translate

TIPS *Group items can contain all of the same page items that a layer can contain, including other nested groups.*

Paths contained within a group or compound path in a document will be returned as individual paths when a script asks for the paths contained in the document. However, paths contained in a group or compound path will not be returned when a script asks for the paths in a layer that contains the group or compound path.

A new group can be created that contains the contents of a vector art file if you provide a file specification to the vector file (EPS or PDF) in the with data parameter of the make command. The resulting group will be the same object as if the user had placed the file from the user interface using the File > Place command with the Link checkbox selected.

mesh item, mesh items

A gradient mesh art object or list of gradient mesh art objects.

Elements

ELEMENT	CAN BE REFERENCED BY
tag	name, index, before/after, range, test

Properties

PROPERTY	VALUE TYPE	EXPLANATION
inheritance*	class	The class that is the parent for this class. Always returns page item.

Properties inherited from the superclass page item:
best type*, blend mode, class*, container*, control bounds*, default type*, editable*, geometric bounds*, height, hidden, index*, isolated, knockout, layer*, locked, name, opacity, position, properties, selected, sliced, URL, visible bounds*, visibility variable, width

Valid Commands

Commands inherited from the superclass page item:
count, delete, duplicate, exists, move, rotate, scale, transform, translate

TIP *Mesh items cannot be created from a script, but they can be duplicated, copied, and pasted.*

path item, path items

A path or list of paths. A path is composed of path points that define its geometry.

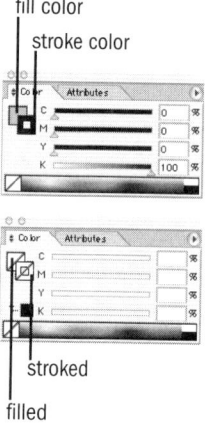

Figure 5.21 *The fundamental path item properties fill color, filled, stroke color, and stroked are accessible from the Color palette. If you set either filled or stroked to false, the value of their corresponding color property is ignored by the application. You can set fill color or stroke color to any of the valid color assignment object classes, such as CMYK color info, gradient color info, or RGB color info, among others.*

Figure 5.22 *A path item object's fill overprint, stroke overprint, evenodd, and note properties are accessed in the Attributes palette of the user interface. The evenodd property sets the color filling rule used for the path. When evenodd is false, the non-zero winding fill rule is applied, filling all overlapping regions of the path the same as any other region. When evenodd is true, the even-odd fill rule is used, so overlapping regions cancel each other out and are not filled.*

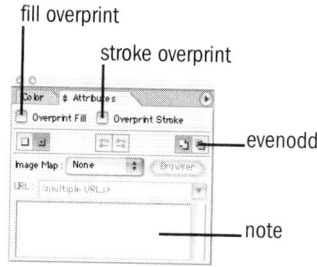

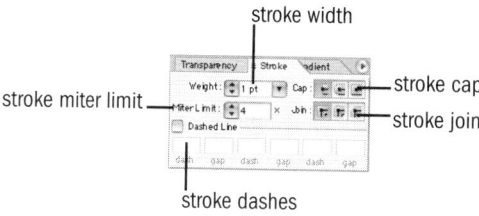

Figure 5.23 *The basic properties for a path's stroke are available in the aptly named Stroke palette of the user interface. The stroke dash offset property specifies where a stroke dash pattern should start in relation to the beginning of any path it is applied to.*

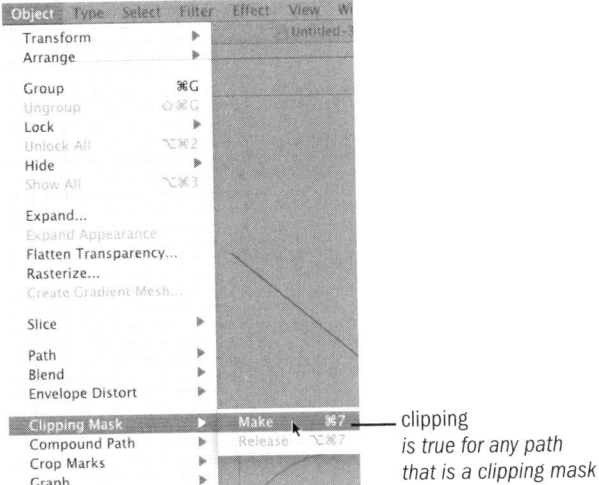

Figure 5.24 *Once you make a clipping mask, the frontmost path item object in the resulting group always has its clipping property set to true.*

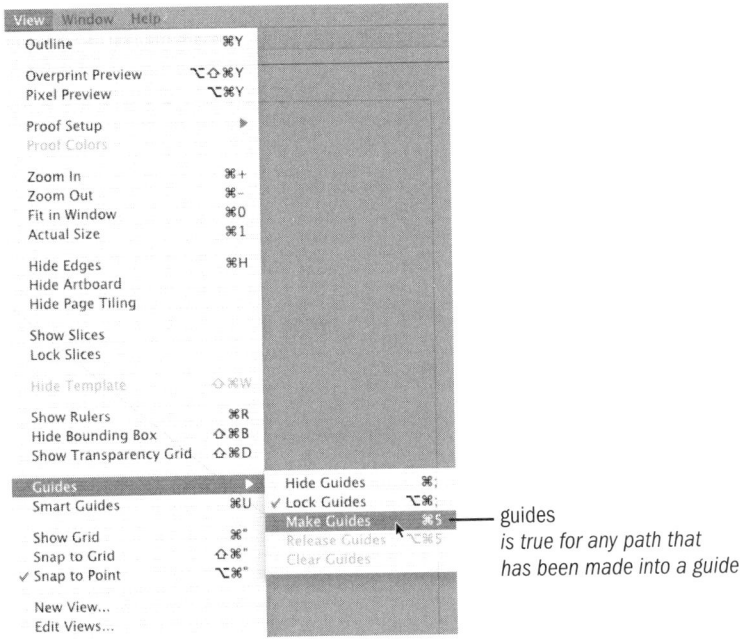

Figure 5.25 *Accessing an entire document's set of guides is easy from a script, since Illustrator treats guides as special paths. The magic path item property that determines whether the path is a guide or not is simple: guides. Just set the guides property of any path item to true to convert it into a guide, or you can test an existing path's guides property to determine if it is a guide.*

Elements

ELEMENT	CAN BE REFERENCED BY
path point	index, before/after, range, test
tag	name, index, before/after, range, test

Properties

PROPERTY	VALUE TYPE	EXPLANATION
area*	real	The area of this path in square points. An area may be negative or even 0. The path's winding order is determined by the sign of area. If the area is negative, the path is wound counter-clockwise. Self-intersecting paths may contain sub-areas that cancel each other out. Therefore, it is possible for a path's area to appear as zero even though it has apparent area.
clipping	boolean	Is this path to be used as a clipping path?
closed	boolean	Is this path closed?
entire path	list (of path point info)	All the path item's path points returned as a list of path point info with each item a record using this format: {anchor, left direction, point type, right direction}. The individual properties of this record are defined in the path point object entry below.
evenodd	boolean	Use the even-odd rule to determine insideness?
fill color	CMYK color info/gray color info/RGB color info/spot color info/pattern color info/gradient color info	The fill color of the path.
fill overprint	boolean	Will art beneath a filled object be overprinted?
filled	boolean	Should the path be filled?
guides	boolean	Is this path a guide object?
inheritance*	class	The class that is the parent for this class. Always returns page item.
note	string	The note text assigned to the path.
polarity	negative/positive	The polarity of the path.
resolution	real	The resolution of the path (in dots per inch).

Properties (continued)

PROPERTY	VALUE TYPE	EXPLANATION
selected path points*	list (of object references)	All of the selected path points in the path.
stroke cap	butted/rounded/projecting	The type of line capping.
stroke color	CMYK color info/gray color info/RGB color info/spot color info/pattern color info/gradient color info	The stroke color for the path.
stroke dash offset	real	The default distance into the dash pattern at which the pattern should be started.
stroke dashes	list (of real numbers)	The lengths for dashes and gaps in dashed lines, starting with the first dash length, followed by the first gap length, and so on. Set to an empty list, {}, for a solid line.
stroke join	mitered/rounded/beveled	Type of joints for the path.
stroke miter limit	real	Are joins mitered (pointed) or beveled (squared-off)?
stroke overprint	boolean	Will art beneath a stroked object be overprinted?
stroke width	real	Width of stroke.
stroked	boolean	Should the path be stroked?

Properties inherited from the superclass page item:
  best type*, blend mode, class*, container*, control bounds*, default type*, editable*, geometric bounds*, height, hidden, index*, isolated, knockout, layer*, locked, name, opacity, position, properties, selected, sliced, URL, visible bounds*, visibility variable, width

Valid Commands

COMMAND	RETURN VALUE	EXPLANATION
make new path item at location-reference [with data {data-list}] [with properties {path-item-properties}]	path-item-reference	Creates new object at location specified within containing object using optional properties.

Commands inherited from the superclass page item:
  count, delete, duplicate, exists, move, rotate, scale, transform, translate

TIP *The path item class gives you complete access to paths in Illustrator.*

path point, path points

A point on a path. A path point is located at the anchor, which has a pair of control points, or handles, named left direction and right direction. Any point can be considered a corner point. Setting the `point type` property of a path point to a corner forces the left and right direction points to be on a straight line when the user attempts to modify them in the user interface.

Properties

PROPERTY	VALUE TYPE	EXPLANATION
anchor	fixed point	The position of the point.
container*	path-item-reference	A reference to the path item that contains this path point.
left direction	fixed point	The position of the in control point.
point type	corner/smooth	The type of path point, either smooth or a corner.
right direction	fixed point	The position of the out control point.
selected	anchor selected/left selected/ left right selected/none/right selected	Are points of this path point selected? If so, which one(s)?

Valid Commands

COMMAND	RETURN VALUE	EXPLANATION
make		make new path point at location-reference [with data {data-list}] [with properties {property-list}]
	path-point-reference	Creates new object at location specified within containing object using optional properties.

Other commands:
   count, delete, duplicate, exists

Path points are always contained in a path. A path point object is not a subclass of page item.

placed item, placed items

An artwork item (optionally stored in an external file) placed in a document. A placed item must correspond to a file containing vector-graphic data, such as a PICT, EPS, or PDF file.

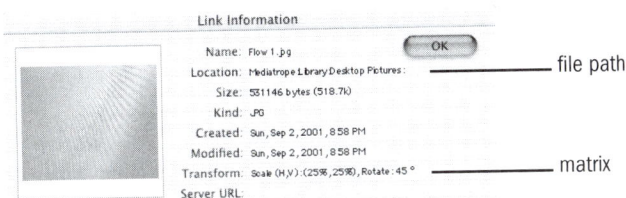

Figure 5.26 *When you double-click an entry for a placed art item in the user interface's Links palette, the Link Information dialog window appears. Here the user can see the placed item's file path and matrix properties, but Illustrator won't let the user change these values. From a script, both the file path and matrix properties are editable, allowing a script to change placed art's file links and appearance easily.*

Elements

ELEMENT	CAN BE REFERENCED BY
tag	name, index, before/after, range, test

Properties

PROPERTY	VALUE TYPE	EXPLANATION
bounding box*	fixed rectangle	Dimensions of placed item regardless of transformations.
content variable	variable object reference	The content variable bound to this placed item.
file path	file specification	The file containing the placed artwork.
inheritance*	class	The class that is the parent for this class. Always returns page item.
matrix	matrix	The transformation matrix applied to the placed item.

Properties inherited from the superclass page item:
   best type*, blend mode, class*, container*, control bounds*, default type*, editable*, geometric bounds*, height, hidden, index*, isolated, knockout, layer*, locked, name, opacity, position, properties, selected, sliced, URL, visible bounds*, visibility variable, width

Valid Commands

COMMAND	RETURN VALUE	EXPLANATION
make new placed item at location-reference [with data {data-list}] [with properties {placed-item-properties}]	placed-item-reference	Creates new object at location specified within containing object using optional properties.

Commands inherited from the superclass page item:
count, delete, duplicate, exists, move, rotate, scale, transform, translate

TIPS When you create a placed item, Illustrator may display a dialog box. To avoid this dialog box, check the box to turn the warning off the first time the dialog box is displayed.

Vector art files, such as EPS and PDF files, can be placed by users with the File > Place command in Illustrator. Placed items can be created from vector art files in a script using the technique illustrated in Script 4.18 in Chapter 4.

plugin item, plugin items

An art object or objects created by an Illustrator plug-in.

Elements

ELEMENT	CAN BE REFERENCED BY
tag	name, index, before/after, range, test

Properties

PROPERTY	VALUE TYPE	EXPLANATION
inheritance*	class	The class that is the parent for this class. Always returns page item.

Properties inherited from the superclass page item:
best type*, blend mode, class*, container*, control bounds*, default type*, editable*, geometric bounds*, height, hidden, index*, isolated, knockout, layer*, locked, name, opacity, position, properties, selected, sliced, URL, visible bounds*, visibility variable, width

Valid Commands

Commands inherited from the superclass page item:
count, delete, duplicate, exists, move, rotate, scale, transform, translate

TIP Plug-in items cannot be created from a script, but they can be duplicated, copied, and pasted.

raster item, raster items

A bitmap art object or list of objects.

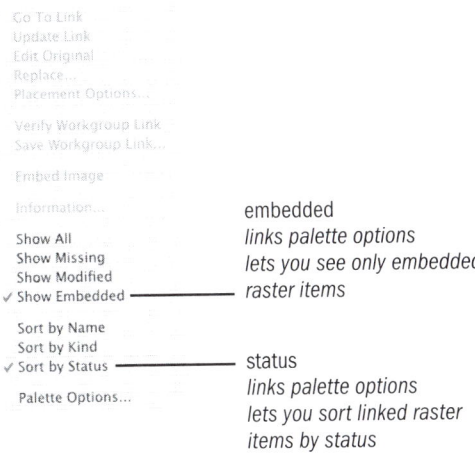

Figure 5.27 *Two important properties of a raster item are available from the Links palette in the user interface, sort of. The embedded property tells you whether or not the raster art object's bitmap is stored entirely inside of the Illustrator document. The status property tells you about the status of externally linked bitmap files. Illustrator lets the user sort the Links palette by these two properties.*

Elements

ELEMENT	CAN BE REFERENCED BY
tag	name, index, before/after, range, test

Properties

PROPERTY	VALUE TYPE	EXPLANATION
bounding box	fixed rectangle	Dimensions of raster item regardless of transformations.
color space *	Gray/RGB/CMYK	The color space of the raster image.
content variable	variable object reference	The content variable bound to this raster item.
embedded	boolean	Is the raster art embedded within the illustration?
file path	file specification	The file containing the raster artwork, if it is stored externally.

Properties (continued)

PROPERTY	VALUE TYPE	EXPLANATION
inheritance*	class	The class that is the parent for this class. Always returns page item.
matrix	matrix	The transformation matrix of the raster art object.
status *	no data/data from file/ modified data	The status of the linked image, if the image is stored externally.

Properties inherited from the superclass page item:
best type*, blend mode, class*, container*, control bounds*, default type*, editable*, geometric bounds*, height, hidden, index*, isolated, knockout, layer*, locked, name, opacity, position, properties, selected, sliced, URL, visible bounds*, visibility variable, width

Valid Commands

COMMAND	RETURN VALUE	EXPLANATION
colorize raster item index-or-name [in object-reference/ whose match-criteria] raster color color-definition-object		Applies color to TIFF raster art item.
make new raster item at location-reference [with data {data-list}] [with properties {raster-item-properties}]	raster-item-reference	Creates new object at location specified within containing object using optional properties.

Commands inherited from the superclass page item:
count, delete, duplicate, exists, move, rotate, scale, transform, translate

> **TIP** Raster items can be created from a script if an external file is used. New raster items can also be created by duplicating or copying and pasting an existing raster item.

symbol item, symbol items

A symbol object or objects.

Elements

ELEMENT	CAN BE REFERENCED BY
tag	name, index, before/after, range, test

Properties

PROPERTY	VALUE TYPE	EXPLANATION
symbol*	symbol-reference	The symbol object used by this symbol item.

Properties inherited from the superclass page item:
best type*, blend mode, class*, container*, control bounds*, default type*, editable*, geometric bounds*, height, hidden, index*, isolated, knockout, layer*, locked, name, opacity, position, properties, selected, sliced, URL, visible bounds*, visibility variable, width

Valid Commands

Commands inherited from the superclass page item:
count, delete, duplicate, exists, move, rotate, scale, transform, translate

TIP *Symbol items cannot be created from a script.*

text art item, text art items

A text art object or objects. From the user interface, this is text created with the Text tool.

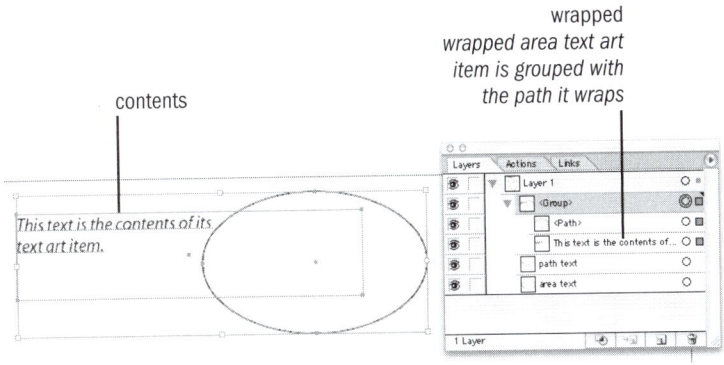

Figure 5.28 *The most basic aspect of a text art item is its textual contents property. Almost complete text art access has been provided to scripts, including the ability to manipulate the wrapped property of area text, which describes whether or not the text art is set to wrap around a path with which it is grouped.*

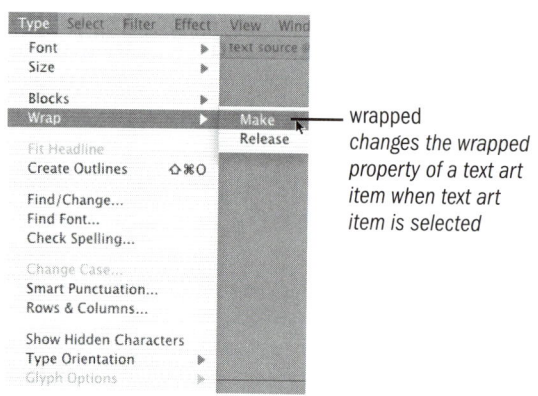

Figure 5.29 To set the wrapped property of a text art item to true from the user interface, select the text art object and a path for it to wrap around and choose Type > Wrap > Make from the menus. A script can do the same thing: create a group item, move a path item and a text art item into the group, and set the text art item's wrapped property to true.

Figure 5.30 The Type tool palette's first three tool choices provide direct access from the user interface to create the three different kinds of text art objects: point text, area text, and path text. Both area text and path text require a path as well.

Elements

ELEMENT	CAN BE REFERENCED BY
character	index, before/after, range, test
insertion point	index, before/after, range, test
line	index, before/after, range, test
paragraph	index, before/after, range, test
path item	name, index, before/after, range, test
tag	name, index, before/after, range, test
text	index, before/after, range
text path	name, index, before/after, range, test
word	index, before/after, range, test

Properties

PROPERTY	VALUE TYPE	EXPLANATION
contents	string	The textual contents of the text art item, represented as a string.

Properties (continued)

PROPERTY	VALUE TYPE	EXPLANATION
content variable	variable object reference	The content variable bound to this text art item.
kind	point text/area text/path text	The type of text art.
selection	object reference	The reference to the text range in this text art item's current selection, if any.
wrapped	boolean	Does the text wrap around other objects? (valid only for area text)

Properties inherited from the superclass page item:
  best type*, blend mode, class*, container*, control bounds*, default type*, editable*, geometric bounds*, height, hidden, index*, isolated, knockout, layer*, locked, name, opacity, position, properties, selected, sliced, URL, visible bounds*, visibility variable, width

Valid Commands

COMMAND	RETURN VALUE	EXPLANATION
convert to paths text art item index-or-name [in object-reference/whose match-criteria]	group-item-reference	Change text art to paths, returning a group with all paths and compound paths created.
make new text art item at location-reference [with data {data-list}] [with properties { text-art-item-properties}]	text-art-item-reference	Creates new object at location specified within containing object using optional properties.

Commands inherited from the superclass page item:
  count, delete, duplicate, exists, move, rotate, scale, transform, translate

> **TIP** *There are three types of text art objects in Illustrator, as specified by the text art item's kind property. See Chapter 3, "Scripting Basics," for more information on working with the three kinds of text art items.*

Text Superclass of Objects

text

Any text in the contents of a text art item.

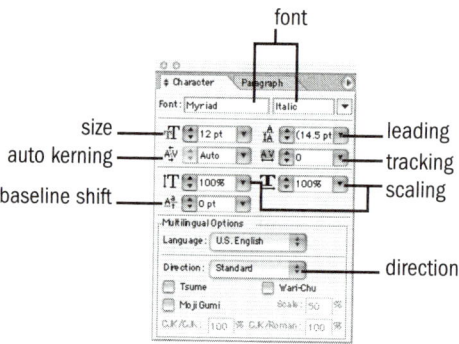

Figure 5.31 *The Character palette provides access to the basic properties for all of the text objects: character, insertion point, line, paragraph, text, and word.*

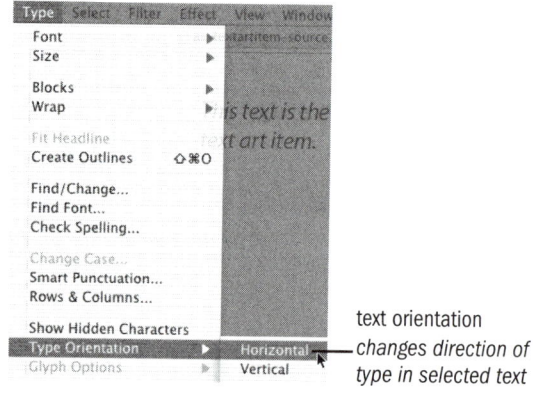

Figure 5.32 *The orientation property lets you change the way the text is drawn in a text object.*

Elements

ELEMENT	CAN BE REFERENCED BY
character	index, before/after, range, test
insertion point	index, before/after, range, test
line	index, before/after, range, test
paragraph	index, before/after, range, test
text	index, before/after, range
word	index, before/after, range, test

Properties

PROPERTY	VALUE TYPE	EXPLANATION
auto kerning	boolean	Should the font's built-in kerning rules be used?
baseline shift	real	The baseline offset.
best type*	class	The best type for the text object. Always returns string.
character offset*	integer	Offset from beginning (in characters).
class*	class	The text object's class, which is text.
clipping*	boolean	Is there a clipping path associated with the text art item containing this text?
container*	object reference	A reference to the text art item that contains this text.
contents	string	The contents of the character as a string.
default type*	class	The default type for the text object, which is string. The string value returned is the value contained in the text's contents property.
direction	normal/rotated/KumiMoji	The direction of characters in a vertical text block.
evenodd	boolean	Should the even-odd rule be used to determine fills?
fill color	CMYK color info/gray color info/RGB color info/spot color info/pattern color info/gradient color info	The character's fill color.
fill overprint	boolean	Should art beneath the filled character be overprinted?
filled	boolean	Should the character's path be filled?
font	string	The name of the text face (font).
index*	integer	The index of this text in the complete string.
leading	real	The leading.
length*	integer	Length (in characters).
note*	string	A note associated with the text.
properties	record	All of the character's properties returned in a single record (properties that are individually read-only remain so in this record).
resolution*	real	The resolution of the path in dots per inch (dpi).

Properties (continued)

PROPERTY	VALUE TYPE	EXPLANATION
scaling	fixed point	Horizontal and vertical scaling specified as a point value.
size	real	The font size.
stroke cap	butted/rounded/projecting	The type of cap on the character's stroke.
stroke color	CMYK color info/gray color info/RGB color info/spot color info/pattern color info/gradient color info	The stroke color of the text.
stroke dash offset	real	The default distance to start the stroke dash pattern.
stroke dashes	list (of reals)	The lengths for dashes and gaps in dashed lines, starting with the first dash length, followed by the first gap length, and so on. Set to an empty list, {}, for a solid line.
stroke join	mitered/rounded/beveled	The type of joins in the text stroke.
stroke miter limit	real	The angle at which a stroke join switches from mitered to beveled.
stroke overprint	boolean	Should art beneath the stroked text be overprinted?
stroke width	real	The width of the stroke.
stroked	boolean	Should the text path be stroked?
text orientation*	horizontal/vertical	The orientation of the text. Use the text path class to modify this value.
text path*	object reference	A reference to the text path associated with the text art item containing this text.
tracking	real	The uniform spacing amount between characters.

Valid Commands

COMMAND	RETURN VALUE	EXPLANATION
count of text [in object-reference/whose match-criteria]	integer	Returns number of text in containing object or found by whose criteria.
delete text index [in object-reference/whose match-criteria]	nothing	Deletes object specified.

Valid Commands (continued)

COMMAND	RETURN VALUE	EXPLANATION
duplicate text index [to location-reference]	layer-reference	Duplicates object specified, returning a reference to the new object.
exists text index [in object-reference/whose match-criteria]	boolean	Tests for the existence of the specified object, returning true or false.
make new text at location-reference [with data {data-list}] [with properties { text-properties}]	text-reference	Creates new object at location specified within containing object using optional properties.

TIP *Text can be accessed using the character, insertion point, word, line, paragraph, and text classes. All text is contained within text art items.*

character, characters

A character or list of characters in the contents of a text art item.

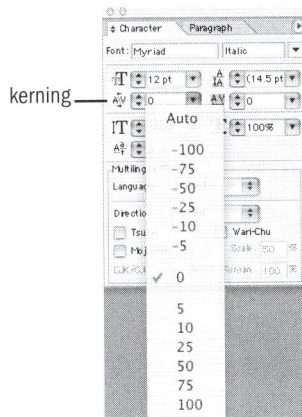

Figure 5.33 *The kerning property of a character object lets you change the individual spacing between it and the next character.*

Elements

ELEMENT	CAN BE REFERENCED BY
character	index, before/after, range, test
insertion point	index, before/after, range, test
line	index, before/after, range, test
paragraph	index, before/after, range, test
text	index, before/after, range
word	index, before/after, range, test

Properties

PROPERTY	VALUE TYPE	EXPLANATION
kerning	real	The character spacing between characters.

Properties inherited from the superclass text:
auto kerning, baseline shift, best type*, character offset*, class*, clipping*, container*, contents, default type*, direction, evenodd, fill color, fill overprint, filled, font, index*, leading, length*, note*, properties, resolution, scaling, size, stroke cap, stroke color, stroke dash offset, stroke dashes, stroke join, stroke miter limit, stroke overprint, stroke width, stroked, text orientation*, text path*, tracking

Valid Commands

COMMAND	RETURN VALUE	EXPLANATION
move character index-or-name [in object-reference/whose match-criteria] to location-reference	layer-reference	Move object to location specified within containing object.

Commands inherited from the superclass text:
count, delete, duplicate, exists, make

TIP *The text contained within text art items in Illustrator can be accessed using the character, insertion point, word, line, paragraph, and text classes. The properties and valid commands for all of these classes are similar but not identical. For example, while character has a kerning property, the other text classes do not.*

insertion point, insertion points

One or more insertion points in the contents of a text art item.

Elements

ELEMENT	CAN BE REFERENCED BY
character	index, before/after, range, test
insertion point	index, before/after, range, test
line	index, before/after, range, test
paragraph	index, before/after, range, test
text	index, before/after, range
word	index, before/after, range, test

Properties

Properties inherited from the superclass text:
auto kerning*, baseline shift*, best type*, character offset*, class*, clipping*, container*, contents, default type*, direction*, evenodd*, fill color*, fill overprint*, filled*, font*, index*, leading*, length*, note*, properties, resolution*, scaling*, size*, stroke cap*, stroke color*, stroke dash offset*, stroke dashes*, stroke join*, stroke miter limit*, stroke overprint*, stroke width*, stroked*, text orientation*, text path*, tracking*

Valid Commands

Commands inherited from the superclass text:
count, exists

> **TIPS** *An insertion point is logically located between two characters in a text art item. Each insertion point is before the corresponding character in a text art item. Insertion point 1 is before character 1, etc.*
>
> *The properties of an insertion point are the same as the character at the same position in the text art item. For example, the font for insertion point 2 of text art item 1 will be the same as the font for character 2 of text art item 1.*
>
> *You can set the properties for an insertion point, but only setting the contents property will have any affect on the text art item. The result of setting the contents of an insertion point to a string value is to insert the string in the text art item at the insertion point's location. Setting the contents to an empty string has no affect.*

line, lines

A line or lines of text in a text art item.

Elements

ELEMENT	CAN BE REFERENCED BY
character	index, before/after, range, test
insertion point	index, before/after, range, test
line	index, before/after, range, test
paragraph	index, before/after, range, test
text	index, before/after, range
word	index, before/after, range, test

Properties

Properties inherited from the superclass text:

auto kerning, baseline shift, best type*, character offset*, class*, clipping*, container*, contents, default type*, direction, evenodd, fill color, fill overprint, filled, font, index*, leading, length*, note*, properties, resolution*, scaling, size, stroke cap, stroke color, stroke dash offset, stroke dashes, stroke join, stroke miter limit, stroke overprint, stroke width, stroked, text orientation*, text path*, tracking

Valid Commands

Commands inherited from the superclass text:
count, delete, duplicate, exists

TIPS *Illustrator's text can be accessed using the character, insertion point, word, line, paragraph, and text classes.*

Lines of text cannot be created. When the contents property of a text art item is modified, Illustrator will create text lines as it reflows the text within the text art item.

paragraph, paragraphs

A paragraph or list of paragraphs of text in the contents of a text art object.

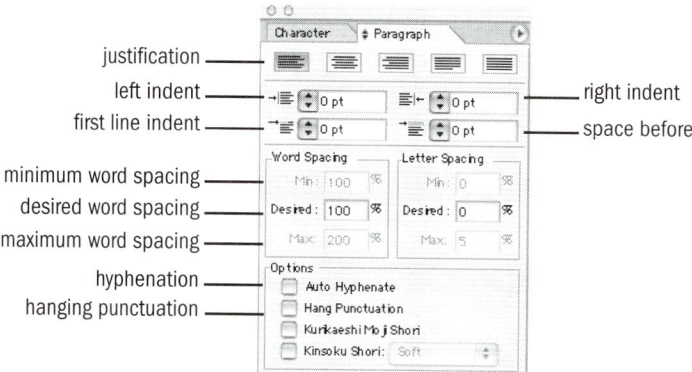

Figure 5.34 *The Paragraph palette provides access to the layout properties of the paragraph object.*

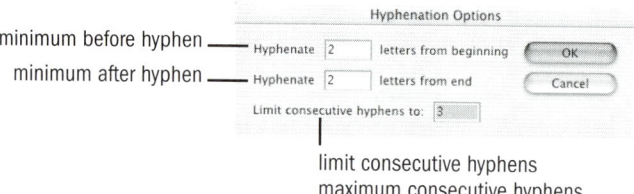

Figure 5.35 *The Hyphenation Options dialog box of the Paragraph palette gives the user access to the detailed hyphenation settings for a paragraph object.*

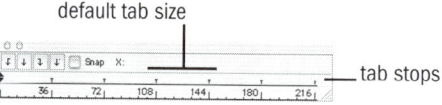

Figure 5.36 *The default tab size property of a paragraph object describes the distance between default tabs on the paragraph's Tab Ruler. The tab stops provide access to individual tab settings for the paragraph. AppleScript provides access to individual tab settings, but Visual Basic does not.*

Elements

ELEMENT	CAN BE REFERENCED BY
character	index, before/after, range, test
insertion point	index, before/after, range, test
line	index, before/after, range, test
paragraph	index, before/after, range, test
text	index, before/after, range
word	index, before/after, range, test

Properties

PROPERTY	VALUE TYPE	EXPLANATION
default tab size	real	The default distance between tab stops.
desired letter spacing	real	The desired letter spacing expressed as a percentage, where 100.0 is 100%.
desired word spacing	real	The desired word spacing expressed as a percentage, where 100.0 is 100%.
first line indent	real	The left indent of the first line of text.
hanging punctuation	boolean	Should punctuation appear outside the margins of the paragraph?
hyphenation	boolean	Is hyphenation enabled for the paragraph?
justification	unknown/left/center/right/justify full lines/justify all lines	The text justification for the paragraph.
left indent	real	The left indent of the margin.
limit consecutive hyphenations	boolean	Is there a limit on the number of consecutive hyphenated lines?
maximum consecutive hyphens	integer	The maximum number of consecutive hyphenated lines if limit consecutive hyphenations is set to true.
maximum letter spacing	real	The maximum letter spacing expressed as a percentage, where 100.0 is 100%.
maximum word spacing	real	The maximum word spacing expressed as a percentage, where 100.0 is 100%.
minimum after hyphen	integer	The minimum number of characters after a hyphen.
minimum before hyphen	integer	The minimum number of characters before a hyphen.

Properties

PROPERTY	VALUE TYPE	EXPLANATION
minimum letter spacing	real	The minimum letter spacing expressed as a percentage, where 100.0 is 100%.
minimum word spacing	real	The minimum word spacing expressed as a percentage, where 100.0 is 100%.
repeated character processing	boolean	Should Repeated Character Processing be used in the paragraph?
right indent	real	The right indent of margin.
space before	real	The spacing before paragraphs.
tab stops	list (of tab stop info)	The tab stop settings for the paragraph returned in a list with each item consisting of a record using this format: {alignment, decimal character, position}. The alignment property of the record accepts these values: center/decimal/left/right/unknown. The decimal character property can be set to a single character for matching decimal tab stops. The position property is a real number defining the tabs position.

Properties inherited from the superclass text:
   48 auto kerning, baseline shift, best type*, character offset*, class*, clipping*, container*, contents, default type*, direction, evenodd, fill color, fill overprint, filled, font, index*, leading, length*, note*, properties, resolution*, scaling, size, stroke cap, stroke color, stroke dash offset, stroke dashes, stroke join, stroke miter limit, stroke overprint, stroke width, stroked, text orientation*, text path*, tracking

Valid Commands

COMMAND	RETURN VALUE	EXPLANATION
move paragraph index-or-name [in object-reference/whose match-criteria] to location-reference	layer-reference	Move object to location specified within containing object.

Commands inherited from the superclass text:
   count, delete, duplicate, exists, make

TIPS *Illustrator's text can be accessed using the character, insertion point, word, line, paragraph, and text classes. All text is contained within text art items.*

The paragraph class has additional properties that other related classes do not share, including properties for margins, tab stop settings, hyphenation, and word/letter spacing.

word

A string of text in a text art item that is separated by white space.

Elements

ELEMENT	CAN BE REFERENCED BY
character	index, before/after, range, test
insertion point	index, before/after, range, test
line	index, before/after, range, test
paragraph	index, before/after, range, test
text	index, before/after, range
word	index, before/after, range, test

Properties

Properties inherited from the superclass text:
auto kerning, baseline shift, best type*, character offset*, class*, clipping*, container*, contents, default type*, direction, evenodd, fill color, fill overprint, filled, font, index*, leading, length*, note*, properties, resolution*, scaling, size, stroke cap, stroke color, stroke dash offset, stroke dashes, stroke join, stroke miter limit, stroke overprint, stroke width, stroked, text orientation*, text path*, tracking

Valid Commands

COMMAND	RETURN VALUE	EXPLANATION
move word index-or-name [in object-reference/whose match-criteria] to location-reference	layer-reference	Move object to location specified within containing object.

Commands inherited from the superclass text:
 count, delete, duplicate, exists, make

> **TIP** Illustrator's text can be accessed using the character, insertion point, word, line, paragraph, and text classes. All text is contained within text art items.

Swatch Palette Color Objects

These objects all reside in the Swatches palette of your document. Using the swatch or swatches object form will give you access to every swatch in the document's palette. Using the spot or spots form will let you access spot color swatches, global process color swatches, and registration color swatches. The gradient swatch and its various parts are all also accessible. Pattern color swatches are the only kind of color swatch you cannot create from a script.

gradient, gradients

A gradient definition or gradient definitions. Gradients are contained in documents.

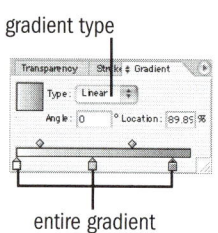

Figure 5.37 *Gradient colors are complicated. The Gradient palette of the user interface provides only basic properties, such as gradient type, and access to each of the gradient stops.*

Elements

ELEMENT	CAN BE REFERENCED BY
gradient stop	index, before/after, range, test

Properties

PROPERTY	VALUE TYPE	EXPLANATION
best type*	class	The best type for the gradient object's value. Always returns reference.
class*	class	The gradient object's class, which is gradient.
container*	object reference	A reference to the document that contains this gradient.
default type*	class	The default type for the gradient object's value. Always returns reference.
entire gradient	list (of gradient stop info)	All of the gradient stops in the gradient.
gradient type	linear/radial	The type of the gradient.
index*	integer	The position of this gradient in the application.
name	string	The gradient's name.
properties	record	All of the gradient's properties returned in a single record (properties that are individually read-only remain so in this record).

Valid Commands

COMMAND	RETURN VALUE	EXPLANATION
count of gradients [in object-reference/whose match-criteria]	integer	Returns number of gradients in containing object or found by whose criteria.
delete gradient index-or-name [in object-reference/whose match-criteria]	nothing	Deletes object specified.
duplicate gradient index-or-name [to location-reference]	layer-reference	Duplicates object specified, returning a reference to the new object.
exists gradient index-or-name [in object-reference/whose match-criteria]	boolean	Tests for the existence of the specified object, returning true or false.
make new gradient at location-reference [with data {data-list}] [with properties { gradient-properties}]	gradient-reference	Creates new object at location specified within containing object using optional properties.

TIP *Illustrator's gradient object represents a gradient as defined in the Illustrator application. Additional gradients may be created by the user within Illustrator or via a script.*

gradient stop, gradient stops

A gradient stop definition or definitions contained in a specific gradient.

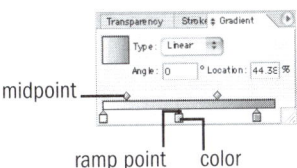

Figure 5.38 Each individual gradient stop in a gradient object defines the color, ramp point (where the color starts), and midpoint (where the color blends 50% with the next stop to the left's color).

Properties

PROPERTY	VALUE TYPE	EXPLANATION
best type*	class	The best type for the gradient stop object's value. Always returns reference.
class*	class	The gradient stop object's class, which is gradient stop.
color	CMYK color info/gray color info/RGB color info/spot color info/pattern color info/gradient color info	The color linked to this gradient stop.

Properties (contiued)

PROPERTY	VALUE TYPE	EXPLANATION
container*	object reference	A reference to the gradient that contains this gradient stop.
default type*	class	The default type for the gradient stop object's value. Always returns reference.
index*	integer	The position of this gradient stop in the gradient.
midpoint	real	The midpoint of the blend between this stop's and the next stop's colors. Range: 13.0–87.0.
properties	record	All of the gradient stop's properties returned in a single record (properties that are individually read-only remain so in this record).
ramp point	real	The location of the color in the gradient. Range: 0.0–100.0.

Valid Commands

COMMAND	RETURN VALUE	EXPLANATION
count of gradient stops [in object-reference/whose match-criteria]	integer	Returns number of gradient stops in containing object or found by whose criteria.
delete gradient stop index-or-name [in object-reference/whose match-criteria]	nothing	Deletes object specified.
duplicate gradient stop index-or-name [to location-reference]	layer-reference	Duplicates object specified, returning a reference to the new object.
exists gradient stop index-or-name [in object-reference/whose match-criteria]	boolean	Tests for the existence of the specified object, returning true or false.
make new gradient stop at location-reference [with data {data-list}] [with properties { gradient-stop-properties}]	gradient-stop-reference	Creates new object at location specified within containing object using optional properties.

TIP *Illustrator's gradient stop object represents a point on a specific gradient defined in the Illustrator application. Each gradient stop specifies a color change in the containing gradient.*

gradient stop info

Gradient stop information of a specific gradient, returned by the entire gradient property of a gradient.

Properties

PROPERTY	VALUE TYPE	EXPLANATION
color	CMYK color info/gray color info/RGB color info/spot color info/pattern color info/gradient color info	The color linked to this gradient stop.
midpoint	real	The midpoint of the blend between this stop's and the next stop's colors. Range: 13.0–87.0.
ramp point	real	The location of the color in the gradient. Range: 0.0–100.0.

TIPS When you get the entire gradient property of a gradient, a list of gradient stop info records is returned—one record for each gradient stop in the gradient.

The gradient stops for a new gradient can be specified by providing a list of gradient stop info records in the entire gradient property. The following applies when creating a gradient from a list of gradient stop info records:

- A gradient stop's location in the gradient is determined by its ramp point value, not the gradient stop info record's order in the entire gradient list.

- The midpoint value of the last gradient stop info record in the entire gradient list is not used for the newly created gradient and need not be provided. If it is present, its value must be in the valid range.

pattern, patterns

A pattern definition or list of definitions contained in a document.

Properties

PROPERTY	VALUE TYPE	EXPLANATION
best type*	class	The best type for the pattern object's value. Always returns reference.
class*	class	The pattern object's class, which is pattern.
container*	object reference	A reference to the document that contains this pattern.
default type*	class	The default type for the pattern object's value. Always returns reference.

Properties (continued)

PROPERTY	VALUE TYPE	EXPLANATION
index*	integer	The position of this pattern in the application.
name	string	The pattern name.
properties	record	All of the pattern properties returned in a single record (properties that are individually read-only remain so in this record).

Valid Commands

COMMAND	RETURN VALUE	EXPLANATION
count of patterns [in object-reference/whose match-criteria]	integer	Returns number of patterns in containing object or found by whose criteria.
delete pattern index-or-name [in object-reference/whose match-criteria]	nothing	Deletes object specified.
exists pattern index-or-name [in object-reference/whose match-criteria]	boolean	Tests for the existence of the specified object, returning true or false.

TIP *Illustrator's pattern object represents a pattern as defined in the Illustrator application.*

spot, spots

A spot color definition or list of definitions contained in a document.

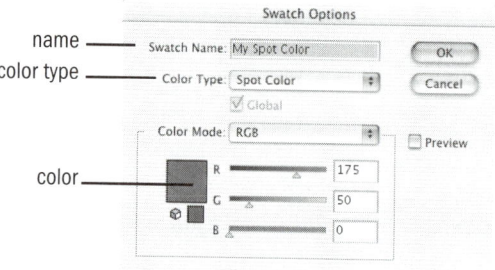

Figure 5.39 *A spot is a spot color swatch saved on the Swatches palette. The Swatch Options dialog box, opened by double-clicking a swatch in the palette, shows some of a spot's properties.*

Properties

PROPERTY	VALUE TYPE	EXPLANATION
best type*	class	The best type for the spot object. Always returns reference.
class*	class	The spot object's class, which is spot.
color	CMYK color info/gray color info/RGB color info/spot color info/pattern color info/gradient color info	The color information for this spot.
color type	spot color/process color/registration color	The type of this spot definition.
container*	object reference	A reference to the document that contains this spot.
default type*	class	The default type for the spot. Always returns reference.
index*	integer	The position of this spot in the document.
name	string	The spot's unique name.
properties	record	All of the spot's properties returned in a single record (properties that are individually read-only remain so in this record).

Valid Commands

COMMAND	RETURN VALUE	EXPLANATION
count of spots [in object-reference/whose match-criteria]	integer	Returns number of spots in containing object or found by whose criteria.
delete spot index-or-name [in object-reference/whose match-criteria]	nothing	Deletes object specified.
duplicate spot index-or-name [to location-reference]	layer-reference	Duplicates object specified, returning a reference to the new object.
exists spot index-or-name [in object-reference/whose match-criteria]	boolean	Tests for the existence of the specified object, returning true or false.
make new spot at location-reference [with data {data-list}] [with properties { spot-properties}]	spot-reference	Creates new object at location specified within containing object using optional properties.

TIP *Illustrator's spot object represents a spot color as defined by Illustrator. All Illustrator documents contain the spot color "[Registration]", which can be used to print to all plates of a separation.*

If no properties are specified when creating a new spot, default properties will be provided. However, if specifying the color, you must use the same color space as the document: either CMYK or RGB. Otherwise, an error will result. When created, the spot is inserted into the Swatches palette at the end.

swatch, swatches

A color swatch or list of swatches contained in a document.

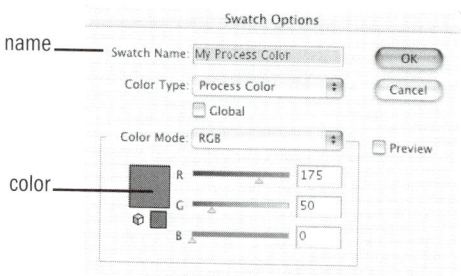

Figure 5.40 *A swatch is a color of any type saved on the Swatches palette.*

Properties

PROPERTY	VALUE TYPE	EXPLANATION
best type*	class	The best type for the swatch. Always returns reference.
class*	class	The swatch object's class, which is swatch.
color	CMYK color info/gray color info/RGB color info/spot color info/pattern color info/gradient color info	The color information for this swatch.
container*	object reference	A reference to the document that contains this swatch.
default type*	class	The default type for the swatch. Always returns reference.
index*	integer	The position of this swatch in the document.
name	string	The unique name of the swatch.
properties	record	All of the swatch's properties returned in a single record (properties that are individually read-only remain so in this record).

Valid Commands

COMMAND	RETURN VALUE	EXPLANATION
count of swatches [in object-reference/whose match-criteria]	integer	Returns number of swatches in containing object or found by whose criteria.
delete swatch index-or-name [in object-reference/whose match-criteria]	nothing	Deletes object specified.
duplicate swatch index-or-name [to location-reference]	layer-reference	Duplicates object specified, returning a reference to the new object.
exists swatch index-or-name [in object-reference/whose match-criteria]	boolean	Tests for the existence of the specified object, returning true or false.
make new swatch at location-reference [with data {data-list}] [with properties { swatch-properties}]	swatch-reference	Creates new object at location specified within containing object using optional properties.

TIP *The swatches correspond to the Swatches palette in Illustrator's user interface. Additional swatches can be created either manually by a user or by a script. The swatch can hold all types of color data (i.e., pattern, gradient, CMYK, RGB, gray, spot).*

Basic Color Definitions

CMYK color info

A CMYK color specification used to specify a CMYK color in conjunction with the color property.

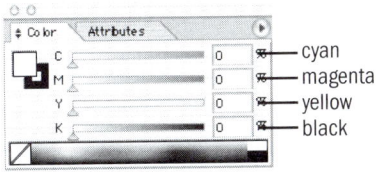

Figure 5.41 *A CMYK color info object is simply an instance of a color definition, as represented by the Color palette. The act of creating a CMYK color info object and setting its properties is just like opening the Color palette with no objects selected and mixing up a new color setting.*

Properties

PROPERTY	VALUE TYPE	EXPLANATION
cyan	real	The cyan color value as a value in the range 0.0–100.0.
magenta	real	The magenta color value as a value in the range 0.0–100.0.
yellow	real	The yellow color value as a value in the range 0.0–100.0.
black	real	The black color value as a value in the range 0.0–100.0.

TIPS *This class is used to define a record that contains the color component values of a CMYK color. It is used for specifying and retrieving color information from an Illustrator document or from page items in a document.*

If the color space of a document is RGB and you specify the color value for a page item in that document using CMYK color info, Illustrator will translate the CMYK color specification into an RGB color specification. The same thing happens if the document's color space is CMYK and you specify colors using RGB color info. Since this translation can cause information loss, you should specify colors using the color info class that matches the document's color space.

gradient color info

A gradient color specification used to specify a gradient color in conjunction with the color property.

angle —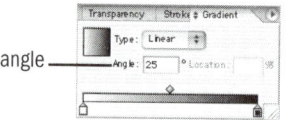

Figure 5.42 *You can set the angle property of a gradient only when you're ready to apply the color and need to define a gradient color info object.*

Properties

PROPERTY	VALUE TYPE	EXPLANATION
angle	real	The gradient vector angle (in degrees).
gradient	object reference	A reference to the gradient object that defines the gradient to use in this color definition.
hilite angle	real	The gradient hilite vector angle (in degrees).
hilite length	real	The gradient hilite vector length.

Properties (continued)

PROPERTY	VALUE TYPE	EXPLANATION
length	real	The gradient vector length.
matrix	matrix	An additional transformation matrix to manipulate the gradient path.
origin	fixed point	The gradient vector origin.

TIP *This class is used to define a record that contains the color component values of a gradient color swatch. It is used for specifying and retrieving color information from an Illustrator document or from page items in a document.*

gray color info

A gray color specification used to specify a gray color in conjunction with the color property.

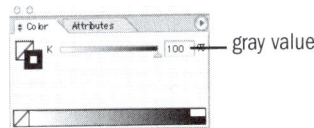

Figure 5.43 *A gray color info object is simply a definition of a gray tint of black, as represented by the Color palette.*

Properties

PROPERTY	VALUE TYPE	EXPLANATION
gray value	real	The tint of the gray as a value in the range 0.0–100.0

TIPS *This class is used to define a record that contains the tint value of a gray color. It is used for specifying and retrieving color information from an Illustrator document or from page items in a document.*

Gray colors are specified using a real value that ranges from 0.0 to 100.0 for the tint of color, where 0.0 represents white and 100.0 represents black.

pattern color info

A pattern color specification is used to specify a pattern color in conjunction with the color property.

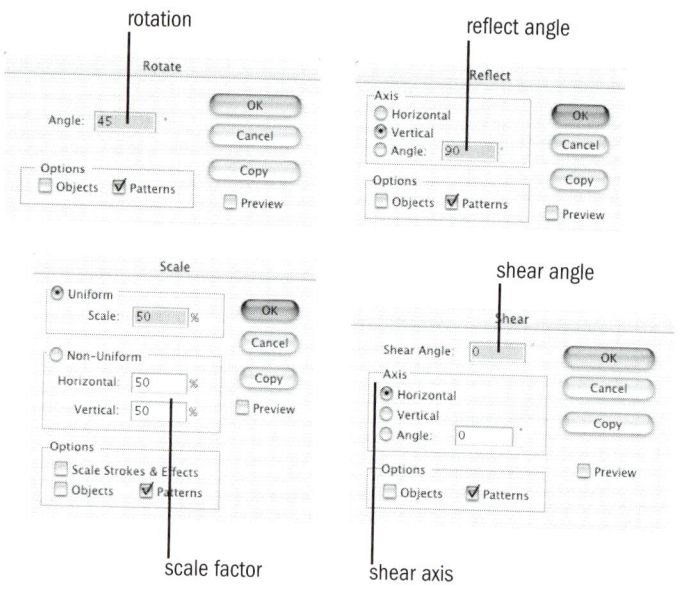

Figure 5.44 *A pattern color info object has a large number of properties to allow you to change the pattern's appearance from a script. These properties correspond to some of the details shown in the various object transformation dialog boxes available in the user interface.*

Properties

PROPERTY	VALUE TYPE	EXPLANATION
matrix	matrix	An additional transformation matrix to manipulate the prototype pattern.
pattern	object reference	A reference to the pattern object that defines the pattern to use in this color definition.
reflect	boolean	Is the prototype reflected before filling?
reflect angle	real	The axis (in degrees) around which to reflect.
rotation	real	The angle (in degrees) to rotate the prototype pattern before filling.
scale factor	fixed point	The horizontal and vertical scaling to scale the prototype pattern expressed as a fixed point.
shear angle	real	The angle (in degrees) to slant the shear by.

Properties

PROPERTY	VALUE TYPE	EXPLANATION
shear axis	real	The axis (in degrees) to shear with respect to.
shift angle	real	The angle (in degrees) to translate the unscaled prototype pattern before filling
shift distance	real	The distance to translate the unscaled prototype pattern before filling.

TIP *Pattern colors are created using a reference to an existing pattern in a document. A matrix may be specified to further transform the pattern color.*

RGB color info

An RGB color specification used to specify an RGB color in conjunction with the color property.

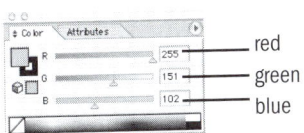

Figure 5.45 *An RGB color info object is simply an instance of a red-green-blue color definition, as represented by the Color palette.*

Properties

PROPERTY	VALUE TYPE	EXPLANATION
red	real	The red color value as a value in the range 0.0–255.0
green	real	The green color value as a value in the range 0.0–255.0.
blue	real	The blue color value as a value in the range 0.0–255.0.

TIP *If the color space of a document is CMYK and you specify the color value for a page item in that document using RGB color info, Illustrator will translate the RGB color specification into a CMYK color specification. The same thing happens if the document's color space is RGB and you specify colors using CMYK color info. Since this translation can cause information loss, you should specify colors using the color info class that matches the document's color space.*

spot color info

A spot color specification used to specify a spot color in conjunction with the color property.

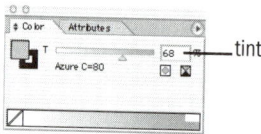

Figure 5.46 *A spot color info object needs to have a spot color to reference. This means that you need to have a spot color swatch defined first.*

Properties

PROPERTY	VALUE TYPE	EXPLANATION
spot	object reference	A reference to the spot object that defines the color.
tint	real	The tint of the color as a value in the range 0.0–100.0.

TIP *The spot property must be set to a reference to an existing spot color definition.*

Objects Related to Save, Export, and Open Options

EPS save options

Options that may be supplied when saving a document as an Illustrator EPS file. See the save command in the command reference for additional details.

Properties

PROPERTY	VALUE TYPE	EXPLANATION
CMYK PostScript	boolean	Use CMYK PostScript? (Default: false)
compatibility	Illustrator 3/Illustrator 4/ Illustrator 5/Illustrator 6/ Illustrator 7/Illustrator 8/ Illustrator 9	Specifies the version of the Illustrator file format to create. (Default: Illustrator 9)
embed all fonts	boolean	Include fonts used in the EPS file? (Default: false)
embed linked files	boolean	Are linked image files to be included in the saved document? (Default: false)

Properties (continued)

PROPERTY	VALUE TYPE	EXPLANATION
flatten output	preserve paths/preserve appearance	How should transparency be flattened for file formats before Illustrator 9. (Default: preserve appearance)
included document thumbnails	boolean	Include thumbnail image of the EPS artwork? (Default: true)
japanese file format	boolean	Save the file using Japanese version of file format? Valid only for Illustrator 3–5 compatibility. (Default: false)
PostScript	level 1/level 2/level 3	Specifies the PostScript level to use when saving the file. (Default: level 3)
preview	none/BW Macintosh/color Macintosh/BW TIFF/color TIFF/transparent color TIFF	Specifies the format for the EPS preview image. (Default: color Macintosh)

Valid Commands

COMMAND	RETURN VALUE	EXPLANATION
save document index-or-name in file-specification [as eps/Illustrator/pdf] [with options save-related-options]	document-reference	Saves document in file as file type specified.

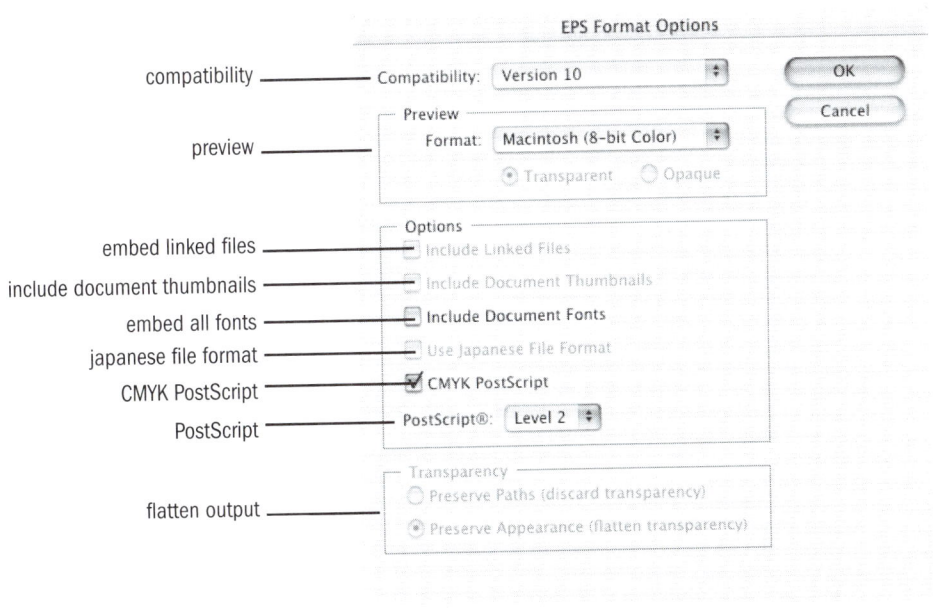

Figure 5.47 *This illustration shows how the EPS Format Options save dialog box maps to properties of the EPS save options object. You need to create a new EPS save options object and set any of its properties to the nondefault values desired before saving a document as an EPS with the save command.*

TIPS *This class is used to define a record containing properties that specify options when saving a document as an EPS file. EPS save options can only be used in conjunction with the save command. It is not possible to get or create an EPS save options object.*

It is not necessary to specify values for all properties. Default values will be provided for any properties not specified.

Flash export options

Options that may be supplied when exporting a document as a Flash .swf file.

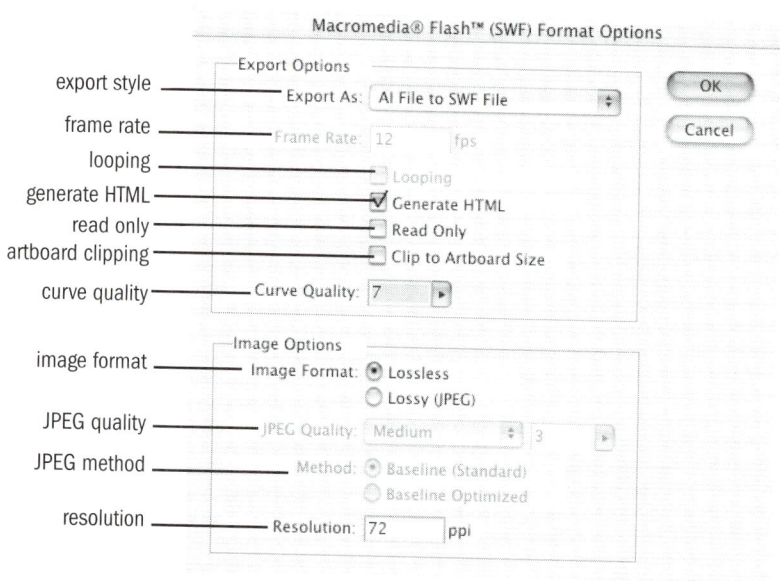

Figure 5.48 *Create a new Flash export options object and set any properties to the values you want before exporting a document as a SWF file with the save command.*

Properties

PROPERTY	VALUE TYPE	EXPLANATION
artboard clipping	boolean	Should the resulting image be clipped to the artboard? (Default: false)
curve quality	integer	How much curve information should be preserved? Range: 0–10. (Default: 7)

Properties (continued)

PROPERTY	VALUE TYPE	EXPLANATION
export style	Flash file/layers to files/layers to frames	How should the Flash file be created? (Default: Flash file)
frame rate	real	Frame rate (per second) when exporting layers to Flash frames. Range: 0.1–120. (Default: 12)
generate HTML	boolean	Create an HTML file as well when exporting Flash file? (Default: true)
image format	lossless/lossy	How should the images in the exported Flash file be compressed? (Default: lossless)
JPEG method	optimized/standard	Which bitmap JPEG compression scheme should be used? (Default: standard)
JPEG quality	integer	Level of JPEG bitmap image compression. Range: 0–10. (Default: 3)
looping	boolean	Should the Flash file be set to loop when run? (Default: false)
read only	boolean	Should the exported Flash file be saved as a read-only file? (Default: false)
replacing	no/ask/yes	If a file with the same name already exists, should it be replaced?
resolution	real	Resolution of bitmap images, in pixels per inch. Range: 72–2400. (Default: 72)

Valid Commands

COMMAND	RETURN VALUE	EXPLANATION
export document index-or-name to file-specification as Flash/GIF/JPEG/PNG24/PNG8/Photoshop/SVG [with options export-related-options]	nothing	Exports document as specified file type with options specified.

TIPS *This class is used to define a record containing properties that specify options when exporting a document as a Flash file. Flash export options can only be used in conjunction with the export command. It is not possible to get or create a Flash export options object.*

It is not necessary to specify values for all properties. Default values will be provided for any properties not specified.

GIF export options

Options that may be supplied when exporting a document as a GIF file. See the export command in the command reference for additional details.

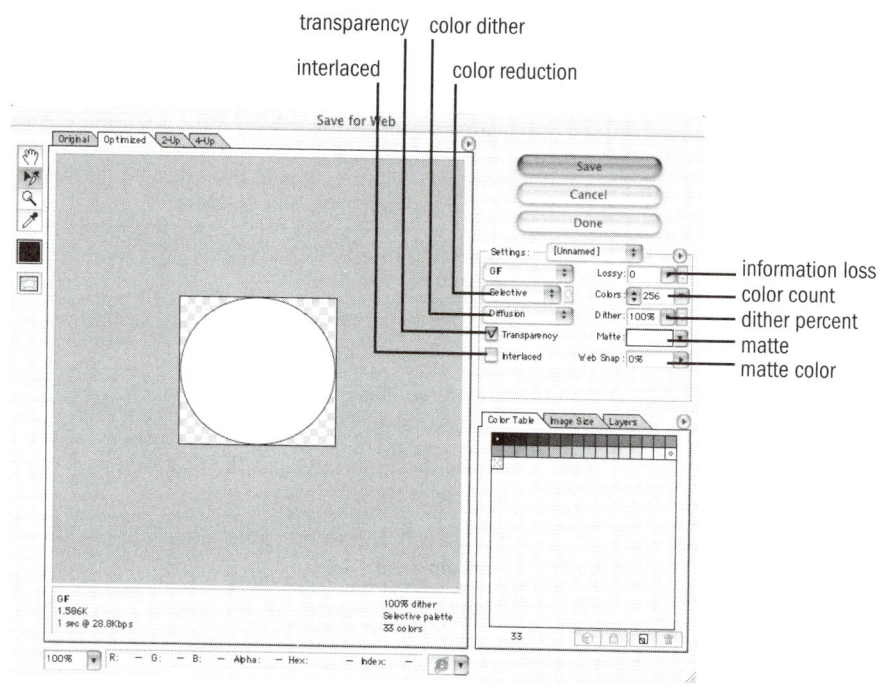

Figure 5.49 *Some of the properties available in the GIF export options object are not made available to the user interface. Can you find any missing? (Hint: anti aliasing and artboard clipping are a couple that seem to be missing to me.)*

Properties

PROPERTY	VALUE TYPE	EXPLANATION
anti aliasing	boolean	Should the resulting image be anti-aliased? (Default: true)
artboard clipping	boolean	Should the resulting image be clipped to the artboard? (Default: false)
color count	integer	The number of colors in the exported color table. Range: 2–256. (Default: 128)
color dither	none/diffusion/pattern dither/white noise/blue noise	The method used to dither colors. (Default: diffusion)
color reduction	selective/adaptive/perceptual/web	The method used to reduce the number of colors in the document. (Default: selective)

Properties (continued)

PROPERTY	VALUE TYPE	EXPLANATION
dither percent	integer	How much should the colors be dithered? Range: 0–100. (Default: 88)
horizontal scaling	real	The horizontal scaling factor to apply to the resulting image. Range: 0.0–100.0. (Default: 100.0)
information loss	integer	The level of information loss during compression (as a percentage). Range: 0–100. (Default: 0)
interlaced	boolean	Should the resulting image be interlaced? (Default: false)
matte	boolean	Should the artboard be matted with a color? (Default: true)
matte color	RGB color info	The color to use when matting the artboard. (Default: {255.0, 255.0, 255.0})
saving as HTML	boolean	Should the resulting image be saved with an accompanying HTML file? (Default: false)
transparency	boolean	Should the resulting image use transparency? (Default: true)
vertical scaling	real	The vertical scaling factor to apply to the resulting image. Range: 0.0–100.0.
web snap	integer	How much should the color table be changed to match the Web palette? Range: 0–100, where 100 is the maximum change. (Default: 0)

Valid Commands

COMMAND	RETURN VALUE	EXPLANATION
export document index-or-name to file-specification as Flash/GIF/JPEG/PNG24/PNG8/Photoshop/SVG [with options export-related-options]	nothing	Exports document as specified file type with options specified.

TIPS *This class is used to define a record containing properties that specify options when exporting a document as a GIF file. GIF export options can only be supplied in conjunction with the export command. It is not possible to get or create a GIF export options object.*

It is not necessary to specify values for all properties. Default values will be provided for any properties not specified.

Illustrator save options

Options that may be supplied when saving a document as an Illustrator file. See the save command in the command reference for additional details.

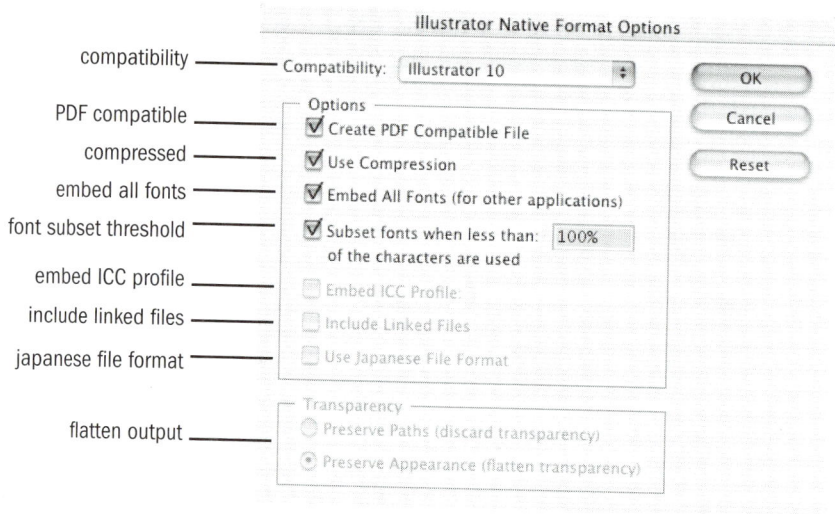

Figure 5.50 *The Illustrator save options object is a mouthful to say, but as an object it provides access to all of the options possible when saving a document from a script with save.*

Properties

PROPERTY	VALUE TYPE	EXPLANATION
compatibility	Illustrator 3/Illustrator 4/ Illustrator 5/Illustrator 6/ Illustrator 7/Illustrator 8/ Illustrator 9/Illustrator 10	Specifies the version of the Illustrator file format to create. (Default: Illustrator 10)
compressed	boolean	Is this file saved in a compressed format? Only for Illustrator 10. (Default: true)
embed all fonts	boolean	Embed all fonts used by the document in the saved file? Only for Illustrator 9 or 10 documents. (Default: false)
embed ICC profile	boolean	Embed the document's ICC profile in the saved file? Only for Illustrator 9 or 10 documents. (Default: false)

Properties (continued)

PROPERTY	VALUE TYPE	EXPLANATION
flatten output	preserve paths/ preserve appearance	How should transparency be flattened for file formats before Illustrator 9/10? (Default: preserve appearance)
font subset threshold	real	Include a subset of fonts when less than this percentage of characters are used. Only for Illustrator 9 or 10 documents. Range: 0.0–100.0. (Default: 100.0)
include linked files	boolean	Are linked image files to be included in the saved document? Only for Illustrator 7 or later documents. (Default: false)
japanese file format	boolean	Save using the Japanese version of the file format? Only for Illustrator 3, 4, or 5 documents. (Default: true)
PDF compatible	boolean	Can the file be opened directly in Acrobat as a PDF? Only for Illustrator 10 documents. (Default: true)

Valid Commands

COMMAND	RETURN VALUE	EXPLANATION
save document index-or-name in file-specification [as eps/Illustrator/pdf] [with options save-related-options]	document-reference	Saves document in file as file type specified.

TIPS *This class is used to define a record containing properties used to specify options when saving a document as an Illustrator file. Illustrator save options can only be supplied in conjunction with the save command. It is not possible to get or create an Illustrator save options object.*

It is not necessary to specify values for all properties. Default values will be provided for any properties not specified.

JPEG export options

Options that may be supplied when exporting a document as a JPEG file. See the export command in the command reference for additional details.

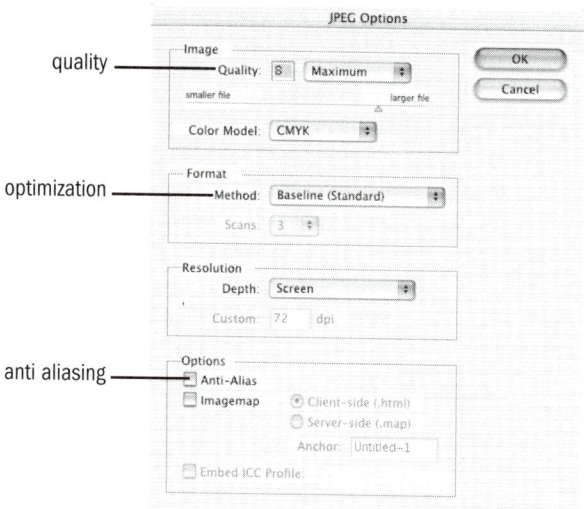

Figure 5.51 Create a new JPEG export options object and set any properties to the values you want before exporting a document as a JPEG file.

Properties

PROPERTY	VALUE TYPE	EXPLANATION
anti aliasing	boolean	Should the resulting image be anti-aliased? (Default: true)
artboard clipping	boolean	Should the resulting image be clipped to the artboard? (Default: false)
blur	real	The amount of blurring to apply to the resulting image. Range: 0.0–2.0. (Default: 0.0)
horizontal scaling	real	The percentage horizontal scaling factor to apply to the resulting image. Range: 0.0–100.0. (Default: 100.0)
matte	boolean	Should the artboard be matted with a color? (Default: true)
matte color	RGB color info	The color to use when matting the artboard. (Default: {255.0, 255.0, 255.0})
optimization	boolean	Should the resulting image be optimized for Web viewing? (Default: true)

Properties (continued)

PROPERTY	VALUE TYPE	EXPLANATION
quality	integer	The quality of the resulting image. Range: 0–100. (Default: 30)
saving as HTML	boolean	Should the resulting image be saved with an accompanying HTML file? (Default: false)
vertical scaling	real	The percentage vertical scaling factor to apply to the resulting image. Range: 0.0–100.0. (Default: 100.0)

Valid Commands

COMMAND	RETURN VALUE	EXPLANATION
export document index-or-name to file-specification as Flash/GIF/JPEG/PNG24/PNG8/Photoshop/SVG [with options export-related-options]	nothing	Exports document as specified file type with options specified.

TIPS *This class is used to define a record containing properties that specify options when exporting a document as a JPEG file. JPEG export options can only be supplied in conjunction with the export command. It is not possible to get or create a JPEG export options object.*

It is not necessary to specify values for all properties. Default values will be provided for any properties not specified.

PDF open options

Options that may be supplied when opening a multipage PDF document.

Properties

PROPERTY	VALUE TYPE	EXPLANATION
page	integer	The page number of the multipage PDF file to open as an Illustrator document.

Valid Commands

COMMAND	RETURN VALUE	EXPLANATION
open file-specification [forcing CMYK/RGB] [with options open-related-options]	document-object-reference	Opens document at specified file.

TIPS *This class is used to define a record containing properties used to specify options when opening a PDF file. PDF open options can only be supplied in conjunction with the open command. It is not possible to get or create a PDF open options object.*

PDF save options

Options that may be supplied when saving a document as an Acrobat PDF file. See the save command in the command reference for additional details.

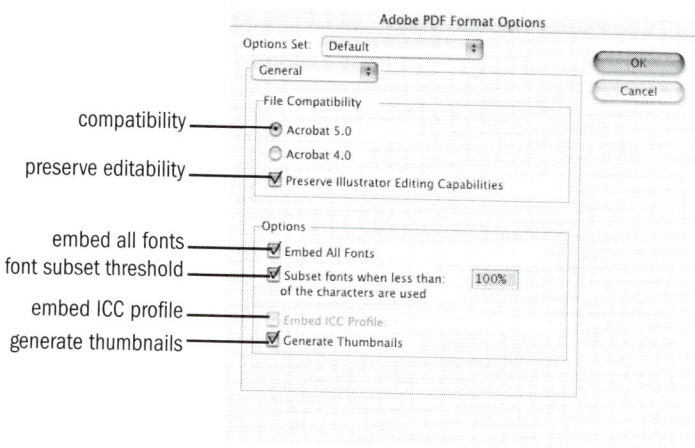

Figure 5.52 *The PDF format is an important one, and the PDF save options object offers full access to all of the properties that user interface dwellers get to play with.*

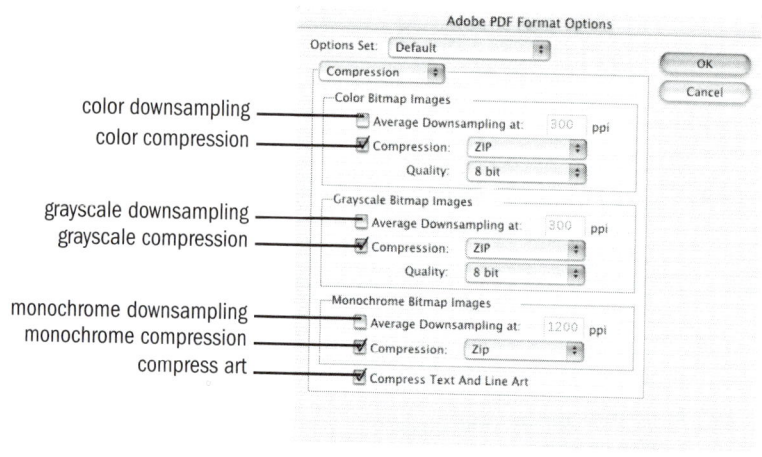

Figure 5.53 *The Compression panel of the Adobe PDF Format Options dialog box shows all of the save properties related to compressing art in the resulting file.*

Properties

PROPERTY	VALUE TYPE	EXPLANATION
color compression	none/automatic/JPEG minimum/JPEG low/ JPEG medium/JPEG high/JPEG maximum/ ZIP4bit/ZIP8bit	The type of color bitmap compression used. (Default: ZIP8bit)
color downsampling	real	The downsampling resolution to use for color images in dots per inch (dpi). If set to zero (0), no downsampling occurs. (Default: 300.0)
compatibility	Acrobat 4/Acrobat 5	Specifies the version of the Acrobat file format to create. (Default: Acrobat 4)
compress art	boolean	Is line art and text to be compressed? (Default: true)
embed all fonts	boolean	Are all fonts to be embedded? (Default: true)
embed ICC profile	boolean	Should the document's ICC profile be embedded in the saved file? (Default: true)
font subset threshold	real	Include a subset of fonts when less than this percentage of characters are used. Range: 0.0–100.0 (Default: 100.0)
generate thumbnails	boolean	Should thumbnails be generated for the saved document? (Default: true)
grayscale compression	none/automatic/JPEG minimum/JPEG low/ JPEG medium/JPEG high/JPEG maximum/ ZIP4bit/ZIP8bit	Specifies type of grayscale bitmap compression used. (Default: ZIP8bit)
grayscale downsampling	real	The downsampling resolution to use for grayscale images in dots per inch (dpi). If set to zero (0), no downsampling occurs. (Default: 300.0)
monochrome compression	none/CCITT3/CCITT4/ ZIP/run length	Specifies type of monochrome bitmap compression used. (Default: ZIP)
monochrome downsampling	real	The downsampling resolution to use for monochrome images in dots per inch (dpi). If set to zero (0), no downsampling occurs. (Default: 1200)

Properties (continued)

PROPERTY	VALUE TYPE	EXPLANATION
preserve editability	boolean	Should Illustrator editing capabilities be preserved when saving the document? (Default: true)

Valid Commands

COMMAND	RETURN VALUE	EXPLANATION
save document index-or-name in file-specification [as eps/Illustrator/pdf] [with options save-related-options]	document-reference	Saves document in file as file type specified.

TIPS *This class is used to define a record containing properties used to specify options when saving a document as a PDF file. PDF save options can only be supplied in conjunction with the save command. It is not possible to get or create a PDF save options object.*

It is not necessary to specify values for all properties. Default values will be provided for any properties not specified.

Photoshop export options

Options that may be supplied when exporting a document as a Photoshop file. See the export command in the command reference for additional details.

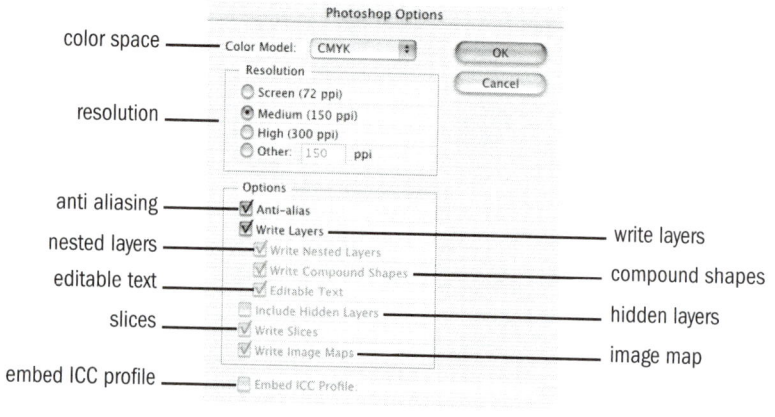

Figure 5.54 *All of the properties available to the user interface for exporting Photoshop files are made available to the Photoshop export options object for use when exporting with the export command.*

Properties

PROPERTY	VALUE TYPE	EXPLANATION
anti aliasing	boolean	Should the exported image be anti-aliased? (Default: true)
color space	Gray/RGB/CMYK	The color space of the exported file. (Default: RGB)
compound shapes	boolean	Should compound shapes be exported as shape layers? (Default: true)
editable text	boolean	Should text objects be exported as editable text layers? (Default: true)
embed ICC profile	boolean	Should an ICC profile be embedded in the exported image? (Default: false)
hidden layers	boolean	Should the hidden layers of the Illustrator document be preserved in the exported image? (Default: false)
image map	boolean	Should image maps be preserved in RGB color space documents using the ImageReady 3.0 format? (Default: true)
nested layers	boolean	Should the nested layers of the Illustrator document be preserved in the exported image? (Default: false)
resolution	real	The resolution of the exported image (in dots per inch). (Default: 150.0)
slices	boolean	Should slices be preserved in the exported file? (Default: true)
warnings	boolean	Should a warning dialog box be displayed because of conflicts in the export settings? (Default: true)
write layers	boolean	Should the layers of the Illustrator document be preserved in the exported image? (Default: true)

Valid Commands

COMMAND	RETURN VALUE	EXPLANATION
export document index-or-name to file-specification as Flash/GIF/JPEG/PNG24/PNG8/Photoshop/SVG [with options export-related-options]	nothing	Exports document as specified file type with options specified.

TIPS *This class is used to define a record containing properties that specify options when exporting a document as a Photoshop file. Photoshop export options can only be supplied in conjunction with the export command. It is not possible to get or create a Photoshop export options object.*

It is not necessary to specify values for all properties. Default values will be provided for any properties not specified.

Photoshop options

Options that may be supplied when opening or placing a Photoshop file.

Properties

PROPERTY	VALUE TYPE	EXPLANATION
best type*	type class	The best type for the object's value.
default type*	type class	The default type for the object's value.
class type*	class	The object's class.
properties	record	All of this object's properties returned in a single record.
preserve image maps	boolean	Should image maps be preserved when the document is converted? (Default: true)
preserve layers	boolean	Should layers be preserved when the document is converted? (Default: true)
preserve slices	boolean	Should slices be preserved when the document is converted? (Default: true)

Valid Commands

COMMAND	RETURN VALUE	EXPLANATION
open file-specification [forcing CMYK/RGB] [with options open-related-options]	document-object-reference	Opens document at specified file.

TIPS *This class is used to define a record containing properties that specify options when opening a Photoshop file. Photoshop options can only be supplied in conjunction with the open command. It is not possible to get or create a Photoshop options object.*

It is not necessary to specify values for all properties. Default values will be provided for any properties not specified.

PNG24 export options

Options that may be supplied when exporting a document as a PNG file with 24-bit color. See the export command in the command reference for additional details.

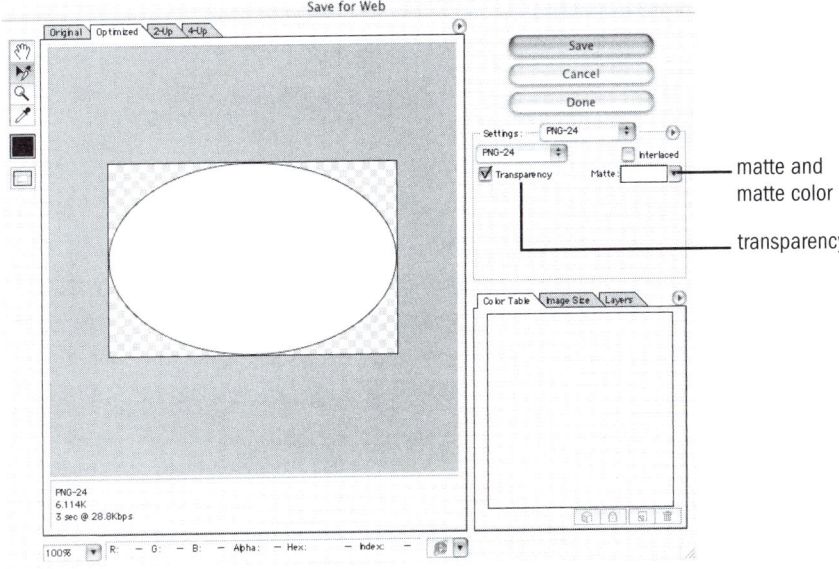

Figure 5.55 *The PNG24 export options object has many more properties available for exporting PNG-24 images from a script than the user interface provides for in Illustrator. But curiously, there is not an interlaced property in PNG24 export options, so the user interface gets access to one property that we, as scripters, do not.*

Properties

PROPERTY	VALUE TYPE	EXPLANATION
anti aliasing	boolean	Should the resulting image be anti-aliased? (Default: true)
artboard clipping	boolean	Should the resulting image be clipped to the artboard? (Default: false)
horizontal scaling	real	The percentage horizontal scaling factor to apply to the resulting image. Range: 0.0–100.0. (Default: 100.0)
matte	boolean	Should the artboard be matted with a color? (Default: true)
matte color	RGB color info	The color to use when matting the artboard. (Default: {255.0, 255.0, 255.0})
saving as HTML	boolean	Should the resulting image be saved with an accompanying HTML file? (Default: false)
transparency	boolean	Should the resulting image use transparency? (Default: true)
vertical scaling	real	The percentage vertical scaling factor to apply to the resulting image. Range: 0.0–100.0. (Default: 100.0)

Valid Commands

COMMAND	RETURN VALUE	EXPLANATION
export document index-or-name to file-specification as Flash/GIF/JPEG/PNG24/PNG8/Photoshop/SVG [with options export-related-options]	nothing	Exports document as specified file type with options specified.

TIPS *This class is used to define a record containing properties that specify options when exporting a document as a PNG-24 file. PNG-24 export options can only be supplied in conjunction with the export command. It is not possible to get or create a PNG-24 export options object.*

It is not necessary to specify values for all properties. Default values will be provided for any properties not specified.

PNG8 export options

Options that may be supplied when exporting a document as a PNG file with 8-bit color. See the export command in the command reference for additional details.

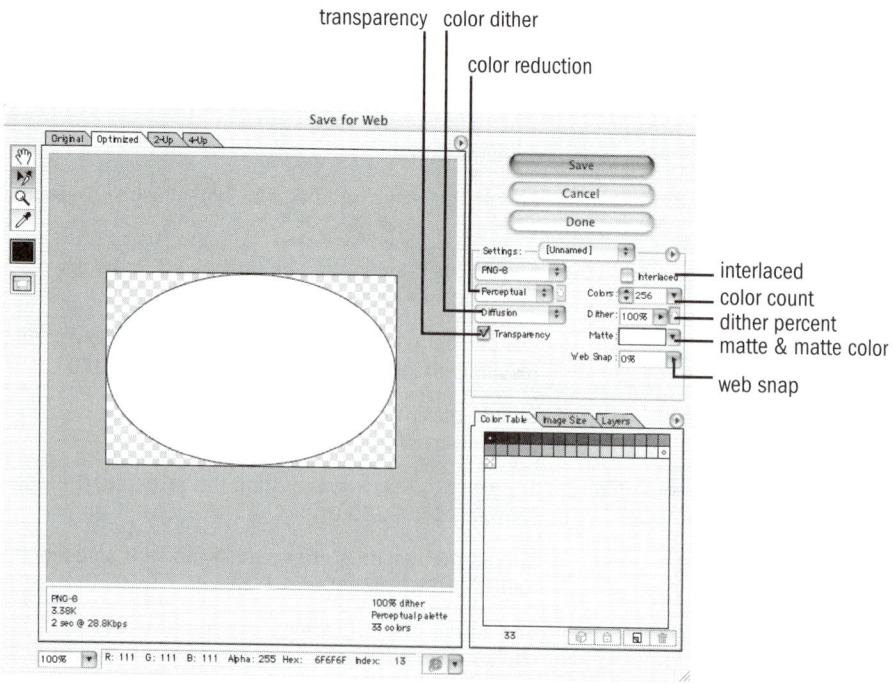

Figure 5.56 *The Save for Web dialog box gives users a good number of options when exporting a PNG-8 image. The PNG8 export options object offers a similar array of properties for use with export.*

Properties

PROPERTY	VALUE TYPE	EXPLANATION
anti aliasing	boolean	Should the resulting image be anti-aliased? (Default: true)
artboard clipping	boolean	Should the resulting image be clipped to the artboard? (Default: false)
color count	integer	The number of colors in the exported color table. Range: 2–256. (Default: 128)
color dither	none/diffusion/ pattern dither/white noise/blue noise	The method used to dither colors. (Default: diffusion)
color reduction	selective/adaptive/ perceptual/web	The method used to reduce the number of colors in the document. (Default: selective)
dither percent	integer	How much should the colors be dithered as a percentage? Range: 0–100. (Default: 88)
horizontal scaling	real	The percentage horizontal scaling factor to apply to the resulting image. Range: 0.0–100.0. (Default: 100.0)
interlaced	boolean	Should the resulting image be interlaced? (Default: false)
matte	boolean	Should the artboard be matted with a color? (Default: true)
matte color	RGB color info	The color to use when matting the artboard. (Default: {255.0, 255.0, 255.0})
saving as HTML	boolean	Should the resulting image be saved with an accompanying HTML file?
transparency	boolean	Should the resulting image use transparency? (Default: true)
vertical scaling	real	The percentage vertical scaling factor to apply to the resulting image. Range: 0.0–100.0. (Default: 100.0)
web snap	integer	How much should the color table be changed to match the Web palette as a percentage? Range: 0–100. (Default: 0)

Valid Commands

COMMAND	RETURN VALUE	EXPLANATION
export document index-or-name to file-specification as Flash/GIF/JPEG/PNG24/ PNG8/Photoshop/SVG [with options export-related-options]	nothing	Exports document as specified file type with options specified.

TIPS *This class is used to define a record containing properties that specify options when exporting a document as a PNG-8 file. PNG-8 export options can only be supplied in conjunction with the export command. It is not possible to get or create a PNG-8 export options object.*

It is not necessary to specify values for all properties. Default values will be provided for any properties not specified.

SVG export options

Options that may be supplied when exporting a document as a SVG file. See the export command in the command reference for additional details.

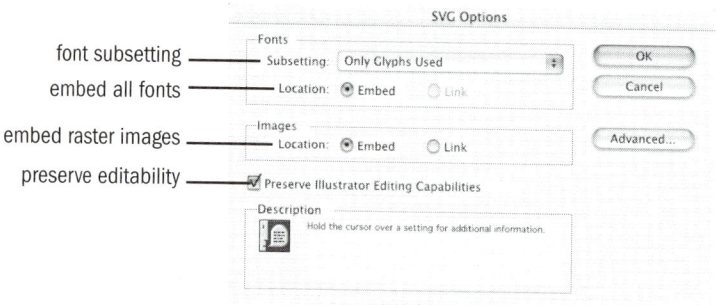

Figure 5.57 *The new format on the block, SVG, is given its due from scripting, with an SVG export options object providing access to all of the export properties shown in the user interface.*

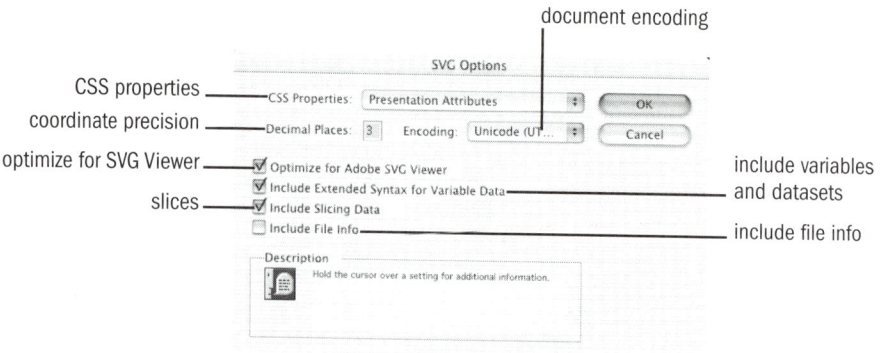

Figure 5.58 *The SVG Advanced Options dialog box shows that every export property possible, including exporting variable and dataset data, is provided for in the SVG export options object's set of properties.*

Properties

PROPERTY	VALUE TYPE	EXPLANATION
CSS properties	entities/presentation attributes/style attributes/style elements	How should the CCS properties of the document be included in the exported file? (Default: style attributes)
compressed	boolean	Should the exported file be compressed? (Default: false)
coordinate precision	integer	The decimal precision for element coordinate values. Range: 1–7. (Default: 3)
document encoding	ASCII/UTF8/UTF16	How should the text in the document be encoded? (Default: ASCII)
embed all fonts	boolean	Should the fonts used in the document be included in the exported file? (Default: true)
embed raster images	boolean	Should the raster images used in the document be included in the exported file? (Default: true)
font subsetting	all glyphs/common english/common roman/glyphs used/glyphs used plus english/glyphs used plus roman/none	What font glyphs should be included in the exported file? (Default: all glyphs)
include file info	boolean	Should file information be included in the SVG file? (Default: false)
include variables and datasets	boolean	Should variables and datasets be included in the SVG file? (Default: false)
optimize for SVG Viewer	boolean	Should the SVG file be optimized for the SVG Viewer plug-in? (Default: false)
preserve editability	boolean	Should the SVG file be editable in Illustrator? (Default: false)
slices	boolean	Should slice data be saved in the SVG file? (Default: false)

Valid Commands

COMMAND	RETURN VALUE	EXPLANATION
export document index-or-name to file-specification as Flash/GIF/JPEG/PNG24/PNG8/Photoshop/SVG [with options export-related-options]	nothing	Exports document as specified file type with options specified.

TIPS *This class is used to define a record containing properties that specify options when exporting a document as a SVG file. SVG export options can only be supplied in conjunction with the export command. It is not possible to get or create a SVG export options object.*

It is not necessary to specify values for all properties. Default values will be provided for any properties not specified.

Other Objects Contained in Document

art style, art styles

An art style or list of art styles. Each art style defines a set of appearance attributes that you can apply nondestructively to page items. Art styles are contained in documents.

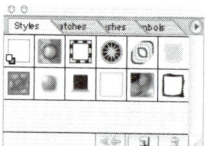

Figure 5.59 *The Styles palette in the user interface displays each of the art style objects in the current document. You cannot create, but may delete styles with a script. You can also apply styles to page items from a script with the apply command.*

Properties

PROPERTY	VALUE TYPE	EXPLANATION
best type*	class	The best type for the art style object's value. Always returns reference.
class*	class	The art style object's class, which is art style.
container*	object reference	A reference to the document that contains this art style.
default type*	class	The default type for the art style object, which is reference.
index*	integer	The index of this art style.
name*	string	The name of this art style.
properties*	record	All of the properties of this object returned as a record.

Valid Commands

COMMAND	RETURN VALUE	EXPLANATION
apply art style index-or-name to page-item-reference	nothing	Applies style to one or more page items.
count of art styles [in object-reference/whose match-criteria]	integer	Returns number of art styles in containing object or found by whose criteria.
exists art style index-or-name [in object-reference/whose match-criteria]	boolean	Tests for the existence of the specified object, returning true or false.

TIP *Illustrator's art styles can be accessed from scripting, but they cannot be created.*

brush, brushes

A brush or list of brushes. Brushes are contained in documents.

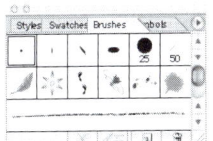

Figure 5.60 The Brushes palette displays all of the brushes contained in the document. Scripts cannot create or delete brushes but can apply them to page items with the apply command method.

Properties

PROPERTY	VALUE TYPE	EXPLANATION
best type*	class	The best type for the brush object's value. Always returns reference.
class*	class	The brush object's class, which is brush.
container*	object reference	A reference to the document that contains this brush.
default type*	class	The default type for the brush object, which is reference.
index*	integer	The index of this brush.
name*	string	The name of this brush.
properties*	record	All of the properties of this object returned as a record.

Valid Commands

COMMAND	RETURN VALUE	EXPLANATION
apply brush index-or-name to page-item-reference	nothing	Applies brush to one or more page items.
count of brushes [in object-reference/whose match-criteria]	integer	Returns number of brushes in containing object or found by whose criteria.
exists brush index-or-name [in object-reference/whose match-criteria]	boolean	Tests for the existence of the specified object, returning true or false.

TIP *Additional brushes may be created by the user within Illustrator. Illustrator's brushes can be accessed from scripting, but they cannot be created.*

dataset, datasets

A dataset or list of datasets. Datasets are contained in documents and accessed from the Variables palette. A document must contain variables to contain datasets.

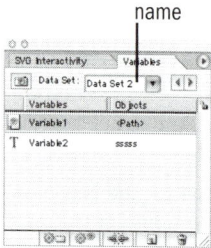

Figure 5.61 *The Variables palette provides access to all of the variables defined in the current document as well as each of the dataset objects. A dataset is a snapshot of all of variables' values. See Chapter 2 for more on working with variables and datasets.*

Properties

PROPERTY	VALUE TYPE	EXPLANATION
best type*	class	The best type for the dataset object's value. Always returns reference.
class*	class	The dataset object's class, which is dataset.
container*	object reference	A reference to the document that contains this dataset.
default type*	class	The default type for the dataset object, which is reference.
index*	integer	The index of this dataset.
name	string	The name of this dataset.
properties	record	All of the properties of this object returned as a record.

Valid Commands

COMMAND	RETURN VALUE	EXPLANATION
count of datasets [in object-reference/whose match-criteria]	integer	Returns number of datasets in containing object or found by whose criteria.
display dataset index-or-name [in object-reference/whose match-criteria]	nothing	Displays data stored in dataset, updating document display.
exists dataset index-or-name [in object-reference/whose match-criteria]	boolean	Tests for the existence of the specified object, returning true or false.
export variables document-reference to file-specification	nothing	Saves all variable and dataset definitions from document specified into an XML-formatted text file.
import variables document-reference from file-specification	nothing	Replaces all variable and dataset definitions for document specified by importing new information from a properly-formatted XML text file.
make new dataset at document-reference	dataset-reference	Creates a new dataset in the document specified, returning a reference to the new dataset object created.
update dataset index-or-name [in object-reference/whose match-criteria]	nothing	Stores current settings of all variables in specified dataset.

TIPS *The Variables palette, if open in Illustrator when created new datasets via script control, may not update its dataset information until closed and reopened.symbol, symbols*

symbol, symbols

A symbol or list of symbols. Symbols are contained in documents.

Properties

PROPERTY	VALUE TYPE	EXPLANATION
best type*	class	The best type for the symbol object's value. Always returns reference.
class*	class	The symbol object's class, which is symbol.
container*	object reference	A reference to the document that contains this brush.

Properties (continued)

PROPERTY	VALUE TYPE	EXPLANATION
default type*	class	The default type for the symbol object, which is reference.
index*	integer	The index of this symbol.
name	string	The name of this symbol.
properties*	record	All of the properties of this object returned as a record.
source art*	anything	The source art object-references used only to create a new symbol.

Valid Commands

COMMAND	RETURN VALUE	EXPLANATION
count of symbols [in object-reference/ whose match-criteria]	integer	Returns number of symbols in containing object or found by whose criteria.
exists symbol index-or-name [in object-reference/whose match-criteria]	boolean	Tests for the existence of the specified object, returning true or false.
make new symbol at location-reference with properties {source art: {page-item-reference(s)}, symbol-properties}	symbol-reference	Creates new symbol in document at location specified using source art referenced with source art property and any optional properties provided.

TIP Additional symbols may be created by the user within Illustrator or from scripting.

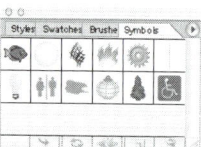

Figure 5.62 The Symbols palette in the user interface displays each of the symbol objects in the current document. You cannot create, but may delete symbols with a script. You can work with symbol items, which are page items composed of symbols.

tag, tags

A tag or list of tags associated with a specific page item.

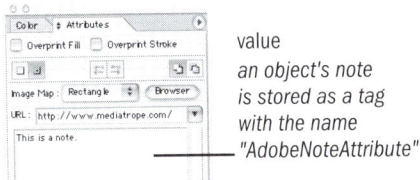

value
an object's note
is stored as a tag
with the name
"AdobeNoteAttribute"

Figure 5.63 *Tags are the most powerful and hidden feature of Illustrator. Each page item in a document can contain as many tags as you wish. Each tag contains a name and a value. This means you can attach data to objects in your documents that get saved within the document. See Chapter 4 for a script that lets you add, edit, and search tags in a document. Adobe uses tags to store some of the metadata for objects, such as notes.*

Properties

PROPERTY	VALUE TYPE	EXPLANATION
best type*	class	The best type for the tag object. Always returns reference.
class*	class	The tag object's class, which is tag.
container*	object reference	A reference to the page item that contains this tag.
default type*	class	The default type for the tag. Always returns reference.
index*	integer	The index of this tag in the page item.
name	string	The tag's name.
properties	record	All of the tag's properties returned in a single record (properties that are individually read-only remain so in this record).
value	string	The data stored in this tag.

Valid Commands

COMMAND	RETURN VALUE	EXPLANATION
count of tags [in object-reference/whose match-criteria]	integer	Returns number of tags in containing object or found by whose criteria.
delete tag index-or-name [in object-reference/whose match-criteria]	nothing	Deletes object specified.
duplicate tag index-or-name [to location-reference]	layer-reference	Duplicates object specified, returning a reference to the new object.

Valid Commands (continued)

COMMAND	RETURN VALUE	EXPLANATION
exists tag index-or-name [in object-reference/whose match-criteria]	boolean	Tests for the existence of the specified object, returning true or false.
make new tag at location-reference [with data {data-list}] [with properties { tag-properties}]	tag-reference	Creates new object at location specified within containing object using optional properties.

TIP *Tags allow you to assign an unlimited number of key-value pairs to any page item in a document. The underlying functionality is used by Illustrator to implement the note property of page items. Try setting the note of a page item and then look at its tags in a script.*

variable, variables

A variable or list of variables found in a specific document.

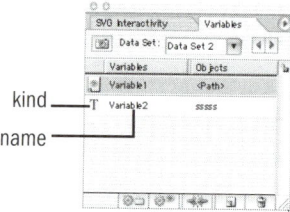

Figure 5.64 *The Variables palette provides access to all of the variables defined in the current document as well as each of the variable objects. A variable can be created and attached to a page item. There are different kinds of variables that may be attached to different kinds of page items. See Chapter 2 for more on working with variables and datasets.*

Properties

PROPERTY	VALUE TYPE	EXPLANATION
best type*	class	The best type for the variable object. Always returns reference.
class*	class	The variable object's class, which is variable.
container*	object reference	A reference to the document that contains this variable.
default type*	class	The default type for the variable. Always returns reference.

Properties (continued)

PROPERTY	VALUE TYPE	EXPLANATION
index*	integer	The index of this variable in the document's variables palette.
kind	graph/image/textual/ unknown/visibility	The variable's type.
name	string	The variable's name.
properties	record	All of the variable's properties returned in a single record (properties that are individually read-only remain so in this record).

Valid Commands

COMMAND	RETURN VALUE	EXPLANATION
count of variables [in object-reference/ whose match-criteria]	integer	Returns number of variables in containing object or found by whose criteria.
delete variable index-or-name [in object-reference/whose match-criteria]	nothing	Deletes object specified.
duplicate variable index-or-name [to location-reference]	layer-reference	Duplicates object specified, returning a reference to the new object.
exists variable index-or-name [in object-reference/whose match-criteria]	boolean	Tests for the existence of the specified object, returning true or false.
export variables document-reference to file-specification	nothing	Saves all variable and dataset definitions from document specified into an XML-formatted text file.
import variables document-reference from file-specification	nothing	Replaces all variable and dataset definitions for document specified by importing new information from a properly-formatted XML text file.
make new variable at location-reference [with data {data-list}] [with properties { variable-properties}]	variable-reference	Creates new object at location specified within containing object using optional properties.

TIP Variables allow you to assign dynamic attributes to certain kinds of page items in a document. You can create new variables and assign variables to page items by using the specific properties visibility variable and content variable.

view, views

A document view or list of views in an Illustrator document.

Properties

PROPERTY	VALUE TYPE	EXPLANATION
best type*	class	The best type for the view object. Always returns reference.
bounds*	fixed rectangle	The bounding rectangle of this view relative to the current document's bounds.
center point	fixed point	The center point of this view relative to the current document's bounds.
class*	class	The view object's class, which is view.
container*	object reference	A reference to the document that contains this view.
default type*	class	The default type for the view object. Always returns reference.
index*	integer	The index of the view in the document.
properties	record	All of the view's properties returned in a single record (properties that are individually read-only remain so in this record).
screen mode	multiwindow/desktop/full screen	The mode of display for this view.
zoom	real	The zoom factor of this view, where 100.0 is 100%.

Valid Commands

COMMAND	RETURN VALUE	EXPLANATION
count of views [in object-reference/whose match-criteria]	integer	Returns number of views in containing object or found by whose criteria.
exists view index-or-name [in object-reference/whose match-criteria]	boolean	Tests for the existence of the specified object, returning true or false.

TIP *Illustrator's view object represents a window view onto a document. New views cannot be created, but some properties of existing views can be modified, including the center point, screen mode, and zoom.*

Other Objects Contained in Application

text face, text faces

A text face (currently available font) or list of faces in the application.

Properties

PROPERTY	VALUE TYPE	EXPLANATION
best type*	class	The best type for the text face. Always returns reference.
class*	class	The text face object's class, which is text face.
default type*	class	The default type for the text face. Always returns string.
index*	integer	The index of this text face in the application.
name*	string	The name of the text face.
properties*	record	All of the text face's properties returned in a single record (properties that are individually read-only remain so in this record).

Valid Commands

COMMAND	RETURN VALUE	EXPLANATION
count of text faces [whose match-criteria]	integer	Returns number of text faces in application or found by whose criteria.
exists text face index-or-name [whose match-criteria]	boolean	Tests for the existence of the specified object, returning true or false.

TIP *Text faces provide access to the name of every font available to the Illustrator application.*

The Matrix Object Class

matrix

A transformation matrix specification used to transform the geometry of objects.

Properties

PROPERTY	VALUE TYPE	EXPLANATION
mvalue_a	real	Matrix property a.
mvalue_b	real	Matrix property b.
mvalue_c	real	Matrix property c.
mvalue_d	real	Matrix property d.
mvalue_tx	real	Matrix property tx.
mvalue_ty	real	Matrix property ty.

Valid Commands

COMMAND	RETURN VALUE	EXPLANATION
concatenate matrix matrix-object-definition with matrix-object-definition	matrix-object-definition	This command combines two matrices using matrix multiplication, thereby combining the transformations each represented into a single returned matrix.
concatenate rotation matrix matrix-object-definition angle real	matrix-object-definition	This command combines a rotation matrix with another supplied matrix using matrix multiplication, thereby combining the transformations each represented into a single returned matrix.
concatenate scale matrix matrix-object-definition horizontal scale real vertical scale real	matrix-object-definition	This command combines a scale matrix with another supplied matrix using matrix multiplication, thereby combining the transformations each represented into a single returned matrix.
concatenate translation matrix matrix-object-definition delta x real delta y real	matrix-object-definition	This command combines a movement matrix with another supplied matrix using matrix multiplication, thereby combining the transformations each represented into a single returned matrix.
equal matrices	boolean	This command compares two supplied matrices to see if they match.

Valid Commands (continued)

COMMAND	RETURN VALUE	EXPLANATION
get identity matrix	matrix-object-definition	This command returns the standard identity matrix that, when applied to transform objects, returns the objects unchanged.
get rotation matrix angle real	matrix-object-definition	This command returns a transformation matrix that, when applied to transform objects, rotates them the specified angle.
get scale matrix horizontal scale real vertical scale real	matrix-object-definition	This command returns a transformation matrix that, when applied to transform objects, scales them the specified percentages.
get translation matrix delta x real delta y real	matrix-object-definition	This command returns a transformation matrix that, when applied to transform objects, moves them the specified distances.
invert matrix matrix-object-definition	matrix-object-definition	This command reverses a supplied matrix, returning its inverse matrix.
singular matrix matrix-object-definition	boolean	This command checks to see if a supplied matrix can be inverted or not.

TIPS *This class is used to define a record that contains the component values of an Illustrator transformation matrix. It is used for specifying and retrieving matrix information from an Illustrator document or from page items in a document.*

Matrices are used in conjunction with the transform command and as a property of a number of objects. A matrix specifies how to transform the geometry of an object. You can generate an original matrix using get identity matrix, get translation matrix, get scale matrix, or get rotation matrix.

A matrix is a record containing the matrix values, not a reference to a matrix object. The matrix commands listed above operate on the values of a matrix record. If a command modifies a matrix, a modified matrix record is returned as the result of the command. The original matrix record passed to the command is not modified.

Special Path Item Creation-Only Objects

Illustrator provides a group of special path-item-related classes that can be used with the make command to create new path items. The ellipse, polygon, rectangle, rounded rectangle, and star objects are available exclusively for use with the make command. The class of the object created will be a path item. Therefore, the properties for an ellipse are write-once in the sense that they can be used only to specify the creation of a new path item. This special class allows you to quickly create complex path items using the straightforward properties provided. If you do not specify any properties when making a new ellipse, default values will be used. Properties usually associated with path items, such as fill color, can also be specified at the time of creation.

Figure 5.65 *The Path pop-out palette of the Tool palette in Illustrator provides access to create the same special path shapes for which AppleScript provides unique object classes.*

Valid Commands

COMMAND	RETURN VALUE	EXPLANATION
make new special-page-item at location-reference [with data {data-list}] [with properties { special-page-item-properties}]	special-page-item-reference	Creates new object at location specified within containing object using optional properties.

ellipse

A class used to create an elliptical path in an Illustrator document. This class can be used only to create new path item objects.

Properties

PROPERTY	VALUE TYPE	EXPLANATION
bounds	fixed rectangle	The bounds of the ellipse. (Default: {0.0, 0.0, 50.0, 100.0})
inscribed	boolean	Is the ellipse path inscribed (drawn inside the rectangle described by the bounds)? (Default: False)
reversed	boolean	Is the ellipse path reversed? (Default: False)

polygon

A class used to create a multisided path in an Illustrator document. This class can be used only to create new path item objects.

Properties

PROPERTY	VALUE TYPE	EXPLANATION
center point	fixed point	The center point for the polygon. (Default: {200.0, 300.0})
radius	real	The radius of the polygon's points. (Default: 50.0)
reversed	boolean	Is the polygon path reversed? (Default: false)
sides	integer (unsigned)	The number of sides for the polygon. (Default: 8)

rectangle

A class used to create a rectangular path in an Illustrator document. This class can be used only to create new path item objects.

Properties

PROPERTY	VALUE TYPE	EXPLANATION
bounds	fixed rectangle	The bounds of the rectangle. (Default: {100.0, 200.0, 175.0, 100.0})
reversed	boolean	Is the path reversed? (Default: false)

rounded rectangle

A class used to create a rectangular path with rounded corners in an Illustrator document. This class can be used only to create new path item objects.

Properties

PROPERTY	VALUE TYPE	EXPLANATION
bounds	fixed rectangle	The bounds of the rectangle to create. (Default: {100.0, 100.0, 150.0, 200.0})
horizontal radius	real	The horizontal radius of the rectangle's rounded corners. (Default: 15.0)
reversed	boolean	Is the rectangle path reversed? (Default: false)
vertical radius	real	The vertical radius of the rectangle's rounded corners. (Default: 20.0)

star

A class used to create a star-shaped path in an Illustrator document. This class can be used only to create new path item objects.

Properties

PROPERTY	VALUE TYPE	EXPLANATION
center point	fixed point	The center point of the star. (Default: {200.0, 300.0})
inner radius	real	The inner radius of the star. (Default: 20.0)
point count	integer	The number of points on the star. (Default: 5)
radius	real	The radius of the star's points. (Default: 50.0)
reversed	boolean	Is the star path reversed? (Default: false)

6: Visual Basic Reference

This reference section illustrates and defines the objects and methods (a synonym for *commands* used in VB) in Illustrator's Visual Basic type library. All the objects in the type library are presented by their importance in the object model. You can use the language-specific object model diagram on the next page to look up page numbers for specific objects or just browse the pages.

Each object listing includes the following:

- Screen shots of the user-interface elements that give users access to the object's properties, with callouts showing the scripting term you can use to access the same properties from your script.

- Collection properties that refer to other objects contained within the object. Layers are contained in documents, for example, and page items are contained in layers. In Visual Basic, you can reference individual objects within a collection only by index number and object name (if any).

- Properties of the object, including the value type for the property, an explanation, and whether the property is read-only. Read-only is indicated by an asterisk (*).

- Valid methods you can use with the object in your script.

- Notes to explain special issues that might be of interest to you.

Throughout this chapter, when an object inherits properties or methods from another object, I reference the superclass object and list all properties or methods inherited.

At the very end of the chapter is a quick reference for the most important value enumerations unique to Illustrator. When you see an object property value type starting with the letters "Ai" listed as an enumeration or when a method parameter starts with the letters "Ai", this is the tip-off that a unique value enumeration is required. See the table at the end for the actual values to use for each enumeration type.

Visual Basic Language Reference

Illustrator's object model

A good understanding of Illustrator's object model will improve your scripting abilities. These diagrams show the containment hierarchy of the object model, starting with the application object. Note that the layer, group item, and all text classes can contain additional objects of the same class, which in turn can contain additional nested objects.

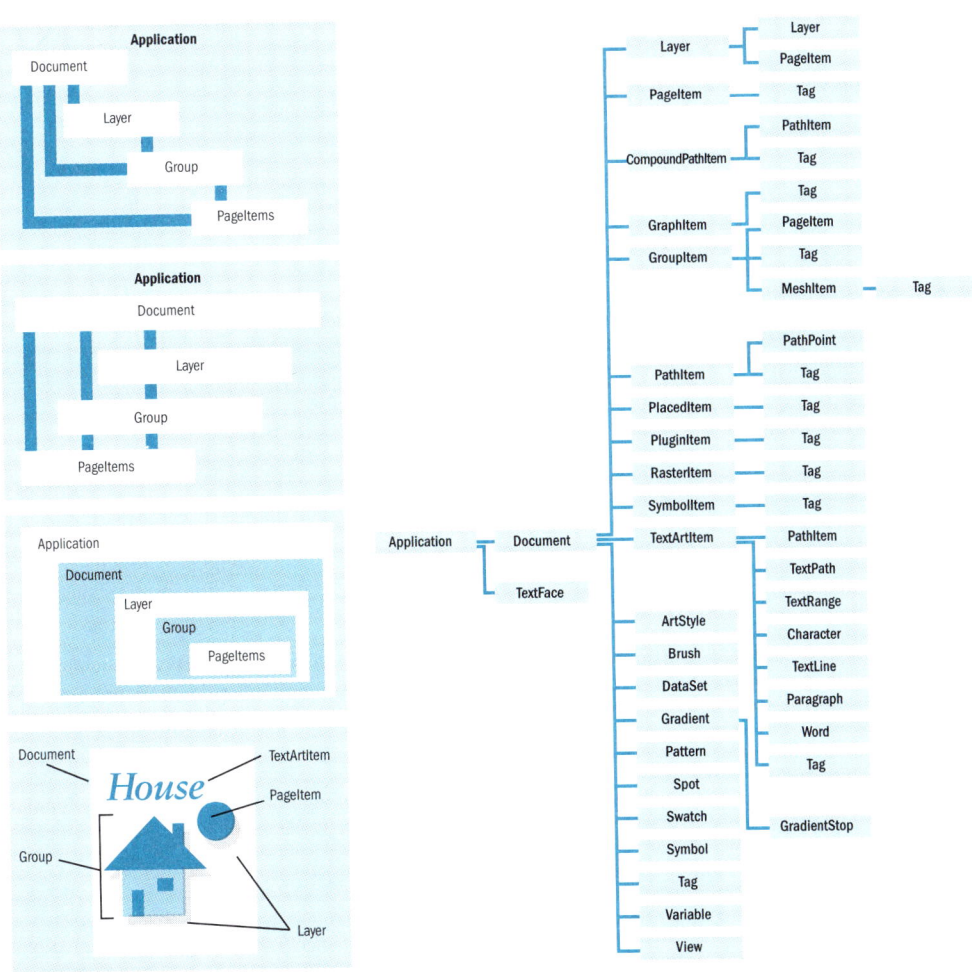

Primary objects

Application

The Adobe Illustrator application object (**Figure 6.1**), which contains all other Illustrator objects.

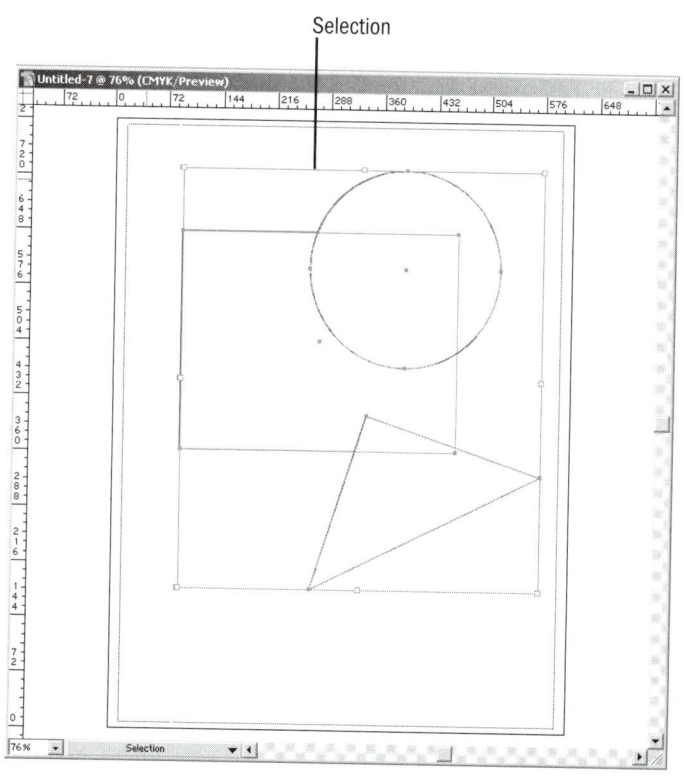

Figure 6.1 *The Application object's Selection property holds an array of references to the selected objects in the Active Document. Each Document also has a selection property that contains references to any selected page items (if any). The Selection is Empty when no page items are highlighted.*

Collection Properties

PROPERTY	VALUE TYPE	EXPLANATION
Documents*	Documents collection object	The documents in the application.
TextFaces*	Textfaces collection object	The text faces (fonts) available to the application.

Other Properties

PROPERTY	VALUE TYPE	EXPLANATION
ActionIsRunning	Boolean	Is an action currently running in Illustrator?
ActiveDocument	Document object	The active (frontmost) document in Illustrator.
Application*	Application object	The Illustrator Application object.
BrowserAvailable*	Boolean	Is a Web browser available?
FreeMemory*	Long	The amount of unused memory (in bytes) within the Adobe Illustrator partition.
Name*	String	The application's name (not related to the name of the application file).
Path*	String	The file path to the application.
Preferences*	Preferences object	A record of the preferences for Illustrator, including defaults used for opening Photoshop files.
ScriptingVersion*	String	The version of the Scripting plug-in.
Selection	Variant Array (of objects)	All the selected objects in the active (frontmost) document. See note for more information.
UserInteractionLevel	AiUserInteractionLevel enumeration	The level of interaction with the user that should be allowed when handling script commands. Use this property carefully; in Illustrator 10, not all application dialogs are aware of this property.
Version*	String	The version of the Adobe Illustrator application.
Visible*	Boolean	Is the application visible?

Methods

METHOD	RETURN VALUE (IF ANY)	EXPLANATION
ConcatenateMatrix(Matrix As Matrix, secondMatrix As Matrix)	Matrix object	Concatenates two matrices.
ConcatenateRotationMatrix(Matrix As Matrix, angle As Single)	Matrix object	Concatenates a rotation translation to a transformation matrix.

Methods

METHOD	RETURN VALUE (IF ANY)	EXPLANATION
ConcatenateScaleMatrix(Matrix As Matrix, [scaleX As Single], [scaleY As Single])	Matrix object	Concatenates a scale translation to a transformation matrix.
ConcatenateTranslationMatrix(Matrix As Matrix, [deltaX As Single], [deltaY As Single])	Matrix object	Concatenates a translation to a transformation matrix.
DoScript(action As String, from As String, [dialogs As Boolean])	Nothing	Plays an action from the Actions palette.
GetIdentityMatrix	Matrix object	Returns an identity matrix.
GetRotationMatrix([angle As Single])	Matrix object	Returns a transformation matrix containing a single rotation.
GetScaleMatrix([scaleX As Single], [scaleY As Single])	Matrix object	Returns a transformation matrix containing a single scale.
GetTranslationMatrix([deltaX As Single], [deltaY As Single])	Matrix object	Returns a transformation matrix containing a single translation.
InvertMatrix(Matrix As Matrix)	Matrix object	Inverts a matrix.
IsEqualMatrix(Matrix As Matrix, secondMatrix As Matrix)	Boolean	Checks whether two matrices are equal.
IsSingularMatrix(Matrix As Matrix)	Boolean	Checks whether a matrix is singular and cannot be inverted.
Open(files as Variant, [DocumentColorSpace As AiDocumentColorSpace])	Document Object	Opens the file(s) specified by the string or array of strings containing file paths.
Quit	Nothing	Quits Illustrator. Note that if the Clipboard contains data, Illustrator may show a dialog prompting the user to save the data for other applications. Prevent the possibility of this dialog by emptying the Clipboard manually with the VB method Clipboard.Clear.
Redraw	Nothing	Allow Illustrator to redraw all its windows.

TIP *In Illustrator, the application's selection can be accessed as well as modified. The selection will contain Empty when no objects are selected. To deselect all objects in the current document, simply set the selection to Empty. A reference to a character is returned when there is an active selection in the contents of a text art item. Similarly, a reference to a range of text is returned when characters are selected in the contents of a text art item. You can set the Selection to change the Application's current selection.*

Document

An Illustrator document (**Figure 6.2**). Documents are contained in the application object.

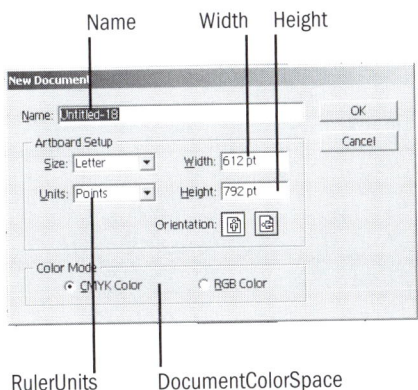

Figure 6.2 *Some of a Document object's most basic properties are accessed from the user interface in the New Document dialog. In a script, you can set only a document's Width, Height, and DocumentColorSpace when you are creating a new document.*

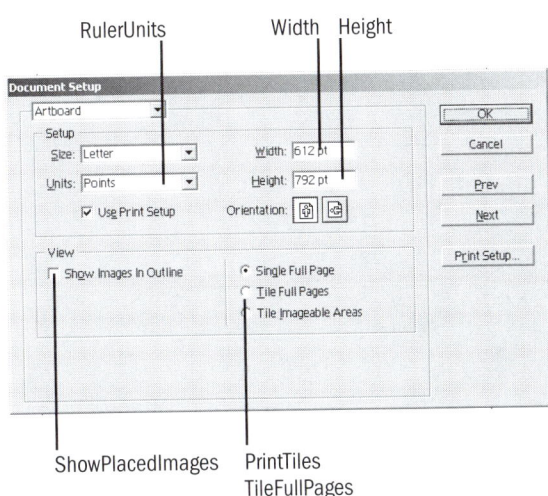

Figure 6.3 *You can access the additional properties ShowPlacedImages, PrintTiles, and TileFullPages of the Document object from the Document Setup dialog in the user interface.*

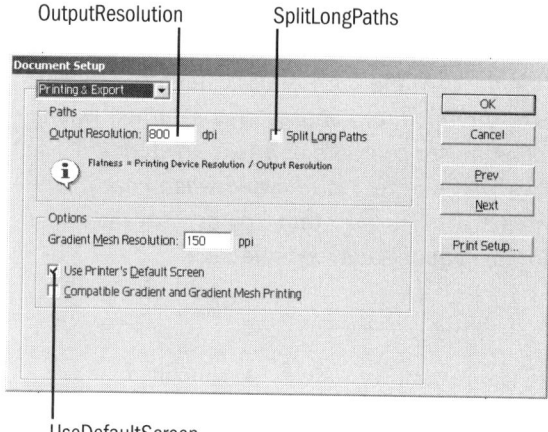

Figure 6.4 The Printing & Export panel of the Document Setup dialog provides access to yet more Document object properties. All these properties are read-only from your scripts, which means that you cannot change their values—only look at them.

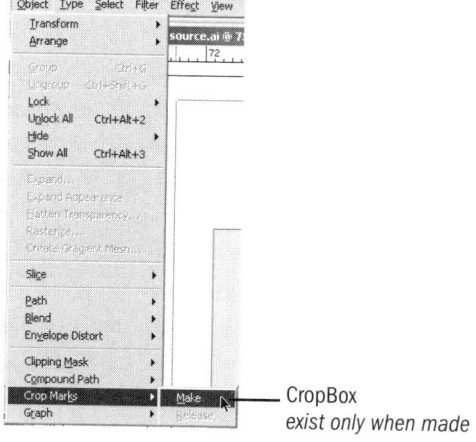

Figure 6.5 The CropBox property of the Document object exists only after the user has made crop marks by choosing Object > Crop Marks > Make in Illustrator. Any scripts that attempt to access this property should be prepared in case the value does not exist. Crop marks cannot be made automatically from the scripting environment.

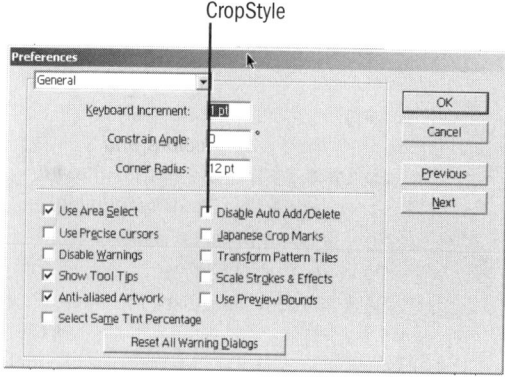

Figure 6.6 The General panel of the Preferences dialog provides access to the rare and mysterious CropStyle property of the Document object, which is called Japanese Crop Marks in the user interface.

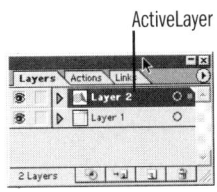

Figure 6.7 A Document object's ActiveLayer property is simply an object reference to the selected layer in the document, as shown in the Layers palette of the user interface.

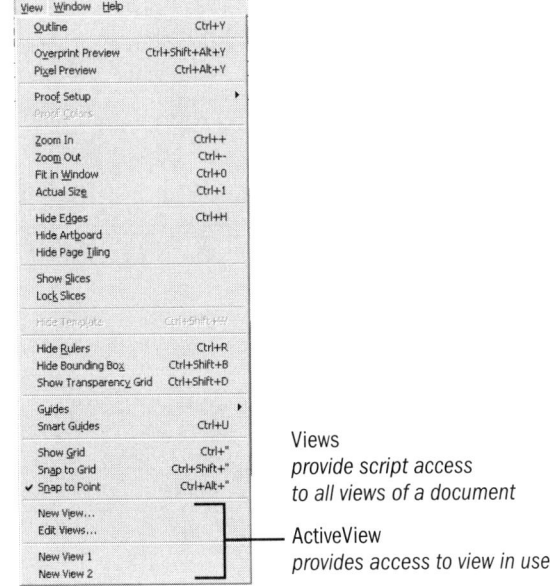

Figure 6.8 The Views collection property is an array that contains an object reference to each of the document's views, which are listed at the bottom of the View menu. The ActiveView property provides a reference to the view being used in the user interface.

Views
provide script access to all views of a document

ActiveView
provides access to view in use

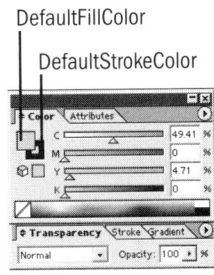

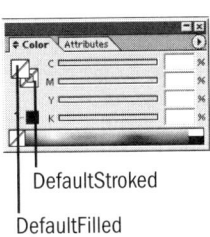

Figure 6.9 All the properties of the Document object that start with the word Default define the settings used for new path items created in the document, such as the fill and stroke colors and states. The default properties DefaultFillColor, DefaultFilled DefaultStrokeColor, and DefaultStroked are also accessible from the Color palette of the user interface. If you set DefaultFilled or DefaultStroked to false, the value of the corresponding color property is ignored by the application.

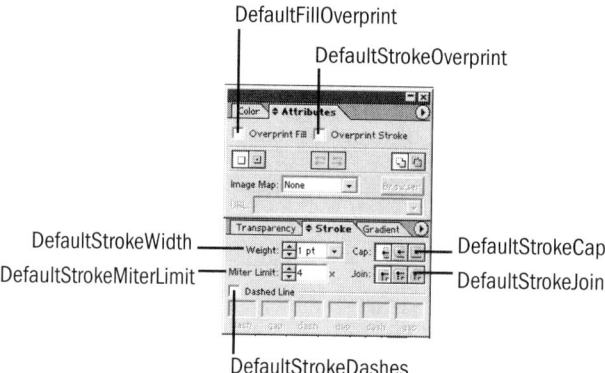

DefaultFillOverprint
DefaultStrokeOverprint
DefaultStrokeWidth
DefaultStrokeMiterLimit
DefaultStrokeCap
DefaultStrokeJoin
DefaultStrokeDashes

Figure 6.10 *The Attributes palette is another place in the user interface where many of the Document object's default path item properties are located. Scripters get access to an additional property for dashed lines with DefaultStrokeDashOffset, which lets you specify where the dash pattern should start in relation to the beginning of a path to which it is applied.*

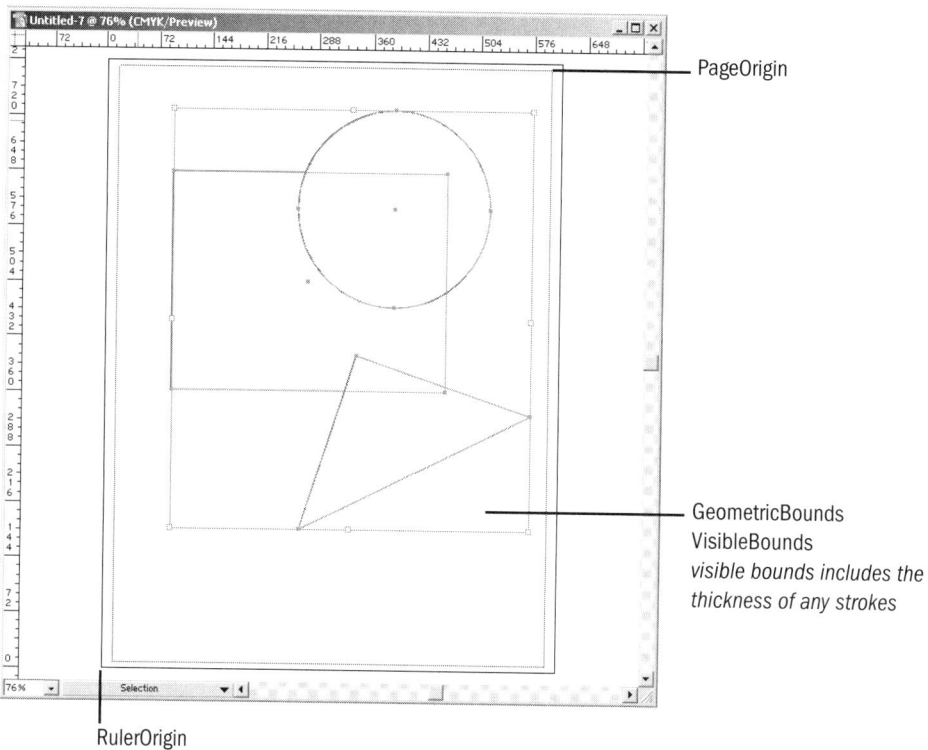

PageOrigin
GeometricBounds
VisibleBounds
visible bounds includes the thickness of any strokes
RulerOrigin

Figure 6.11 *The basic geometric properties of a Document object are things we take for granted in the user interface of Illustrator. But having access to basic orientation information, such as PageOrigin and RulerOrigin, enables your scripts to know all about the positioning geometry details of a document and its contents. Your script can figure out where the zero point of a document's coordinate system (RulerOrigin) is in relation to its artboard (PageOrigin). A more curious, but potentially useful, pair of properties is GeometricBounds and VisibleBounds. The GeometricBounds property provides the overall rectangle that contains all objects in a document, based on the object's actual coordinates. VisibleBounds is the same, except that it adds in the thicknesses of any strokes applied and accounts for any object clipping.*

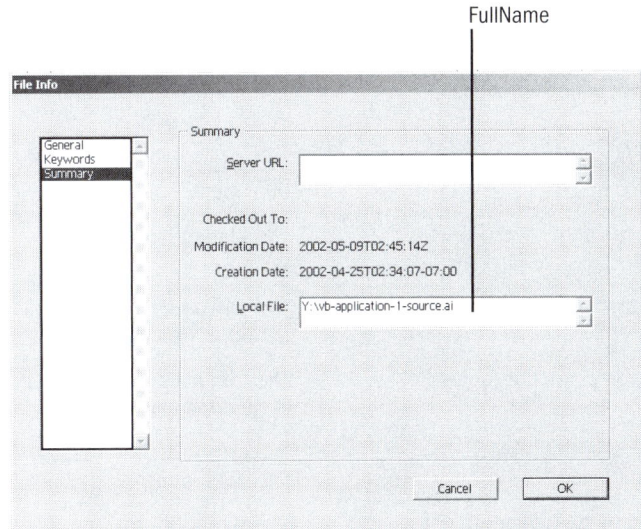

Figure 6.12 Hidden from users in the Summary panel of the File Info dialog, the Document's FullName property is fundamentally important to scripts that want to know the full path to the document in the file system.

Collection Properties

PROPERTY	VALUE TYPE	EXPLANATION
ArtStyles*	ArtStyles collection object	The art styles contained in the document.
Brushes*	Brushes collection object	The brushes contained in the document.
CompoundPathItems*	CompoundPathItems collection object	The compound path items contained in the document.
Datasets*	Datasets collection object	The datasets contained in the document.
Gradients*	Gradients collection object	The gradients contained in the document.
GraphItems*	GraphItems collection object	The graph items contained in the document.
GroupItems*	GroupItems collection object	The group items contained in the document.
Layers*	Layers collection object	The layers contained in the document.
MeshItems*	MeshItems collection object	The mesh art items contained in the document.
PageItems*	PageItems collection object	The page items (including all art object classes) contained in the document.

Collection Properties (continued)

PROPERTY	VALUE TYPE	EXPLANATION
PathItems*	PathItems collection object	The path items contained in this document.
Patterns*	Patterns collection object	The patterns contained in this document.
PlacedItems*	PlacedItems collection object	The placed items contained in this document.
PluginItems*	PluginItems collection object	The plug-in items contained in this document.
RasterItems*	RasterItems collection object	The raster items contained in this document.
Symbols*	Symbols collection object	The symbols contained in this document.
SymbolItems*	SymbolItems collection object	The symbol items contained in this document.
Swatches*	Swatches collection object	The swatches contained in this document.
Tags*	Tags collection object	The tags contained in this document.
TextArtItems*	TextArtItems collection object	The text art items contained in this document.
Variables*	Variables collection object	The variables contained in this document.
Views*	Views collection object	The views contained in this document.

Other Properties

PROPERTY	VALUE TYPE	EXPLANATION
ActiveDataSet	DataSet object	The active dataset in the document.
ActiveLayer	Layer object	The active layer in the document.
ActiveView*	View object	The document's current view.
Application*	Application object	The Illustrator Application object.
CropBox	Variant Array (of four Singles)	The boundary of the document's cropping box for output. A document does not have a default CropBox. To read this property, you have to set the CropBox first.
CropStyle	AiCropOptions enumeration	The style of the document's cropping box.

Other Properties (continued)

PROPERTY	VALUE TYPE	EXPLANATION
DefaultFillColor	Color object	The color to fill new paths if DefaultFilled is true.
DefaultFilled	Boolean	Should a new path be filled?
DefaultFillOverprint	Boolean	Will art beneath a filled object be overprinted by default?
DefaultStrokeCap	AiStrokeCap enumeration	Default type of line capping for paths created.
DefaultStrokeColor	Color object	The stroke color for new paths if DefaultStroked is true.
DefaultStroked	Boolean	Should a new path be stroked?
DefaultStrokeDashes	Variant Array (of Singles)	Default lengths for dashes and gaps in dashed lines, starting with the first dash length, followed by the first gap length, and so on. Set to an empty variant array for a solid line.
DefaultStrokeDashOffset	Single	The default distance into the dash pattern at which the pattern should be started for new paths.
DefaultStrokeJoin	AiStrokeJoin enumeration	Default type of joints in new paths.
DefaultStrokeMiterLimit	Single	Specifies when a join is mitered (pointed) or beveled (squared off) by default when DefaultStrokeJoin is set to mitered.
DefaultStrokeOverprint	Boolean	Will art beneath a stroked object be overprinted by default?
DefaultStrokeWidth	Single	Default width of stroke for new paths.
DocumentColorSpace*	AiDocumentColorSpace enumeration	The color specification system to use for this document's color space.
FullName*	String	The file associated with the document, which includes the complete path to the file.
GeometricBounds*	Variant Array (of four Singles)	The bounds of the illustration, excluding the stroke width of any objects in the document.
Height*	Single	The height of the document.
Name*	String	The document's name (not the complete path to the document).
OutputResolution*	Single	The current output resolution for the document, in dots per inch (dpi).

Other Properties (continued)

PROPERTY	VALUE TYPE	EXPLANATION
PageOrigin	Variant Array (of two Singles)	The zero point of the page in the document without margins, relative to the overall height and width.
Parent*	Application object	The application that contains this document.
Path*	String	The file associated with the document, which includes the complete path to the file.
PrintTiles*	Boolean	Does this document print as tiled output?
RulerOrigin	Variant Array (of two Singles)	The zero point of the rulers in the document, relative to the bottom-left corner of the document.
RulerUnits*	AiRulerUnits enumeration	The default measurement units for the rulers in the document.
Saved	Boolean	False if the document has never been saved or if the document has been changed since the last time it was saved.
Selection	Variant Array (of objects)	The array of references to the objects in this document's current selection.
ShowPlacedImages	Boolean	Are placed images displayed in the document?
SplitLongPaths*	Boolean	Are long paths to be split when printing?
Spots*	Spots collection object	The spot colors contained in this document.
Stationery*	Boolean	Is the document saved as a stationery file?
TileFullPages*	Boolean	Should full pages be tiled when printing this document?
UseDefaultScreen*	Boolean	Should the printer's default screen be used when printing this document?
VariablesLocked	Boolean	Are the variables in this document locked?
VisibleBounds*	Variant Array (of four Singles)	The visible bounds of the document, including the stroke width of any objects in the illustration.
Width*	Single	The width of this document.

Methods

METHOD	RETURN VALUE (IF ANY)	EXPLANATION
Activate	Nothing	Bring the first window associated with the document to the front.
Close([saving As AiSaveOptions])	Nothing	Closes a document.
Copy	Nothing	Copies the current selection in the document to the Clipboard. The associated document must be the frontmost document.
Cut	Nothing	Cuts the current selection in the document to the Clipboard. The associated document must be the frontmost document.
Export(exportFile As String, exportFormat as AiExportType, [options As ExportOptionsGIF/ ExportOptionsJPEG/ExportOptionsPNG24/ExportOptionsPNG8/ExportOptionsPhotoshop/ExportOptionsSVG]	Nothing	Exports the document to the specified file, using one of the export file formats.
ExportVariables(exportFile as String)	Nothing	Creates an XML-formatted export text file of all variables and datasets defined in the document.
ImportVariables(importFile as String)	Nothing	Replaces existing variables and datasets in document using XML-formatted data stored in specified import text file.
Paste	Nothing	Pastes the contents of the Clipboard into the current layer of the document. If the document is frontmost, all pasted objects remain selected after the paste.
PrintOut([showDialog As Boolean])	Nothing	Prints the document.
Save	Nothing	Saves the document in its current location.
SaveAs([saveIn As String], [options As EPSSaveOptions/Illustrator SaveOptions/PDFSaveOptions])	Nothing	Saves the document in the specified file as an Illustrator, EPS, or PDF file.

Documents

A collection of one or more documents. Documents are contained in the Application object.

Properties

PROPERTY	VALUE TYPE	EXPLANATION
Application*	Application object	The Illustrator Application object.
Count*	Long	The number of objects in the collection.
Index(item As Document)	Long	Returns the index position of the object within the collection.
item(itemKey)	Document object	Returns an object reference to the object identified by itemKey.
Parent*	Object	The parent of this object.

Methods

METHOD	RETURN VALUE (IF ANY)	EXPLANATION
Add([DocumentColorSpace As AiDocumentColorSpace], [Width As Single], [Height As Single])	Document object	Creates a new document, using optional parameters, and returns a reference to the new document.

TIPS *Illustrator's default document settings—those properties starting with the word Default—are global settings that affect the current document. Be sure to modify these default properties only when a document is open. Note that if you set default properties to desired values before creating new objects, you can streamline your scripts, eliminating the need to specify properties (such as FillColor and Stroked) that have analogous default properties.*

A document's DocumentColorSpace, Height, and Width can be set only when the document is created. After a document is created, these properties cannot be changed.

The frontmost document can be referred to as either Application.ActiveDocument or Application.Documents(1).

Layer

A layer in a document. Layers may contain nested layers, which are called *sublayers* in the user interface.

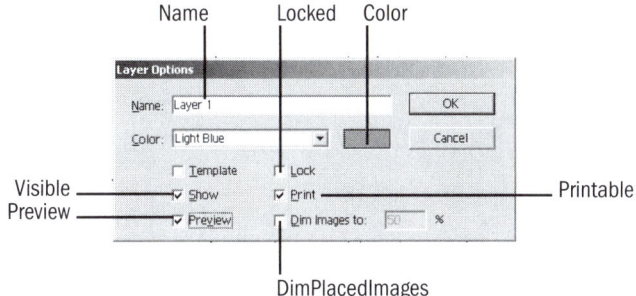

Figure 6.13 Double-click any layer in the Layers palette of Illustrator, and you get access to a plethora of properties. This illustration maps the property names to the controls in the Layer Options dialog of the user interface.

Collection Properties

PROPERTY	VALUE TYPE	EXPLANATION
CompoundPathItems*	CompoundPathItems collection object	The compound path items contained in this layer.
GraphItems*	GraphItems collection object	The graph items contained in the document.
GroupItems*	GroupItems collection object	The group items contained in this layer.
Layers*	Layers collection object	The layers contained in this layer.
MeshItems*	MeshItems collection object	The mesh items contained in this layer.
PageItems*	PageItems collection object	The page items contained in this layer.
PathItems*	PathItems collection object	The path items contained in this layer.
PlacedItems*	PlacedItems collection object	The placed items contained in this layer.
PluginItems*	PluginItems collection object	The plug-in items contained in this layer.
RasterItems*	RasterItems collection object	The raster items contained in this layer.

Collection Properties (continued)

PROPERTY	VALUE TYPE	EXPLANATION
SymbolItems*	SymbolItems collection object	The symbol items contained in this document.
TextArtItems*	TextArtItems collection object	The text art items contained in this layer.

Other Properties

PROPERTY	VALUE TYPE	EXPLANATION
Application*	Application object	The Illustrator Application object.
ArtworkKnockout	AiKnockoutState enumeration	Is this layer used to create a knockout? If so, what kind of knockout?
BlendingMode	AiBlendModes enumeration	The mode used when compositing an layer.
Color	RGBColor object	The layer's selection mark color.
DimPlacedImages	Boolean	Are placed images to be rendered as dimmed in this layer?
HasSelectedArtwork	Boolean	Is any object in this layer selected? Setting this property to false deselects all objects in the layer.
IsIsolated	Boolean	Is this layer isolated?
Locked	Boolean	Is this layer editable? Setting this property to true locks the layer.
Name	String	The name of this layer.
Opacity	Single	The opacity of the layer. The value is between 0.0 and 100.0.
Parent*	Document object or Layer Object	The document or layer that contains this layer.
Preview	Boolean	Is this layer displayed in preview mode?
Printable	Boolean	Is this layer printed when printing the document?
Visible	Boolean	Is this layer visible?
ZOrderPosition*	Long	The position of this layer within the stacking order of layers in the document.

Methods

METHOD	RETURN VALUE (IF ANY)	EXPLANATION
Paste	Nothing	Pastes the contents of the Clipboard into the layer. If the associated document is frontmost, all pasted objects remain selected after the paste.
ZSetOrder(zOrderCmd As AiZOrderMethod)	Nothing	Arranges the layer's position in the stacking order of layers in this document.

Layers

A collection of layers in a document or layer.

Properties

PROPERTY	VALUE TYPE	EXPLANATION
Application*	Application object	The Illustrator Application object.
Count*	Long	The number of objects in the collection.
Index(item As Layer)	Long	Returns the index position of the object within the collection.
item(itemKey)	Layer object	Returns an object reference to the object identified by itemKey.
Parent*	Object	The parent of this object.

Methods

METHOD	RETURN VALUE (IF ANY)	EXPLANATION
Add	Layer object	Creates a new object.
Remove(item As Layer)	Nothing	Deletes a layer from this collection.
RemoveAll	Nothing	Deletes all objects in this collection.

TIP *Illustrator's layer object contains all the page items in the specific layer as elements. Your script can access page items as elements of the layer object or as elements of the document object. When the script is accessing page items as elements of a layer, only objects in that layer can be accessed. To access page items throughout the entire document, be sure to refer to them as elements of the document.*

PageItem superclass of objects

PageItem

Any art object or list of art objects. Every art object and group in a document is a page item. Page items may be referenced as an element of a document, layer(s), or group(s).

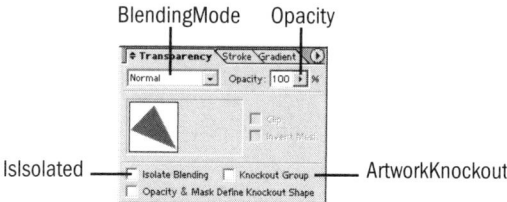

Figure 6.14 *A PageItem object is the meat and potatoes of any good Illustrator document. The Transparency palette is where some of the most powerful visual properties of a page item can be changed from the UI. Most of these properties are available to scripts as well.*

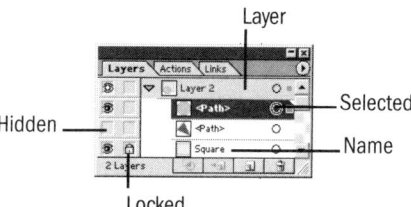

Figure 6.15 *Many of a PageItem object's fundamental properties are viewed in the user interface from the hierarchical Layers palette. Most of the PageItem properties shown are editable directly from a script. The exception is the read-only Layer property, which must be changed via the page item's MoveToBeginning or MoveToEnd methods.*

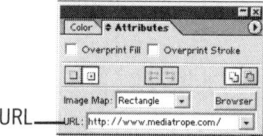

Figure 6.16 *The URL property of a page item can be set from a script, enabling you to create scripts that export images and HTML complete with hyperlinks.*

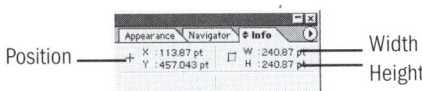

Figure 6.17 The three most basic properties—Position, Width and Height—are visible in the Info palette of the user interface.

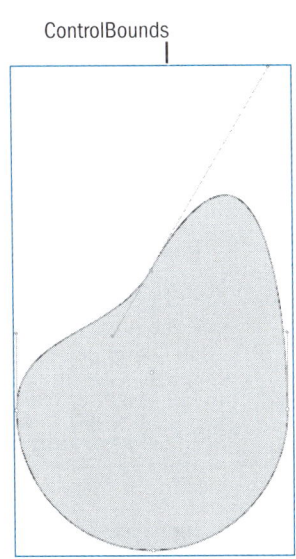

ControlBounds

Figure 6.18 Script access to geometric bounding properties is abundant in Illustrator. In addition to GeometricBounds and VisibleBounds, you have ControlBounds, which, believe me or not, actually provides the rectangular bounds created by the extent of all control handles (LeftDirection and RightDirection) of any path points in the object.

Collection Properties

PROPERTY	VALUE TYPE	EXPLANATION
Tags*	Tags collection object	The tags contained in this page item.

Other Properties

PROPERTY	VALUE TYPE	EXPLANATION
Application*	Application object	The Illustrator Application object.
ArtworkKnockout	AiKnockoutState enumeration	Is this object used to create a knockout? If so, what kind of knockout? You cannot set this value to aiKnockoutUnknown.

Other Properties (continued)

PROPERTY	VALUE TYPE	EXPLANATION
BlendingMode	AiBlendModes enumeration	The mode used when compositing an object.
CompoundPathItem*	CompoundPathItem object	If the page item is a compound path item, a reference to object as a compound path item.
ControlBounds *	Variant Array (of four Singles)	The bounds of the object, including stroke width and controls.
Editable*	Boolean	Is this page item editable?
GeometricBounds *	Variant Array (of four Singles)	The bounds of the object, excluding stroke width.
GraphItem*	GraphItem object	If the page item is a graph item, a reference to object as a graph item.
GroupItem*	GroupItem object	If the page item is a group item, a reference to object as a group item.
Height	Single	The height of the page item.
Hidden	Boolean	Is this page item hidden?
IsIsolated	Boolean	Is this object isolated?
Layer *	Layer object	The layer to which this page item belongs.
Left	Single	The left X coordinate of the page item's position.
Locked	Boolean	Is this page item locked?
MeshItem*	MeshItem object	If the page item is a mesh item, a reference to object as a mesh item.
Name	String	The name of this page item.
Opacity	Single	The opacity of the object . The value is between 0.0 and 100.0.
PageItemType*	AiPageItemType enumeration	The type (class) of art object that is represented by this page item.
Parent*	Layer object or GroupItem object	The parent of this object.
PathItem*	PathItem object	If the page item is a path item, a reference to object as a path item.
PlacedItem*	PlacedItem object	If the page item is a placed item, a reference to object as a placed item.
PluginItem*	PluginItem object	If the page item is a plug-in item, a reference to object as a plug-in item.

Other Properties (continued)

PROPERTY	VALUE TYPE	EXPLANATION
Position	Variant Array (of two Singles)	The position of the top-left corner of the page item.
RasterItem*	RasterItem object	If the page item is a raster item, a reference to object as a raster item.
Selected	Boolean	Is this object selected?
Sliced	Boolean	Is this object sliced?
SymbolItem*	SymbolItem object	If the page item is a symbol item, a reference to object as a symbol item.
TextArtItem*	TextArtItem object	If the page item is a text art item, a reference to object as a text art item.
Top	Single	The top Y coordinate of the page item's position.
URL	String	The value of the Adobe URL tag assigned to this page item.
VisibilityVariable	Variable object	The visibility variable bound to this page item, if any.
VisibleBounds *	Variant Array (of four Singles)	The visible bounds of the page item, including stroke width.
Width	Single	The width of the page item.
ZOrderPosition*	Long	The position of this page item within the stacking order of the group or layer (Parent) that contains the page item.

Methods

METHOD	RETURN VALUE (IF ANY)	EXPLANATION
Copy	Nothing	Copies the art object to the Clipboard. The associated document must be the frontmost document.
Cut	Nothing	Cuts the art object to the Clipboard. The associated document must be the frontmost document.
Duplicate	PageItem object	Duplicates the page item and returns a reference to the newly created page item.

Methods (continued)

METHOD	RETURN VALUE (IF ANY)	EXPLANATION
MoveAfter(PageItem As Object)		Moves page item after another page item.
MoveBefore(PageItem As Object)		Moves page item before another page item.
MoveToBeginning(Container As Object)		Moves page item to the beginning of a containing object, such as a layer or group.
MoveToEnd(Container As Object)		Moves page item to the end of a containing object, such as a layer or group.
Resize(scaleX As Single, scaleY As Single, [changePositions As Boolean], [changeFillPatterns As Boolean], [changeFillGradients As Boolean], [changeStrokePattern As Boolean], [changeLineWidths As Single], [scaleAbout As AiTransformation])	Nothing	Scales the art object, where scaleX is the horizontal scaling factor and scaleY is the vertical scaling factor; 100.0 = 100%.
Rotate(Angle As Single, [changePositions As Boolean], [changeFillPatterns As Boolean], [changeFillGradients As Boolean], [changeStrokePattern As Boolean], [rotateAbout As AiTransformation])	Nothing	Rotates the art object relative to the current rotation. The object is rotated counterclockwise if the Angle value is positive and clockwise if the value is negative.
Transform(transformationMatrix As Matrix, [changePositions As Boolean], [changeFillPatterns As Boolean], [changeFillGradients As Boolean], [changeStrokePattern As Boolean], [changeLineWidths As Single], [transformAbout As AiTransformation])	Nothing	Transforms the art object by applying a transformation matrix.
Translate([deltaX As Single], [deltaY As Single], [transformObjects As Boolean], [transformFillPatterns As Boolean], [transformFillGradients As Boolean], [transformStrokePatterns As Boolean])	Nothing	Repositions the art object relative to the current position, where deltaX is the horizontal offset and deltaY is the vertical offset.
ZSetOrder(zOrderCmd As AiZOrderMethod)	Nothing	Arranges the art object's position in the stacking order of the group or layer (Parent) of this object.

PageItems

A collection of one or more page items.

Properties

PROPERTY	VALUE TYPE	EXPLANATION
Application*	Application object	The Illustrator Application object.
Count*	Long	The number of objects in the collection.
Index(item As PageItem)	Long	Returns the index position of the object within the collection.
item(itemKey)	PageItem object	Returns an object reference to the object identified by itemKey.
Parent*	Object	The parent of this object.

Methods

METHOD	RETURN VALUE (IF ANY)	EXPLANATION
Remove(item As PageItem)	Nothing	Deletes a page item from this collection.
RemoveAll	Nothing	Deletes all objects in this collection.

> **TIPS** *The page item class gives you complete access to every art object contained in an Illustrator document. The page item class is the superclass of all artwork objects in a document. The classes compound path item, group item, mesh item, path item, placed item, plug-in item, raster item, and text art item each inherit a set of properties from the page item class.*
>
> *You cannot create a page item directly. You must use create one of the specific page item subclasses, such as path item.*

CompoundPathItem

A compound path composed of more than one path object. *Compound paths* are objects composed of multiple intersecting paths, resulting in transparent interior spaces where the original paths overlap.

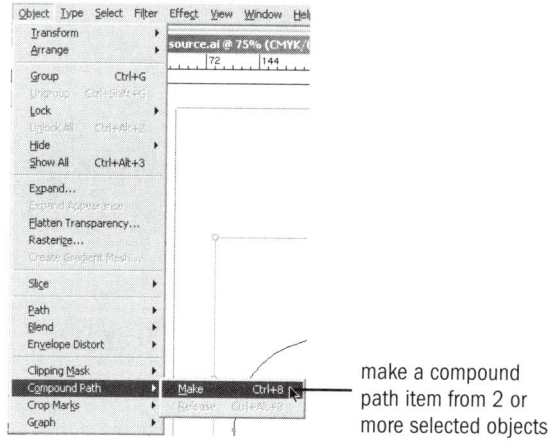

make a compound path item from 2 or more selected objects

Figure 6.19 *Making compound paths in the user interface is a multiple-step process: Select two or more objects, and choose Object > Compound Path > Make. As soon as you do this, your selected objects appear as one in the UI. But from the script perspective, you have added an object—a CompoundPathItem—that contains all the PathItems you had selected.*

Collection Properties

PROPERTY	VALUE TYPE	EXPLANATION
PathItems*	PathItems collection object	The path art items in this compound path.
Tags*	Tags collection object	The tags contained in this object.

Other Properties

PROPERTY	VALUE TYPE	EXPLANATION
PageItem*	PageItem object	The page item object corresponding to the compound path item.

Properties inherited from the superclass PageItem:
Application*, ArtworkKnockout, BlendingMode, ControlBounds*, Editable*, GeometricBounds*, Height, Hidden, IsIsolated, Layer*, Left, Locked, Name, Opacity, Parent*, Position, Selected, Sliced, Top, URL, VisibleBounds*, VisibilityVariable, Width, ZOrderPosition*

Methods

Methods inherited from the superclass PageItem:
Copy, Cut, Duplicate, MoveAfter, MoveBefore, MoveToBeginning, MoveToEnd, Resize, Rotate, Transform, Translate, ZSetOrder

CompoundPathItems

A collection of compound paths.

Properties

PROPERTY	VALUE TYPE	EXPLANATION
Application*	Application object	The Illustrator Application object.
Count*	Long	The number of objects in the collection.
Index(item As CompoundPathItem)	Long	Returns the index position of the object within the collection.
item(itemKey)	CompoundPathItem object	Returns an object reference to the object identified by itemKey.
Parent*	Object	The parent of this collection, either a Layer or a GroupItem.

Methods

METHOD	RETURN VALUE (IF ANY)	EXPLANATION
Add	CompountPathItem object	Creates a new CompoundPathItem.
Remove(item As CompoundPathItem)	Nothing	Deletes a compound path item from this collection.
RemoveAll	Nothing	Deletes all objects in this collection.

> **TIPS** *Paths contained within a compound path or group in a document will be returned as individual paths when a script asks for the paths contained in the document. Paths contained in a compound path or group, however, will not be returned when a script asks for the paths in a layer that contains the compound path or group.*
>
> *All paths inside a compound path share property values. Therefore, if you set the value of a property of any of the paths in the compound path, all other paths' matching properties will be updated to the new value.*

GraphItem

A graph art object.

Collection Properties

PROPERTY	VALUE TYPE	EXPLANATION
Tags*	Tags collection object	The tags contained in this object.

Other Properties

PROPERTY	VALUE TYPE	EXPLANATION
PageItem*	PageItem object	The page item object corresponding to the compound path item.

Properties inherited from the superclass PageItem:
Application*, ArtworkKnockout, BlendingMode, ControlBounds*, Editable*, GeometricBounds*, Height, Hidden, IsIsolated, Layer*, Left, Locked, Name, Opacity, Parent*, Position, Selected, Sliced, Top, URL, VisibleBounds*, VisibilityVariable, Width, ZOrderPosition*

Methods

Methods inherited from the superclass PageItem:
Copy, Cut, Duplicate, MoveAfter, MoveBefore, MoveToBeginning, MoveToEnd, Resize, Rotate, Transform, Translate, ZSetOrder

GraphItems

A collection of one or more graph items.

Properties

PROPERTY	VALUE TYPE	EXPLANATION
Application*	Application object	The Illustrator Application object.
Count*	Long	The number of objects in the collection.
Index(item As GraphItem)	Long	Returns the index position of the object within the collection.
item(itemKey)	GraphItem object	Returns an object reference to the object identified by itemKey.
Parent*	Object	The parent of this collection, either a Layer or a GroupItem.

Methods

METHOD	RETURN VALUE (IF ANY)	EXPLANATION
Remove(item As GraphItem)	Nothing	Deletes a graph item from this collection.
RemoveAll	Nothing	Deletes all objects in this collection.

TIP *Graph items cannot be created from a script. You can modify existing graph objects from a script by binding a variable to the graph object and then importing datasets under script control to update the values in the graph object. See Chapter 4 for an example of this technique.*

GroupItem

A grouped set of art objects.

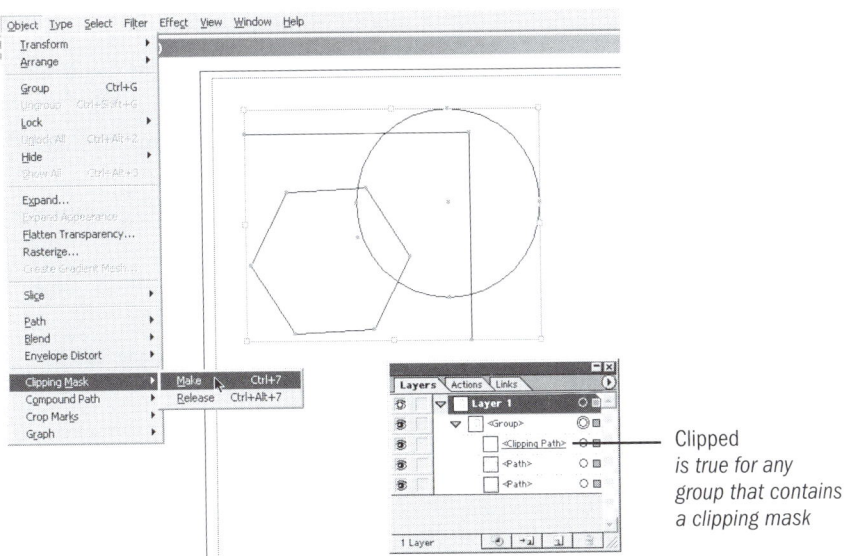

Figure 6.20 You can make a clipping mask from the user interface by selecting the objects you want to mask as well as the masking path itself, making sure that it is frontmost, and then choosing Object > Clipping Mask > Make. The result is that the objects get grouped and the group object's Clipped property is set to True. A script can make a clipping mask simply by doing the same. Create a group object, add page items to it, and set the Clipped property to True for the group object. Or you can set the Clipping property of the first path item in the group to True. This property is also editable and in turn changes the group's Clipped property value automatically.

Collection Properties

PROPERTY	VALUE TYPE	EXPLANATION
CompoundPathItems*	CompoundPathItems collection object	The compound path items contained in this group.
GraphItems*	GraphItems collection object	The graph items contained in the document.
GroupItems*	GroupItems collection object	The group items contained in this group.
MeshItems*	MeshItems collection object	The mesh items contained in this group.
PageItems*	PageItems collection object	The page items contained in this group.

Collection Properties (continued)

PROPERTY	VALUE TYPE	EXPLANATION
PathItems*	PathItems collection object	The path items contained in this group.
PlacedItems*	PlacedItems collection object	The placed items contained in this group.
PluginItems*	PluginItems collection object	The plug-in items contained in this group.
RasterItems*	RasterItems collection object	The raster items contained in this group.
SymbolItems*	SymbolItems collection object	The symbol items contained in this document.
Tags*	Tags collection object	The tags contained in this group.
TextArtItems*	TextArtItems collection object	The text art items contained in this group.

Other Properties

PROPERTY	VALUE TYPE	EXPLANATION
Clipped	Boolean	Is the group clipped to its first path item?
PageItem*	PageItem object	The page item object corresponding to the group item.

Properties inherited from the superclass PageItem:
  Application*, ArtworkKnockout, BlendingMode, ControlBounds*, Editable*, GeometricBounds*, Height, Hidden, IsIsolated, Layer*, Left, Locked, Name, Opacity, Parent*, Position, Selected, Sliced, Top, URL, VisibleBounds*, VisibilityVariable, Width, ZOrderPosition*

Methods

METHOD	RETURN VALUE (IF ANY)	EXPLANATION
Paste	Nothing	Inserts the contents of the Clipboard at the beginning of the group item. You may paste only into a group that is contained in the active document.

Methods inherited from the superclass PageItem:
  Copy, Cut, Duplicate, MoveAfter, MoveBefore, MoveToBeginning, MoveToEnd, Resize, Rotate, Transform, Translate, ZSetOrder

GroupItems

A collection of one or more group items.

Properties

PROPERTY	VALUE TYPE	EXPLANATION
Application*	Application object	The Illustrator Application object.
Count*	Long	The number of objects in the collection.
Index(item As GroupItem)	Long	Returns the index position of the object within the collection.
item(itemKey)	GroupItem object	Returns an object reference to the object identified by itemKey.
Parent*	Object	The parent of this object.

Methods

METHOD	RETURN VALUE (IF ANY)	EXPLANATION
Add	GroupItem object	Creates a new object.
CreateFromFile (imageFile As String)	GroupItem object	Places an external vector art file in the document as a group item.
Remove(item As GroupItem)	Nothing	Deletes a group item from this collection.
RemoveAll	Nothing	Deletes all objects in this collection.

TIPS *Group items can contain all the same page items that a layer can contain, including other nested groups.*

Paths contained within a group or compound path in a document will be returned as individual paths when a script asks for the paths contained in the document. Paths contained in a group or compound path, however, will not be returned when a script asks for the paths in a layer that contains the group or compound path.

You can create a new group that contains the contents of a vector art file if you provide a file specification to the vector file (EPS or PDF) in the with data *parameter of the* make *command. The resulting group will be the same object as though the user had placed the file from the user interface, choosing File > Place and checking the Embed checkbox.*

MeshItem

A gradient mesh art object.

Collection Properties

PROPERTY	VALUE TYPE	EXPLANATION
Tags*	Tags collection object	The tags contained in this mesh item.

Other Properties

PROPERTY	VALUE TYPE	EXPLANATION
PageItem*	PageItem object	The page item object corresponding to the mesh item.

Properties inherited from the superclass PageItem:
Application*, ArtworkKnockout, BlendingMode, ControlBounds*, Editable*, GeometricBounds*, Height, Hidden, IsIsolated, Layer*, Left, Locked, Name, Opacity, Parent*, Position, Selected, Sliced, Top, URL, VisibleBounds*, VisibilityVariable, Width, ZOrderPosition*

Methods

Methods inherited from the superclass PageItem:
Copy, Cut, Duplicate, MoveAfter, MoveBefore, MoveToBeginning, MoveToEnd, Resize, Rotate, Transform, Translate, ZSetOrder

MeshItems

A collection of one or more mesh art items.

Properties

PROPERTY	VALUE TYPE	EXPLANATION
Application*	Application object	The Illustrator Application object.
Count*	Long	The number of objects in the collection.
Index(item As MeshItem)	Long	Returns the index position of the object within the collection.
item(itemKey)	MeshItem object	Returns an object reference to the object identified by itemKey.
Parent*	Object	The parent of this object.

Methods

METHOD	RETURN VALUE (IF ANY)	EXPLANATION
Remove(item As MeshItem)	Nothing	Deletes a mesh item from this collection.
RemoveAll	Nothing	Deletes all objects in this collection.

TIP *Mesh items cannot be created from a script but can be duplicated, copied, and pasted.*

PathItem

A path art object. A path is composed of path points that define its geometry.

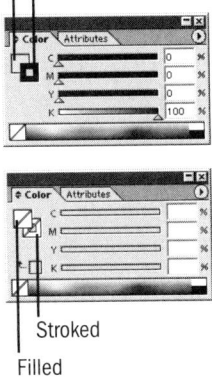

Figure 6.21 The fundamental PathItem properties FillColor, Filled StrokeColor, and Stroked are accessible from the Color palette. If you set Filled or Stroked to False, the value of the corresponding color property is ignored by the application. You can set FillColor or StrokeColor to any of the valid color assignment object classes, such as CMYKColor, GradientColor, and RGBColor.

Figure 6.22 A PathItem object's FillOverprint, StrokeOverprint, Evenodd, and Note properties are accessed in the Attributes palette. The Evenodd property sets the color filling rule used for the path. When Evenodd is false, the nonzero winding fill rule is applied, filling all overlapping regions of the path the same as any other region. When Evenodd is true, the even–odd fill rule is used, so overlapping regions cancel one another out and are not filled.

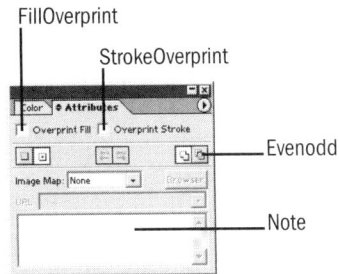

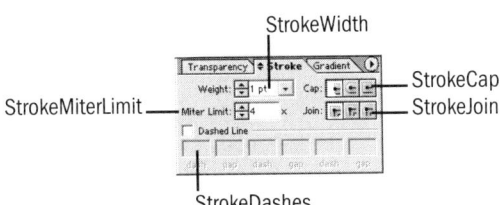

Figure 6.23 The basic properties for a path's stroke are available in the aptly named Stroke palette of the user interface. StrokeDashOffset specifies where a stroke dash pattern should start in relation to the beginning of any path to which it is applied.

421

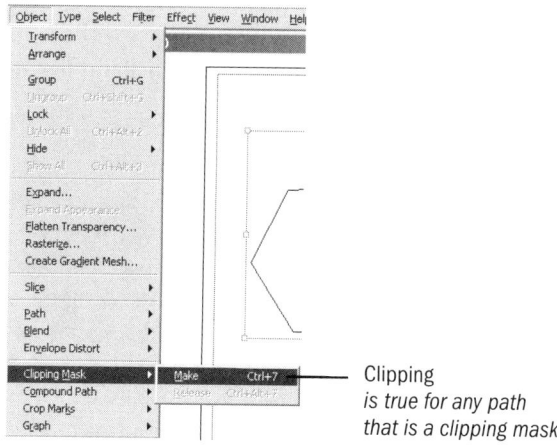

Clipping
*is true for any path
that is a clipping mask*

Figure 6.24 *After you make a clipping mask, the frontmost PathItem object in the resulting group always has its Clipping property set to True.*

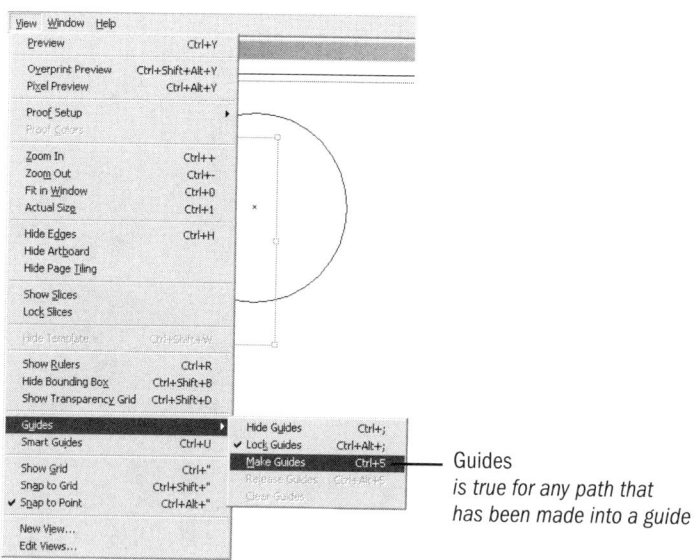

Guides
*is true for any path that
has been made into a guide*

Figure 6.25 *Accessing an entire document's set of guides from a script is easy, because Illustrator treats guides like special paths. The magic PathItem property that determines whether the path is a guide is simple. Just set the Guides property of any PathItem to true to convert it to a guide. Or you can test an existing path's Guides property to determine whether it is a guide.*

Collection Properties

PROPERTY	VALUE TYPE	EXPLANATION
PathPoints*	PathPoints collection object	The path points contained in this path item.
SelectedPathPoints*	PathPoints collection object	All the selected path points in the path.
Tags*	Tags collection object	The tags contained in this path item.

Other Properties

PROPERTY	VALUE TYPE	EXPLANATION
Area*	Single	The area of this path, in square points. An area may be negative or even 0. The path's winding order is determined by the sign of the area. If the area is negative, the path is wound counter-clockwise. Self-intersecting paths may contain subareas that cancel one another out. Therefore, it is possible for a path's area to appear as 0, even though it has apparent area.
Clipping	Boolean	Is this path to be used as a clipping path?
Closed	Boolean	Is this path closed?
Evenodd	Boolean	Use the even-odd rule to determine insideness?
FillColor	Color object	The fill color of the path.
Filled	Boolean	Should the path be filled?
FillOverprint	Boolean	Will art beneath a filled object be over-printed?
Guides	Boolean	Is this path a guide object?
Note	String	The note text assigned to the path.
PageItem*	PageItem object	The page item object corresponding to the path item.
Polarity	AiPolarityValues	Is the polarity of the path positive or negative?
Resolution*	Single	The resolution of the path (in dots per inch).
StrokeCap	AiStrokeCap enumeration	The type of line capping.
StrokeColor	Color object	The stroke color for the path.
Stroked	Boolean	Should the path be stroked?

Other Properties (continued)

PROPERTY	VALUE TYPE	EXPLANATION
StrokeDashes	Variant Array	Dash lengths, set to an empty array for a solid line.
StrokeDashOffset	Single	The default distance into the dash pattern at which the pattern should be started.
StrokeJoin	AiStrokeJoin enumeration	Type of joints for the path.
StrokeMiterLimit	Single	Are joins mitered (pointed) or beveled (squared off)?
StrokeOverprint	Boolean	Will art beneath a stroked object be overprinted?
StrokeWidth	Single	Width of stroke.

Properties inherited from the superclass PageItem:
Application*, ArtworkKnockout, BlendingMode, ControlBounds*, Editable*, GeometricBounds*, Height, Hidden, IsIsolated, Layer*, Left, Locked, Name, Opacity, Parent*, Position, Selected, Sliced, Top, URL, VisibleBounds*, VisibilityVariable, Width, ZOrderPosition*

Methods

METHOD	RETURN VALUE (IF ANY)	EXPLANATION
SetEntirePath(path Specification As Variant Array of Variant Array of two Singles)	Nothing	Defines path points for this path, using the supplied array of fixed points (each comprised of a Variant Array of two Singles). Each fixed point represents the Anchor for a path point.

Methods inherited from the superclass PageItem:
Copy, Cut, Duplicate, MoveAfter, MoveBefore, MoveToBeginning, MoveToEnd, Resize, Rotate, Transform, Translate, ZSetOrder

PathItems

A collection of one or more path items.

Properties

PROPERTY	VALUE TYPE	EXPLANATION
Application*	Application object	The Illustrator Application object.
Count*	Long	The number of objects in the collection.
Index(item As PathItem)	Long	Returns the index position of the object within the collection.
item(itemKey)	PathItem object	Returns an object reference to the object identified by itemKey.
Parent*	Object	The parent of this object.

Methods

METHOD	RETURN VALUE (IF ANY)	EXPLANATION
Add	PathItem object	Creates a new object.
Ellipse([top As Single], [left As Single], [Width As Single], [Height As Single], [reversed As Boolean], [inscribed As Boolean])	PathItem object	Creates a new path item in the shape of an ellipse, using the supplied parameters.
Polygon([centerX As Single], [centerY As Single], [radius As Single], [sides As Long], [reversed As Boolean])	PathItem object	Creates a new path item in the shape of an polygon, using the supplied parameters.
Rectangle([top As Single], [left As Single], [Width As Single], [Height As Single], [reversed As Boolean])	PathItem object	Creates a new path item in the shape of an polygon, using the supplied parameters.
Remove(item As PathItem)	Nothing	Deletes a path item from this collection.
RemoveAll	Nothing	Deletes all objects in this collection.
RoundedRectangle([top As Single], [left As Single], [Width As Single], [Height As Single], [horizontalRadius As Single], [verticalRadius As Single], [reversed As Boolean])	PathItem object	Creates a new path item in the shape of a rectangle with rounded corners, using the supplied parameters.
Star([centerX As Single], [centerY As Single], [radius As Single], [innerRadius As Single], [points As Long], [reversed As Boolean])	PathItem object	Creates a new path item in the shape of a star, using the supplied parameters.

TIPS The path item class gives you complete access to paths in Illustrator.

The methods Ellipse, Polygon, Rectangle, RoundedRectangle, and Star allow you to create complex path items with straightforward parameters. If you do not provide any parameters when calling these methods, default values will be used.

PathPoint

A PathPoint represents a point on a path.

Properties

PROPERTY	VALUE TYPE	EXPLANATION
Anchor	Variant Array (of two Singles)	The position of this point's anchor point.
Application*	Application object	The Illustrator Application object.
LeftDirection	Variant Array (of two Singles)	The position of this path point's in control point.
Parent*	PathItem object	The path item that contains this path point.
PointType	AiPointType enumeration	The type of path point, either a curve or a corner.
RightDirection	Variant Array (of two Singles)	The position of this path point's out control point.
Selected	AiPathPointSelection enumeration	Are points of this path point selected? If so, which one(s)?.

TIP *Anchor, with its pair of control points, or handles, LeftDirection and RightDirection. Any point can be considered to be a corner point. Setting the PointType property of a path point to a corner forces the left and right direction points to be on a straight line when the user attempts to modify them in the user interface.*

PathPoints

A collection of one or more PathPoints.

Properties

PROPERTY	VALUE TYPE	EXPLANATION
Application*	Application object	The Illustrator Application object.
Count*	Long	The number of objects in the collection.
Index(item As PathPoint)	Long	Returns the index position of the object within the collection.
item(itemKey)	PathPoint object	Returns an object reference to the object identified by itemKey.
Parent*	Object	The parent of this object.

METHOD	DETAILED FORMAT	RETURN VALUE
Add	PathPoint object	Creates a new object.
Remove(item As PathPoint)	Nothing	Deletes a path point from this collection.
RemoveAll	Nothing	Deletes all objects in this collection.

PlacedItem

An artwork item (optionally stored in an external file) placed in a document. A placed item must correspond to a file containing vector-graphic data, such as a PICT, EPS, or PDF file.

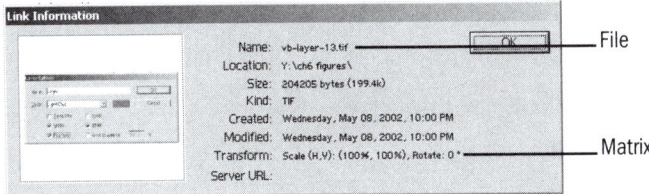

Figure 6.26 *When you double-click an entry for a placed art item in the user interface's Links palette, the Link Information dialog appears. Here, the user can see the PlacedItem's File and Matrix properties, but Illustrator won't let the user change these values. From a script, both the File and Matrix properties are editable, allowing a script to change placed art's file links and appearance easily.*

Collection Properties

PROPERTY	VALUE TYPE	EXPLANATION
Tags*	Tags collection object	The tags contained in this placed item.

Other Properties

PROPERTY	VALUE TYPE	EXPLANATION
BoundingBox*	Variant Array (of four Singles)	Dimensions of placed item regardless of transformations.
ContentVariable	Variable object	The content variable bound to this placed item, if any.
File	String	The file containing the placed object.
Matrix	Matrix object	The transformation matrix applied to the placed item.

Other Properties (continued)

PROPERTY	VALUE TYPE	EXPLANATION
PageItem*	PageItem object	The page item object corresponding to the placed item.

Properties inherited from the superclass PageItem:
Application*, ArtworkKnockout, BlendingMode, ControlBounds*, Editable*, GeometricBounds*, Height, Hidden, IsIsolated, Layer*, Left, Locked, Name, Opacity, Parent*, Position, Selected, Sliced, Top, URL, VisibleBounds*, VisibilityVariable, Width, ZOrderPosition*

Methods

Methods inherited from the superclass PageItem:
Copy, Cut, Duplicate, MoveAfter, MoveBefore, MoveToBeginning, MoveToEnd, Resize, Rotate, Transform, Translate, ZSetOrder

PlacedItems

A collection of one or more placed art items.

Properties

PROPERTY	VALUE TYPE	EXPLANATION
Application*	Application object	The Illustrator Application object.
Count*	Long	The number of objects in the collection.
Index(item As PlacedItem)	Long	Returns the index position of the object within the collection.
item(itemKey)	PlacedItem object	Returns an object reference to the object identified by itemKey.
Parent*	Object	The parent of this object.

Methods

METHOD	RETURN VALUE (IF ANY)	EXPLANATION
Add	PlacedItem object	Creates a new object.
Remove(item As PlacedItem)	Nothing	Deletes a placed item from this collection.
RemoveAll	Nothing	Deletes all objects in this collection.

TIPS When you create a placed item, Illustrator may display a dialog. To prevent this dialog from appearing, check the checkbox to turn the warning off the first time the dialog is displayed.

Vector art files, such as EPS and PDF files, can be placed by users with the File > Place command in Illustrator. Placed items can be created from vector art files in a script via the technique illustrated in the following example.

PluginItem

An art object or objects created by an Illustrator plug-in.

Collection Properties

PROPERTY	VALUE TYPE	EXPLANATION
Tags*	Tags collection object	The tags contained in this placed item.

Properties

PROPERTY	VALUE TYPE	EXPLANATION

Properties inherited from the superclass PageItem:
Application*, ArtworkKnockout, BlendingMode, ControlBounds*, Editable*, GeometricBounds*, Height, Hidden, IsIsolated, Layer*, Left, Locked, Name, Opacity, Parent*, Position, Selected, Sliced, Top, URL, VisibleBounds*, VisibilityVariable, Width, ZOrderPosition*

Methods

Methods inherited from the superclass PageItem:
Copy, Cut, Duplicate, MoveAfter, MoveBefore, MoveToBeginning, MoveToEnd, Resize, Rotate, Transform, Translate, ZSetOrder

PluginItems

A collection of one or more plug-in art items.

Properties

PROPERTY	VALUE TYPE	EXPLANATION
Application*	Application object	The Illustrator Application object.
Count*	Long	The number of objects in the collection.
Index(item As PluginItem)	Long	Returns the index position of the object within the collection.
item(itemKey)	PluginItem object	Returns an object reference to the object identified by itemKey.
Parent*	Object	The parent of this object.

Methods

METHOD	RETURN VALUE (IF ANY)	EXPLANATION
Remove(item As PluginItem)	Nothing	Deletes a plug-in item from this collection.
RemoveAll	Nothing	Deletes all objects in this collection.

TIP *Plug-in items cannot be created from a script but can be duplicated as well as copied.*

RasterItem

A bitmap art object linked to an external bitmap file or embedded in the document.

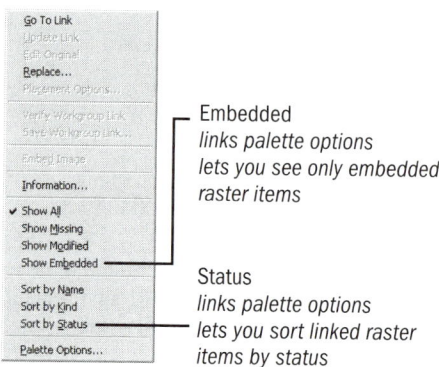

Embedded
links palette options lets you see only embedded raster items

Status
links palette options lets you sort linked raster items by status

Figure 6.27 *Two important properties of a RasterItem are available from the Links palette in the user interface, sort of. The Embedded property tells you whether the raster art object's bitmap is stored entirely inside the Illustrator document. The Status property tells you about the status of externally linked bitmap files. Illustrator lets the user sort the Links palette by these two properties.*

Collection Properties

PROPERTY	VALUE TYPE	EXPLANATION
Tags*	Tags collection object	The tags contained in this raster art item.

Properties

PROPERTY	VALUE TYPE	EXPLANATION
BoundingBox	Variant Array (of four Singles)	Dimensions of raster item regardless of transformations.
ContentVariable	Variable object	The content variable bound to this raster item, if any.
Embedded	Boolean	Is the raster art embedded within the illustration?
File	String	The file containing the raster object, if it is stored externally.
ImageColorSpace	AiImageColorSpace enumeration	The color space of the raster image.
Matrix	Matrix object	The transformation matrix of the raster art object.

Properties (continued)

PROPERTY	VALUE TYPE	EXPLANATION
PageItem*	PageItem object	The page item object corresponding to the raster item.
Status	AiRasterLinkState enumeration	The status of the linked image, if the image is stored externally.

Properties inherited from the superclass PageItem:
Application*, ArtworkKnockout, BlendingMode, ControlBounds*, Editable*, GeometricBounds*, Height, Hidden, IsIsolated, Layer*, Left, Locked, Name, Opacity, Parent*, Position, Selected, Sliced, Top, URL, VisibleBounds*, VisibilityVariable, Width, ZOrderPosition*

Methods

Methods inherited from the superclass PageItem:
Copy, Cut, Duplicate, MoveAfter, MoveBefore, MoveToBeginning, MoveToEnd, Resize, Rotate, Transform, Translate, ZSetOrder

RasterItems

A collection of one or more raster art items.

Properties

PROPERTY	VALUE TYPE	EXPLANATION
Application*	Application object	The Illustrator Application object.
Count*	Long	The number of objects in the collection.
Index(item As RasterItem)	Long	Returns the index position of the object within the collection.
item(itemKey)	RasterItem object	Returns an object reference to the object identified by itemKey.
Parent*	Object	The parent of this object.

Methods

METHOD	RETURN VALUE (IF ANY)	EXPLANATION
Add	RasterItem object	Creates a new object.
Remove(item As RasterItem)	Nothing	Deletes a raster item from this collection.
RemoveAll	Nothing	Deletes all objects in this collection.

TIP *Raster items can be created from a script if an external file is used. New raster items can also be created by duplicating or copying and pasting an existing raster item.*

SymbolItem

A symbol art object.

Collection Properties

PROPERTY	VALUE TYPE	EXPLANATION
Tags*	Tags collection object	The tags contained in this raster art item.

Other Properties

PROPERTY	VALUE TYPE	EXPLANATION
Symbol*	Symbol object	The symbol to which this symbol art item is linked.

Properties inherited from the superclass PageItem:
Application*, ArtworkKnockout, BlendingMode, ControlBounds*, Editable*, GeometricBounds*, Height, Hidden, IsIsolated, Layer*, Left, Locked, Name, Opacity, Parent*, Position, Selected, Sliced, Top, URL, VisibleBounds*, VisibilityVariable, Width, ZOrderPosition*

Methods

Methods inherited from the superclass PageItem:
Copy, Cut, Duplicate, MoveAfter, MoveBefore, MoveToBeginning, MoveToEnd, Resize, Rotate, Transform, Translate, ZSetOrder

SymbolItems

A collection of one or more symbol art items.

Properties

PROPERTY	VALUE TYPE	EXPLANATION
Application*	Application object	The Illustrator Application object.
Count*	Long	The number of objects in the collection.
Index(item As SymbolItem)	Long	Returns the index position of the object within the collection.
item(itemKey)	SymbolItem object	Returns an object reference to the object identified by itemKey.
Parent*	Object	The parent of this object.

Methods

METHOD	RETURN VALUE (IF ANY)	EXPLANATION
Add	SymbolItem object	Creates a new object.
Remove(item As SymbolItem)	Nothing	Deletes a symbol item from this collection.
RemoveAll	Nothing	Deletes all objects in this collection.

TextArtItem

A text art object. From the user interface, this object is text created with one of the Text tools.

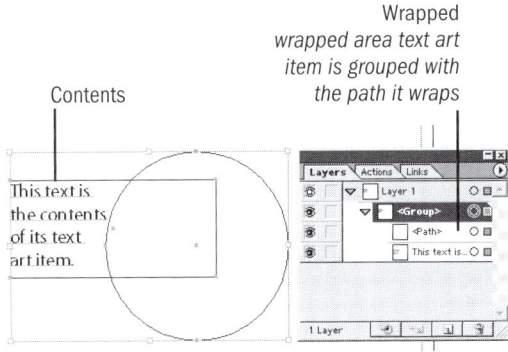

Figure 6.28 *The most basic aspect of a TextArtItem is its textual Contents property. Almost complete text art access has been provided to scripts, including the ability to manipulate the Wrapped property of area text, which describes whether or not the text art is set to wrap around a path it is grouped with.*

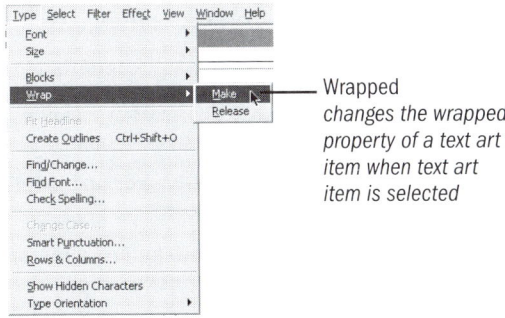

Figure 6.29 *To set the Wrapped property of a TextArtItem to true from the user interface, select the text art object and a path for it to wrap around; then choose Type > Wrap > Make. A script can do the same thing. Create a GroupItem, move a PathItem and a TextArtItem into the group, and set the TextArtItem's Wrapped property to true.*

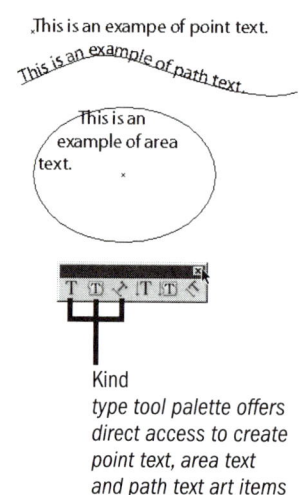

Figure 6.30 The type tool palette's first three tool choices provide direct access from the UI to create the three kinds of text art objects: point text, area text, and path text. Both area text and path text require a path as well.

Kind
type tool palette offers direct access to create point text, area text and path text art items

Collection Properties

PROPERTY	VALUE TYPE	EXPLANATION
Selection	TextRange collection object	The selected text in the contents of this text art item.
Tags*	Tags collection object	The tags contained in this raster art item.
TextPath_PathItems*	PathItems collection object	The path items associated with in-path and on-path text.
TextPaths*	TextPaths collection object	The text paths contained in this text art item.

Other Properties

PROPERTY	VALUE TYPE	EXPLANATION
Contents	String (default property)	The text contents of the text art item.
ContentVariable	Variable Object	The content variable bound to this text art item, if any.
Kind	AiTextType enumeration	The type of text art displayed by this object.
Wrapped	Boolean	Does the text wrap around other objects (valid only for area text)?

Properties inherited from the superclass PageItem:
  Application*, ArtworkKnockout, BlendingMode, ControlBounds*, Editable*, GeometricBounds*, Height, Hidden, IsIsolated, Layer*, Left, Locked, Name, Opacity, Parent*, Position, Selected, Sliced, Top, URL, VisibleBounds*, VisibilityVariable, Width, ZOrderPosition*

Methods

METHOD	RETURN VALUE (IF ANY)	EXPLANATION
CreateOutline	GroupItem object	Converts a text art item to a group item consisting of paths and compound paths.

Methods inherited from the superclass PageItem:
Copy, Cut, Duplicate, MoveAfter, MoveBefore, MoveToBeginning, MoveToEnd, Resize, Rotate, Transform, Translate, ZSetOrder

TextArtItems

A collection of one or more text art items.

Properties

PROPERTY	VALUE TYPE	EXPLANATION
Application*	Application object	The Illustrator Application object.
Count*	Long	The number of objects in the collection.
Index(item As TextArtItem)	Long	Returns the index position of the object within the collection.
item(itemKey)	TextArtItem object	Returns an object reference to the object identified by itemKey.
Parent*	Object	The parent of this object.

Methods

METHOD	RETURN VALUE (IF ANY)	EXPLANATION
Add	TextArtItem object	Creates a new object.
Remove(item As TextArtItem)	Nothing	Deletes a text art item from this collection.
RemoveAll	Nothing	Deletes all objects in this collection.

> **TIP** Illustrator has three types of text art objects, specified by the text art item's kind property. See Chapter 3 for more information on working with the three kinds of text art items.

Text superclass of objects

TextRange

Any text in the contents of a text art item.

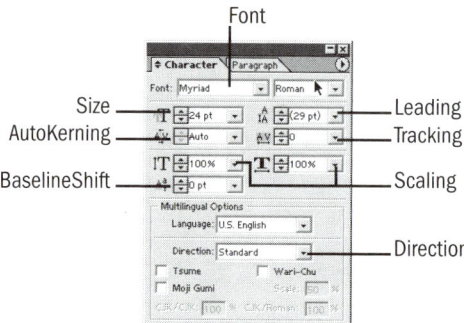

Figure 6.31 *The Character palette provides access to the basic properties for all the text objects: Character, Paragraph, TextLine, TextRange, and Word.*

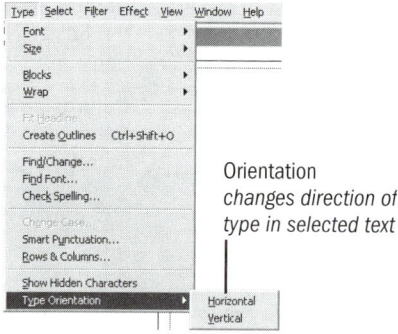

Figure 6.32 *The Orientation property lets you change the way the text is drawn in a text object.*

Collection Properties

PROPERTY	VALUE TYPE	EXPLANATION
Characters*	Characters collection object	The characters contained in this text range.
Paragraphs*	Paragraphs collection object	The paragraphs contained in this text range.
TextLines*	TextLines collection object	The lines of text contained in this text range.
Words*	Words collection object	The words contained in this text range.

Properties

PROPERTY	VALUE TYPE	EXPLANATION
Application*	Application object	The Illustrator Application object.
AutoKerning	Boolean	Should a font's built-in kerning information be used?
BaselineShift	Single	Baseline offset of text.
Clipping*	Boolean	Is a clipping path associated with the text art item containing this text range?
Contents	String (default property)	The text contained in the text range.
Direction	AiCharDirection enumeration	The orientation of the characters in a vertical text block.
Evenodd	Boolean	Should the even–odd rule be used to determine insideness?
FillColor	Color	Fill color of text.
Filled	Boolean	Should the text be filled?
FillOverprint	Boolean	Should the art beneath the text be overprinted?
Font	String	The text face of the text.
Leading	Single	The vertical leading of the text.
Length	Long	The number of character in the text.
Note*	String	The note associated with this text.
Offset*	Long	Offset of selected text in text range (in characters).
Orientation*	AiTextOrientation enumeration	The orientation of the text. Use the TextPath class to alter this property.
Parent*	TextArtItem object	The parent of this object.
Resolution*	Single	The resolution of the object (in dots per inch).
Scaling	Variant Array (of two Singles)	The character scaling supplied as a point, with the first coordinate as the horizontal scale and the second coordinate as the vertical scale, where 100.0 is 100%.
Size	Single	Font size of text.
StrokeCap	AiStrokeCap enumeration	The type of line capping.
StrokeColor	Color object	The stroke color for the path.

Properties (continued)

PROPERTY	VALUE TYPE	EXPLANATION
Stroked	Boolean	Should the path be stroked?
StrokeDashes	Variant Array	Dash lengths, set to an empty array for a solid line.
StrokeDashOffset	Single	The default distance into the dash pattern at which the pattern should be started.
StrokeJoin	AiStrokeJoin enumeration	Type of joints for the path.
StrokeMiterLimit	Single	Are joins mitered (pointed) or beveled (squared off)?
StrokeOverprint	Boolean	Will art beneath a stroked object be overprinted?
StrokeWidth	Single	Width of stroke.
TextPath*	TextPath object	A reference to the text path associated with the text art item containing this text.
Tracking	Single	The spacing between multiple characters.

Methods

METHOD	RETURN VALUE (IF ANY)	EXPLANATION
Copy	Nothing	Copies the text range to the Clipboard. The associated document must be the frontmost document.
Cut	Nothing	Cuts the text range to the Clipboard. The associated document must be the frontmost document.
DeleteRange	Nothing	Deletes the text range.
Paste	Nothing	Replaces text range with the contents of the Clipboard.
TextRange([rangeStart As Long], [rangeEnd As Long])	TextRange object	Returns a text range object referencing a substring of the current text range, where rangeStart is the beginning character position and rangeEnd is the ending position. The first character position is 0. If omitted, rangeStart defaults to 0. If omitted, rangeEnd defaults to the last character of the range.

TIP *Text can be accessed via the Character, Word, TextLine, Paragraph, and TextRange classes. All text is contained within text art items.*

Character

A character of text in the text contained in a text art item.

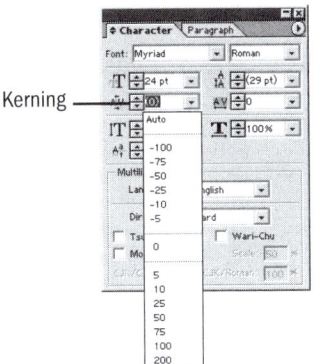

Figure 6.33 *The Kerning property of a Character object lets you change the individual spacing between it and the next character.*

Properties

PROPERTY	VALUE TYPE	EXPLANATION
Kerning	Single	The spacing between two characters, in milli-ems, or thousandths of an em.
Paragraph*	Paragraph object	The paragraph containing the character.
TextLine*	TextLine object	The line of text containing the character.
Word*	Word object	The word containing this character.

Properties inherited from the superclass TextRange:
   Application*, AutoKerning, BaselineShift, Clipping*, Contents, Direction, Evenodd, FillColor, Filled, FillOverprint, Font, Leading, Length, Note*, Offset*, Orientation*, Parent*, Resolution*, Scaling, Size, StrokeCap, StrokeColor, Stroked, StrokeDashes, StrokeDashOffset, StrokeJoin, StrokeMiterLimit, StrokeOverprint, StrokeWidth, TextPath*, Tracking

Methods

Methods inherited from the superclass TextRange:
Copy, Cut, Paste

> **TIP** You can access the text contained within text art items in Illustrator by using TextRange and its subclasses. The properties and valid commands for all these classes are similar but not identical. Character has a kerning property, for example, but the other text classes do not.

Characters

A collection of one or more characters.

Properties

PROPERTY	VALUE TYPE	EXPLANATION
Application*	Application object	The Illustrator Application object.
Count*	Long	The number of characters in the collection.
Index(item As Character)	Long	Returns the index position of the object within the collection.
item(itemKey)	Character object	Returns an object reference to the object identified by itemKey (which can be only index for Character).
Parent*	Object	The text art item that contains this character.

Methods

METHOD	RETURN VALUE (IF ANY)	EXPLANATION
Add	Character object	Adds a character after the last character in the current collection.
AddBefore	Character object	Adds a character before the first character in the current collection.
Remove(item As Character)	Nothing	Deletes a character from this collection.
RemoveAll	Nothing	Deletes all objects in this collection.

Paragraph

A paragraph of text in a text art object.

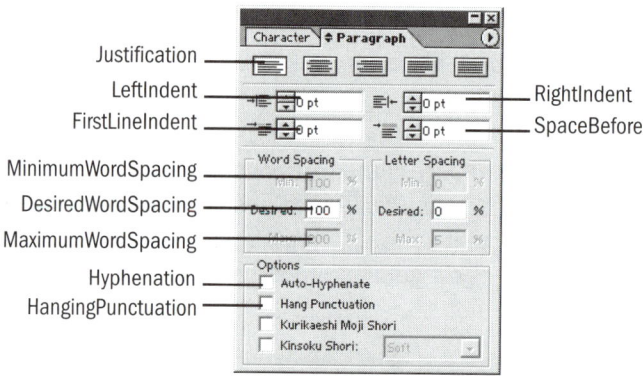

Figure 6.34 *The Paragraph palette provides access to the layout properties of the Paragraph object.*

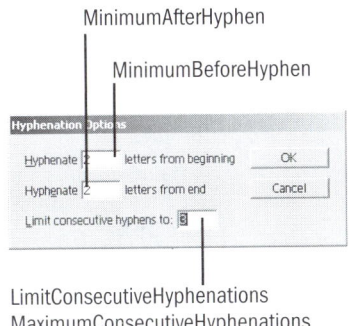

Figure 6.35 The Hyphenation Options dialog (accessible from the Paragraph palette) gives the user access to the detailed hyphenation settings for a Paragraph object.

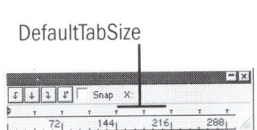

Figure 6.36 The DefaultTabSize property of a Paragraph object describes the distance between default tabs on the paragraph's Tab Ruler. There is no access to individual tab settings in Visual Basic—only in AppleScript.

Collection Properties

PROPERTY	VALUE TYPE	EXPLANATION
Characters*	Characters collection object	The characters contained in this text range.
TextLines*	TextLines collection object	The lines of text contained in this paragraph.
Words*	Words collection object	The words contained in this paragraph.

Other Properties

PROPERTY	VALUE TYPE	EXPLANATION
DefaultTabSize	Single	The default distance for tab stops.
DesiredLetterSpacing	Single	The desired letter spacing. 100.0 is normal letter spacing.
DesiredWordSpacing	Single	The desired word spacing. 100.0 is normal word spacing.
FirstLineIndent	Single	The indent of the first line.
HangingPunctuation	Boolean	Should punctuation appear outside the margins of the paragraph?
Hyphenation	Boolean	Is hyphenation enabled for the paragraph?
Justification	AiJustification enumeration	The paragraph alignment or justification.

Other Properties (continued)

PROPERTY	VALUE TYPE	EXPLANATION
LeftIndent	Single	The left indent of the paragraph's margin.
LimitConsecutiveHyphenations	Boolean	Is there a limit on the number of consecutive hyphenated lines in this paragraph?
MaximumConsecutiveHyphenations	Long	The maximum number of consecutive hyphenated lines.
MaximumLetterSpacing	Single	The maximum letter. 100.0 is normal letter spacing.
MaximumWordSpacing	Single	The maximum letter spacing. 100.0 is normal word spacing.
MinimumAfterHyphen	Long	The minimum number of characters after a hyphen.
MinimumBeforeHyphen	Long	The minimum number of characters before a hyphen.
MinimumLetterSpacing	Single	The minimum letter spacing.100.0 is normal letter spacing.
MinimumWordSpacing	Single	The minimum letter spacing.100.0 is normal word spacing.
RepeatedCharacterProcessing	Boolean	Should RepeatedCharacterProcessing be used?
RightIndent	Single	The right indent of the paragraph's margin.
SpaceBefore	Single	The spacing before this paragraph.

Properties inherited from the superclass TextRange:
   Application*, AutoKerning, BaselineShift, Clipping*, Contents, Direction, Evenodd, FillColor, Filled, FillOverprint, Font, Leading, Length, Note*, Offset*, Orientation*, Parent*, Resolution*, Scaling, Size, StrokeCap, StrokeColor, Stroked, StrokeDashes, StrokeDashOffset, StrokeJoin, StrokeMiterLimit, StrokeOverprint, StrokeWidth, TextPath*, Tracking

Methods

Methods inherited from the superclass TextRange:
Copy, Cut, Paste, TextRange

Paragraphs

A collection of one or more paragraphs.

Properties

PROPERTY	VALUE TYPE	EXPLANATION
Application*	Application object	The Illustrator Application object.
Count*	Long	The number of paragraphs in the collection.
Index(item As Paragraph)	Long	Returns the index position of the object within the collection.
item(itemKey)	Paragraph object	Returns an object reference to the object identified by itemKey (which can be only index for Paragraph).
Parent*	Object	The text art item that contains this paragraph.

Methods

METHOD	RETURN VALUE (IF ANY)	EXPLANATION
Add	Paragraph object	Adds a paragraph after the last paragraph in the current collection.
AddBefore	Paragraph object	Adds a paragraph before the first paragraph in the current collection.
Remove(item As Paragraph)	Nothing	Deletes a paragraph from this collection.
RemoveAll	Nothing	Deletes all objects in this collection.

TIP *The Paragraph class has additional properties that related classes do not share, including properties for margins, justification, hyphenation, and word/letter spacing.*

TextLine

A line of text in a text art item.

Collection Properties

PROPERTY	VALUE TYPE	EXPLANATION
Characters*	Characters collection object	The characters contained in this text line.

Other Properties

PROPERTY	VALUE TYPE	EXPLANATION
Paragraph*	Paragraph object	The paragraph containing the character.

Properties inherited from the superclass TextRange:
 Application*, AutoKerning, BaselineShift, Clipping*, Contents, Direction, Evenodd, FillColor, Filled, FillOverprint, Font, Leading, Length, Note*, Offset*, Orientation*, Parent*, Resolution*, Scaling, Size, StrokeCap, StrokeColor, Stroked, StrokeDashes, StrokeDashOffset, StrokeJoin, StrokeMiterLimit, StrokeOverprint, StrokeWidth, TextPath*, Tracking

Methods

Methods inherited from the superclass TextRange:
Copy, Cut, Paste

TextLines

A collection of one or more lines of text.

Properties

PROPERTY	VALUE TYPE	EXPLANATION
Application*	Application object	The Illustrator Application object.
Count*	Long	The number of text lines in the collection.
Index(item As TextLine)	Long	Returns the index position of the object within the collection.
item(itemKey)	TextLine object	Returns an object reference to the object identified by itemKey (which can be only index for TextLine).
Parent*	Object	The text art item that contains this text line.

Methods

METHOD	RETURN VALUE (IF ANY)	EXPLANATION
Remove(item As TextLine)	Nothing	Deletes a line of text from this collection.
RemoveAll	Nothing	Deletes all objects in this collection.

TIP *Lines of text cannot be created. When the contents property of a text art item is modified, Illustrator will create text lines as it reflows the text within the text art item.*

Word

A string of text in a text art item that is separated by white space.

Collection Properties

PROPERTY	VALUE TYPE	EXPLANATION
Characters*	Characters collection object	The characters contained in this word.

Other Properties

PROPERTY	VALUE TYPE	EXPLANATION
Paragraph*	Paragraph object	The paragraph containing the character.

Properties inherited from the superclass TextRange:
Application*, AutoKerning, BaselineShift, Clipping*, Contents, Direction, Evenodd, FillColor, Filled, FillOverprint, Font, Leading, Length, Note*, Offset*, Orientation*, Parent*, Resolution*, Scaling, Size, StrokeCap, StrokeColor, Stroked, StrokeDashes, StrokeDashOffset, StrokeJoin, StrokeMiterLimit, StrokeOverprint, StrokeWidth, TextPath*, Tracking

Methods

Methods inherited from the superclass text:
count, delete, duplicate, exists, make

Words

A collection of one or more words of text.

Properties

PROPERTY	VALUE TYPE	EXPLANATION
Application*	Application object	The Illustrator Application object.
Count*	Long	The number of words in the collection.
Index(item As Word)	Long	Returns the index position of the object within the collection.
item(itemKey)	Word object	Returns an object reference to the object identified by itemKey (which can be only index for Word).
Parent*	Object	The text art item that contains this word.

Methods

METHOD	RETURN VALUE (IF ANY)	EXPLANATION
Remove(item As Word)	Nothing	Deletes a word from this collection.
RemoveAll	Nothing	Deletes all objects in this collection.

Swatch-palette color objects

All these objects reside in the Swatches palette of your document. Using the swatch or swatches object form will give you access to every swatch in the document's palette. Using the spot or spots form will let you access spot color swatches, global process color swatches, and registration color swatches. The gradient swatch and its various parts are also accessible. Pattern color swatches are the only kind of color swatch you cannot create from a script.

Gradient

A gradient definition stored as a document swatch. Gradients are contained in documents.

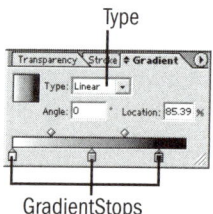

Figure 6.37 *Gradient colors are complicated. The Gradient palette of the UI provides only basic properties, such as Type, and access to each of the GradientStops.*

Collection Properties

PROPERTY	VALUE TYPE	EXPLANATION
GradientStops*	GradientStops collection object	The gradient stops contained in this gradient.

Properties

PROPERTY	VALUE TYPE	EXPLANATION
Application*	Application object	The Illustrator Application object.
Name	String	The gradient's name.
Parent*	Document object	The document that contains this gradient.
Type	AiGradientType enumeration	The kind of the gradient, either radial or linear.

Gradients

A collection of one or more gradient definitions.

Properties

PROPERTY	VALUE TYPE	EXPLANATION
Application*	Application object	The Illustrator Application object.
Count*	Long	The number of objects in the collection.
Index(item As Gradient)	Long	Returns the index position of the object within the collection.
item(itemKey)	Gradient object	Returns an object reference to the object identified by itemKey.
Parent*	Object	The parent of this object.

Methods

METHOD	RETURN VALUE (IF ANY)	EXPLANATION
Add	Gradient object	Creates a new object.
Remove(item As Gradient)	Nothing	Deletes a gradient from this collection.
RemoveAll	Nothing	Deletes all objects in this collection.

TIP *Because a gradient is a swatch element, it has no methods. You can create a new gradient by using the Add method of the Gradients collection. Additional gradients may be created by the user within Illustrator or via a script.*

GradientStop

A gradient stop definition contained in a specific gradient.

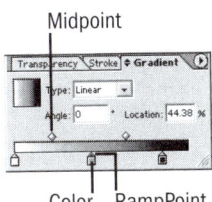

Figure 6.38 *Each individual GradientStop in a Gradient object defines the Color, RampPoint (where the color starts), and Midpoint (where the color blends 50% with the color of the next stop to the left).*

Properties

PROPERTY	VALUE TYPE	EXPLANATION
Application*	Application object	The Illustrator Application object.
Color	Color object	The color linked to this gradient stop.
Midpoint	Single	The midpoint key value in a range from 0.0 to 1.0.
Parent	Gradient object	The gradient that contains this gradient stop.
RampPoint	Single	The location of the color in the blend in a range from 0.0 to 100.0, where 100.0 is 100%.

GradientStops

A collection of one or more gradient stop definitions contained in a specific gradient.

Properties

PROPERTY	VALUE TYPE	EXPLANATION
Application*	Application object	The Illustrator Application object.
Count*	Long	The number of objects in the collection.
Index(item As GradientStop)	Long	Returns the index position of the object within the collection.
item(itemKey)	GradientStop object	Returns an object reference to the object identified by itemKey.
Parent*	Object	The parent of this object.

Methods

METHOD	RETURN VALUE (IF ANY)	EXPLANATION
Add	GradientStop object	Creates a new object.
Remove(item As GradientStop)	Nothing	Deletes a gradient stop from this collection.
RemoveAll	Nothing	Deletes all objects in this collection.

TIP *Illustrator's gradient stop object represents a point on a specific gradient defined in the Illustrator application. Each gradient stop specifies a color change in the containing gradient.*

Pattern

A pattern definition contained in a document.

Properties

PROPERTY	VALUE TYPE	EXPLANATION
Application*	Application object	The Illustrator Application object.
Name*	String	The pattern name.
Parent*	Document object	The document that contains this pattern.

Patterns

A collection of one or more pattern definitions.

Properties

PROPERTY	VALUE TYPE	EXPLANATION
Application*	Application object	The Illustrator Application object.
Count*	Long	The number of objects in the collection.
Index(item As Pattern)	Long	Returns the index position of the object within the collection.
item(itemKey)	Pattern object	Returns an object reference to the object identified by itemKey.
Parent*	Object	The parent of this object.

Methods

METHOD	RETURN VALUE (IF ANY)	EXPLANATION
Add	Pattern object	Creates a new object.
Remove(item As Pattern)	Nothing	Deletes a pattern from this collection.
RemoveAll	Nothing	Deletes all objects in this collection.

TIP *Illustrator's pattern object represents a pattern as defined in the Illustrator application.*

Spot

A spot color definition contained in a document.

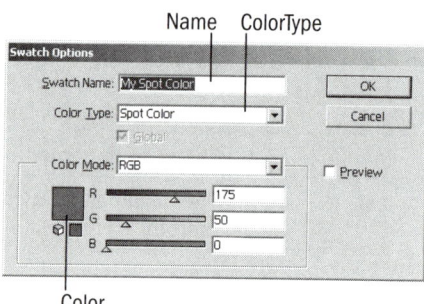

Figure 6.39 *A Spot is a spot color swatch saved in the Swatch palette. The Swatch Options dialog, which you open by double-clicking a swatch in the palette, shows some of a Spot's properties.*

Properties

PROPERTY	VALUE TYPE	EXPLANATION
Application*	Application object	The Illustrator Application object.
Color	Color object	The color information for this spot color.
Name*	String	The spot color's name.
Parent*	Document object	The document that contains this spot color.

Spots

A collection of one or more spot color definitions.

Properties

PROPERTY	VALUE TYPE	EXPLANATION
Application*	Application object	The Illustrator Application object.
Count*	Long	The number of objects in the collection.
Index(item As Spot)	Long	Returns the index position of the object within the collection.
item(itemKey)	Spot object	Returns an object reference to the object identified by itemKey.
Parent*	Object	The parent of this object.

Methods

METHOD	RETURN VALUE (IF ANY)	EXPLANATION
Add	Spot object	Creates a new object.
Remove(item As Spot)	Nothing	Deletes a spot color from this collection.
RemoveAll	Nothing	Deletes all objects in this collection.

TIPS *Illustrator's spot object represents a spot color as defined by Illustrator. All Illustrator documents contain the spot color "[Registration]", which can be used to print to all plates of a separation.*

If you specify no properties when you create a new spot, default properties will be provided. If you're specifying the color, however, you must use the same color space as the document—either CMYK or RGB. Otherwise, an error will result. When created, the spot is inserted at the end of the swatch palette.

Swatch

A color swatch contained in a document.

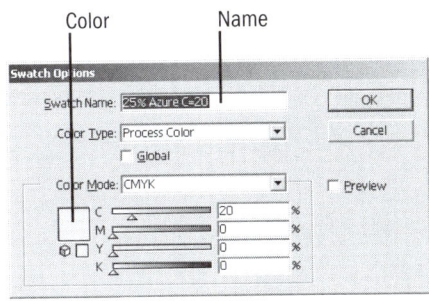

Figure 6.40 *A Swatch is a color of any type saved in the Swatch palette.*

Properties

PROPERTY	VALUE TYPE	EXPLANATION
Application*	Application object	The Illustrator Application object.
Color	Color object	The color information for this swatch.
Name	String	The swatch's name.
Parent*	Document object	The document that contains this swatch.

Swatches

A collection of one or more color swatches.

Properties

PROPERTY	VALUE TYPE	EXPLANATION
Application*	Application object	The Illustrator Application object.
Count*	Long	The number of objects in the collection.
Index(item As Swatch)	Long	Returns the index position of the object within the collection.
item(itemKey)	Swatch object	Returns an object reference to the object identified by itemKey.
Parent*	Object	The parent of this object.

Methods

METHOD	RETURN VALUE (IF ANY)	EXPLANATION
Add	Spot object	Creates a new object.
Remove(item As Swatch)	Nothing	Deletes a swatch from this collection.
RemoveAll	Nothing	Deletes all objects in this collection.

TIP *The swatches correspond to the swatch palette in Illustrator's user interface. Additional swatches can be created manually by a user or by a script. The swatch can hold all types of color data, including pattern, gradient, CMYK, RGB, gray, and spot.*

Basic color definitions

CMYKColor

A CMYK color specification, used to specify a CMYK color in conjunction with the Color property.

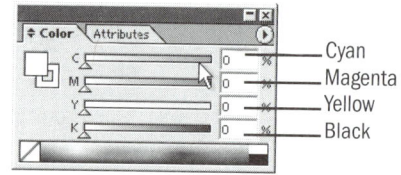

Figure 6.41 *A CMYKColor object is simply an instance of a color definition, as represented by the Color palette. The act of creating a CMYKColor object and setting its properties is just like opening the Color palette with no objects selected and mixing up a new color setting.*

Properties

PROPERTY	VALUE TYPE	EXPLANATION
Application*	Application object	The Illustrator Application object.
Black	Single	The black color value as a value in the range 0.0 to 100.0.
Cyan	Single	The cyan color value as a value in the range 0.0 to 100.0.
Magenta	Single	The magenta color value as a value in the range 0.0 to 100.0.
Yellow	Single	The yellow color value as a value in the range 0.0 to 100.0.

TIPS This class is used to define a record that contains the color component values of a CMYK color. It is used for specifying and retrieving color information from an Illustrator document or from page items in a document.

If the color space of a document is RGB, and you specify the color value for a page item in that document by using CMYKColor, Illustrator will translate the CMYK color specification to a RGB color specification. The same thing happens if the document's color space is CMYK and you specify colors by using RGBColor. Because this translation can cause information loss, you should specify colors by using the color info class that matches the document's color space.

GradientColor

A gradient color specification, used to specify a gradient color in conjunction with the color property.

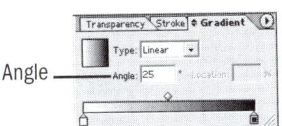

Figure 6.42 You can set the Angle property of a gradient only when you're ready to apply the color and need to define a GradientColor object.

Properties

PROPERTY	VALUE TYPE	EXPLANATION
Angle	Single	The gradient vector angle (in degrees).
Application*	Application object	The Illustrator Application object.
Gradient	Gradient object	Reference to the object defining the gradient.

Properties (continued)

PROPERTY	VALUE TYPE	EXPLANATION
HiliteAngle	Single	The gradient highlight vector angle (in degrees).
HiliteLength	Single	The gradient highlight vector length.
Length	Single	The gradient vector length.
Matrix	Matrix object	An additional transformation matrix to manipulate the gradient path.
Origin	Variant Array (of two Singles)	The gradient vector origin.

TIP *This class is used to define a record that contains the color component values of a gradient color swatch. It is used for specifying and retrieving color information from an Illustrator document or from page items in a document.*

GrayColor

A gray color specification, used to specify a gray color in conjunction with the color property.

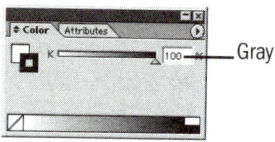

Figure 6.43 *A GrayColor object is simply a definition of a gray tint of black, as represented by the Color palette.*

Properties

PROPERTY	VALUE TYPE	EXPLANATION
Application*	Application object	The Illustrator Application object.
Gray	Single	The tint of the gray as a value in the range 0.0 to 100.0, where 0.0 is black and 100.0 is white.

TIPS *This class defines a record that contains the tint value of a gray color. It is used for specifying and retrieving color information from an Illustrator document or from page items in a document.*

You specify gray colors by using a real value that ranges from 0.0 to 100.0 for the tint of color, where 0.0 represents white and 100.0 represents black.

PatternColor

A pattern color specification, used to specify a pattern color in conjunction with the color property.

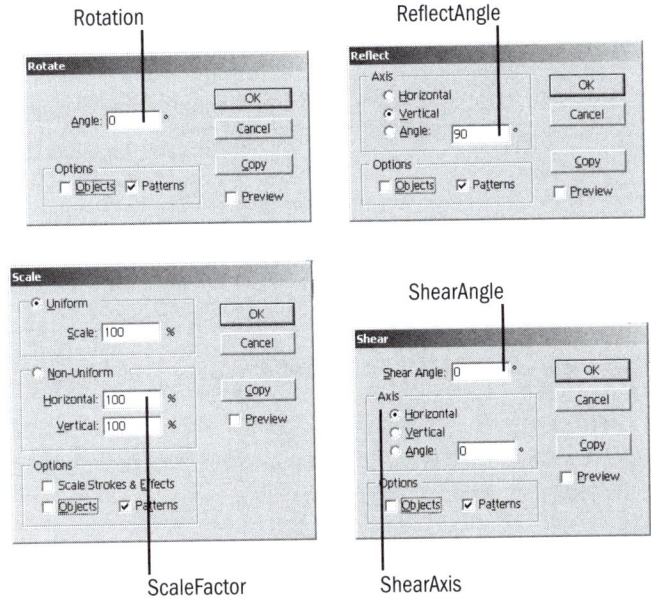

Figure 6.44 A PatternColor object has a large number of properties that allow you to change the pattern's appearance from a script. These properties correspond to some of the details shown in the various object-transformation dialogs available in the user interface.

Properties

PROPERTY	VALUE TYPE	EXPLANATION
Application*	Application object	The Illustrator Application object.
Matrix	Matrix object	An additional transformation matrix to manipulate the prototype pattern,
Pattern	Pattern object	A reference to the pattern object that defines the pattern to use in this color definition.
Reflect	Boolean	Is the prototype reflected before filling?
ReflectAngle	Single	The axis (in degrees) around which to reflect.
Rotation	Single	The angle (in degrees) to rotate the prototype pattern before filling.

Properties (continued)

PROPERTY	VALUE TYPE	EXPLANATION
ScaleFactor	Variant Array (of two Singles)	The fraction to scale the prototype pattern before filling, represented as a point containing horizontal and vertical scaling percentages.
ShearAngle	Single	The angle (in degrees) by which to slant the shear.
ShearAxis	Single	The axis (in degrees) to shear the pattern about.
ShiftAngle	Single	The angle (in degrees) to translate the unscaled prototype pattern before filling.
ShiftDistance	Single	The distance to translate the unscaled prototype pattern before filling.

TIP *Pattern colors are created via a reference to an existing pattern in a document. A matrix may be specified to transform the pattern color further.*

RGBColor

An RGB color specification, used to specify a RGB color in conjunction with the color property.

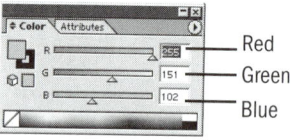

Figure 6.45 *A RGBColor object is simply an instance of a red-green-blue color definition, as represented by the Color palette.*

Properties

PROPERTY	VALUE TYPE	EXPLANATION
Blue	Single	The blue color value as a value in the range 0.0 to 255.0.
Green	Single	The green color value as a value in the range 0.0 to 255.0.
Red	Single	The red color value as a value in the range 0.0 to 255.0.

TIP *If the color space of a document is CMYK, and you specify the color value for a page item in that document by using RGB color info, Illustrator will translate the RGB color specification to a CMYK color specification. The same thing happens if the document's color space is RGB and you specify colors by using CMYK color info. Because this translation can cause information loss, you should specify colors by using the color info class that matches the document's color space.*

SpotColor

A spot color specification, used to specify a spot color in conjunction with the color property.

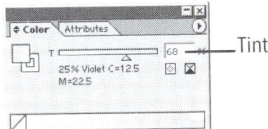

Figure 6.46 *A SpotColor object needs to have a spot color to reference, so you need to have a Spot color swatch defined first.*

Properties

PROPERTY	VALUE TYPE	EXPLANATION
Spot	Spot object	A reference to the spot color object that defines the color.
Tint	Single	The tint of the color as a value in the range 0.0 to 100.0.

TIP *The spot property must be set to a reference to an existing spot color definition.*

Objects related to save, export, and open options

EPSSaveOptions

Options that may be supplied when saving a document as an Illustrator EPS file. See the save command in the command reference for additional details.

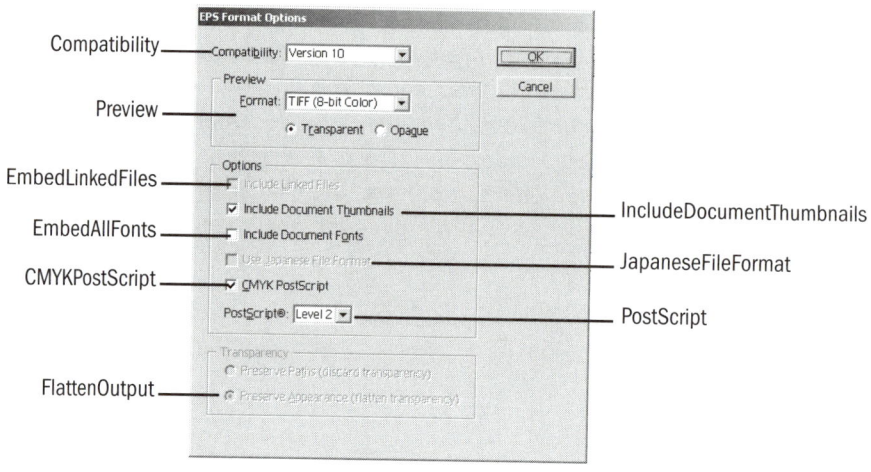

Figure 6.47 *This illustration shows how the EPS Format Options dialog maps to properties of the EPSSaveOptions object. You need to create a new EPSSaveOptions object and set any of its properties to the desired nondefault values before saving a document as an EPS with the Document.SaveAs method.*

Properties

PROPERTY	VALUE TYPE	EXPLANATION
Application*	Application object	The Illustrator Application object.
CMYKPostScript	Boolean	Use CMYK PostScript?
Compatibility	AiCompatibility enumeration	Specifies the version of the EPS file format to save.
EmbedAllFonts	Boolean	Include fonts used in the EPS file?
EmbedLinkedFiles	Boolean	Are linked image files to be included in the saved document?
FlattenOutput	AiOutputFlattening enumeration	How should transparency be flattened for file formats older than Illustrator 9?
IncludeDocumentThumbnails	Boolean	Include thumbnail image of the EPS artwork?
JapaneseFileFormat	Boolean	Save file using Japanese version of file format?
PostScript	AiPostScriptLevel enumeration	Specifies the PostScript level to use when saving the file.
Preview	AiEPSPreview enumeration	Specifies the format for the EPS preview image.

Methods

This object can be used only in conjunction with the Document.SaveAs method.

> **TIP** *This class is used to define a record containing properties that specify options when saving a document as an EPS file. It is not necessary to specify values for all properties. Default values will be provided for any properties that are not specified.*

ExportOptionsFlash

Options that may be supplied when exporting a document as a Flash .swf file.

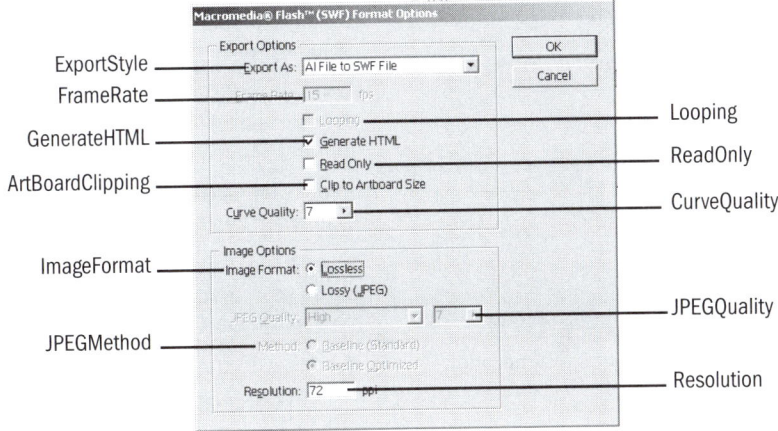

Figure 6.48 Create a new ExportOptionsFlash object and set any properties to the values you want before exporting a document as a SWF file with the Document.Export method.

Properties

PROPERTY	VALUE TYPE	EXPLANATION
Application*	Application object	The Illustrator Application object.
ArtBoardClipping	Boolean	Should the exported image be clipped to the artboard? The default value is false.
CurveQuality	Long	How much curve information should be preserved? Range: 0 to 10 (default: 7).
ExportStyle	AiFlashExportStyle enumeration	How should the Flash file be created?

Properties (continued)

PROPERTY	VALUE TYPE	EXPLANATION
FrameRate	Single	Frame rate (per second) when exporting layers to Flash frames. Range: 0.1 to 120 (default: 12).
GenerateHTML	Boolean	Create an HTML file as well when exporting Flash file? (Default: true.)
ImageFormat	AiFlashImageFormat enumeration	How should the images in the exported Flash file be compressed? (Default: lossless.)
JPEGMethod	AiFlashJPEGMethod enumeration	Which bitmap JPEG compression scheme should be used? (Default: standard.)
JPEGQuality	Long	Level of JPEG bitmap image compression. Range: 0 to 10 (default: 3).
Looping	Boolean	Should the Flash file be set to loop when run? (Default: false.)
ReadOnly	Boolean	Should the exported Flash file bed saved as a read-only file? (Default: false.)
Replacing	AiSaveOptions enumeration	If a file with the same name already exists, should it be replaced?
Resolution	Single	Resolution of bitmap images, in pixels per inch. Range: 72 to 2400 (default: 72).

Methods

This object can be used only in conjunction with the Document.Export method.

TIP *This class is used to define a record containing properties that specify options when exporting a document as a Flash file. It is not necessary to specify values for all properties. Default values will be provided for any properties that are not specified.*

ExportOptionsGIF

Options that may be supplied when exporting a document as a GIF file.

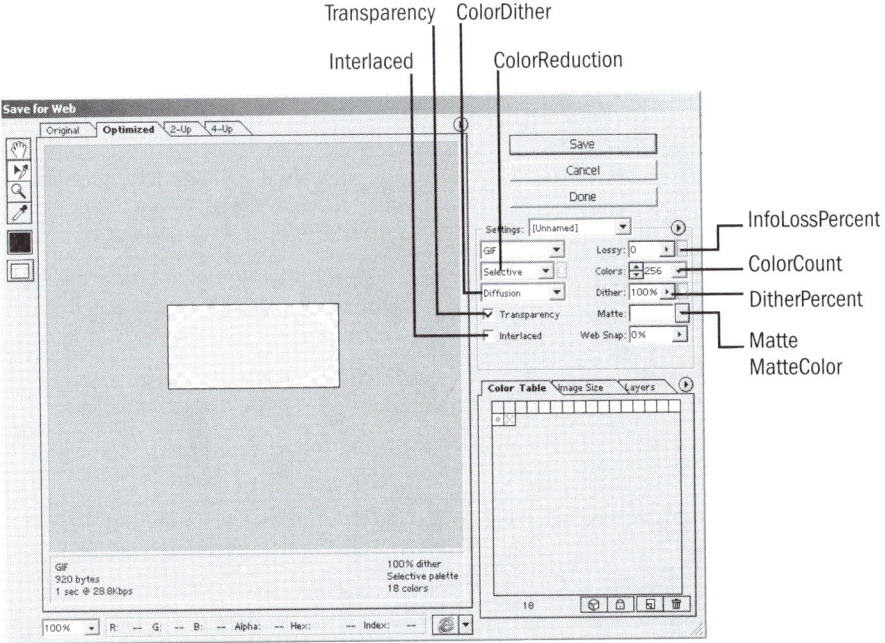

Figure 6.49 Some of the properties available in the ExportOptionsGIF object are not made available to the user interface. Can you find any missing?

Properties

PROPERTY	VALUE TYPE	EXPLANATION
AntiAliasing	Boolean	Should the exported image be antialiased? The default value is true.
Application*	Application object	The Illustrator Application object.
ArtBoardClipping	Boolean	Should the exported image be clipped to the artboard? The default value is false.
ColorCount	Long	The number of colors in the exported image's color table. Acceptable values range from 2 to 256. The default value is 128.
ColorDither	AiColorDitherMethod enumeration	The method used to dither colors in the exported image. The default value is aiDiffusionDither.

Properties (continued)

PROPERTY	VALUE TYPE	EXPLANATION
ColorReduction	AiColorReductionMethod enumeration	The method used to reduce the number of colors in the exported image. The default value is aiSelective.
DitherPercent	Long	How much should the colors of the exported image be dithered? 100.0 is 100%.
HorizontalScale	Single	The horizontal scaling factor to apply to the exported image, where 100.0 is 100%. The default value is 100.0.
InfoLossPercent	Long	The level of information loss allowed during compression, where 100.0 is 100%.
Interlaced	Boolean	Should the exported image be interlaced? The default value is false.
Matte	Boolean	Should the artboard be matted with a color? The default value is true.
MatteColor	RGBColor object	The color to use when matting the artboard. The default value is white.
SaveAsHTML	Boolean	Should the exported image be saved with an accompanying HTML file? The default value is false.
Transparency	Boolean	Should the exported image use transparency? The default value is true.
VerticalScale	Single	The vertical scaling factor to apply to the exported image, where 100.0 is 100%. The default value is 100.0.
WebSnap	Long	How much should the color table be changed to match the Web palette? 100 is maximum. The default value is 0.

Methods

This object can be used only in conjunction with the Document.Export method.

TIP *This class is used to define a record containing properties that specify options when exporting a document as a GIF file. It is not necessary to specify values for all properties. Default values will be provided for any properties that are not specified.*

ExportOptionsJPEG

Options that may be supplied when exporting a document as a JPEG file.

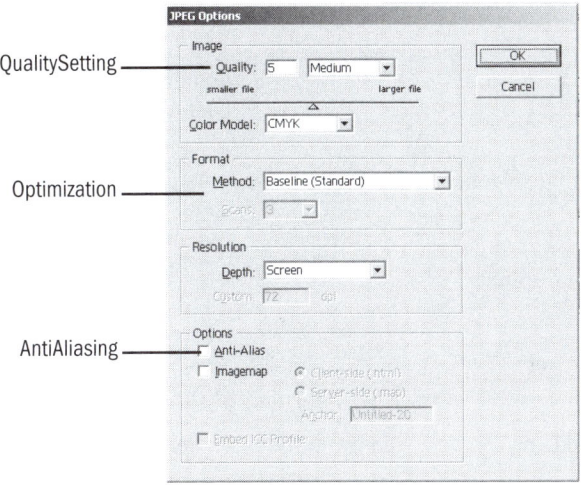

Figure 6.50 Create a new ExportOptionsJPEG object and set any properties to the values you want before exporting a document as a JPEG file.

Properties

PROPERTY	VALUE TYPE	EXPLANATION
AntiAliasing	Boolean	Should the exported image be antialiased? The default value is true.
Application*	Application object	The Illustrator Application object.
ArtBoardClipping	Boolean	Should the exported image be clipped to the artboard? The default value is false.
BlurAmount	Single	The amount of blur to apply to the exported image. This value ranges from 0.0 to 2.0. The default value is 0.0.
HorizontalScale	Single	The horizontal scaling factor to apply to the exported image, where 100.0 is 100%. The default value is 100.0.
Matte	Boolean	Should the artboard be matted with a color? The default value is true.
MatteColor	RGBColor object	The color to use when matting the artboard. The default value is white.

Properties (continued)

PROPERTY	VALUE TYPE	EXPLANATION
Optimization	Boolean	Should the exported image be optimized for Web viewing? The default value is true.
QualitySetting	Long	The quality of the exported image. This value ranges from 0 to 100. The default value is 30.
SaveAsHTML	Boolean	Should the exported image be saved with an accompanying HTML file? The default value is false.
VerticalScale	Single	The vertical scaling factor to apply to the exported image, where 100.0 is 100%. The default value is 100.0.

Methods

This object can be used only in conjunction with the Document.Export method.

TIP *This class is used to define a record containing properties that specify options when exporting a document as a JPEG file. It is not necessary to specify values for all properties. Default values will be provided for any properties that are not specified.*

ExportOptionsPhotoshop

Options that may be supplied when exporting a document as a Photoshop file.

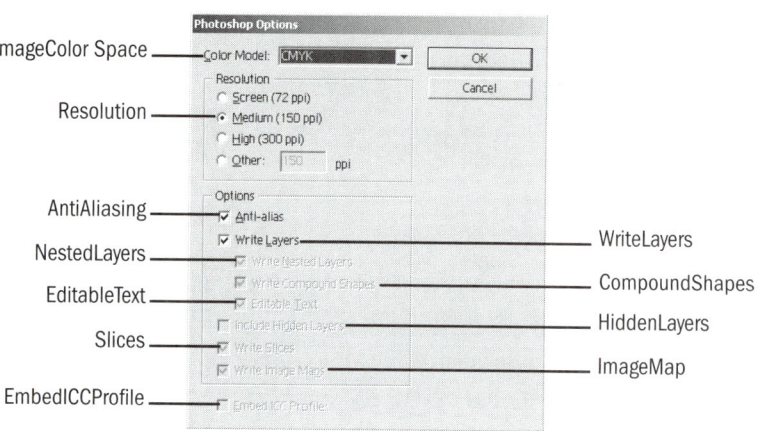

Figure 6.51 *All the properties available to the user interface for exporting Photoshop files are made available to the ExportOptionsPhotoshop object for use when exporting with the Document.Export method.*

Properties

PROPERTY	VALUE TYPE	EXPLANATION
AntiAliasing	Boolean	Should the exported image be antialiased? The default value is true.
Application*	Application object	The Illustrator Application object.
CompoundShapes	Boolean	Should compound shapes be exported as shape layers? (Default: true.)
EditableText	Boolean	Should text objects be exported as editable text layers? (Default: true.)
EmbedICCProfile	Boolean	Should a ICC profile be embedded in the exported file?
HiddenLayers	Boolean	Should hidden layers be included in the exported file?
ImageColorSpace	AiImageColorSpace enumeration	The color space of the exported file.
ImageMap	Boolean	Should image maps be preserved in RGB color space documents, using the ImageReady 3.0 format? (Default: true.)
NestedLayers	Boolean	Should nested layers be included in the exported file?
Resolution	Single	The resolution of the exported file (in dots per inch).
Slices	Boolean	Should slices be preserved in the exported file? (Default: true.)
Warnings	Boolean	Should a warning dialog be displayed because of conflicts in the export settings? (Default: true.)
WriteLayers	Boolean	Should the document layers be preserved in the exported file? (Default: true.)

Methods

This object can be used only in conjunction with the Document.Export method.

TIP *This class is used to define a record containing properties that specify options when exporting a document as a Photoshop file. It is not necessary to specify values for all properties. Default values will be provided for any properties that are not specified.*

ExportOptionsPNG24

Options that may be supplied when exporting a document as a PNG file with 24-bit color.

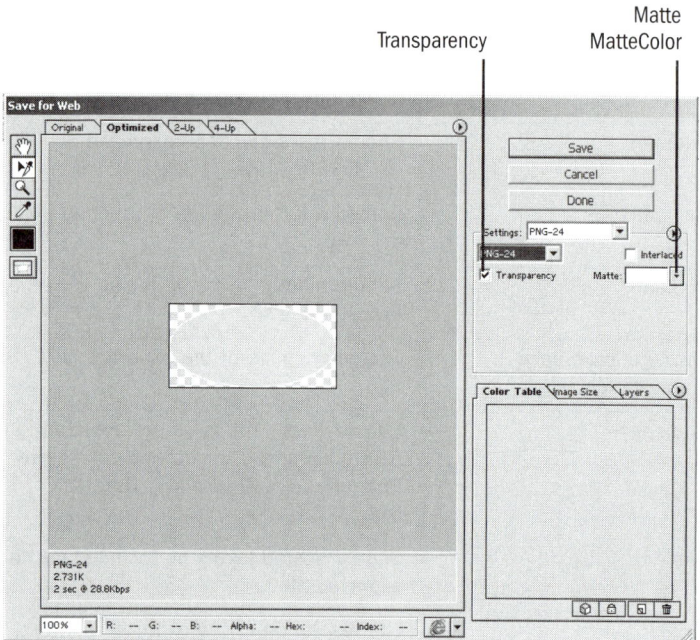

Figure 6.52 As you can see looking at the Save for Web dialog, the ExportOptionsPNG24 object has many more properties available for exporting PNG24 images from a script than the user interface provides for in Illustrator. But curiously, there is no Interlaced property in ExportOptionsPNG24 so the user interface gets access to one property that we, as scripters, do not.

Properties

PROPERTY	VALUE TYPE	EXPLANATION
AntiAliasing	Boolean	Should the exported image be antialiased? The default value is true.
Application*	Application object	The Illustrator Application object.
ArtBoardClipping	Boolean	Should the exported image be clipped to the artboard? The default value is false.
HorizontalScale	Single	The horizontal scaling factor to apply to the exported image, where 100.0 is 100%. The default value is 100.0.
Matte	Boolean	Should the artboard be matted with a color? The default value is true.
MatteColor	RGBColor object	The color to use when matting the artboard. The default value is white.
SaveAsHTML	Boolean	Should the exported image be saved with an accompanying HTML file? The default value is false.

Properties (continued)

PROPERTY	VALUE TYPE	EXPLANATION
Transparency	Boolean	Should the exported image use transparency? The default value is true.
VerticalScale	Single	The vertical scaling factor to apply to the exported image, where 100.0 is 100%. The default value is 100.0.

Methods

This object can be used only in conjunction with the Document.Export method.

> **TIP** *This class is used to define a record containing properties that specify options when exporting a document as a PNG24 file. It is not necessary to specify values for all properties. Default values will be provided for any properties that are not specified.*

ExportOptionsPNG8

Options that may be supplied when exporting a document as a PNG file with 8-bit color.

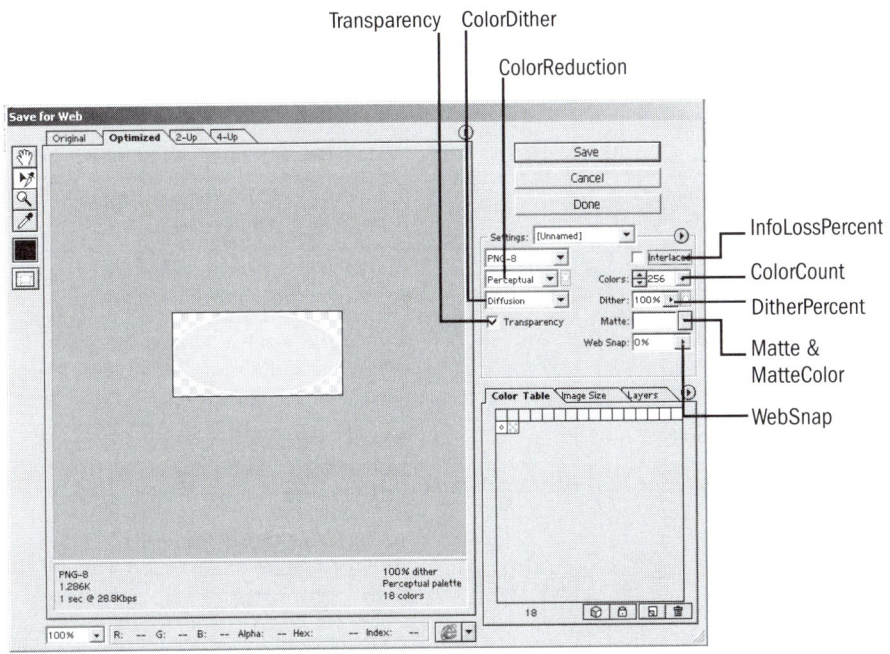

Figure 6.53 *The Save for Web dialog gives users a good number of options for exporting a PNG8 image. The ExportOptionsPNG8 object offers a similar array of properties for use with Document.Export.*

Properties

PROPERTY	VALUE TYPE	EXPLANATION
AntiAliasing	Boolean	Should the exported image be antialiased? The default value is true.
Application*	Application object	The Illustrator Application object.
ArtBoardClipping	Boolean	Should the exported image be clipped to the artboard? The default value is false.
ColorCount	Long	The number of colors in the exported image's color table. Acceptable values range from 2 to 256. The default value is 128.
ColorDither	AiColorDitherMethod enumeration	The method used to dither colors in the exported image. The default value is aiDiffusionDither.
ColorReduction	AiColorReductionMethod enumeration	The method used to reduce the number of colors in the exported image. The default value is aiSelective.
DitherPercent	Long	How much should the colors of the exported image be dithered? 100.0 is 100%.
HorizontalScale	Single	The horizontal scaling factor to apply to the exported image, where 100.0 is 100%. The default value is 100.0.
Interlaced	Boolean	Should the exported image be interlaced? The default value is false.
Matte	Boolean	Should the artboard be matted with a color? The default value is true.
MatteColor	RGBColor object	The color to use when matting the artboard. The default value is white.
SaveAsHTML	Boolean	Should the exported image be saved with an accompanying HTML file? The default value is false.
Transparency	Boolean	Should the exported image use transparency? The default value is true.
VerticalScale	Single	The vertical scaling factor to apply to the exported image, where 100.0 is 100%. The default value is 100.0.
WebSnap	Long	How much should the color table be changed to match the Web palette? 100 is maximum. The default value is 0.

Methods

This object can be used only in conjunction with the Document.Export method.

> **TIP** *This class is used to define a record containing properties that specify options when exporting a document as a PNG8 file. It is not necessary to specify values for all properties. Default values will be provided for any properties that are not specified.*

ExportOptionsSVG

Options that may be supplied when exporting a document as a SVG file.

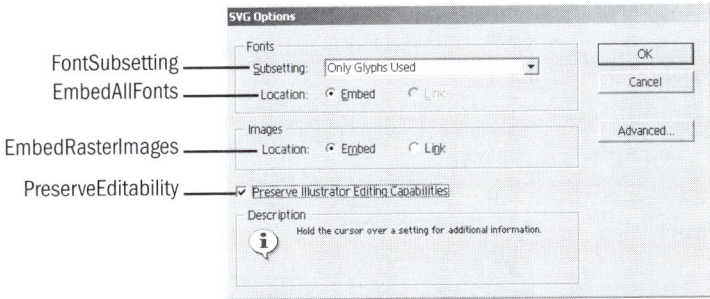

Figure 6.54 *The new format on the block, SVG, is given its due from scripting, with an ExportOptionsSVG object providing access to all the export properties shown in the user interface.*

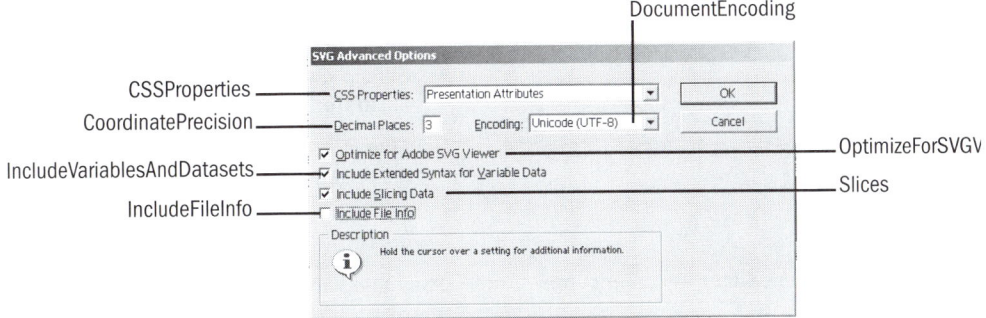

Figure 6.55 *The SVG Advanced Options dialog shows that every export property possible, including exporting variable and dataset data, is provided for in the ExportOptionsSVG object's set of properties.*

Properties

PROPERTY	VALUE TYPE	EXPLANATION
Application*	Application object	The Illustrator Application object.
Compressed	Boolean	Should the exported file be compressed? The default value is false.
CoordinatePrecision	Long	The decimal precision for element coordinate values. This value can range from 1 to 7. The default value is 3.
CSSProperties	AiSVGCSSPropertyLocation enumeration	How should the CSS properties of the document be included in the exported file?
DocumentEncoding	AiSVGDocumentEncoding enumeration	How should the text in the document be encoded?
EmbedAllFonts	Boolean	Embed all fonts used by the document in the saved file?
EmbedRasterImages	Boolean	Embed raster images contained in the document in the saved file?
FontSubsetting	AiSVGFontSubsetting enumeration	What font glyphs should be included in the export file?
IncludeFileInfo	Boolean	Should file information be included in the SVG file? (Default: false.)
IncludeVariablesAndDatasets	Boolean	Should variables and datasets be included in the SVG file? (Default: false.)
OptimizeForSVGViewer	Boolean	Should the SVG file be optimized for the SVG Viewer plug-in? (Default: false.)
PreserveEditability	Boolean	Should the SVG file be editable in Illustrator? (Default: false.)
Slices	Boolean	Should slice data be saved in the SVG file? (Default: false.)

Methods

This object can be used only in conjunction with the Document.Export method.

> **TIP** This class is used to define a record containing properties that specify options when exporting a document as a SVG file. It is not necessary to specify values for all properties. Default values will be provided for any properties that are not specified.

IllustratorSaveOptions

Options that may be supplied when saving a document as an Illustrator file. Used with the Document.SaveAs method.

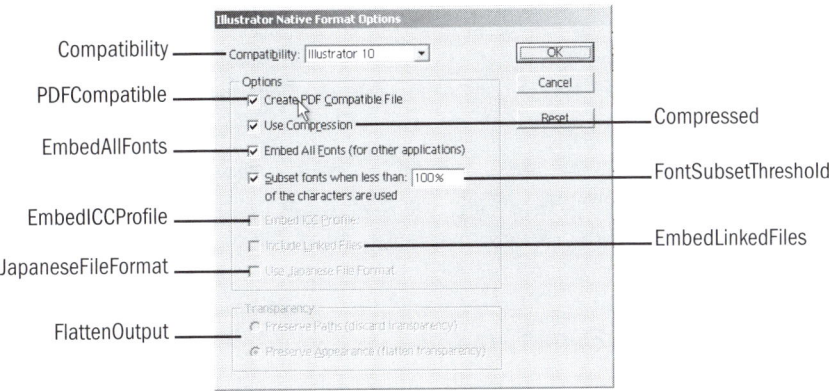

Figure 6.56 The IllustratorSaveOptions object is a mouthful to say, but it provides access to all the options possible when you're saving a document from a script with Document.SaveAs.

Properties

PROPERTY	VALUE TYPE	EXPLANATION
Application*	Application object	The Illustrator Application object.
Compatibility	AiCompatibility enumeration	Specifies the version of the Illustrator file format to create.
EmbedAllFonts	Boolean	Are all fonts used in the document to be embedded in the saved document? Valid only for Illustrator 9 file format.
EmbedICCProfile	Boolean	Should a ICC profile be embedded in the saved file?
EmbedLinkedFiles	Boolean	Are linked image files to be included in the saved document? Valid only for SaveOptions that specify an Illustrator compatibility of version 7 or later.
FlattenOutput	AiOutputFlattening enumeration	How should transparency be flattened for file formats older than Illustrator 9?
FontSubsetThreshold	Single	Include a subset of fonts when less than this percentage of characters is used in the document. Valid for Illustrator 9 file format.

Properties (continued)

PROPERTY	VALUE TYPE	EXPLANATION
JapaneseFileFormat	Boolean	Save using the Japanese version of the file format?

Methods

This object can be used only in conjunction with the Document.SaveAs method.

> **TIP** This class is used to define a record containing properties used to specify options when saving a document as an Illustrator file. It is not necessary to specify values for all properties. Default values will be provided for any properties that are not specified.

PDFOpenOptions

Options that may be supplied when opening a multipage PDF document.

Properties

PROPERTY	VALUE TYPE	EXPLANATION
Application*	Application object	The Illustrator Application object.
PageToOpen	Long	The page number of the multipage PDF file to open as an Illustrator document.

Methods

This object can be used only in conjunction with the Application.Open method.

> **TIP** This class is used to define a record containing properties used to specify options when opening a PDF file. PDF open options can be supplied only in conjunction with the Open command.

PDFSaveOptions

Options that may be supplied when saving a document as an Acrobat PDF file. See the save command in the command reference for additional details.

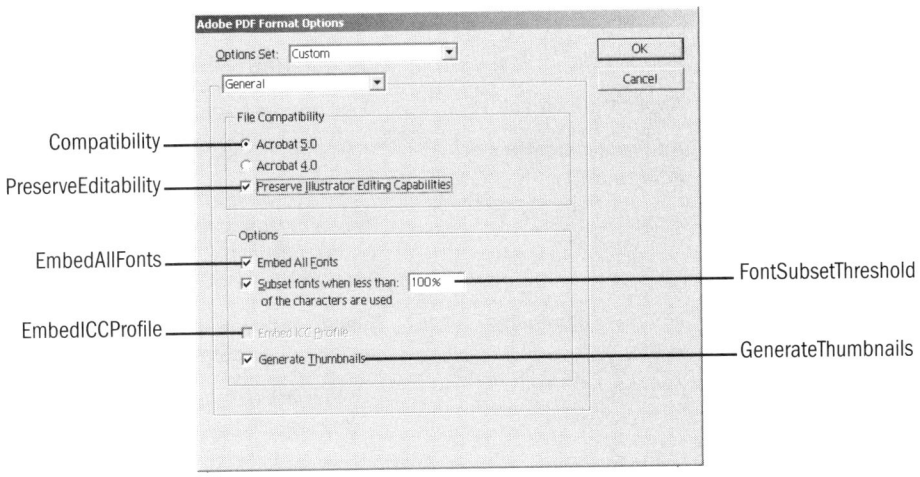

Figure 6.57 *The PDF format is an important one, and the PDFSaveOptions object offers full access to all the properties that user-interface dwellers get to play with.*

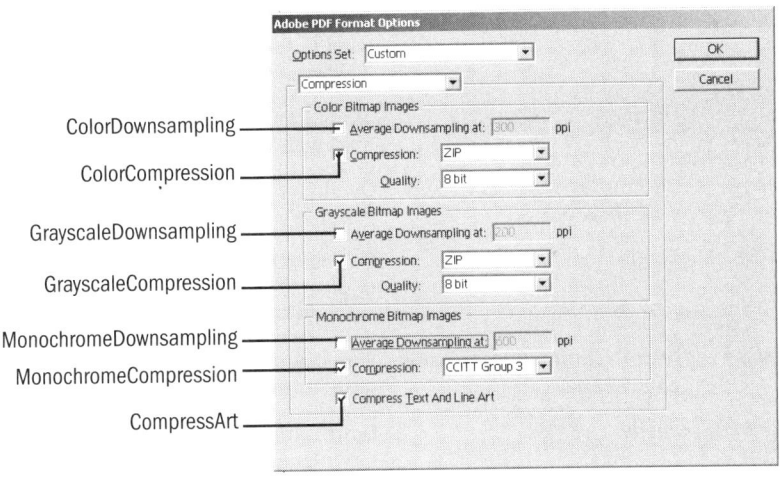

Figure 6.58 *The Compression panel of the Adobe PDF Format Options dialog shows all the save properties related to compressing art in the resulting file.*

Properties

PROPERTY	VALUE TYPE	EXPLANATION
Application*	Application object	The Illustrator Application object.
ColorCompression	AiCompressionQuality enumeration	The type of color bitmap compression used.
ColorDownsampling	Single	The color downsampling resolution, in dots per inch (dpi). If the value is 0, no downsampling is performed.
Compatibility	AiPDFCompatibility enumeration	Specifies the version of the Acrobat file format to create.
CompressArt	Boolean	Are line art and text to be compressed?
EmbedAllFonts	Boolean	Are all fonts to be embedded?
EmbedICCProfile	Boolean	Should a ICC profile be embedded in the saved file?
FontSubsetThreshold	Single	Include a subset of fonts when less than this percentage of characters is used in the document. Valid for Illustrator 9 file format.
GenerateThumbnails	Boolean	Should thumbnail images be generated with the saved file?
GrayscaleCompression	AiCompressionQuality enumeration	Quality of grayscale bitmap compression.
GrayscaleDownsampling	Single	Downsampling resolution, in dots per inch (dpi). If the value is 0, no downsampling is performed.
MonochromeCompression	AiMonochromeCompression enumeration	Specifies type of monochrome bitmap compression used.
MonochromeDownsampling	Single	Downsampling resolution, in dots per inch (dpi). If the value is 0, no downsampling is performed.
PreserveEditability	Boolean	Should Illustrator editing capabilities be preserved when saving the document?

Methods

This object can be used only in conjunction with the Document.SaveAs method.

> **TIP** *This class is used to define a record containing properties used to specify options when saving a document as a PDF file. It is not necessary to specify values for all properties. Default values will be provided for any properties that are not specified.*

PhotoshopFileOptions

Options that may be supplied when opening or placing a Photoshop file.

Properties

PROPERTY	VALUE TYPE	EXPLANATION
Application*	Application object	The Illustrator Application object.
Parent*	Object	The object that contains this object.
class type*	class	The object's class.
PreserveImageMaps	Boolean	Should image maps be preserved when the document is converted? (Default: true.)
PreserveLayers	Boolean	Should layers be preserved when the document is converted? (Default: true.)
PreserveSlices	Boolean	Should slices be preserved when the document is converted? (Default: true.)

Methods

This object can be used only in conjunction with the Application.Open method.

> **TIP** This class is used to define a record containing properties that specify options when opening a Photoshop file. It is not necessary to specify values for all properties. Default values will be provided for any properties that are not specified.

Other objects contained in document

ArtStyle

An art style. Each art style defines a set of appearance attributes that you can apply nondestructively to page items. Art styles are contained in documents.

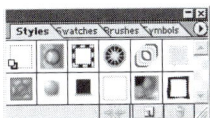

Figure 6.59 The Styles palette in the user interface displays each of the ArtStyle objects in the current document. You cannot create but may delete styles with a script. You can also apply styles to page items from a script via the ApplyTo method.

Properties

PROPERTY	VALUE TYPE	EXPLANATION
Application*	Application object	The Illustrator Application object.
Name*	String	The art style name.
Parent*	Document object	The document that contains this art style.

Methods

METHOD	RETURN VALUE (IF ANY)	EXPLANATION
ApplyTo(artItem As PageItem)	Nothing	Applies the art style to a specific art object.

ArtStyles

A collection of one or more art styles.

Properties

PROPERTY	VALUE TYPE	EXPLANATION
Application*	Application object	The Illustrator Application object.
Count*	Long	The number of art styles in the document.
Index(item As ArtStyle)	Long	Returns the index position of the object within the collection.
item(itemKey)	ArtStyle object	Returns an object reference to the object identified by itemKey.
Parent*	Object	The document that contains this art styles collection.

Methods

METHOD	RETURN VALUE (IF ANY)	EXPLANATION
Remove(item As ArtStyle)	Nothing	Deletes an art style from this collection.
RemoveAll	Nothing	Deletes all objects in this collection.

TIP *Illustrator's art styles can be accessed from scripting but cannot be created.*

Brush

A brush. Brushes are contained in documents.

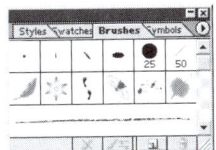

Figure 6.60 *The Brushes palette displays all the brushes contained in the document. Scripts cannot create or delete brushes but can apply them to page items via the ApplyTo method.*

Properties

PROPERTY	VALUE TYPE	EXPLANATION
Application*	Application object	The Illustrator Application object.
Name*	String	The brush name.
Parent*	Document object	The document that contains this brush.

Methods

METHOD	RETURN VALUE (IF ANY)	EXPLANATION
ApplyTo(artItem As PageItem)	Nothing	Applies the brush to a specific art object.

Brushes

A collection of one or more brushes.

Properties

PROPERTY	VALUE TYPE	EXPLANATION
Application*	Application object	The Illustrator Application object.
Count*	Long	The number of objects in the collection.
Index(item As Brush)	Long	Returns the index position of the object within the collection.
item(itemKey)	Brush object	Returns an object reference to the object identified by itemKey.
Parent*	Object	The document that contains this brushes collection.

> **TIP** *Additional brushes may be created by the user within Illustrator. Illustrator's brushes can be accessed from scripting but cannot be created or deleted.*

DataSet

A dataset in the Variables palette. Datasets are contained in documents and accessed from the Variables palette. A document must contain variables to contain datasets.

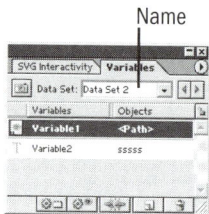

Figure 6.61 The Variables palette provides access to all the variables defined in the current document, as well as each of the DataSet objects. A DataSet is a snapshot of all variables' values. See Chapter 2 for more information on working with variables and datasets.

Properties

PROPERTY	VALUE TYPE	EXPLANATION
Application*	Application object	The Illustrator Application object.
Name	String	The name of this dataset.
Parent*	Document object	The document that contains this dataset.

Methods

METHOD	RETURN VALUE (IF ANY)	EXPLANATION
Display	Nothing	Changes the current dataset used by document's page items bound to variables and updates visual display of document to reflect dataset values.
Update	Nothing	Replaces existing values in dataset for variables bound to document's page items.

DataSets

A collection of one or more datasets.

Properties

PROPERTY	VALUE TYPE	EXPLANATION
Application*	Application object	The Illustrator Application object.
Count*	Long	The number of datasets in the document.
Index(item As ArtStyle)	Long	Returns the index position of the object within the collection.

Properties (continued)

PROPERTY	VALUE TYPE	EXPLANATION
item(itemKey)	DataSet object	Returns an object reference to the object identified by itemKey.
Parent*	Object	The document that contains this datasets collection.

Methods

METHOD	RETURN VALUE (IF ANY)	EXPLANATION
Add	DataSet object	Adds a dataset to the collection of datasets in the document.
Remove(item As DataSet)	Nothing	Deletes a dataset from this collection.
RemoveAll	Nothing	Deletes all objects in this collection.

TIP *Illustrator's datasets can be created under script control. See also the ExportVariables and ImportVariables methods of the Document object.*

Symbol

A symbol from the Symbols palette. Symbols are contained in documents.

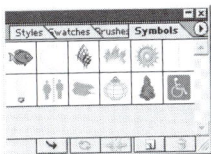

Figure 6.62 *The Symbols palette in the user interface displays each of the Symbol objects in the current document. You cannot create but may delete symbols with a script. You can work with SymbolItems, which are page items comprised of symbols.*

Properties

PROPERTY	VALUE TYPE	EXPLANATION
Application*	Application object	The Illustrator Application object.
Name	String	The symbol name.
Parent*	Document object	The document that contains this symbol.

Methods

METHOD	RETURN VALUE (IF ANY)	EXPLANATION
Duplicate()	Symbol object	Duplicates the symbol by creating a new symbol object with same source art, returning a reference to new symbol object.

Symbols

A collection of one or more symbols.

Properties

PROPERTY	VALUE TYPE	EXPLANATION
Application*	Application object	The Illustrator Application object.
Count*	Long	The number of objects in the collection.
Index(item As Symbol)	Long	Returns the index position of the object within the collection.
item(itemKey)	Symbol object	Returns an object reference to the object identified by itemKey.
Parent*	Object	The document that contains this brushes collection.

Methods

METHOD	RETURN VALUE (IF ANY)	EXPLANATION
Add(PageItem object)	Symbol object	Creates a new symbol using the page item passed to the function as source art, returning a reference to new symbol object.
Remove(item As Symbol)	Nothing	Deletes a symbol from this collection.
RemoveAll	Nothing	Deletes all objects in this collection.

TIP *Additional symbols may be created by the user within Illustrator or under script control.*

Tag

A tag associated with a specific page item in a document.

Figure 6.63 Tags are the most powerful and hidden features of Illustrator. Each page item in a document can contain as many tags as you want. Each tag contains a name and a value, which means that you can attach to objects in your document's data that gets saved within the document. See Chapter 4 for a script that lets you add, edit, and search tags in a document. Adobe uses tags to store some of the metadata for objects, such as notes.

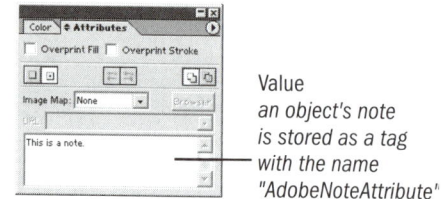

Value
an object's note is stored as a tag with the name "AdobeNoteAttribute"

Properties

PROPERTY	VALUE TYPE	EXPLANATION
Application*	Application object	The Illustrator Application object.
Name	String	The tag's name.
Parent*	Object	The object that contains this tag.
Value	String	The data stored in this tag.

Tags

A collection of one or more tags.

Properties

PROPERTY	VALUE TYPE	EXPLANATION
Application*	Application object	The Illustrator Application object.
Count*	Long	The number of tags in the collection.
Index(item As Tag)	Long	Returns the index position of the object within the collection.
item(itemKey)	Tag object	Returns an object reference to the object identified by itemKey.
Parent*	Object	The document that contains this tags collection.

Methods

METHOD	RETURN VALUE (IF ANY)	EXPLANATION
Add	Tag object	Adds a tag to the collection of tags.
Remove(item As Tag)	Nothing	Deletes a tag from this collection.
RemoveAll	Nothing	Deletes all objects in this collection.

TIP *Tags allow you to assign an unlimited number of key–value pairs to any page item in a document. This data is stored with the document and can be searched and modified. See Chapter 4 for more information.*

Variable

A variable in a specific document.

Collection Properties

PROPERTY	VALUE TYPE	EXPLANATION
PageItems*	PageItems collection object	The page items bound to this variable.

Properties

PROPERTY	VALUE TYPE	EXPLANATION
Application*	Application object	The Illustrator Application object.
Kind	AiVariableKind enumeration	What kind of variable is this one?
Name	String	The variable's name.
Parent*	Document object	The document that contains this variable.

Variables

A collection of one or more variables.

Properties

PROPERTY	VALUE TYPE	EXPLANATION
Application*	Application object	The Illustrator Application object.
Count*	Long	The number of variables in the collection.
Index(item As Variable)	Long	Returns the index position of the object within the collection.
item(itemKey)	Variable object	Returns an object reference to the object identified by itemKey.
Parent*	Object	The document that contains this variables collection.

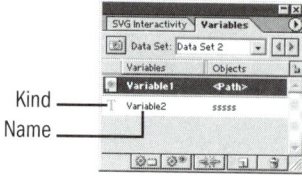

Figure 6.64 *The Variables palette provides access to all the variables defined in the current document, as well as each of the Variable objects. A Variable can be created and attached to a page item. Different kinds of variables can be attached to different kinds of page items See Chapter 2 for more information on working with variables and datasets.*

Methods

METHOD	RETURN VALUE (IF ANY)	EXPLANATION
Add	Variable object	Adds a variable to the collection of variables.
Remove(item As Variable)	Nothing	Deletes a variable from this collection.
RemoveAll	Nothing	Deletes all objects in this collection.

TIP *Variables allow you to assign dynamic attributes to certain kinds of page items in a document. You can create new variables and assign variables to page items by using the specific properties' visibility variable and content variable. See also the ExportVariables and ImportVariables methods of the Document object.*

View

A document view in an Illustrator document.

Properties

PROPERTY	VALUE TYPE	EXPLANATION
Application*	Application object	The Illustrator Application object.
Bounds*	Variant Array (of four Singles)	The bounding rectangle of this view relative to the current document's bounds.
CenterPoint	Variant Array (of two Singles)	The center point of this view relative to the current document's bounds.
Parent*	Document object	The document that contains this view.
ScreenMode	AiScreenMode enumeration	The mode of display for this view.
Zoom	Single	The zoom factor of this view, where 100.0 is 100%.

Views

A collection of one or more views.

Properties

PROPERTY	VALUE TYPE	EXPLANATION
Application*	Application object	The Illustrator Application object.
Count*	Long	The number of views in the collection.
Index(item As View)	Long	Returns the index position of the object within the collection.

Properties (continued)

PROPERTY	VALUE TYPE	EXPLANATION
item(itemKey)	View object	Returns an object reference to the object identified by itemKey.
Parent*	Document object	The document containing this view.

TIP *Illustrator's view object represents a window view of a document. You cannot create new views, but you can modify some properties of existing views, including the center point, screen mode, and zoom.*

Other objects contained in application

TextFace

A text face (currently available font) in the application.

Properties

PROPERTY	VALUE TYPE	EXPLANATION
Application*	Application object	The Illustrator Application object.
Name*	String	The text face's name.
Parent*	Application object	The Illustrator Application object.

TextFaces

A collection of one or more text faces.

Properties

PROPERTY	VALUE TYPE	EXPLANATION
Application*	Application object	The Illustrator Application object.
Count*	Long	The number of text faces in the collection.
Index(item As TextFace)	Long	Returns the index position of the object within the collection.
item(itemKey)	TextFace object	Returns an object reference to the object identified by itemKey.
Parent*	Object	The Illustrator Application object.

TIP *TextFace provides access to the names of all fonts available to the Illustrator application.*

The matrix object

Matrix

A transformation matrix specification, used to transform the geometry of objects.

Properties

PROPERTY	VALUE TYPE	EXPLANATION
Application*	Application object	The Illustrator Application object.
MValueA	Single	Matrix property a.
MValueB	Single	Matrix property b.
MValueC	Single	Matrix property c.
MValueD	Single	Matrix property d.
MValueTX	Single	Matrix property tx.
MValueTY	Single	Matrix property ty.

TIPS *This class is used to define an object that contains the component values of an Illustrator transformation matrix. It is used for specifying and retrieving matrix information from an Illustrator document or from page items in a document.*

Matrices are used in conjunction with the `transform` *command and as a property of several objects. A matrix specifies how to transform the geometry of an object. You can generate an original matrix by using* `get identity matrix,` `get translation matrix,` `get scale matrix,` *or* `get rotation matrix.`

A matrix is a record containing the matrix values, not a reference to a matrix object. The matrix commands listed in the preceding table operate on the values of a matrix record. If a command modifies a matrix, a modified matrix record is returned as the result of the command. The original matrix record passed to the command is not modified.

Important Value Enumerations

Visual Basic lets applications like Illustrator use special value enumeration types for object properties and method parameters. Whenever you see a reference to a term starting with the letters "Ai", that's a good sign that it is a unique Adobe Illustrator value enumeration type (individual value enumerations are prefixed by the letters "ai"). The most important enumeration types and their corresponding values are noted below.

Value Enumerations

ENUMERATION TYPE	POSSIBLE VALUES
AiBlendModes	aiColorBlend, aiColorBurn, aiColorDodge, aiDarken, aiDifference, aiExlcusion, aiHardLight, aiHue, aiLighten, aiLuminosity, aiMultiply, aiNormalBlend, aiOverlay, aiSaturationBlend, aiScreen, aiSoftLight
AiCharDirection	aiKumiMoji, aiNormal, aiRotated
AIColor	aiColorCMYK, aiColorGradient, aiColorGray, aiColorNone, aiColorPattern, aiColorRGB, aiColorSpot
AiColorDitherMethod	aiDiffusion, aiNoise, aiNoReduction, aiPatternDither
AiColorReductionMethod	aiAdaptive, aiPerceptual, aiSelective, aiWeb
AiCompatibility	aiIllustrator10, aiIllustrator3, aiIllustrator4, aiIllustrator5, aiIllustrator6, aiIllustrator7, aiIllustrator8, aiIllustrator9
AiCompressionQuality	aiAutomatic, aiJPEGHigh, aiJPEGLow, aiJPEGMaximum, aiJPEGMedium, aiJPEGMinimum, aiNoCompression, aiZIP4Bit, aiZIP8Bit
AiCropOptions	aiCropJapanese, aiCropStandard
AiDocumentColorSpace	aiDocumentCMYKColor, aiDocumentRGBColor
AiEPSPreview	aiBWMacintosh, aiBWTIFF, aiColorMacintosh, aiColorTIFF, aiNoPreview, aiTransparentColorTIFF
AiExportType	aiFlash, aiGIF, aiJPEG, aiPhotoshop, aiPNG24, aiPNG8, aiSVG
AiFlashExportStyle	aiAsFlashFile, aiLayersAsFiles, aiLayersAsFrames
AiFlashImageFormat	aiLossless, aiLossy
AiFlashJPEGMethod	aiJPEGOptimized, aiJPEGStandard
AiGradientType	aiLinearGradient, aiRadialGradient
AiImageColorSpace	aiImageCMYK, aiImageGrayScale, aiImageRGB
AiJustification	aiAllLines, aiCenter, aiFullLines, aiLeft, aiRight, aiUnknown
AiKnockoutState	aiDisabled, aiEnabled, aiInherited, aiKnockoutUnknown
AiMonochromeCompression aiRunLength	aiCCIT3, aiCCIT4, aiMonoZIP, aiNoMonoCompression,
AiOutputFlattening	aiPreserveAppearance, aiPreservePaths
AiPageItemType	aiCompoundPathItem, aiGraphItem, aiGroupItem, aiMeshitem, aiPathItem, aiPlacedItem, aiPluginItem, aiRasterItem, aiSymbolItem, aiTextArtItem
AiPathPointSelection	aiAnchorPoint, aiLeftDirection, aiLeftRightPoint, aiNoSelection, aiRightDirection
AiPDFCompatibility	aiAcrobat4, aiAcrobat5

Value Enumerations (continued)

ENUMERATION TYPE	POSSIBLE VALUES
AiPointType	aiCorner, aiSmooth
AiPolarityValues	aiNegative, aiPositive
AiPostScriptLevel	aiLevel1, aiLevel2, aiLevel3
AiRasterLinkState	aiDataFromFile, aiDataModified, aiNoData
AiRulerUnits	aiUnitsCM, aiUnitsInches, aiUnitsMM, aiUnitsPicas, aiUnitsPoints, aiUnitsQ, aiUnitsUnknown
AiSaveOptions aiSaveChanges	aiDoNotSaveChanges, aiPromptToSaveChanges,
AiScreenMode	aiDesktop, aiFullScreen, aiMultiWindow
AiStrokeCap	aiButtEndCap, aiProjectingEndCap, aiRoundEndCap
AiStrokeJoin	aiBevelEndJoin, aiMiterEndJoin, aiRoundEndJoin
AiSVGCSSPropertyLocation	aiEntities, aiPresentationAttributes, aiStyleAttributes, aiStyleElements
AiSVGDocumentEncoding	aiASCII, aiUTF16, aiUTF8
AiSVGFontSubsetting	aiAllGlyphs, aiCommonEnglish, aiCommonRoman, aiGlyphsUsed, aiGlyphsUsedPlusEnglish, aiGlyphsUsedPlusRoman, aiNoFonts
AiTextOrientation	aiHorizontal, aiVertical
AiTextType	aiAreaText, aiPathText, aiPointText
AiTransformation	aiTransformationBottom, aiTransformationBottomLeft, aiTransformationBottomRight, aiTransformationCenter, aiTransformationDocumentOrigin, aiTransformationLeft, aiTransformationRight, aiTransformationTop, aiTransformationTopLeft, aiTransformationTopRight
AiUserInteractionLevel	aiDisplayAlerts, aiDontDisplayAlerts
AiVariableKind	aiGraph, aiImage, aiTextual, aiUnknownKind, aiVisibility
AiZOrderMethod	aiBringForward, aiBringToFront, aiSendBackward, aiSendToBack

7: Learning More

Books

AppleScript for Applications: Visual QuickStart Guide, by yours truly, Ethan Wilde, is a great text to expand your AppleScript skills across dozens of applications you use every day already.

AppleScript for the Internet: Visual QuickStart Guide, by me again, covers AppleScript tricks specifically for Internet power users and developers.

Danny Goodman's AppleScript Handbook, is the well-worn mainstay of all AppleScript reference books.

Physics for Game Developers, by David M. Bourg, is a wonderful title for learning more about the mathematical and physics-based graphical visualization possibilities opened up by scripting support in Illustrator.

Real World Adobe Illustrator 10, by Deke McClelland, is one of the best all-around Illustrator 10 texts available.

The Illustrator 10 Wow! Book, by Sharon Steuer, is the latest edition of a long-lauded title that deals with specific tricks in Illustrator, many of which could inspire a worthy script.

VB & VBA in a Nutshell, by Paul Lomax, is my favorite and most reliable reference text for working with Visual Basic.

Magazines

MacTech Magazine

http://www.mactech.com/

This print magazine covers development technologies for Mac OS, including AppleScript. In-depth coverage of AppleScript Studio can become commonplace in recent issues of MacTech.

Visual Studio Magazine

http://www.fawcette.com/vsm/

This print magazine covers all of Microsoft's development technologies with a special focus on Visual Basic and its related languages like VBScript and VBA.

Web Sites

Adobe.com's Scripting Adobe Applications Forum

http://www.adobe.com/support/forums/main.html

Choose Scripting Adobe Applications from the Topic forum index to access this Web-based threaded discussion of scripting with Adobe's products. This forum is often visited by Adobe engineers responsible for scripting in various products, including Illustrator 10.

Apple's AppleScript Discussion

http://discussions.info.apple.com/

Choose AppleScript from the System Software Discussions index to enter this threaded discussion Web site. Topics range from working with AppleScript Studio and Script Editor to specific scripting implementation questions.

DevX

http://www.devx.com/

This broad site on Microsoft development technologies like Visual Basic provides links to other sites that cover aspects of Visual Basic in more depth.

MacScripter.net AppleScript site

http://www.macscripter.net/

This is an all-purpose information site about AppleScript, scripting additions, scriptable applications and related technologies. It provides a good entry-point to finding information about AppleScript on the Web.

Microsoft's MSDN Newsgroups site

http://msdn.microsoft.com/newsgroups/

Choose Visual Basic from the Visual Tools and Languages menu to access directories of the many Internet newsgroups that cover Microsoft's Visual Basic language and its variants like VBScript and VBA.

Planet Source Code

http://www.planet-source-code.com

This site provides an extensive downloadable library of Visual Basic source code for various projects without charge.

Index

-- (two dashes), 42
- (minus sign), 54
/ (slash), 54
& (ampersand), 47, 52–53
* (asterisk), 54
*) (asterisk and parenthesis), 42
^ (carat symbol), 54
= (equals sign), 55
≥ (greater-than-or-equals sign), 55
<> (less-than/greater-than signs), 54
≤ (less-than-or-equals sign), 55
≠ (not-equals sign), 53
¬ (not sign), 43
(* (parenthesis and asterisk), 42
+ (plus sign), 54
' (single straight quote), 42
_ (underscore), 43, 51
{ } (curly brackets), 298

A

About window
    Script Editor, 3
    Visual Basic, 4
About.com, 252
Access, Microsoft, 270, 274–275
Acrobat, Adobe, 91
actions, 11, 12, 16–17
Actions palette, 10, 16–17
activate command, 103
Activate method, 104
ActiveLayer property, 397
ActiveView property, 397
Add method, 55
addition operator, 54
Adobe
    Acrobat, 91
    forums, 490
    Illustrator (*See* Illustrator)
    PDF Format Options dialog box, 364, 473
    Solutions Network, 91
"Ai" enumeration types, 390, 485–487
aiDocumentCMYKColor enumeration, 132, 486

aiDocumentRGBColor enumeration, 245, 486
AlterCast, 14–16
anchor point property, 90
anchor points, defining, 91
AnchorPoint property, 90
and operator, 57
Angle property, 453
animated GIF, 15
animation
    creating/exporting, 184–190
    resources for physics-based, 184
Apple Developer Connection, 5
Apple Extras folder, 26
AppleScript. *See also* Script Editor
    advantages over JavaScript, 20
    annotating scripts in, 42
    basic color definition objects, 92–93, 349–354
    commands
        additional libraries of, 24 (*See also* scripting additions)
        purpose of, 54
        reference, 293–388
        viewing, 27
    conditional statements/comparisons, 55–57
    dealing with long lines in, 43
    debugging tools, 64
    defining/calling functions in, 61–62, 63
    error-handling in, 66
    getting input from users with, 59–61
    getting list of installed fonts with, 95, 167–171
    launching/quitting Illustrator with, 103–104
    numerical operators, 54
    objects
        reference, 293–388
        referring to, 41, 49, 81–83, 85–88
        viewing, 27, 71

    purpose of, 2, 24
    saving scripts in, 67, 107
    script examples (*See* script examples)
    scripting object model for Illustrator, 69, 295
    setting variables in, 52
    sources of additional information on, 489–490
    user-interface capabilities, 107, 109
    using coordinates in, 77–79, 239
    using loops in, 58–59 (*See also* loops)
    using measurement units in, 76
    using transformation matrix in, 100, 164–165
    value types, 50–51
    Web-services support, 232
    working with objects in documents/layers in, 85–86
    working with selected objects in, 86–88
    working with values in, 43–52
    writing scripts in, 72, 74–75, 105–111 (*See also* script examples)
AppleScript folder, 26
AppleScript for Applications: Visual QuickStart Guide, 489
AppleScript for the Internet: Visual QuickStart Guide, 489
AppleScript Handbook, Danny Goodman's, 489
AppleScript Studio, 5, 6
application object, 48, 296–297, 392–395
applications, saving scripts as, 67–68
Applications folder, Mac, 26
Aqua interface, 2
area text, 98
Array function, 48
arrays
    advantages of, 47

arrays *(continued)*
    assigning values to, 79
    defined, 51
    defining, 48–49, 79
    looping through items in, 59
    and x-/y-coordinates, 78
art style(s) object, 104, 374–375
ArtStyle(s) object, 475–476
Ashlar, 205
assignment operator, 55
Attributes palette, 302, 398
AutoCAD, 205
Autodesk, 205
automation, 2, 9

B

Babelfish, 227, 230, 232, 234
basic color definition objects
    AppleScript, 92–93, 349–354
    Visual Basic, 93–94, 452–457
batch processing
    of nested folders, 106–112
    of objects in current
        document, 117–123
    of objects in current selection,
        123–129
    of open documents, 113–116
Bézier curves, 90, 91
bitmap art object, 327, 430
booklet, creating two-up, 252–269
books, recommended, 489
Boolean operators, 57
Boolean values, 46, 50, 51, 135, 144
bouncing-ball animation, 184–190
Bourg, David M., 184
Brush(es) object, 477
brush(es) object, 104, 375–376
Brushes palette, 375, 477
business-card template, 272, 276
button-click subroutine. *See*
    `Command1_Click()`
    subroutine

C

`call soap` function, 232
Carbon applications, 5
centimeters, 77
Character palette, 332, 436
Character(s) object, 439–440
character(s) object, 335–336
Check Syntax button, 24

child classes, 40
classes
    object, 39–40, 49
    value, 43–44
`Clear` command, 104
`Clipboard.Clear` command, 104
clipping masks, 239, 244–245, 318, 321, 417
CMYK color, 13–14, 92–94
CMYK color info object, 92, 349–350
CMYKColor object, 452–453
Cocoa applications, 5
code. *See also* scripts
    reusing, 61, 62, 106
    storing in functions, 105
    viewing, 29, 30
Code window, Visual Basic, 29, 30
Collect for Output command, 167
collect-for-output script, 167–173
collection properties, 390
    Application object, 392
    CompoundPathItem object, 414
    Document object, 399–400
    Gradient object, 446
    GraphItem object, 415
    GroupItem object, 417
    Layer object, 405–406
    MeshItem object, 420
    PageItem object, 409
    Paragraph object, 441
    PathItem object, 423
    PlacedItem object, 427
    PluginItem object, 429
    RasterItem object, 430
    SymbolItem object, 432
    TextArtItem object, 434
    TextLine object, 443
    TextRange object, 436
    Variable object, 482
    Word object, 445
color definition objects
    AppleScript, 92–93, 349–354
    Visual Basic, 93–94, 452–457
Color Mode options, 14
color objects, swatch palette, 92–94, 341–349
color space, defining, 14, 132
`Combo1_Click()` subroutine, 224
command reference
    AppleScript, 293–388
    Visual Basic, 389–487
CommandButton tool, 108, 116
`Command1_Click()` subroutine

and attaching-tags script, 223
and batch-processing scripts, 114, 120, 126
and exporting script, 144
and language-translation script, 234
and multipage-PDF script, 194
purpose of, 111
and sliced-graphics script, 244
and title-block script, 182
and two-up-booklet script, 260
comments, script, 41–42
comparison operators, 53, 55–56
compound path item(s) object, 315–316
CompoundPathItem(s) object, 413–415
Compression panel, 473
computer-aided design
    applications, 205
concatenation operator, 47, 52–53
conditional statements, 55–57. *See also* `if...then...` statement
constants, 49
continuation character, 43
`control bounds` property, 81
control points, 91
`ControlBounds` property, 81
conversion formulas, measurement unit, 77
coordinates, 77–79, 239
creative process, tasks that interfere with, 1
Crop Marks option, Japanese, 300, 396
`crop marks` property, 300
`CropBox` property, 396
`CropStyle` property, 396
curves, Bézier, 90, 91

D

Danny Goodman's AppleScript Handbook, 489
Data Source Name. *See* DSN
databases
    creating, 270
    defining fields in, 271
    FileMaker Pro, 270
    Illustrator, 215
    importing as datasets, 284–291
    ODBC (*See* ODBC)
    querying, 282
    testing, 272

datasets
    creating, 17, 479
    defined, 19, 376
    importing database data as, 284–291
    switching between, 18
DataSet(s) object, 478–479
dataset(s) object, 376–377
date values, 46–47
debugging tools, 25, 64, 65
default document settings, 130–133, 307, 397, 404
DefaultTabSize property, 441
deleteAllStyles() subroutine, 152, 154, 155, 157
deleteUnusedSwatches() function, 154, 157
deleteUnusedSymbols() function, 154, 157
Developer Connection, Apple, 5
DevX, 490
DHTML, 184
dictionaries, 25, 27–28
Dictionary window, Script Editor, 25, 28
Dim statement, 52, 132, 244
Dir1_Change() subroutine, 259
Director, Macromedia, 184
display dialog command, 64
div operator, 54
divide-without-remainder operator, 54
division operator, 54
.dll files, 24, 36, 37, 182
Do Until loop, 59
Do While loop, 59, 225, 283, 290
document-processing function. *See* doProcessDocument() function
Document Setup dialog box, 299, 396
documents
    assigning names to objects in, 13
    batch processing objects in current, 117–123
    batch processing open, 113–116
    creating, 72–73
        with doMakeDocument() function, 130–133
        for use as templates, 13–16
        for use with AlterCast, 14–16
    creating/autocompleting title blocks for, 174–183

default settings for, 130–133, 307, 397, 404
exporting, 134–151
mass-producing from template, 269
merging database/template to create custom, 269–283
recording position of objects in, 77–78
reducing size of, 152–161
referencing objects in, 84–86
removing unused palette collections from, 152–161
setting color space for, 132
setting height/width for, 132
setting up for use with scripts, 13–14
tagging items in, 215–227
translating text in, 227–235
using color in, 13–14
working with parametric shapes in, 205–214
zero point for, 78–79
Document(s) object, 395–404
document(s) object, 298–307
Document.SaveAs method, 471
doMakeDocument() function, 130–133
doProcessDocument() function, 107, 110, 154, 157
doProcessObjects() function, 117, 120, 123
doProcessSelection() function, 126
doRefreshControls() subroutine, 223
doReplace() function, 280
doTranslate() function, 232, 234
double values, 51
Drive1_Change() subroutine, 244, 259
DriveListBox tool, 108
DSN, 271, 276, 282, 289
duplicating objects, 162–166
dynamic linked library, 24. *See also* .dll files

E

elements, object, 40. *See also* command reference; specific objects
Ellipse method, 425

ellipse object, 386
else clause, 55, 56–57, 134
Embedded property, 430
empty lists, 298
enumerations. *See* value enumerations
EPS Format Options dialog box, 355
EPS save options object, 354–356
EPSSaveOptions object, 457–459
errFlag variable, 232
error-handling techniques, 65–66, 113, 232
Event Log window, Script Editor, 25, 64
Excel, 6, 29
.exe files, 68, 107
export-document script, 134–151
export options, objects related to, 356–374, 457–475
exportDocument() function, 134, 135–136, 144, 157, 186, 189
exporting
    animations, 184–190
    documents, 134–151
    GIF files, 358, 461–462
    graphics, 236–251
    JPEG files, 463–464
    Photoshop files, 464–465
    PNG files, 466–469
    SVG files, 372–374, 469–470
    SWF files, 459–460
ExportOptionsFlash object, 459–460
ExportOptionsGIF object, 461–462
ExportOptionsJPEG object, 463–464
ExportOptionsPhotoshop object, 464–465
ExportOptionsPNG8 object, 467–469
ExportOptionsPNG24 object, 466–467
ExportOptionsSVG object, 469–470
exportPSDDocument() function, 197–198, 202
expressions, 52–54

F

File Info dialog box, 303, 399
FileMaker Pro, 270, 272–273

files. *See also* specific file formats
    collecting for prepress output, 167–173
    exporting, 134–151
    reducing size of, 152–161
fixed point, 78, 80
Flash export options object, 356–357
folder-processor script, 106–112
FolderListBox tool, 108
folders, batch processing of nested, 106–112
font-report text file, 167, 168, 171
fonts, producing list of installed, 95–96, 167–173
Fonts directory, Windows 2000, 97
Fonts folder, Mac OS X, 96
Fonts menu, 96
foreign languages, translating, 227, 230
For...Next loop
    and batch-processing scripts, 120–121, 127
    and file-collection script, 171
    how they work, 58
    and multipage-PDF script, 194
    and sliced-graphics script, 244
forums, Adobe, 490
`FullName` property, 399
functions. *See also* specific functions
    calling, 63
    defined, 61
    defining, 61–63
    naming, 61, 62
    passing data to, 62
    storing code in, 105

G

geographic information system, 215
`geometric bounds` property, 81, 302, 312
geometric transformation matrix. *See* transformation matrix
`GeometricBounds` property, 81, 398, 409
`get` command, 54
`getBounds()` function, 209, 212
`GetUserName()` function, 182
GIF export options object, 358–359
GIF files, 15, 358, 461–462
GIS database, 215

Google, 184
gradient color info object, 350–351
Gradient palette, 94, 342
gradient stop info object, 344–345
gradient stop(s) object, 343–344
GradientColor object, 453–454
Gradient(s) object, 446–447
gradient(s) object, 342–343
GradientStop(s) object, 447–448
graph item(s) object, 316–317, 415–416
graph variables, 18, 285
graphics
    cropping, 15
    exporting for Web use, 236–251
    resizing, 15
    reusing, 14
    slicing along guides, 236
    updating, 14
GraphItem(s) object, 415–416
graphs, 104
gray color info object, 351
GrayColor object, 454
group item(s) object, 317–319
GroupItem(s) object, 417–419
guides, slicing graphics along, 236, 238

H

handlers
    building, 117
    defined, 105
    purpose of, 61
    using in scripts, 110, 113, 117
`height` property, 80
Hyphenation Objects dialog box, 441

I

IDE, 7, 21
identity matrix, 164
`if...then...` statement, 12, 46, 55–57
Illustrator
    automation tools/techniques, 2, 9–10
    built-in database, 215
    and JavaScript, 2, 20
    launching/quitting, 103–104
    Mac *vs.* Windows versions, 2–4
    scripting languages supported by, 20–21

    scripting limitations, 104
    scripting object model, 68–71, 295, 391
    Software Development Kit, 91
    sources of additional information on, 489
    using actions with, 16–17
    viewing commands/objects for, 71
    working with multipage PDFs in, 191–192
    writing scripts for, 72–76, 105–106 (*See also* script examples)
Illustrator 10 Wow! Book, The, 489
Illustrator Native Format Options dialog box, 471
Illustrator save options object, 360–361
IllustratorSaveOptions object, 471–472
image servers, 14, 15
image variables, 18
images
    cropping, 15
    exporting for Web use, 236–251
    resizing, 15
    reusing, 14
    slicing along guides, 236
    updating, 14
imposition
    creating two-up booklet, 252–269
    defined, 252
    setting page count for, 255
    source of additional information on, 252
inches, 77
index position, object, 81
inheritance, 40
InputBox function, 60
insertion point(s) object, 336–337
integer values, 50
Integrated Development Environment. *See* IDE
Interface Builder, AppleScript Studio, 5
Internet. *See* Web
ITypeLib Viewer, 34, 35

J

Japanese Crop Marks option, 300, 396

JavaScript
    and AlterCast, 16
    contrasted with other
        scripting languages, 20
    Illustrator support for, 2
    and physics-based
        animations, 184
JPEG export options object,
    362–363
JPEG files, 362–363, 463–464
JScript, 20

K

`Kerning/kerning` property, 335,
    336, 439
`Kind/kind` property, 98

L

language-translation service,
    227–235
Late Night Software, 6
Layer Options dialog box, 308, 405
layers
    nested, 308, 405
    referencing objects in, 84–86
Layer(s) object, 405–407
layer(s) object, 308–310
Layers palette, 308
`left direction` property, 90
`LeftDirection` property, 90, 426
libraries, command, 24. *See also*
    type libraries
`line` property, 98
line(s) object, 337–338
Lingo, 184
Links palette, 325
list values, 47, 51
lists
    adding items to, 53
    empty, 298
    looping through items in, 59
logic, 12, 55
logical operators, 57
long values, 51
loops
    `Do Until`, 59
    `Do While`, 59, 225, 283, 290
    `For...Next`, 58, 120–121, 127,
        171, 194, 244
    nested, 280, 282, 287, 289
    `repeat`, 58, 169, 193, 239, 280

M

Mac OS
    Apple Extras folder, 26
    AppleScript folder, 26
    Applications folder, 26
    boot volume, 96, 97
    creating applications for, 5
    Fonts folder, 96, 97
    and `say` command, 64
    Script Editor icons, 4, 24
    and Scripting Additions, 27, 28
    using this book with, 4
Macintosh
    operating systems
        (*See* Mac OS)
    requirements for writing
        scripts on, 4–6, 24
    using Script Editor on, 24–26
        (*See also* Script Editor)
Macromedia Director, 184
MacScripter.net, 490
MacTech Magazine, 490
mail-merge applications,
    11, 12, 269
`make` command, 54, 386, 419
Make Project.exe command, 68
math-based animation, 184
matrix object, 99, 101,
    383–385, 485
measurement units
    conversion formulas, 77
    using in scripts, 76–77
mesh art, 104
mesh item(s) object, 104, 319
MeshItem(s) object, 420
methods, 54, 55, 389–487. *See also*
    specific methods
Microsoft
    Access, 270, 274–275
    Excel, 6, 29
    Visual Studio, 29
    Word, 6, 29
Millennium Edition, Windows, 6
millimeters, 77
mod operator, 54
movement transformations, 101
mpr.dll file, 182
MsgBox function, 114, 126
mssoapinit method, 234
multimedia development
    environment, 184
multiplication operator, 54
`Mvalue/mValue` property, 101

`myBounds` variable, 209, 212
`myDefaultLayers` variable, 130
`myDefaults` variable, 130
`myFieldNames` variable, 280
`myFolder` variable, 171
`myFormat` variable, 135–136, 144
`myFrameCount` variable, 186, 188
`myFriction` variable, 186, 189
`myGuide` variables, 244
`myHeight` variable, 132
`myNameExtra` variable, 135, 144
`myPage` variable, 193
`myPageItem` variable, 223
`myRestoreFlag` variable,
    135–136, 144
`mySaveFolder` variable, 135, 144
`myTagName` variable, 219, 223
`myTranslationMode` variable, 232
`myWidth` variable, 132

N

naming
    functions, 61, 62
    objects, 13
    tags, 219
    text art items, 178
    variables, 51–52, 284, 286
Native Format Options dialog box,
    Illustrator, 471
nested folders, 106–112
nested layers, 308, 405
nested loops, 280, 282, 287, 289
nested objects, 295, 391
New in Script Editor command, 74
New Project command, 108, 176
New Script command, 107
nonequality operator, 53–54
not operator, 57
Note feature, 215
null-terminated strings, 182
numeric values, 45–46
numerical operators, 54

O

Object Browser window, Visual
    Basic, 31, 33
object classes, 39–40, 49
object inheritance, 40
object model
    for Illustrator in AppleScript,
        69, 295

object model *(continued)*
    for Illustrator in Visual Basic, 70, 391
    for spaceship, 39
object-oriented programming, 38–41
object-processing function. *See* doProcessObjects() function
object properties. *See* properties
object reference values, 48–50, 51
objects. *See also* specific objects
    assigning properties to, 54
    associating interactivity with, 16
    associating variables with, 16
    batch processing, 117–129
    collections of, 40
    creating, 54, 55
    defining properties for, 27, 32
    duplicating with step-and-repeat, 162–166
    examples of, 27, 32
    index position for, 81
    moving, 99
    naming, 13
    nested, 295, 391
    reference
        AppleScript, 293–388
        Visual Basic, 389–487
    referring to, 40–41, 48–50, 81–84
    retrieving, 54
    rotating, 99
    scaling, 99
    working with selected, 86–89
ODBC, 36, 271, 275–276, 282, 289
OLE/COM Viewer, 33–35
OLEVIEW.exe, 34
On Error GoTo statement, 194
on error resume next statement, 65, 66, 182
on error statement, 65–66
on/off flags, 46
on statement, 61–62
Open Data Base Connectivity. *See* ODBC
Open Dictionary command, 27
open handler, 110
open options, objects-related, 363–364, 368, 472, 475
Open Scripting Architecture, 20
Open Scripting Architecture eXtension, 24, 28

openFolder subroutine, 111
operators, 52–54. *See also* specific operators
Option Base 1 statement, 244
Option Explicit declaration, 111, 244
or operator, 57
OrderValues() function, 239, 240, 244, 245
Orientation property, 98, 436
orientation property, 98, 332
OS X. *See* Mac OS
OSA, 20
OSAX, 24, 28. *See also* scripting additions

P

page items, attaching tags to, 215–227
page item(s) objects, 80–81, 311–315, 408–413
page origin property, 78
PageItem(s) object, 408–413
PageOrigin property, 78, 245, 398
Paragraph(s) object, 440–444
paragraph(s) object, 338–340
parametric shapes, 205–208
path item(s) object, 40, 90–91, 320–323, 386–388, 421–425
path point(s) object, 90, 91, 324, 426–427
Path pop-out palette, 386
path text, 98
PathItem(s) object, 421–425
PathPoint(s) object, 426–427
pattern color info object, 352–353
PatternColor object, 455–456
Pattern(s) object, 449
pattern(s) object, 93, 94, 345–346
PC. *See* Windows systems
PDF files
    opening, 363–364, 472
    saving, 364–366, 472–474
    working with multipage, 191–195, 363
PDF Format Options dialog box, 364, 473
PDF open options object, 363–364
PDF save options object, 364–366
PDFOpenOptions object, 472
PDFSaveOptions object, 472–474

Photoshop export options object, 366–367
Photoshop Options dialog box, 366
Photoshop options object, 368
PhotoshopFileOptions object, 475
physics-based animation, 184
Physics for Game Developers, 184, 489
picas, 77
placed item(s) object, 325–326
PlacedItem(s) object, 427–428
placeholders
    handler, 117
    script, 123
    text, 13, 269, 272
plug-in art, 104, 326
plug-ins, third-party, 20
plugin item(s) object, 326
PluginItem(s) object, 429
PNG8 export options object, 370–372
PNG24 export options object, 368–370
PNG files
    and AlterCast, 15
    exporting, 368–372, 466–469
point text, 98
point type property, 324
points, 76, 77
PointType property, 426
Polygon method, 425
polygon object, 387
Portable Document Format, 91. *See also* PDF files
position property, 80
prepress output, collecting files for, 167–173
printer's spreads, 252
Printing & Export panel, 299, 396
Project Builder, AppleScript Studio, 5
Project window, Visual Basic, 178
properties
    assigning to objects, 54
    defining, 27, 32
    examples of, 27, 32
    read-only, 390
    reference
        AppleScript, 293–388
        Visual Basic, 389–471
PSD format
    and AlterCast, 15
    exporting raster art in, 202
public function statement, 62–63

Q

Qs, 77
QuarkXPress, 167
Quick Watch command, 65
quit command, 103

R

raster art, resizing and embedding, 195–205
raster item(s) object, 327–328
RasterItem(s) object, 430–431
read-only properties, 390
real values, 50
Real World Adobe Illustrator 10, 489
record values, 51
Rectangle method, 425
rectangle object, 387
reference
    AppleScript, 293–388
    Visual Basic, 389–487
References window, Visual Basic, 36–37
Rem command, 42
repeat loop, 58, 169, 193, 239, 280
repetitive tasks, automating, 1–2, 16, 20
Replace() function, 282
Result window, Script Editor, 25, 64
resume next statement, 65, 66
RGB color, 13–14, 92–94
RGB color info object, 93, 353
RGBColor object, 456–457
right direction property, 90
RightDirection property, 90, 426
rotation transformations, 99, 101
rounded rectangle object, 387
RoundedRectangle method, 425
RulerOrigin property, 398
Run button, 24
run handler, 110, 113, 117

S

save command, 457
Save for Web dialog box, 369, 370, 461, 466, 467
save options objects
    AppleScript, 354–356, 360–361, 364–366, 374
    Visual Basic, 457–459, 471–474

say command, 64
scaling transformations, 99, 101
Script Debugger, 6, 49
script-editing applications, 3, 6, 23. *See also* specific applications
Script Editor. *See also* AppleScript
    debugging tools, 64
    finding on Mac, 26
    icon, 4, 24
    purpose of, 4, 21
    reading dictionaries in, 27–28
    windows, 3, 24–25
script examples, 106–291
    attaching searchable data to objects, 215–227
    autocompleting title blocks, 174–183
    batch processing
        nested folders, 106–112
        objects in current document, 117–123
        objects in current selection, 123–129
        open documents, 113–116
    collecting files for prepress output, 167–173
    converting multipage PDF to multiple Illustrator files, 191–195
    creating/exporting animations, 184–190
    creating new document with default settings, 130–133
    creating two-up booklet imposition, 252–269
    creating/working with parametric shapes, 205–214
    duplicating objects with step-and-repeat, 162–166
    exporting current document, 134–151
    generating font report, 167–173
    importing database data as datasets, 284–291
    merging database text with template, 269–283
    removing unused swatch/symbol/style, 152–161
    resizing/embedding raster art, 195–205
    slicing/exporting graphics for Web use, 236–251

    using Web service to translate text, 227–235
Script window, Script Editor, 24
scripting. *See also* scripts
    as creative tool, 20
    on Macintosh, 24–29 (*See also* Script Editor)
    modular approach to, 106
    object model for Illustrator
        in AppleScript, 69, 295
        in Visual Basic, 70, 391
    object-oriented approach to, 38–41
    questions to ask prior to, 2, 12–13
    sources of additional information on, 489
    use of logic in, 12, 55
    on Windows systems, 29–37 (*See also* Visual Basic)
scripting additions
    defined, 24
    icons for, 28
    and Mac OS X, 27
    purpose of, 28–29
    storing, 29
Scripting Additions folder, 28, 29
scripting languages, 20, 23. *See also* specific languages
scriptlets, 106–151
    for batch processing
        nested folders, 106–112
        objects in current document, 117–123
        objects in current selection, 123–129
        open documents, 113–116
    for creating new document, 130–133
    for exporting current document, 134–151
    purpose of, 106
scripts
    contrasted with actions, 16–17
    dealing with long lines in, 43
    debugging, 25, 64–65
    defined, 19
    defining/calling functions in, 61–63
    describing, 24
    determining need for, 11–13
    getting user input while running, 59–61
    handling errors in, 65–66, 113

scripts *(continued)*
   including type libraries in, 36–37
   launching/quitting Illustrator with, 103–104
   purpose of, 1–2
   running, 24, 107
   saving, 67–68, 107
   setting up documents for use with, 13–14
   testing/troubleshooting, 24, 30, 63–65
   using commands/methods in, 54–55
   using comments in, 41–42
   using comparisons in, 55, 57
   using conditional statements in, 55–57
   using coordinates in, 77–79, 239
   using expressions/operators in, 52–54
   using loops in, 58–59 (*See also* loops)
   using measurement units in, 76–77
   using transformation matrix in, 99–101, 164–166
   using values in, 43–52
   working with color in, 92–94
   for working with objects in documents/layers, 84–86
   for working with selected objects, 86–89
   writing, 29, 72–76, 105–112
   (*See also* script examples)
Scripts menu, 10
SDK, Illustrator, 91
selected objects, working with, 86–89
selection
   batch processing objects in current, 123–129
   duplicating with step-and-repeat, 162–166
service bureau, preparing files for, 167–173
set command, 52, 54
Set statement, 55
setBounds() function, 209, 212
Sherlock, 26
Simple Object Access Protocol. *See* SOAP
skewing transformations, 101

SOAP
   and doTranslate() function, 234
   purpose of, 235
   Toolkit, 227, 228, 232
soft-return character, 43
spirals, 104
Split function, 212
spot color info object, 354
SpotColor object, 457
Spot(s) object, 450–451
spot(s) object, 346–348
SQL, 282, 289
stacking order, 84
Standard .EXE projects, 68
Star method, 425
star object, 388
start log command, 64
Status property, 430
step-and-repeat script, 162–166
Step Into command, 65
stop log command, 64
string values
   accessing individual characters in, 44–45
   blank, 135
   combining, 52
   defined, 44, 50, 51
   null-terminated, 182
Stroke palette, 421
styles
   art, 374–375, 475–476
   removing unused, 152–161
   viewing list of, 153
Styles palette, 153, 374, 475
subclasses, 40
sublayers, 308, 405
subroutines, 61, 63, 105
subtraction operator, 54
SVG export options object, 372–374
SVG files
   and AlterCast, 15, 16
   exporting, 372–374, 469–470
SVG Interactivity palette, 16
SVG Options dialog box, 372, 469
Swatch Options dialog box, 346, 348, 450
swatch palette color objects, 92–94, 341–349
swatches
   removing unused, 152–161
   viewing list of, 153
Swatch(es) object, 451–452
swatch(es) object, 348–349

Swatches palette, 153, 341
SWF files, 459–460
symbol item(s) object, 328–329
SymbolItem(s) object, 432–433
symbols
   removing unused, 152–161
   viewing list of, 153
Symbol(s) object, 479–480
symbol(s) object, 377–378
Symbols palette, 153, 378, 479
System 7.1, Mac, 24

T

tags, 215–227
   attaching to page items, 215–227
   checking for existence of, 219
   creating/storing, 209
   defined, 215
   editing, 220, 224
   naming, 219
   searching, 215, 220, 223
Tag(s) object, 480–481
tag(s) object, 379–380
templates
   creating documents for use as, 13–16
   merging with database text, 269–283
testing scripts, 63–65
text, dynamically updating, 16
text art item(s) object, 74–76, 98, 178, 328–331, 433–435
text face(s) object, 383
text object, 331–335
text path offset property, 98
text path property, 98
TextArtItem(s) object, 433–435
TextFace(s) object, 484
TextLine property, 98
TextLines object, 444
TextPath property, 98
TextPathOffset property, 98
TextRange object, 436–438
textual variables, 18
TIFF files, 15
title blocks, 174–183
   creating, 174–179
   information typically included in, 174
   purpose of, 174
   scripts for autocompleting, 180–183

Toggle Breakpoint command, 65
Toolbar, Visual Basic, 30, 31
transform command, 485
transformation matrix, 99–103. *See also* matrix object
    defined, 99
    math behind, 102–103
    source of additional information on, 101
    using in scripts, 100–101, 164–166
translation service, language, 227–235
translation transformations, 101
troubleshooting scripts, 63–65
true/false operators, 57
true/false values, 46, 135, 144
try statement, 64, 65–66, 154, 193
type libraries, 32–37
    defined, 24
    including in Visual Basic scripts, 36–37
    opening, 31
    printing definitions from, 33–35
    purpose of, 31, 32
    sources of, 37
    viewing, 31
Type tool palette, 330

U

UBound function, 48
user-defined values, 51
users, interacting with, 59–61, 107, 109

V

value enumerations, 390, 485–487
values, 43–52
    defined, 43
    saving as variables, 51–52
    types/classes of, 43–44, 50–51
    ways of using, 43
    working with specific types, 44–50
        array, 47, 48
        Boolean, 46
        date, 46–47
        list, 47
        numeric, 45–46
        object reference, 48–50
        string, 44–45

Variable Options dialog, 284, 286
variables
    advantage of using, 19
    assigning value types to, 52
    associating with objects, 16
    defined, 51
    naming, 51–52, 284, 286
    types of, 18, 52
Variable(s) object, 482–483
variable(s) object, 380–381
Variables palette
    as alternative to scripting, 11, 13
    and DataSet/dataset objects, 376, 478
    purpose of, 17
    setting up documents for use with, 13
    and Variable/variable objects, 380, 482
    and XML-based datasets, 10, 17–19, 284
variant array, 48, 78
VB & VBA in a Nutshell, 489
VB6 IDE, 29
VBA, 6
VB6.exe, 32
vector graphics, 325, 326, 427, 428
Vellum, 205
View(s) object, 483–484
view(s) object, 382
visibility variables, 18
visible bounds property, 81, 302, 312
VisibleBounds property, 81, 398, 409
Visio, 6, 29
Visual Basic
    adding Web-services support to, 232
    advantages over JavaScript, 20
    advice for new users of, 106
    annotating scripts in, 42
    basic color definition objects, 93–94, 452–457
    conditional statements/comparisons, 56–57
    creating new projects in, 176–177
    dealing with long lines in, 43
    defining/calling functions in, 61, 62–63
    defining variables in, 52

    development environment, 4, 6–7
    editors, 6–7
    error-handling in, 66
    finding editor on PC, 32
    getting input from users with, 59–61
    getting list of installed fonts with, 95–96, 171–173
    icon, 29
    launching/quitting Illustrator with, 104
    methods, 54, 55, 389–487
    numerical operators, 54
    object/method reference, 389–487
    purpose of, 2
    referring to objects in, 41, 50, 83–86
    saving scripts in, 67, 68, 107
    script examples (*See* script examples)
    scripting object model for Illustrator, 70, 391
    sources of additional information on, 489
    Toolbar, 31
    type libraries, 24, 32–37
    user-interface capabilities, 107
    using coordinates in, 78–79
    using loops in, 58–59 (*See also* loops)
    using measurement units in, 77
    using transformation matrix in, 101, 165–166
    value types, 51
    viewing commands/objects for, 33
    viewing Illustrator commands/objects in, 71
    windows, 4, 29–31
    working with objects in documents/layers in, 86
    working with selected object(s) in, 89
    working with values in, 43–52
    writing scripts in, 73, 75–76, 106–109, 111–112 (*See also* script examples)
Visual Basic for Applications, 6
Visual Editor, 29
Visual QuickStart Guides, 489
Visual Studio, Microsoft, 29
Visual Studio Magazine, 490

W

Watches window, Visual Basic, 31, 65
WBMP format, 15
Web
    recommended sites on, 490
    slicing/exporting graphics for use on, 236–251
Web services
    and AppleScript, 232
    defined, 235
    source of additional information on, 235
    translating documents using, 227–235
    and Visual Basic, 232
    ways of accessing, 235
`width` property, 80
Windows 98, 6
Windows 2000, 6, 32, 97
Windows Millennium Edition, 6
Windows NT, 6
Windows systems
    additional libraries of commands for, 24
    finding Visual Basic editor on, 32
    requirements for writing scripts on, 6–7
    using Visual Basic on, 29–37 (*See also* Visual Basic)
Windows XP, 6
`with data` parameter, 419
Word, Microsoft, 6, 29
Word(s) object, 445
`word(s)` object, 341
World Wide Web. *See* Web
`Wrapped` property, 433
`wrapped` property, 330

X

x-coordinate, 78. *See also* coordinates
XMethods, 227, 230, 234
XML, importing/exporting, 17–18
XML-RPC, 232, 235

Y

y-coordinate, 78. *See also* coordinates
yes/no flags, 46

Z

zero point, 78–79